Family Entrepreneurship

Family business is the most prominent form of business organization, and its importance to the global economy cannot be underestimated. Until recently, the impact of the family on entrepreneurial firms has been under researched, leading to a conceptual gap between the two areas of study, and an underestimation of the contribution of family systems to entrepreneurial success.

Starting from the consideration that family is an intimate and essential aspect of entrepreneurship, this book considers connections between family, family members, entrepreneurial behavior, family business, society and the economy. Bringing together a unique range of international contributions, it offers new theoretical perspectives and empirical insights as well as an in-depth consideration of the diversity of contexts and processes associated with entrepreneurship in family settings.

Above all, this book opens up a comprehensive research agenda on the linkages between family, family firms and entrepreneurship and will be of interest to researchers, educators and advanced students of entrepreneurship, small firms and family business.

Kathleen Randerson is Associate Professor of Entrepreneurship at EDC Paris Business School and Visiting Professor at the University of Bergamo, Italy.

Cristina Bettinelli is Assistant Professor at the University of Bergamo, Italy and also a researcher at the ELab Research Center, University of Bergamo, Italy and research fellow at the Cambridge Institute for Family Enterprise, Cambridge, USA.

Giovanna Dossena is Professor of Entrepreneurship and Management at the University of Bergamo, Italy and Director of ELab – Center for Research on Entrepreneurship.

Alain Fayolle is Professor of Entrepreneurship and the Founder and Director of the Entrepreneurship Research Centre at EM Lyon Business School, France.

Routledge Rethinking Entrepreneurship Research
Edited by Alain Fayolle and Philippe Riot

The current focus on entrepreneurship as a purely market-based phenomenon and an unquestionably desirable economic and profitable activity leads to undervaluing and under researching important issues in relation to power, ideology or phenomenology. New postures, new theoretical lenses and new approaches are needed to study entrepreneurship as a contextualized and socially embedded phenomenon. The objective of this series therefore is to adopt a critical and constructive posture toward the theories, methods, epistemologies, assumptions and beliefs which dominate mainstream thinking. It aims to provide a forum for scholarship which questions the prevailing assumptions and beliefs currently dominating entrepreneurship research and invites contributions from a wide range of different communities of scholars, which focus on novelty, diversity and critique.

Rethinking Entrepreneurship
Debating research orientations
Edited by Alain Fayolle and Philippe Riot

Family Entrepreneurship
Rethinking the research agenda
Edited by Kathleen Randerson, Cristina Bettinelli, Giovanna Dossena and Alain Fayolle

Family Entrepreneurship

Rethinking the research agenda

**Edited by
Kathleen Randerson,
Cristina Bettinelli,
Giovanna Dossena
and Alain Fayolle**

Routledge
Taylor & Francis Group

LONDON AND NEW YORK

First published 2016 by Routledge

2 Park Square, Milton Park, Abingdon, Oxfordshire OX14 4RN
52 Vanderbilt Avenue, New York, NY 10017

Routledge is an imprint of the Taylor & Francis Group, an informa business

First issued in paperback 2019

British Library Cataloguing in Publication Data
A catalogue record for this book is available from the British Library

Library of Congress Cataloging in Publication Data
A catalog record for this book has been requested

ISBN: 978-1-138-84119-2 (hbk)
ISBN: 978-0-367-27903-5 (pbk)

Typeset in Baskerville
by Wearset Ltd, Boldon, Tyne and Wear

Contents

Figures

Tables

Appendices

Contributors

Ishrat Ali, Assistant Professor of Entrepreneurship and Innovation in Bloch School of Management at University of Missouri at Kansas City, USA.

Alistair Anderson, Professor and Director of the Centre for Entrepreneurship at Aberdeen Business School, Robert Gordon University, UK.

Céline Barrédy, Associate Professor at the University Paris Ouest Nanterre La Défense, France.

Jonathan Bauweraerts, FNRS-FRESH research fellow at the University of Mons – Warocqué School of Business and Economics, Belgium.

Cristina Bettinelli, Assistant Professor at the University of Bergamo, Italy and research fellow at the Cambridge Institute for Family Enterprise, Cambridge, USA.

Joern Block, Professor of Management at University of Trier, Germany and is a member of the Erasmus Institute of Management, Erasmus University Rotterdam.

Vincent Blok, Assistant Professor in Sustainable Entrepreneurship and Responsible Innovation at Wageningen University, the Netherlands and a research fellow in Philosophy at Radboud University, the Netherlands.

Giovanna Campopiano, Assistant Professor at the Chair of Business Administration and Family Entrepreneurship at the Witten Institute for Family Business (WIFU), University of Witten/Herdecke, Germany.

Lucio Cassia, Professor of Strategic and Global Management, and Chairman of the Research Center for Young and Family Enterprise (CYFE), University of Bergamo, Italy.

Sara Carter, Professor of Entrepreneurship and Associate Deputy Principal at the University of Strathclyde, UK and Associate Director of the UK Enterprise Research Centre and Visiting Professor at Nordland Research Institute, Norway.

Olivier Colot, is Professor at Warocqué School of Business and Economics (University of Mons – Belgium). He is coordinator of the "STEP Academy". His research focuses on entrepreneurial field and family firms, particularly the use of management accounting information and performance measurement systems.

Justin B. Craig, Clinical Professor of Family Enterprise and Co-Director of the Center of Family Enterprises at the Kellogg School of Management at Northwestern University in Chicago, USA.

Sharon M. Danes, Professor, Family Social Science Department, University of Minnesota, USA.

Alfredo De Massis, Full Professor, Chair of Entrepreneurship and Family Business at Lancaster University, UK and Director of the School's Centre for Family Business.

Clay Dibrell, is Associate Professor of Management, University of Mississippi, USA and Associate Editor for the *Journal of Family Business Strategy*. He is also associate editor for *the Journal of Family Business Strategy*.

Giovanna Dossena, Professor of Entrepreneurship and Management at the University of Bergamo, Italy and Director of ELab – Center for Research on Entrepreneurship.

Sarah Drakopoulou Dodd, Professor at the Hunter Centre for Entrepreneurship, University of Strathclyde, UK.

Hanqinq "Chevy" Fang, a PhD candidate in the Department of Management and Information Systems at Mississippi State University, USA.

Alain Fayolle, Professor of Entrepreneurship and Founder and Director of the Entrepreneurship Research Centre at EM Lyon Business School, France.

Robert Garrett, Assistant Professor of Entrepreneurship at the University of Louisville, USA.

Richard T. Harrison, Professor of Entrepreneurship and Innovation and Co-Director of the Centre for Strategic Leadership at the University of Edinburgh Business School, UK.

Sarah Jack, Professor of Entrepreneurship at the Institute for Entrepreneurship and Enterprise Development, Lancaster University, UK.

Claire M. Leitch, Professor of Management Learning and Leadership at Lancaster University Management School, UK.

Rob Lubberink, a PhD candidate at the Management Studies Department of the Wageningen University, the Netherlands.

Eva Lutz, holds the Riesner Endowed Professorship in Entrepreneurship at Heinrich Heine University (HHU) Düsseldorf, Germany.

S.W.F. Onno Omta, Professor at Wageningen University, the Netherlands and Editor-in-Chief of the *Journal on Chain and Network Science*.

Johan A.C. van Ophem, Associate Professor of Economics, Consumers and Households at Wageningen University, the Netherlands.

Kathleen Randerson, Associate Professor at EDC Paris Business School, France and Visiting Professor at the University of Bergamo, Italy.

Robert V.D.G. Randolph, Assistant Professor of Management at the University of Nevada, Las Vegas, USA.

Angelo Renoldi, Professor in Management and Value Creation at the Department of Management, Economics, and Quantitative Methods, Bergamo University, Italy.

Saras Sarasvathy, Isidore Horween Research Professor at University of Virginia's Darden Graduate School of Business, USA.

Salvatore Sciascia, Associate Professor at IULM University, Milan, Italy.

PramoDITA Sharma, the Sanders Chair and Professor of Family Enterprise studies at the University of Vermont. She is the editor in chief of *Family Business Review*.

James Vardaman, Assistant Professor of Management at Mississippi State University, USA.

Friederike Welter, Professor at University of Siegen, Germany and Visiting Professor at Jönköping University in Sweden and also leads the IfM Bonn (Institut für Mittelstandsforschung). She is Senior Editor of *Entrepreneurship: Theory and Practice*.

Preface

PramoDITA Sharma

Family Entrepreneurship is the scholarly overlap between the rapidly growing research fields of entrepreneurship, family science, and family business. It is the playground of an individual managing the paradoxes at the overlap of family and business systems. Choices must be made between two rights as the life cycle changes affect the two systems and the individual in unique ways.

Family Entrepreneurship: Rethinking the research agenda is a thought-provoking book in which editors Kathleen Randerson, Cristina Bettinelli, Giovanna Dossena and Alain Fayolle, have painstakingly compiled leading edge thoughts on this important interface of fields. For the past five years, these editors have devoted diligent efforts to consolidate, build, and refine knowledge on Family Entrepreneurship. Often, their leadership effectively brought together interested scholars to discuss and debate the key constructs, offer theoretical frameworks, asking bold and interesting questions.

Research scientists interested in entrepreneurship, family science, and family business fields will enjoy this thought-provoking book as it will inspire deeper bolder multi-disciplinary and multi-level investigations. Thoughtful practitioners and advisors are likely to enjoy several chapters as well.

The book starts with an introductory review chapter entitled: "What we know about Family Entrepreneurship". Although the idea of bringing more family into family business research is not new, this chapter makes a compelling case of the rationale for looking at the intersection of family, family business, and entrepreneurship to deepen our understanding of all three domains.

Part I, the intersection family business and entrepreneurship, features chapters that explore topics such as effectual thinking in family enterprise, internal corporate venturing, corporate and social entrepreneurship in multi-generational family firms. Each chapter examines the issues using different conceptual lenses, thereby adding to the richness of knowledge at this interface.

Part II, the intersection family business and family, has received significant scholarly attention particularly in the last two decades. The focus has typically been on the question of how family affects the family business. Leveraging on this literature, in an attempt to deepen and grow the field, chapters in this section focus on the dynamic relationships between the two systems of family and business focusing on topics such as identity construction in the family business, financial rewards in family firms, and family level socio-emotional wealth.

Part III, the intersection of entrepreneurship and family, investigates how the family supports entrepreneurial behaviors and how entrepreneurial behaviors can impact the family. Themes such as couple-hood, the family as network, socioemotional wealth and how it affects habitual entrepreneurship, or domestic drivers and barriers are considered.

The conclusion synthesizes the contributions providing an exciting agenda for future research. Congratulations to the authors for their work and to the editors for successfully bringing together communities of scholars who treaded on their respective scientific pathways in oblivious parallelism. This book is an important foundational step in the study of Family Entrepreneurship.

PramoDITA Sharma
Editor, *Family Business Review*
Sanders Professor of Family Business
School of Business Administration
University of Vermont, USA

Introduction

What we know about Family Entrepreneurship

Cristina Bettinelli and Kathleen Randerson

Both the entrepreneurship and the family business fields are reaching their momentum (Melin, Nordqvist, & Sharma, 2014; Venkataraman, Sarasvathy, Dew, & Forster, 2012) and scholars acknowledge the importance of considering not only the family business dimension, but also the individual and family dimensions of entrepreneurship phenomena (e.g., Aldrich & Cliff, 2003; Marchisio, Mazzola, Sciascia, Miles, & Astrachan, 2010; Nordqvist & Zellweger, 2010).

The idea of looking at the intersection of the family business and entrepreneurship fields has become relatively common in the early 2000s, thanks to some scholars (e.g., Chrisman, Chua, & Steier, 2003; Habbershon & Pistrui, 2002; Hall, Melin, & Nordqvist, 2001; Rogoff & Heck, 2003; Zahra, Hayton, & Salvato, 2004) whose efforts have encompassed promising new perspectives. While several papers have focused on themes that can be considered as part of the Family Entrepreneurship field, rare are the cases where an explicit definition of Family Entrepreneurship can be found. For example, among the first special issues dedicated to the topic, Rogoff and Heck (2003) compare entrepreneurship and family business research and conclude that *families* are the oxygen that feed the entrepreneurial fire. In the same issue, Aldrich and Cliff (2003) demonstrate the interrelatedness of family and entrepreneurship by showing how changes in the family have altered the landscape of entrepreneurship.

Among the first inspiring contributions, Habbershon, Williams, and MacMillan (2003) define *enterprising families* as those with a vision forged by the controlling family which "directs the enterprising activities of the family unit, business entity, and individual family members so as to pursue the maximum potential wealth for current and future generations of family members." This paper was one of the first to introduce also a robust theorizing about transgenerational wealth creation, a concept to which we will return later. A few years later, in their seminal work, Heck and colleagues define *Family Entrepreneurship* as a phenomenon involving "the underpinnings and interactions of two systems, namely, the family system and the business system" and show how promising could be studying these fields as well as the overlap between them (Heck, Hoy, Poutziouris, & Steier, 2008: 324). Later on, Nordqvist and Melin (2010), contributed by identifying two separate, yet related dimensions – the dimensions of the entrepreneurial family and the entrepreneurial family business. They use the concept of *the entrepreneurial family* to refer to "the family as an institution, or social structure, that can both drive and constrain entrepreneurial activities," while they consider *the entrepreneurial family business* as "a type of organization, or organizational context, with certain characteristics that can facilitate or constrain entrepreneurial activities, processes and outcomes" (Nordqvist & Melin, 2010: 214). In the same vein, Uhlaner, Kellermanns, Eddleston, and Hoy (2012), examined the intersection of entrepreneurship and family business and offer a paradigm to explain the entrepreneurial behaviors of family firms. In this case the authors specifically focused on *entrepreneuring families*, defined as "the subset of business-owning families focused on entrepreneurial objectives or motives" (Uhlaner, Kellermanns, Eddleston, & Hoy, 2012: 2).

Thus, in the general literature, the concepts of entrepreneurial families and/ or family businesses seem to be quite common, and perceived as fascinating. For example, Poutziouris, Steier, and Smyrnios (2004) talk about "family business entrepreneurial development" while Campbell calls for more transgressive research that aims at revealing the full entrepreneurial potential of family firms and shifts away from the paradigm of the single, heroic entrepreneur to legitimize approaches that also take into account emotional resources, shared values, and underlie "the integration of head and heart" (2011: 41).

A sub-theme – and probably one of the most studied recently – of Family Entrepreneurship is *transgenerational entrepreneurship* which links entrepreneurship and family business theory (Nordqvist & Zellweger, 2010) and is defined as "the processes through which a family uses and develops entrepreneurial mindsets and family-influenced resources and capabilities to create new streams of entrepreneurial, financial and social value across generations" (Habbershon, Nordqvist, & Zellweger, 2010: 1). In this vein, to explore the entrepreneurial process within business families across the globe both qualitatively and quantitatively, the STEP (Successful Transgenerational Entrepreneurship Practices) project has been founded and involves now more than 30 countries and 125 researchers. Kraus and colleagues (2012: 135) similarly to the works mentioned above, do not define Family Entrepreneurship explicitly but stress that family business and entrepreneurship are not contradictory or exact synonyms. For the authors, "family businesses are entrepreneurial … they just go about it differently by leveraging their distinct familiness (Habbershon et al., 2003)." As Kraus and colleagues (2012) note, family firms are a unique form of ownership which relies heavily on the overlap among family, business, and ownership systems (Gersick, Davis, McCollom, & Lansberg, 1997). These authors implicitly talk about Family Entrepreneurship by stressing that successful family firms are the ones that are able to keep the entrepreneurial spirit alive and vigorous for the next generations.

Recently, Fayolle and Begin (Begin & Fayolle A., 2014; Fayolle & Begin, 2009) have focused their attention on the family dimension of individual and organizational entrepreneurial behaviors and the entrepreneurial dimension of family businesses. *Building on and extending this perspective, in this volume we define Family Entrepreneurship as the research field that studies entrepreneurial behaviors of family, family members, and family businesses* (Bettinelli, Fayolle, & Randerson, 2014). We accompany this definition with two visual frameworks that (hopefully) help us offer a clearer view of the concept (Figure I.1).

This conceptualization (represented in Figure I.1) presents three loci (i.e., individual, family, and family business) and identifies the main nexus, between the individual and the family, between the family and the family business, and between the individual and the family business. Each nexus – represented by the arrows – symbolizes the influences on the entrepreneurial behaviors of each loci.

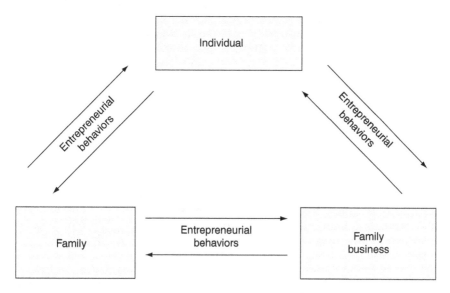

Figure I.1 A conceptualization of Family Entrepreneurship.[1]

Note
1 This figure was originally published as Fig 2.1 in Cristina Bettinelli, Alain Fayolle, and Kathleen Randerson (2014: 169).

With the framework illustrated in Figure I.1 we aim at adopting a holistic view and to take into consideration that not only *entrepreneurial behaviors* of an individual are in most of the cases rooted in the *family context*, the sustainability of the *family firm* depends on individual and/or collective *entrepreneurial behaviors*. Additionally, family firms are qualified as such by virtue of *family* ownership, management, or participation in an *entrepreneurial* firm. Finally, both *entrepreneurial behaviors* and the success or failure of the *family firm* impact the *family unit* (Bettinelli, Fayolle, & Randerson, 2014).

This broad definition allows us to incorporate the previously mentioned concepts and to integrate them into a framework that should help scholars systematize knowledge on the topic. By focusing on behaviors, this definition takes into proper consideration the dynamic nature of Family Entrepreneurship, additionally by considering different loci (i.e., the individual, the family, and family business) it allows us to disentangle the intrinsic complexity of the phenomena under study (Bettinelli, Fayolle, & Randerson, 2014).

While previous research has tended to focus on entrepreneurial phenomena that occur where family and family business overlap, this conceptualization underscores the importance of Family Entrepreneurship as a holistic phenomenon that affects, and is affected by, the three different loci above identified. Thus, not only the family and the family firms are considered, but also the individual, and circular effects are presented in the figure (e.g., family firms are affected by the family but also the family can be affected by family firms' behaviors, individuals' behaviors affect family firms, and vice versa, and so on). This is in line with research that has acknowledged that a large part of the entrepreneurial phenomena can be better understood when both the family effects on the family business and the family business effects on the family are taken into account (e.g., Marchisio, Mazzola, Sciascia, Miles, & Astrachan, 2010; Pieper, 2010; Zellweger, Sieger, & Halter, 2011). However, rare remain the cases where such reverse causality is explored.

Another important aspect is that our definition of Family Entrepreneurship connects the fields of family, family business, and entrepreneurship in an integrative framework and thus offers a first attempt to avoid fragmented approaches that hinder the advancement of the field. Specifically, as shown in Figure I.2, Randerson and colleagues (2015) identify Family Entrepreneurship at the overlap of family, family business, and entrepreneurship fields of research.

We believe that this approach could help move a significant step forward the family, the family business, and the entrepreneurship fields. As shown above, extant literature lying at the intersection of family business and entrepreneurship literatures has mainly used terms such as "the entrepreneuring family" (Uhlancr, Kellermanns, Eddleston, & Hoy, 2012), "entrepreneurial families and family firms" (Nordqvist & Zellweger, 2010), or "family business entrepreneurial development" (Poutziouris, Steier, & Smyrnios, 2004). Interestingly, in these initial integration attempts the focus remained on entrepreneurship in family firms, leaving the role of, and consequences on the family relatively unstudied (Jennings, Breitkreuz, & James, 2014). Moreover, even when the "family side" of entrepreneurship in family firms is acknowledged, the main focus remains on the "business side" (Sciascia & Bettinelli, in this volume).

This edited book aims at contributing to the extant knowledge by offering novel perspectives on the topic of Family Entrepreneurship with a focus on the intersection of the fields of entrepreneurship, family, and family business. The approach that we offer enriches the existent knowledge by going beyond

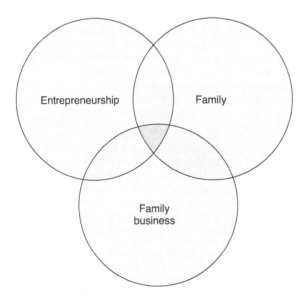

Figure I.2 Family entrepreneurship and the fields that it involves.

the typical firm level of analysis to integrate also individual and family theories, levels of analysis and perspectives. The framework in Figure I.2 guides the structure of this book, based in it, we will now explain how the book is structured to shed some new light on this promising topic.

The intersection of family business and entrepreneurship

The first part of this book is dedicated to research topics that lay at the intersection of family business and entrepreneurship. We start with a contribution by *Sarasvathy, Ali, Block, and Lutz* who have reviewed the empirical family business literature through an effectual lens. Interestingly, with their analysis, the authors extended the empirical findings to a theoretical specification of relationships between socioemotional wealth and the use of effectual principles. What is remarkable is that they were able to separate socioemotional wealth into two sets of factors. First, those that are driven by the need for family control and, second, those that result in stewardship behavior toward both family and nonfamily stakeholders. According to this review, the use of effectual logic in family firms is hindered by the former and facilitated by the latter. The main implication of this study is that it clearly outlines the need to partition the notion of socioemotional wealth into issues of family-centered and other-centered components.

The debate is further developed thanks to the critical literature review by *Sciascia and Bettinelli*. The authors aimed at reviewing past literature on corporate entrepreneurship in family firms (i.e., Corporate Family Entrepreneurship, CFE) to propose future research directions. The papers that are reviewed originated from a literature collection strategy that arrived at 83 articles published up to September 2013, 54 of them were empirically based. With a relatively new approach, the authors review the literature using the Hermagoras method of the "seven Ws" or "seven circumstances": who, what, when, where, why, in what way, by what means. The chapter consequently addresses the definitional issue (what), the levels of analysis in CFE (who), the reasons why CFE is developed (why), how CFE is developed, meaning in what way and by what means CFE is carried out, the role of time in CFE (when), and the role of industrial and geographical context (where). This effort will be of help for readers interested to know more about Family Entrepreneurship in the corporate context and to develop future research about it.

Interesting patterns of research at the intersection of entrepreneurship and family business are also those that consider social issues. In this vein, *Campopiano, De Massis and Cassia* dedicate their research efforts to social Family Entrepreneurship. Drawing on stakeholder and social identity theories, these authors analyze the role of internal stakeholders in shaping the way family firms address social issues. Particular attention was devoted to the understanding of what characterizes small- and medium-sized family firms in their behavior as social entrepreneurs. Starting with a review of the social entrepreneurship and corporate social responsibility literatures, Campopiano and colleagues develop a framework that represents the connections between entrepreneurs' motivations to engage in socially responsible activities, and stakeholders' claims. This framework is then used for the analysis of four case studies. This chapter contributes to extant literature by highlighting the role of internal stakeholders in shaping the way family firms address social issues, and provides relevant implications for academics, practitioners, and policy makers.

The discussion on entrepreneurship in family firms is alimented by *Craig, Garret, and Dibrell,* who focus on Internal Corporate Venturing (ICV) in multi-generational family firms. This topic is one of the most challenging yet under-studied corporate entrepreneurship behaviors in family firms. In their chapter, Craig and colleagues provide new insight into factors that determine which ventures are pursued within a business and how internal corporate venturing is pursued. The authors offer a robust theorization about how the relatedness of ICVs undertaken by the family firm may change as new generations begin to participate in the ownership and control of the firm. This chapter is significant in that it suggests a framework that links interesting elements, such as parent–venture relationships, stewardship, venture autonomy, and governance mecha-nisms, to explain transgenerational sustainability and corporate venturing success.

This first part of the book is dedicated to a better understanding of family business and entrepreneurship from different angles such as the entrepreneur-ial approach (Sarasvathy et al.), corporate venturing (Craig et al.), corporate entrepreneurship (Sciascia & Bettinelli) and social entrepreneurship (Campio-piano et al.). Sarasvathy and colleagues' work represents a good start to under-stand how family firms can learn to be effectual and how they can successfully expand their membership through committed stakeholders. Future research dedicated at testing empirically their propositions, and those included in the chapters in this part, may represent an important step forward in this fascinat-ing realm.

Both the empirical and conceptual work that is included here support the idea that, in order to analyze this realm in a robust way, a shift in terms of types of research questions, theory, and methodology is needed. Particular attention has been paid to the importance of taking into proper consideration the pres-ence of different levels of analysis, a discourse that is continued in the second and third parts of the book.

The intersection of family and family business

When considering different levels of analysis in Family Entrepreneurship the family unit and its relationships with the family business comes to mind. In this second part, the authors' efforts have been dedicated to show the implications of considering how family issues and family business' ones intersect and the nature of the consequent relationships. Importantly it has emerged that these are not necessarily unidirectional or simply causal.

For example, with their discursive psychology approach *Harrison and Leitch* argue that the focus of research on identity construction in family firms should ask questions of "how is entrepreneurial identity formed?" and "how do we develop, change and transform entrepreneurial identity?" Thus, these authors define a new theoretical approach to study the process of identity construction in family firms which is original and very coherent with the issues faced in this part. With their chapter, the authors contribute in at least three ways. First, they re-conceptualize identity not as something that describes who we "are" but as a process that explains how we "do," which is created, presented, and re-presented through talk-in-action in situational and social interactions. Second, they move beyond identity and identity categories as variables used to explain variations to replace this with a focus on how, when, and to what effect identity categories are invoked in particular interactions. Third, they outline a discursive psychology perspective as the basis for further research, which embodies both our onto-logical and methodological positions in a broadly social constructionist tradition and gives due place to the primacy of talk-in-interaction as the basis for analysis by engaged reflexive researchers. By doing so, the authors provide us with a fresh perspective that considers a formal analysis of identity and identity formation in family firms. This chapter is particularly relevant for our line of inquiry as it not only takes into account the relevance of both family and family firms, it also takes into consideration the individual level of analysis and the interactive dynamics among them.

Carter and Welter contribute to this picture with their investigation of how families influence value extraction from family-owned businesses and, con-versely, how the business influences family life in terms of its consumption behavior and relative lifestyle. Specifically, in their contribution, Carter and Welter explain how reward decisions are taken in entrepreneurial fam-ilies. The authors take up the challenge of disentangling complex deci-sions that are bounded both by the revenue-generating capacity of the business and the financial needs of the family. They do so by adopting a conceptual approach and focusing on relevant aspects such as the role of altruism and trust as key dimensions in the allocation of financial rewards. Thus, they explore financial rewards in Family Entrepreneurship, and the influence of factors, specific to this field, that are likely to impact on the allocation of financial rewards. In so doing, they offer an important contribution by illu-minating a relatively unknown dimension – how families influence value extraction from family-owned businesses and, conversely, how the business influences family life in terms of its consumption behavior and relative lifestyle.

Another important conceptual development is provided by *Bauweraerts and Colot* who focus on the creation of a theoretical framework that considers the pursuit of different socioemotional needs as potential drivers of corporate entrepreneurship in family firms. Not only do the authors illuminate previous inconsistencies on the topic, they also represent an important literature review and show how the socioemotional wealth (SEW) model may explain the role of families in developing entrepreneurial activities so that our understanding of family firm and Family Entrepreneurship will be increased. Specifically, Bauweraerts and Colot introduce the SEW – intrafamily entrepreneurship model with a number of intriguing propositions that should be built upon by others interested in the relationship between business families and entrepreneurship.

This second part is closed by *Renoldi*'s note which describes some of the most relevant characteristics of entrepreneurial family firms and offers sugges-tions for future research development. The author's main argument is that family firms can be considered as entrepreneurial when a dynamic balance between the economic growth challenges and the internal human resources spheres is pursued. This contribution identifies the main levers that allow finding of this balance and to maintain in the long run the entrepreneurial spirit in family firms. Among the levers that are analyzed are the ability to simultaneously consider different types of life cycles while remaining innov-ative and the consideration of possible effects of family firm managers' charac-teristics. In addition, the chapter comments on some of the most relevant family entrepreneur's characteristics: long-term vision and value orientation, risk taking, innovativeness, and the capacity to work in a team. While illuminating a few key elements of entrepreneurial family firms, this final contribution is important in that it leaves the door open for new intriguing research projects that could address the many open questions that the Family Entrepreneurship field offers.

This second set of contributions sheds some light on the issues that emerge when a researcher considers topics and approaches that lie at the intersection of the family and family business literatures. Original research questions have been asked and some input has been offered in this direction, in particular, the need to consider the family as a core unit of analysis and to integrate family science in our research have clearly emerged. The third and last part will be dedicated to deepening our understanding of topics at the intersection of family and entrepreneurship.

The intersection of family and entrepreneurship

After the above-mentioned pieces that lie at the intersection of family and family business, the third and last part of the book is dedicated to a better understanding of topics that lie on the juncture between family and entrepreneurship.

Family entrepreneurship can also be significantly informed thanks to a cross-fertilization with the family science field of knowledge. According to family science, couples represent the smallest decision unit and *Sharon M. Danes*' study offers both a theoretical and empirical perspective on the entrepreneur's immediate decision in the venture creation context. Grounded in the Sustainable Family Business Theory (SFBT), this chapter focuses on interactions within the entrepreneurial couple and the resource flows between spouses to deal with the liability of newness in venture creation. The work consists of a longitudinal study that captures decision processes from prior to business launch to approximately one year after the business began operating. Danes' findings indicate that strong couple relationships prior to business launch lead to quality communication about new venture goals. Additionally, according to the author, this spousal social capital stock based in strong couplehood is the foundation for spousal commitment to new venture goals and emotional and instrumental support for the entrepreneur. The synergistic effect of spousal commitment for business goals and quality couple communication about new venture goals forms a copreneurial identity and goal congruence that lead to shorter breakeven points and greater venture viability over time.

Thus, Danes complements the previous empirical results by showing how spousal social capital stock is the foundation for spousal commitment to new venture goals and an emotional and instrumental support for the entrepreneur which leads to greater competitiveness over time. One of the main strengths of this chapter refers to the fact that it uses unique longitudinal data which are quite difficult to retrieve and precious for the added value that they can generate when the task is to establish strong causal inferences. Moreover, the sample is composed of multi-informants with responses from entrepreneurs and their spouses within venture-creating couples thus allowing to account for interaction processes between couples during decision making. Finally, being grounded in the SFBT this chapter provides conceptual development of core concepts such as copreneurial identity.

Drakopoulou Dodd, Anderson, and Jack present the results of their analysis of the role of family networking in the growth process of entrepreneurial family firms and offer a commentary on the implications of their novel findings. Starting with the consideration that social ties shape information, skills, knowledge availability, and perception of specific opportunities, the authors show how network relationships frame access to resources, customers, and strategic partners, as well as configuring the entrepreneur's own perceived legitimacy. Thus, networking is important both in the start-up phase and during the subsequent entrepreneurial developments of the enterprise. However, ventures which survive start-up, show signs of quite substantial evolution in their networking practices and relationships. Drawing on family business and entrepreneurial networking literatures, 12 case studies (in Scotland, England, and Greece), are analyzed in depth by means of the constant comparative method. This chapter is relevant in that it sheds light on divergence in the patterns of networking enacted by family firm entrepreneurs during venture growth. For example, growth strategies for many of the family firms studied tended to be driven by resources available within the family–firm nexus. Additionally, the usage of weak ties appeared to be more significant for family-firm growth than for non-family firms. These findings stress the importance of, and call for additional empirical research on the role of, networking in Family Entrepreneurship.

The discussion on the impact of networks on Family Entrepreneurship is also developed by *Lubberink, Blok, van Ophem, and Omta*, who offer their qualitative analysis of the impact of the family network on start-up and contribute with a deep overview of the antecedents of these impacts. The results allow us to move a step forward and generate new insights on the family drivers and barriers to Family Entrepreneurship. Interestingly, the authors use a work–family conflict approach and discriminate between three different family life cycle stages. Data are based on 45 young Scandinavian start-up entrepreneurs. The findings in this study show thought-provoking results. For example, being in a one-person household allows full devotion to the start-up but does not offer intra-household social capital. Conversely, the support from the partner is emerged to be essential in households with high family time demands and involvement. The authors conclude that the domestic network exerts influence when it comes to starting the company and that this depends mainly on the level of family time demands, family involvement, and the fixed costs of living.

Business families are fertile ground for promoting entrepreneurship among family members. In their chapter, *Randolph, Vardaman, and Fang*, draw upon three literatures: research on habitual entrepreneurship, research on the dynastic family enterprise, and research on socioemotional wealth (SEW) to present a theoretical framework that explains habitual Family Entrepreneurship. What is valuable in this chapter is that it explains the fundamental differences in the process of habitual entrepreneurship as it emerges among members of dynastic business families and recognizes its differences when compared to the entrepreneurial process utilized by others. Additionally, the authors discuss a set of possible lines of inquiry that may yield significant insight to our understanding of habitual Family Entrepreneurship and allow future research to distinguish between these ostensibly distinct, but commonly associated phenomena.

Barredy closes this part with a methodological note that offers a typology of interactions and data content in qualitative family case study research. The author's focus on qualitative case study research allows the researcher to pay attention to the role played by individuals in the process observed and the interactions between them. Interesting insights are suggested. First, thanks to this chapter, a typology of the specific interactions in family business is presented. Second, this chapter contributes to distinguishing the different levels of data collected during interviews thanks to a typology of interactions in four types, one at each level of the family business: individual level interactions, family level interactions, professional level interactions, and systemic level interactions. The third main contribution is to prove a link between the type of interaction, the actor's intention while delivering data, and the data content. This typology should be useful to qualitative researchers and inform their data gathering and analysis processes when studying Family Entrepreneurship and in particular when focusing on the intersection of family and family business aspects.

Conclusion

This book contains both fresh and new empirical findings on relevant issues in Family Entrepreneurship and a synthesis of the existing body of research findings that serves to systematically connect the fragmented landscape of Family Entrepreneurship research, and thus gradually build a cumulative and evidence-based body of knowledge on this topic.

Throughout this book the chapters are organized with the specific aim to connect the various elements that compose Family Entrepreneurship research. Instead of offering pieces on broad and very general topic, each author has put effort to delve into a specific aspect of Family Entrepreneurship that we deem essential to build a cumulative body of knowledge. Starting from the consideration that the field of Family Entrepreneurship can be illuminated by considering the research topics that emerge at the intersection of the fields of family, family business entrepreneurship, we have introduced a number of fresh contributions and positioned them according to this framework. What emerges from this first analysis is that the chapters included in this book are very well linked together and collectively contribute to advance our understanding of Family Entrepreneurship. All of these contributions acknowledge, as well as concretely take into consideration in their research approaches, the complexity of Family Entrepreneurship. We genuinely hope that these manuscripts contribute to building new knowledge and to inspire new research questions especially on topics at the intersection of family business, entrepreneurship, and family sciences.

References

Aldrich, H. E. & Cliff, J. E. 2003. The pervasive effects of family on entrepreneurship: Toward a family embeddedness perspective. *Journal of Business Venturing*, 18(5): 573–596.

Begin, L. & Fayolle A. 2014. Family entrepreneurship: what we know, what we need to know. In A. Fayolle (Ed.), *Handbook of research on entrepreneurship* (pp. 183–214). Cheltenham, UK: Edward Elgar Publishing.

Bettinelli, C., Fayolle, A., & Randerson, K. 2014. Family entrepreneurship: A developing field. *Foundations and Trends® in Entrepreneurship*, 10(3): 161–236.

Campbell, K. 2011. Caring and daring entrepreneurship research. *Entrepreneurship and Regional Development*, 23(1–2): 37–47.

Chrisman, J. J., Chua, J. H., & Steier, L. P. 2003. An introduction to theories of family business. *Journal of Business Venturing*, 18(4): 441–448.

Fayolle, A. & Begin, L. 2009. Entrepreneuriat familial: Croisement de deux champs ou nouveau champ issu d'un double croisement? *Management International/Gestion International/International Management*, 14(1): 11–23.

Gersick, K. E., Davis, J. A., McCollom, H. M., & Lansberg, I. 1997. *Generation to generation: Life cycles of the family business.* Cambridge, MA: Harvard Business Press.

Habbershon, T. G. & Pistrui, J. 2002. Enterprising families domain: Family-influenced ownership groups in pursuit of transgenerational wealth. *Family Business Review*, 15(3): 223–237.

Habbershon, T., Nordqvist, M., & Zellweger, T. 2010. Transgenerational entrepreneurship. In M. Nordqvist & T. Zellweger (Eds.), *Transgenerational entrepreneurship: Exploring growth and performance in family firms across generations* (pp. 1–38). Cheltenham, UK: Edward Elgar Publishing.

Habbershon, T. G., Williams, M., & MacMillan, I. C. 2003. A unified systems perspective of family firm performance. *Journal of Business Venturing*, 18(4): 451–465.

Hall, A., Melin, L., & Nordqvist, M. 2001. Entrepreneurship as radical change in the family business: Exploring the role of cultural patterns. *Family Business Review*, 14(3): 193–208.

Heck, R. K. Z., Hoy, F., Poutziouris, P. Z., & Steier, L. P. 2008. Emerging paths of family entrepreneurship research. *Journal of Small Business Management*, 46(3): 317–330.

Jennings, J. E., Breitkreuz, R. S., & James, A. E. 2014. Theories from family science: A review roadmap for family business research. In L. Melin, M. Nordqvist, & P. Sharma (Eds.), *SAGE handbook of family business* (pp. 25–46). London: Sage.

Kraus, S., Craig, J. B., Dibrell, C., & Maerk, S. 2012. Family firms and entrepreneurship: Contradiction or synonym? *Journal of Small Business and Entrepreneurship*, 25(2): 135–139.

Marchisio, G., Mazzola, P., Sciascia, S., Miles, M., & Astrachan, J. 2010. Corporate venturing in family business: The effects on the family and its members. *Entrepreneurship and Regional Development*, 22(3–4): 349–377.

Melin, L., Nordqvist, M., & Sharma, P. (Eds.). 2014. *SAGE handbook of family business.* London: Sage.

Nordqvist, M. & Melin, L. 2010. Entrepreneurial families and family firms. *Entrepreneurship and Regional Development*, 22(3–4): 211–239.

Nordqvist, M. & Zellweger, T. M. 2010. *Transgenerational entrepreneurship: Exploring growth and performance in family firms across generations.* Cheltenham, UK: Edward Elgar Publishing.

Pieper, T. M. (2010). Non solus: Toward a psychology of family business. *Journal of Family Business Strategy*, 1(1): 26–39.

Poutziouris, P. Z., Steier, L., & Smyrnios, K. X. 2004. Guest editorial: A commentary on family business entrepreneurial developments. *International Journal of Entrepreneurial Behaviour and Research*, 10(1/2): 7–11.

Randerson, K., Bettinelli, C., Fayolle, A., & Anderson, A. (2015). Family entrepreneurship as a field of research: Exploring its contours and contents. *Journal of Family Business Strategy*, 6(3): 143–154. DOI:10.1016/j.jfbs.2015.08.002.

Rogoff, E. G. & Heck, R. K. Z. 2003. Evolving research in entrepreneurship and family business: Recognizing family as the oxygen that feeds the fire of entrepreneurship. *Journal of Business Venturing*, 18(5): 559–566.

Uhlaner, L. M., Kellermanns, F. W., Eddleston, K. A., & Hoy, F. 2012. The entrepreneuring family: A new paradigm for family business research. *Small Business Economics*, 38(1): 1–11.

Venkataraman, S., Sarasvathy, S. D., Dew, N., & Forster, W. R. 2012. Reflections on the 2010 AMR decade award: Whither the promise? Moving forward with entrepreneurship as a science of the artificial. *Academy of Management Review*, 37(1): 21–33.

Zahra, S. A., Hayton, J. C., & Salvato, C. 2004. Entrepreneurship in family vs. non-family firms: A resource-based analysis of the effect of organizational culture. *Entrepreneurship: Theory and Practice*, 28(4): 363–381.

Zellweger, T., Sieger, P., & Halter, F. (2011). Should I stay or should I go? Career choice intentions of students with family business background. *Journal of Business Venturing*, 26(5): 521–536.

Part I

Intersection family business and entrepreneurship

1 Partitioning socioemotional wealth to stitch together the effectual family enterprise

Saras Sarasvathy, Ishrat Ali, Joern Block, and Eva Lutz

This chapter seeks to bring together two recent and growing literatures – family business and effectuation. The use of effectual logic by expert entrepreneurs has begun to be empirically validated through a series of recent publications (Dew, Read et al., 2009; Read et al., 2009; Sarasvathy & Venkataraman, 2011; Wiltbank et al., 2009). In light of this consider the scope of family business – for example, Miller and Miller (2005) estimates that between one- and two-thirds of public companies around the world are family controlled and over three-fourths of all jobs in the US are created by them (La Porta, Lopez-de-Silanes, & Shleifer, 1999; Villalonga & Amit, 2010). Yet, little work has been done on the use of effectual logic by family firms.

To kick start future research at the intersection of family business and entrepreneurial expertise, we begin by summarizing what we have learned empirically about each of them as separate streams of literature. Thereafter we examine the implications of the empirical results for theoretical overlaps and finally push forward with an integrated theoretical specification for future research in this space.

Whereas our first instinct was to seek to analyze the variance between family and nonfamily firms in their use of effectual logic, a deeper examination of both extant literatures suggested a pair of more nuanced approaches. These approaches are also very much in line with how the two separate literatures have been evolving. First, in the case of family firms, although early work focused on patterns of variation *between* family and nonfamily firms (Anderson & Reeb, 2003, 2004; Dyer & Whetten, 2006; Gallo, Tapies, & Cappuyns, 2004; Harris, Martinez, & Ward, 1994; Lee & Rogoff, 1996), more recently, heterogeneity *within* family firms has emerged as an interesting phenomenon in itself (Bammens, Voordeckers, & Van Gils, 2008; Chrisman et al., 2007; Dawson, 2011; Eddleston & Kellermanns, 2007; Schulze, Lubatkin, & Dino, 2003b; Schulze et al., 2001; Westhead & Howorth, 2007). Second, attempts to measure the use of effectual logic by average (as opposed to expert) entrepreneurs have shown that effectuation may be a formative construct better studied at the level of individual principles and heuristics than as a reflective uni-dimensional one (Chandler et al., 2011). Therefore, in our theoretical specification, we construct propositions around the differential use of individual effectual principles within family firms. This twin focus on the relationship between the deconstruction of effectuation and heterogeneity within the population of family enterprises led us to an unexpected insight. In particular, it led us to undertake a theoretically meaningful partitioning of a construct that has become increasingly important and central to the study of family business – namely, socioemotional wealth (Berrone et al., 2010; Gómez-Mejía et al., 2007). We separate socioemotional wealth into factors that are focused on and driven by the need for family control and those that result in stewardship behavior toward both family and nonfamily stakeholders. We propose that the former hinder the use of effectual logic, whereas the latter enable and should facilitate it.

The chapter is structured as follows. A brief introduction to effectuation including a summary of recently published work in the area is followed by a more detailed review of the empirical literature on family business, which we then organize, interpret, and analyze in terms of facilitating or hindering the use of individual effectual principles. The propositions arising out of this analysis highlight a contradiction – on the one hand, a major barrier in family firms to the use of the crazy quilt principle and, on the other, a natural facilitation of the same. Consequently, we conclude the chapter outlining the need to partition the notion of socioemotional wealth into issues of family-centered and other-centered components.

A brief introduction to effectuation research

Effectuation is a collection of heuristics induced from a cognitive science based study of expert entrepreneurs. The heuristics are internally consistent and hence form a useful logic that is practically and pedagogically relevant as well. Drawing on well-established rigorous methodology from the field of cognitive expertise (Ericsson & Simon, 1993), the original study developed and used a representative sample of expert entrepreneurs who were asked to think aloud continuously as they solved the exact same set of typical decisions that need to be made in starting new ventures. "Expert" was defined as someone with ten or more years of experience founding multiple ventures including successes and failures with at least one company taken public. Expertise, therefore, is not the same as success (as it includes both successes and failures and every other type of experience involved in a long career in entrepreneurship), yet it is more than experience alone (for it includes considerable proof of superior performance). And the fact that the sample was deliberately varied widely in terms of the industries in which the entrepreneurs had founded firms ensured the likelihood that the protocols extracted would embody "entrepreneurial" as opposed to technical or other types of expertise.

Once the key principles and heuristics involved in effectuation were extracted from the expert entrepreneurs, the original study was directly replicated with novices and corporate managers (Dew, Read et al., 2009; Read et al., 2009). Thereafter, some of the key principles and heuristics were incorporated into other methodological instruments such as a scenario-based survey, a conjoint experiment and meta-analytical constructs with a view to using a multi-method approach to cumulating evidence (Read, Song, & Smit, 2009; Wiltbank et al., 2009).

These were concurrently supplemented with a collection of in-depth case studies and histories as well as new quantitative and qualitative metrics and measures. For example, Brettel et al. (2011) have documented its use in R&D and Fischer and Reuber (2011) have shown how entrepreneurs effectuate using social media. Attempts at developing better measures are also under way (Chandler et al., 2011). The research stream appears to be moving beyond evidencing the use of effectuation toward fleshing out the principles in greater depth (Dew,

Sarasvathy et al., 2009; Dew, 2009; Dew, Sarasvathy, & Venkataraman, 2004) and constructing connections to other intellectual streams such as Austrian economics (Chiles, Bluedorn, & Gupta, 2007; Chiles, Gupta, & Bluedorn, 2008; Sarasvathy & Dew, 2008; Sarasvathy & Venkataraman, 2011), evolutionary economics (Endres & Woods, 2010), entrepreneurship education (Harmeling, Sarasvathy, & Freeman, 2009), trust (Goel & Karri, 2006), and resilience (Hayward et al., 2009).

In the following three-part outline of what we know about effectuation so far, we begin with the overall process, then list and explain the five specific principles, and end with a brief look at what these imply about human behavior in general and business creation, management, and performance in particular.

Elements of the effectual process

Expert entrepreneurs begin with who they are, what they know, and whom they know, and immediately start taking action and interacting with other people. They focus on what they can do and do it, without worrying much about what they ought to do. Some of the people they interact with self-select into the process by making commitments to the venture. Each commitment results in new means and new goals for the venture. Note that it is not preset goals that lead to targeted stakeholder selection. Instead, people self-select into the process – and the commitments they may make specify their role and help co-create the goals and vision on the venture and its environment. As resources accumulate in the growing network, constraints begin to accrete. The constraints reduce possible changes in future goals and restrict who may or may not be admitted into the stakeholder network. Assuming the stakeholder accumulation process does not prematurely abort, goals and network concurrently converge into artifacts that may include not only new ventures but also new products, services, markets, opportunities, institutions, and other possibilities.

The process is graphically represented in Figure 1.1 and explicated in greater detail in Sarasvathy and Dew (2005). The process diagram also illustrates how the principles listed below iterate and dynamically drive the process over time.

Five principles of effectuation

At each step of the effectual process, expert entrepreneurs use the following principles, each of which allows them to shape and co-create the venture and its environment without having to predict the future. In short, most conventional approaches to decision making involve trying to predict better. For conceptual clarity we group these predictive approaches under the rubric "causal" – to theoretically contrast it with what expert entrepreneurs do using an "effectual" logic. In the brief descriptions of each effectual principle below, notice the contrasting causal inversion to the same decision problems.

The bird-in-hand principle

This is a principle of means-driven (as opposed to goal-driven) action. The emphasis here is on creating something new with existing means than discovering new ways to achieve given goals. This principle partially overlaps with the notion of bricolage (Baker & Nelson, 2005). Whereas bricolage is focused on

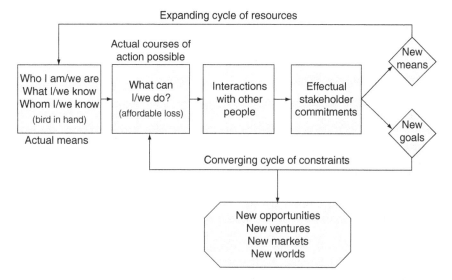

Figure 1.1 The stakeholder self-selection process (the dynamics of the crazy quilt principle).

means-driven strategies as well, bricolage does not require decision makers to be untethered to goals as the bird-in-hand principle does (Baker, Miner, & Eesley, 2003).

The affordable loss principle

This principle prescribes committing in advance to what one is willing to lose rather than investing in calculations about expected returns to the project. While affordable loss can be used as part of a net present value analysis as well as a real options analysis, effectual entrepreneurs tend to use it without trying to accurately predict the upside (Dew, Sarasvathy et al., 2009). In other words, the emphasis here is to control the downside and seek out non-economic upsides that are worthwhile even if the financial investment is completely lost.

The crazy quilt principle

This principle involves negotiating with any and all stakeholders who are willing to make actual commitments to the project, without worrying about opportunity costs, or carrying out elaborate competitive analyses. Furthermore, who comes on board and what they commit shapes the goals of the enterprise and the roles that they play. Not vice versa. This principle is at the heart of the dynamics of effectual entrepreneurship as we will see throughout the rest of this manuscript.

The lemonade principle

This principle suggests acknowledging and appropriating contingency by leveraging surprises rather than trying to avoid them, overcome them, or adapt to them (Dew, 2009). Conventional wisdom advocates starting with clear goals, making accurate predictions, careful plans, and then, of course, avoiding surprises to the extent possible. Effectuation advocates openness to surprises and a creative stance toward even unpleasant surprises with a view to transforming them into useful inputs into the effectual process.

The pilot-in-the-plane principle

This principle urges relying on and working with human agency as the prime driver of opportunity rather than limiting entrepreneurial efforts to exploiting exogenous factors such as technological trajectories and socio-economic trends. It also acknowledges and embraces the pragmatist view that William James stated with characteristic eloquence: "The trail of the human serpent is thus over everything." (James, 1948).

In sum, each of the five principles above embodies techniques of non-predictive control – i.e., reducing the use of predictive strategies to control uncertain situations – rather than trying to predict the future more accurately in the hope of being one step ahead of others in exploiting it. The overall world-view of the effectual entrepreneur is one of making, as well as finding opportunities and advantages, co-creating the future with self-selected stakeholders, as well as executing on pre-commitments from them in conjunction with one's own aspirations and goals.

Effectuation is the inverse of causation. Causal models begin with an effect to be created. They seek either to select between means to achieve those effects or to create new means to achieve pre-selected ends. Effectual models, in contrast, begin with given means and seek to create new ends using non-predictive strategies. In addition to altering conventional relationships between means and ends and between prediction and control, effectuation rearranges many other traditional relationships such as those between organism and environment, parts and whole, subjective and objective, individual and social, and so on. In particular, it makes these relationships a matter of design rather than one of decision.

Implications for behavioral assumptions at the level of individuals and firms

Empirically, entrepreneurs use both causal and effectual approaches, in a variety of combinations. Use of and preference for particular modes is related to the entrepreneur's level of expertise (the higher the expertise, the more the preference for effectual logic in starting new ventures) and where the firm is in its lifecycle (the earlier stages are likely to be more effectual than the later stages). Theoretically, however, it makes sense to analyze causal and effectual approaches as a strict dichotomy. This dichotomy extends beyond the decision making strategies of expert entrepreneurs to certain interesting implicit behavioral assumptions both at the level of the individual and that of the firm.

Effectuators see the world as open, still in-the-making. They see a genuine role for human action in history. In fact, they see both firms and markets as human-made artifacts. In this sense, effectual entrepreneurship is not a social science. It is a science of the artificial (Sarasvathy & Venkataraman, 2011; Simon, 1996; Venkataraman et al., 2012). Human behavior in this view is at once myopic and creative, especially when in collaboration with free agents.

Furthermore, they are intelligently altruistic (knowing when to be selfish and when to be altruistic) and bi-directionally docile (capable of giving and taking advice, persuasive and persuadable, leading and being led – often concurrently across different domains) (Simon, 1990, 1991, 1993). Structural factors – social, institutional, and otherwise – constrain, but do not determine behavior. In other words, collaborations among small groups of people blossoming into intersecting lattices of partial coalitions of varying strengths and intensity are more powerful more often than large faceless social forces as arbiters of progressive change. And performance is measured not only in terms of the financial bottom lines of firms but also in terms of personal, career, and societal aspirations of the people involved.

Effectuators do not seek to avoid failure; they seek to make success happen. This entails a recognition that failing is an integral part of venturing well. Through their willingness to fail, effectuators create temporal portfolios of ventures whose successes and failures they manage – learning to outlive failures by keeping them small and killing them young, and cumulating successes through continual leveraging. In an effectual universe, success/failure is not a Boolean variable and the success/failure of the entrepreneur does not equal the success/failure of the firm.

Effectuation matters, not merely because expert entrepreneurs prefer an effectual logic over a causal one, but because of the details it offers of a comprehensive alternate frame for tackling entrepreneurial problems. Which frame people use influences how they formulate problems; what alternatives they perceive and generate; which constraints they accept, reject, and/or manipulate and how; and why they heed certain criteria rather than others in fabricating and implementing new solutions. Logical framing matters because it makes a real difference in the world and makes a world of difference in the reality entrepreneurs and firms perceive and make possible or impossible.

Although there is not yet an active field of research at the intersection of family business and effectuation, several of the issues raised by the literature on effectuation, including some of the constitutive elements of the principles mentioned above are already familiar to family business research. We now turn to enumerating those next.

Review of extant empirical work in family business research

With a view to carving out overlaps and differences in the use of effectual principles by family firms, we decided to begin with (1) a comprehensive review of abstracts and then (2) narrow down to full readings of empirical works followed by (3) an in-depth examination of a small selection of theory papers evoked by the empirical readings. In Step (2), we compiled a list of all empirical papers published after 1985 in the most reputed management and entrepreneurship journals including *Academy of Management Journal, Strategic Management Journal, Administrative Science Quarterly, Journal of Business Venturing, Entrepreneurship: Theory and Practice*, and *Small Business Economics* from which we chose the most relevant from the point of view of linking family business research to effectuation research. We supplemented this list with inputs from reputed family business research scholars who suggested additions to our selection. The entire selection that we actually read in detail is listed in Table 1.1 and will be discussed in more detail below.

Table 1.1 Mapping to effectuation

Author year	Journal	Category: topic	Data	Method	Relevant findings	Mapping to effectuation
(Davis & Harveston, 1998)	ETP	*Succession:* Family influence on processes attendant to succession	N = 1616 family business (at least 10 employees and min. 2 million in revenue) surveys done by Gallup for Massachusetts Mutual Insurance Company	Telephone surveys, stepwise regression	(1) Extensiveness of succession planning is positively related to age of the owner manager, number of family members involved on a regular basis with the business, level of formalization, and level of capitalization. (2) The relationships are not really affected much by the level of generation of the family business. (3) The more closely related family members were to the owner manager and the higher the role or position they occupy, the greater the collective influence over extensiveness of succession planning process.	Importance of pre-commitment of family stakeholders. Pro bird-in-hand. Anti crazy quilt.
(Shepherd & Zacharakis, 2000)	ETP	*Succession:* Structuring successions in family business, decision making of future business leaders	N = 53 potential business leaders of family businesses	Conjoint analysis, regressions	(1) Future family business leaders value the business more when they have invested both financial and behavioral sunk costs and earned the right to take over the family business. (2) Findings suggest that succession should be planned to encourage future leaders to invest financial and behavioral resources.	Importance of pre-commitment of family stakeholders. Pro bird-in-hand. Anti crazy quilt.

(Sharma, Chrisman, & Chua, 2003)	JBV	*Succession:* Satisfaction with succession process	N = 604 survey respondent family firms in Canada	Descriptive, regression	(1) Satisfaction with the succession process in family firms is enhanced by the incumbent's propensity to step aside, the successor's willingness to take over, agreement among family members to maintain family involvement in business, acceptance of individual roles, and succession planning. (2) Incumbents and successors disagree as to the importance of each other's role in the succession process.	Importance of pre-commitment of family stakeholders. Pro bird-in-hand. Anti crazy quilt.
(Bammens, Voordeckers, & Van Gils, 2008)	SBE	*Succession:* Generational effect on board of directors in family firms	N = 286 respondent family firms from Belgium (2002–2003)	ANOVA and regression analysis	(1) Advice needs decrease from the first generation to the second, and rise again in the third and subsequent generation firms. (2) This convex trend can be explained by two underlying opposing generational evolutions – increase in task conflict among family members and rise in family experience. (3) Mounting trend in number of family directors over generations.	Role of experience and the effectual-causal balance.
(Chaganti & Damanpour, 1991)	SMJ	*Capital structure:* Institutional ownership, capital structure, and firm performance	N = 40 pairs of companies surveyed by Value Line in the US manufacturing sector	Regression analysis	In corporate settings where institutional stockholdings are relatively low, higher levels of family ownership correspond to higher corporate long term debt-capital ratios.	Affordable loss – willing to lose more to retain family control.

continued

Table 1.1 Continued

Author year	Journal	Category: topic	Data	Method	Relevant findings	Mapping to effectuation
(Bopaiah, 1998)	SBE	*Capital structure:* Access to capital for family businesses	N=3404, US – National Survey of Small Business Finance (1988–1989)	Regression – family ownership and discounts offered	(1) Family ownership is statistically significantly associated with easier availability of credit. (2) Lenders may see family ownership as providing incentives for behavior that reduce moral hazard problem with lenders.	Preference for retaining family control. Anti affordable loss.
(Mishra & McConaughy, 1999)	ETP	*Capital structure:* Family control and aversion to debt	N=1000 firms from the Business Week CEO 1000 and Compustat	Regression	FFCRs are more averse to control risk and therefore are debt averse.	Tension between bird-in-hand and crazy quilt principle.
(Romano et al., 2001)	JBV	*Capital structure:* Capital structure decisions of family firms	1059 Australian family businesses complete the 250 item Australian Family and Private Business Questionnaire.	Principal components Analysis (PCA), Confirmatory Factor Analysis (CFA) and Structural Equation Modeling (SEM) to build a hypothesized model and a resultant accepted model	(1) Firm size, family control, business planning and business objective are positively associated with debt. (2) Large family businesses whose owners have a high preference for retaining family control and formal planning practices in place, and whose objective is to create a lifestyle rather than growth, are more likely to derive funds from outside entities. (3) Equity is a consideration for owners of large businesses, young firms, and owners who plan to achieve growth through increasing profit margins. Equity is less likely to be considered by older family business owners and owners who have a preference for retaining family control.	Preference for retaining family control. Anti affordable loss.

(Schulze, Lubatkin, & Dino, 2003a)	AMJ	Capital structure: Agency consequence of ownership dispersion on debt decisions	N= 1464 privately held family firms screened from 1995 survey of American family businesses	Regression analysis	(1) Whereas ownership is expected to align incentives in public firms, how ownership is dispersed among the various family owners of privately held family firms affect decisions to use debt. (2) During periods of market expansion, use of debt has U-shaped relationship to the three modes of dispersion of ownership (controlling owner, sibling partnership, and cousin consortium).	Bird-in-hand vs. crazy quilt principle. Strategic flexibility in capital structure decisions can be reduced when conflict arises in sibling partnerships.
(Steijvers, Voordeckers, & Vanhoof, 2010)	SBE	Capital structure: Collateral, relationship lending, and family firms	N= 2525 loans granted to US SMEs from 1998 NSSBF survey by US Small Business Administration	Decision Tree analysis, Classification Models	(1) In collateral/no collateral decision, the most important classifier is the loan amount. Within high loan amount category, family firms have a higher likelihood of pledging collateral. (2) In low loan amount category, firms that obtain bank loans from their main bank have a higher likelihood of pledging collateral. (3) Private family ownership increases potential shareholder-bondholder agency problems when obtaining high amount loans. (4) Family ownership seems to increase the likelihood of pledging personal collateral.	Preference for retaining family control. Anti affordable loss.

continued

Table 1.1 Continued

Author year	Journal	Category: topic	Data	Method	Relevant findings	Mapping to effectuation
(Dawson, 2011)	JBV	*Capital structure:* Private equity investment decisions in family firms	41 individuals from 35 private equity firms in Italy	Conjoint analysis, Hierarchical Linear Modeling (HLM)	(1) The likelihood of PE professionals investing in a family firm is higher if family members working in the firm have gained outside work experience. (2) The likelihood of PE professionals investing in a family firm is higher if there are nonfamily members. (3) The likelihood of PE professionals investing in family firm is higher if there are family members wishing to sell their shares and exit the firm.	Preference for outside work experience by equity investors. Crazy quilt principle.
(Chua et al., 2011)	JBV	*Capital structure:* Family involvement and new venture debt financing	N=1267 new ventures with varying level of family involvement from the SBDC survey from 2002	Regression, logit	Family involvement increases the ability of a new venture to borrow family social capital. Positive influence of family involvement on new venture debt financing.	Bird-in-hand principle. Using family social capital for debt financing.
(Palmer et al., 1987)	ASQ	*Familiness – nonfamily stakeholders:* Emergence of multidivisional forms in large US corporations	N=147 firms from the fortune 500 list in the mid 1960s	Structural Equations Modeling (SEM)	Family controlled firms were less likely to develop a multi divisional organizational form that is highly correlated with dispersed growth.	Retaining family control inhibits dispersed growth. Tension between bird-in-hand and crazy quilt principle.
(Atkinson & Galaskiewicz, 1988)	ASQ	*Familiness – nonfamily stakeholders:* Ownership and corporate contribution to charity	N=69 corporations from 1981–1982 in Minnesota	Interviews, regression	No difference between family owned firms and other firms in charitable giving.	Pilot-in-the-plane principle (stewardship toward outside stakeholders).

(Chaganti & Schneer, 1994)	JBV	*Familiness – nonfamily stakeholders*: Owners mode of entry, venture performance and management patterns	N=345 firms in northeastern US including 227 owner started, 61 family firms, and 57 small buyout firms	Descriptive, regression	Sales performance was greatest in family firms when they had owner managers with extensive industry experience, were conservative in adding workers, emphasized product customization, relied on written reports, and avoided long-range operations planning.	Bird-in-hand (industry experience), affordable loss (adding workers), pilot-in-the-plane (planning avoidance), crazy quilt (product customization).
(Fiegener et al., 2000)	ETP	*Familiness – nonfamily stakeholders*: CEO ownership stakes and board composition in small private firms	N=5558 questionnaires from independently owned US businesses in 1993. Original database from NFIB.	Regression analysis	CEOs with greater ownership and family stakes have less independent board compositions.	Tension between bird-in-hand and crazy quilt principle.
(Gomez-Mejia, Nuñez-Nickel, & Gutierrez, 2001)	AMJ	*Familiness – nonfamily stakeholders*: Family ties of executives, business risk, firm performance, and executive tenure	N=276 newspapers in Spain published during 1966–1993.	Life time data models, regression analysis	(1) Links between performance, business risk, and executive tenure are stronger when agents have no family ties (vs. executives from family) and also stronger at the lower level (editor vs. CEO).	Family executives are monitored more softly than nonfamily executives. Bird-in-hand vs. crazy quilt principle.
(Gomez-Mejia, Larraza-Kintana, & Makri, 2003)	AMJ	*Familiness – nonfamily stakeholders*: Family ties and executive compensation	N=253 randomized sample of family controlled public firms from COPUSTAT database over the period of 1995–1998	Regression analysis	(1) Executives with family ties to owners receive lower total pay than professional managers. (2) Pay disparity increases as family ownership position and R&D investment increases. (3) Altruistic family motives are at work when family CEOs are at the helm, but these motives manifest themselves not in higher pay but in risk protection.	Affordable loss – attracting resources at a lesser cost.

continued

Table 1.1 Continued

Author year	Journal	Category: topic	Data	Method	Relevant findings	Mapping to effectuation
(Anderson & Reeb, 2004)	ASQ	*Familiness – nonfamily stakeholders:* Independent directors' influence on mitigating conflicting shareholder groups (atomistic shareholders vs. large founding family shareholders) interest	N = 2686 firm year observations for 403 non-utility/non-banking firms from S&P 500 for periods of 1992–1999. Founding family hold stakes in 141 of these firms (average equity 17.9% and 20% of board seats) and 262 were nonfamily firms.	2 way fixed effects model and regression	(1) Most valuable public firms are those in which independent directors balance family board representation. (2) Firms that have continued founding-family ownership and relatively few independent directors, perform significantly worse than nonfamily firms. (3) Moderate family board presence provides substantial benefits to the family firm.	Importance of self-selected outside stakeholders. Crazy quilt principle.
(Zahra, Hayton, & Salvato, 2004)	ETP	*Familiness – nonfamily stakeholders:* Organizational culture in family firms and entrepreneurship	N = 536 completed responses in 1997 by manufacturing companies in five states of USA. 218 were family firms.	Survey, hierarchical regression	(1) Family firms whose cultures strongly favor an individual orientation may find it easy to spur the entrepreneurial initiatives; however, to flourish a certain level of group orientation is also required. Entrepreneurship flourishes at moderate level of individualism. (2) External orientation in family firms is a strong antecedent to entrepreneurship. (3) Decentralization of control and coordination is positively associated with entrepreneurial activity. (4) Longer term focus on strategic control has strong association with entrepreneurship. (5) Influence of culture on entrepreneurship is greater among family than nonfamily firms.	Importance of external orientation (ideas and stakeholders). Crazy quilt principle.

(Ensley & Pearson, 2005)	ETP	*Familiness – nonfamily stakeholders*: Behavioral dynamics of TMT in family and nonfamily ventures	N=242 TMT of new ventures from the Inc. 500 companies in US	Discriminant analysis	TMT with family membership were likely to achieve higher cohesion and strategic consensus than teams without kinship ties.	Bird-in-hand principle. Benefits of working from the TMTs' own means (who they know).
(Dyer & Whetten, 2006)	ETP	*Familiness – nonfamily stakeholders*: Family firms and social responsibility	N=261 S&P 500 firms from 1991–2000. Social performance from KLD database.	T-test, regression, random effects panel model	(1) Family firms and nonfamily firms behave similarly in regard to positive social initiatives. (2) Family firms are more adept at avoiding social concerns than their nonfamily counterparts.	Pilot-in-the-plane principle. Family firms can focus on longer term concerns.
(Gómez-Mejía et al., 2007)	ASQ	*Familiness – nonfamily stakeholders*: Socioemotional wealth and risk taking in family controlled firms	N=1237 family owned oil mills in southern Spain. Secondary data for 54 years	Regression analysis	(1) Family firms frame the relinquishing of socioemotional endowment as a major loss and are willing to accept a greater performance hazard to mitigate that loss. (2) Willingness to give up family control is lowest in those stages in which family influence is strongest, when socioemotional endowment is highest. (3) Family firms are willing to accept lower performance in order to retain their socioemotional wealth.	Crazy quilt plus pilot-in-the-plane principle.
(Gabrielsson, 2007)	ETP	*Familiness – nonfamily stakeholders*: Correlates of board empowerment in small companies	N=135 small companies CEOs in Sweden.	Regression analysis	Board empowerment is largely a response to satisfy the demands of external stakeholders.	Family control vs. crazy quilt principle.

continued

Table 1.1 Continued

Author year	Journal	Category: topic	Data	Method	Relevant findings	Mapping to effectuation
(Eddleston & Kellermanns, 2007)	JBV	*Familiness – nonfamily stakeholders*: How family relationships and interactions affect family firm performance	107 questionnaire responses from 60 family firms in northeast of USA	Structural Equations Modeling (SEM)	(1) Altruism can diminish the occurrence of relationship conflict and can also contribute to a participative strategy process in family firms. As such, altruism may explain why in some family firms members are able to successfully work together and run a business, while in others, family members are laden with animosity that deteriorates performance. Altruism therefore may constitute an important source of competitive advantage. (2) Relationship conflict significantly harms a family firm's performance. (3) Participative strategy process is positively related to firm performance.	Importance of self-selection and commitment to negate conflict.
(Uhlaner, Floren, & Geerlings, 2007)	SBE	*Familiness – nonfamily stakeholders*: Owner commitment and relational governance	N= 233 respondents from Dutch companies	Multiple regressions	(1) Owner commitment and financial performance are positively related. (2) Collective norms and goals as well as perceived organization rewards are positively related to owner commitment.	Bird-in-hand principle.
(Jones, Makri, & Gomez-Mejia, 2008)	ETP	*Familiness – nonfamily stakeholders*: Affiliate directors affecting decisions in family controlled public firms	N= 403 public firms included in COMPUSTAT database. 203 are family controlled.	Panel data analysis	(1) Role of affiliate directors differs from independent directors. (2) Affiliate directors play a more active role in enabling family firms to pursue growth through diversification.	Crazy quilt principle – affiliate directors encouraging diversification.

| (Chrisman, Chua, & Kellermanns, 2009) | ETP | *Familiness – nonfamily stakeholders:* Family influence, resource stocks, and short term firm performance | $N=505$ firms who are SBDC clients and responded to questionnaire, employee size 10–100 | Hierarchical regression | (1) Family influence has positive moderating effect on the relationship between firm performance and external resource stocks. (2) Nonfamily influence has positive moderating effect on relationship between firm performance and resource stocks based on functional skills. (3) External connections of family firms are different in some material way from those of nonfamily firms. (4) Except perhaps in the face of unusual opportunities, continuity and command priorities may make family firms a more stable organizational form. (5) Nonfamily firm priorities may make them more likely to be decentralized along functional lines and, consequently, better suited to capitalize on higher levels of functional resource stocks than family firms, at least in the short term. | Pilot-in-the-plane principle. |

As an additional robustness check, we also scanned the abstracts of empirical papers published in *Family Business Reviews, Organization Studies,* and *Journal of Management Studies* to make sure our list did not miss important scholars who may have chosen to publish in outlets outside of the journals we chose. We were happy to find that authors of the most cited papers in these journals were well represented in the journals we had chosen. By limiting ourselves to the journals listed above along with inputs from more experienced scholars in the field, we could make our task of reviewing more tractable than if we read all the articles published in *FBR,* at the same time achieving a reasonably satisfactory depth of understanding of the field.

We made three overarching observations from our literature reviews – both the one focused on empirical work that we will describe in more depth below as well as the broader sweep of theoretical development in the field over time.

1   In the early stages, the literature seems to have been more focused on differences between family firms and nonfamily firms (Anderson & Reeb, 2003; Gallo, Tapies, & Cappuyns, 2004; Harris, Martinez, & Ward, 1994; Lee & Rogoff, 1996; Villalonga & Amit, 2005; Westhead & Cowling, 1998).

2   As empirical studies such as (Anderson & Reeb, 2004; Bennedsen et al., 2005) brought to light the fact that most valuable public firms require the assimilation of nonfamily stakeholders in substantial ways, the field began to have more of an interest in heterogeneity within family firms, while continuing to delve deeper into positive aspects of "familiness" and how these differentiate family firms that perform well from those that don't (Eddleston & Kellermanns, 2007; Habbershon, Williams, & MacMillan, 2003).

3   More recently, with the publication of Gómez Mejía et al. (2007) that highlighted the role of socioemotional wealth, the field is increasingly interested in moving beyond traditional measures of performance (mostly financial) to honing in on variables of particular interest to family business research, several of which are non-financial and based on non-traditional behavioral assumptions such as altruism and stewardship (Zellweger et al., 2013).

Before we begin integrating these broad observations into possibilities for future research, we will outline key findings from our detailed review of empirical studies in family business and draw out specific implications that cohere into testable propositions at the intersection of effectuation and family business.

In Table 1.1 we have grouped the empirical studies into four categories based on the dependent variables of interest in each study and then chronologically ordered the studies within each category. The four categories we found consisted in the following:

1   succession;
2   capital structure – particularly the issue of retaining strong family control;
3   nonfamily stakeholders and familiness;
4   strategic flexibility.

We will now summarize the findings from each of these categories and discuss their implications for the use of effectual principles in family enterprises. In the process, we will also identify specific variables of interest that help define the intersection between family business research and effectuation research.

Succession

A major theme of interest in family business research has to do with succession planning, its antecedents, consequences, and drivers. Succession is important, for as Diwisch, Voithofer, and Weiss (2009) show, succession impacts not only the firm's own performance, but also has an effect on employment growth. Furthermore, three of the four articles in this category emphasize the importance of family members engaged in the day-to-day decision making and running of the business. In other words, it was not enough for family members to be part of the business, it was necessary for them to be active and engaged as well as pre-commit to involvement after succession in order to positively impact the succession process. Davis and Harveston (1998) found that the more closely related family members were to the owner/manager, and the higher the role or position they occupied, the greater their collective influence over the extensiveness of the succession planning process. Shepherd and Zacharakis (2000) reached the conclusion that future successors to the business should have incurred both financial and behavioral sunk costs and also be more stringently held accountable for firm performance even before the succession. And Sharma, Chrisman, and Chua (2003) showed the importance of agreement among family members to stay involved in the business after succession. These findings evoke a parallel in effectuation with regard to stakeholder commitments to the new venture creation process. Commitment from stakeholders is a matter of great importance to all new ventures that seek to survive and grow. This is even more so when a firm is created effectually because the effectual process is explicitly stakeholder focused, even more so than causally created firms that are mostly resource-focused – using resources to tackle key stakeholders, for example. Yet, the family business literature on succession is worried about one narrow category of stakeholders – namely family members. Therefore these studies also point to a possible tension between the use of the bird-in-hand principle (namely working with the "whom you know" aspect of means at hand – i.e., internal family members) and the crazy quilt principle (namely allowing outside stakeholders to self-select into the process to become key players that help shape the sub-goals and even the long-term vision of the firm). We will see this tension between several of the effectual principles and the crazy quilt principle reappear in each of the other themes of interest to family business researchers as well.

Capital structure

As Bopaiah (1998) shows, family-controlled firms are more likely to obtain debt, perhaps because lenders perceive familiness as a deterrent of moral hazard problems. More recently, Chua et al. (2011) finds evidence with the explanation based on family firms' social capital. Yet several studies show that family firms are debt averse, because they do not wish to give up control to nonfamily stakeholders (Mishra & McConaughy, 1999). Family firms' debt aversion is also evidenced by other studies that show that family firms are more likely to have 100 percent equity, or exhibit no difference in capital structure when compared with nonfamily firms (Agrawal & Nagarajan, 1990; Gallo, Tapies, & Cappuyns, 2004)

Yet the issue of capital structure in family firms is more complex than this. Although they tend to be conservative in seeking funding from outside and prefer internal sources for funding, when they do go out for funding, they appear to prefer debt over equity for the same reason – namely, preserving family control of the firm. Even when the internal source of funding consists of hiring family members and having to pay lesser than market value, resulting in lower costs, family firms may be trading that off against the flexibility of firing them when needed (Gomez-Mejia, Larraza-Kintana, & Makri, 2003; Gomez-Mejia, Nuñez-Nickel, & Gutierrez, 2001). Cruz, Justo, and De Castro (2012) identified another such tradeoff – they found that employing family members increased sales but decreased profitability as measured by ROA (return on assets). The use of equity as opposed to debt is less likely in firms that exhibit higher preferences for strong family control and formal planning practices (Romano, Tanewski, & Smyrnios, 2001). This echoes an earlier finding by Chaganti and Damanpour (1991, p. 489) that, "With respect to capital structure, in corporate settings where institutional stockholdings are relatively low, higher levels of family ownership correspond to higher corporate long-term debt-capital ratios." Arguing for a more nuanced view, in a field study of 1464 family firms, Schulze, Lubatkin, and Dino (2003a) found that the relationship between the use of debt and the dispersion of ownership took a u-shaped form. However, more recently, Steijvers, Voordeckers, and Vanhoof (2010) found that family firms, as opposed to nonfamily firms, are also more likely to pledge collateral even in the low loan amount category.

Taken together, these studies seem to provide a mixed picture about the use of affordable loss in family firms. On the one hand, most family firms are not willing to risk what they cannot afford to lose, namely family control. Paradoxically, this means that they either have to be satisfied to grow slower or seek debt for growth, the latter being more of a burden than equity funding in the event of downside outcomes. In effectual terms, this amounts to closing off one avenue for effectively using affordable loss, namely, reducing risk by spreading it across a more diverse group of stakeholders. That the desire for family control restricts the availability of equity financing is also evidenced by Dawson (2011) that documents the higher likelihood of private equity professionals investing in firms with nonfamily members and where family members are more likely to have outside working experience.

Nonfamily stakeholders and familiness

In spite of the ubiquity of family firms in the world and the benefits of family influence argued for by the empirical evidence, the importance of external stakeholders and their empowerment in terms of decision making within the family firm appears to be a key driver of performance. Anderson and Reeb (2004, p. 209) conducted a compelling empirical examination of this issue using board compensation in S&P 500 firms. They summarize their findings as follows:

> we find that the most valuable public firms are those in which independent directors balance family board representation. In contrast, in firms with continued founding-family ownership and relatively few independent directors, firm performance is significantly worse than in nonfamily firms. We also find that a moderate family board presence provides substantial benefits to the firm.

In an early study, Chaganti and Schneer (1994) found that sales performance was greatest when family firms had owner-managers with extensive industry experience, were conservative in adding workers, emphasized product customization, relied on written reports, but avoided long-range operations planning – several of these may be directly mapped to effectual principles such as bird-in-hand (industry experience), affordable loss (conservative in adding workers) and pilot-in-the-plane (planning avoidance), with slight indirect support for the crazy quilt principle (product customization). Also, in a more recent study of manufacturing firms in five states in the US, Zahra, Hayton, and Salvato (2004) found a positive impact of external orientation and decentralized control on entrepreneurial activity both in family and nonfamily firms – providing some indirect evidence for the role of the crazy quilt principle. But studies show that family controlled firms are less likely to welcome independent board members (Fiegener et al., 2000), and when they do, it is usually as a response to owners not directly managing the company and other contingency factors including the advice of affiliates that push them beyond the focus on family control (Gabrielsson, 2007; Jones, Makri, & Gomez-Mejia, 2008). The issue of allowing stakeholders (whether family members or otherwise) to self-select into the venture creation process is one of the most important principles in effectuation (Sarasvathy & Dew, 2005, 2008). Yet, family firms seek to limit entry by nonfamily members thereby restricting the use of effectual logic in this regard. Before we examine the implications of this challenge to implementing effectual strategies in family firms, we need to understand the unique aspects that family firms seek to preserve and leverage.

Recent research into family enterprise has sought to provide a more rigorous in-depth understanding of these unique aspects through the concept of "familiness" (Habbershon, Williams, & MacMillan, 2003). Chrisman, Chua, and Steier (2005) provide a succinct summary:

> because a family business is an embodiment of the aspirations and capabilities of family members, it has a strong social element affecting the decisions that determine its strategy, operations, and administrative structure. Furthermore, because the social element itself has value to the organizing family, it tends to persist over time, giving the family organization a unique character and culture. Habbershon et al., following Chua, Chrisman, and Sharma (1999), suggest that the uniqueness is manifested through the purposeful transgenerational pursuance of a vision held in common by a family.

Among the empirically investigated concepts of interest to this "social element" that characterizes familiness are included – participative culture (Mahto et al., 2010), altruism (Eddleston & Kellermanns, 2007), owner commitment (Uhlaner, Floren, & Geerlings, 2007), stewardship (Davis, Allen, & Hayes, 2010), and socioemotional endowment (Gómez-Mejía et al., 2007). Several of these are related in interesting ways to positive performance and other factors leading to better performance as well as the possibility of trading off economic performance for non-economic satisfaction. Ensley and Pearson (2005) for example, found that top management teams with family membership were likely to achieve higher cohesion and strategic consensus than teams without kinship ties. And from a societal perspective, Dyer and Whetten (2006, p. 795) found that while family and nonfamily firms are no different in undertaking positive social responsibility initiatives, family firms were more adept at avoiding socially irresponsible behavior, especially in terms of their reputation in the community. The struggle to hold on to family control versus the positive influence of nonfamily stakeholders, however, appears to play a more complex role in achieving better performance in a variety of domains. Chrisman, Chua, and Kellermanns (2009), for example, find a series of differences in relationships between family/ nonfamily influence and different types of resource stocks leading to differential impacts on performance. Even one of the earliest empirical studies that included family and nonfamily firm data found that family controlled firms were less likely to develop a multi-division organizational form that is highly correlated with more dispersed growth (Palmer et al., 1987). Interestingly, however, when examined through a sample of Fortune 1000 firms, Miller, Le Breton-Miller, and Lester (2010) found that family-owned firms were likely to pursue more diversified acquisitions – thereby obtaining some diversification benefits without dilution of wealth concentration with the family.

In sum, the large and growing list of studies in this category point even more strongly to the need to focus future research on the particular elements of family business that facilitate and/or hinder the use of the crazy quilt principle. We will take up that task after we discuss the studies in the fourth category in Table 1.1.

Strategic flexibility

The family's commitment to the business, measured using the F-PEC scale in conjunction with its measure of overlap between family and business values, was also found to have a significant positive impact on strategic flexibility (Zahra et al., 2008). This effect on strategic flexibility was positively moderated by stewardship behaviors. Strategic flexibility refers to the ability of a firm to seize opportunities and deflect threats from its competitive environment. This ability is important as a driver of growth and innovativeness in firms. Kellermanns and Eddleston (2006) found, for example, that "willingness to change and technological opportunity recognition are positively related to corporate entrepreneurship in family firms." Yet achieving strategic flexibility may not be very easy for family controlled firms.

In this and other connections, an interesting distinction made in recent studies in the literature has to do with family control as opposed to family influence. Sirmon et al. (2008, p. 980) define the difference as follows:

> Family control provides the family ultimate control of the firm and represents a complete or majority family ownership (Nordqvist, 2005). Alternatively, family influence does not infer unilateral control. Instead, family influence represents situations where a family has a substantial ownership stake and managerial presence in a firm that together allows the family to affect strategic action without providing unilateral control.
>
> (Chua, Chrisman, & Sharma, 1999)

This distinction is important because while family influence may have several benefits, concentration of ownership in the hands of a family may cause problems even at the level of the economy or society. Consider, for example, the findings from Morck and Yeung (2003) when they divided up the world's US dollar billionaires into two categories – self-made billionaires and those who inherited their wealth. They aggregated the wealth owned by each type of billionaire in each country. As might be expected, they found that a country's per capita GDP grows faster if its self-made billionaire wealth is larger as a fraction of GDP. Counter-intuitively, however, they also found that per capita GDP growth is slower in countries where inherited billionaire wealth is larger as a fraction of GDP. Building on this curious empirical finding, a recent comprehensive review of the topic in the *Journal of Economic Literature* makes a strong case to distinguish highly concentrated corporate control in the hands of family firms from firms in which the concentration of ownership is less onerous (Morck, Wolfenzon, & Yeung, 2005).

The literature we have been reviewing here suggests that this distinction between family control and family influence may also be important at the micro-level. Thomsen and Pedersen (2000) found that while ownership concentration had a positive impact on shareholder value and profits, the effect leveled off for very high levels of concentration. More recently, Sirmon et al. (2008), found that firms with family influence, as opposed to those with family control were less rigid under threats of imitation. Moreover, family-influenced firms had to retract less from their levels of R&D investment and internationalization, allowing them to position themselves for future growth and flexibility. These studies seem to reinforce the finding from Anderson and Reeb (2004) that family firms with an overly strong focus on family control jeopardize their own survival and growth when compared with family firms that are more welcoming to outside stake-holders – even when strategic flexibility is defined simply as the ability to respond to threats and opportunities exogenous to the firm's actions. This coheres with findings from recent studies that family-controlled firms tend to invest less in R&D (Block, 2012; Chen & Hsu, 2009; Munari, Oriani, & Sobrero, 2010).

Effectuation, of course, argues for a different measure of strategic flexibility, namely, the propensity to take one's goals, not as exogenous givens, but shape them as endogenous to how one uses one's means. Interestingly, even though the studies above measured strategic flexibility in terms of responses to exogenous opportunities and threats, the outcomes of flexible strategies did consist in new goals for the firm. Moreover, Sirmon et al.'s (2008) examination of R&D investment and internationalization provided evidence for fewer changes in means in family-influenced firms than in firms with no family influence. The two studies combined argue for the possibility that family-influenced firms are capable of effectual logic, to a substantially greater extent than family-controlled firms.

In sum, after a careful review of selective yet representative empirical studies of family enterprises published in major journals, we have identified at least one persistent source of difficulty in implementing effectual logic – namely, an excessive focus on family control. Yet, it is this difficulty that also offers fertile soil for future work at the intersection of the two burgeoning fields of research. To begin sowing the seeds for such future work, we turn to the development of a few preliminary propositions derived from our detailed investigation of the empirical work in family business to date.

Empirically derived propositions: factors that facilitate and hinder the use of effectual logic in family firms

As mentioned at the beginning of the previous section, one objective of our detailed discussions of findings from the four empirical categories above was to discover relevant variables that help define the intersection between family business research and effectuation research. Assuming our dependent variable is the use of effectual logic in family firms, it is clear that the single most important defining variable in this space is family control, and its variant, family influence. More precisely, the discussion of empirical findings in the previous section suggests the following propositions for future research into the effectual family enterprise:

- Proposition 1:
  The higher the emphasis on family control, the more likely the use of the bird-in-hand principle.
- Complementary Propositions 2a and 2b:
  a   The higher the emphasis on family control, the lower the strategic flexibility – i.e., lower the likelihood of using the lemonade principle.
  b   Family influence, as opposed to family control is more likely to aid in the use of the lemonade principle.
- Proposition 3:
  The higher the desire for and strategic focus on family control or family influence, the more difficult the use of the crazy quilt principle.
- Competing Propositions 4a and 4b:
  a   The higher the desire for and focus on family control, the lower the likelihood of using equity to bring external sources of funding in, and hence the more difficulty in using the affordable loss principle.
  b   The higher the desire for and focus on family control, the higher the likelihood of avoiding external sources of funding altogether, and hence the more likely the use of the affordable loss principle.

Whereas we cannot directly derive a specific proposition with regard to the pilot-in-the-plane principle from our review of the empirical literature listed in Table 1.1, we believe that the following proposition quoted verbatim from Miller (Miller & Le Breton-Miller, 2006, p. 79) captures some aspects relevant to it:

Proposition 2.2. Compared to their competitors, FCBs run by family CEOs are apt to manifest more beneficial stewardship behaviors: specifically, fewer shortsighted acquisition and downsizing decisions and more R&D, training, and capital expenditures, and thus more distinctive capabilities that produce higher long-term financial returns.

The above quote from the Miller and Le Breton-Miller book is reinforced by other studies such as Stavrou,Kassinis, and Filotheou (2007). To the extent that stewardship behaviors entail a focus on what current stakeholders do and care about as opposed to a focus on short-run expected returns, such behaviors are less likely to be based entirely on inevitable trends. This leads us to the following conjecture about the likely use of the pilot-in-the-plane principle in family firms. (Note: we call this "conjecture" as opposed to "proposition" because it is not derived from previous empirical work as the other propositions are. Yet we believe this would be worth investigating in future empirical work at the intersection of family business and effectuation.)

- Conjecture 1:
  The lower the focus on family control, the more likely the stewardship behavior toward outside stakeholders – namely, the higher the use of the pilot-in-the-plane principle.

It is important to clarify in the context of this conjecture that while family-controlled businesses may show stewardship behaviors, they are less likely to show stewardship behaviors toward nonfamily stakeholders. Moreover, we use the term "stewardship" in the technical sense in which it is not the same as socially responsible behavior. While one would expect some overlap between stewardship and social responsibility, as Deniz and Suarez (2005) show, the two concepts are not congruent and can get into conflict when the interests of internal stakeholders are not aligned with those of external stakeholders including those of the natural environment. Atkinson and Galaskiewicz (1988), for example, showed no difference between family-owned firms (that are presumably more likely to show stewardship behavior) and other firms in charitable giving. In sum, a closer examination of the intersection between stewardship theory and effectuation may offer in itself a high-potential opportunity for future research. In recent studies, stewardship has been included in a cluster of attributes within the family business literature under the rubric of "socioemotional wealth." Therefore, in the final sections of our current investigation, we zoom in on these recent developments.

Socioemotional wealth and its relationship to the effectual family enterprise

According to research by Gómez-Mejía et al. (2007) and Berrone et al. (2010), owners of family firms are concerned about both financial returns and socioemotional wealth (SEW) derived through the ownership share in their firms. SEW concerns a variety of non-financial aspects of firm ownership meeting the family's needs. Among these aspects are the family's possibility to be altruistic to family members (Schulze, Lubatkin, & Dino, 2003b), the desire for a high social status in the local community in which the firm is located (Dyer & Whetten, 2006; Wiklund, 2006), the fulfillment of needs for organizational identification (Kepner, 1983; Zellweger et al., 2013), the ability to exercise influence and retain control (Berrone et al., 2010; Olson et al., 2003), and to maintain and create a family dynasty (Jaffe & Lane, 2004).

The preservation of SEW shapes the strategic decision making and the risk behavior in family firms. The behavioral risk literature (Kahneman & Tversky, 1979; Wiseman & Gomez-Mejia, 1998) argues that an individual's risk preference depends on the framing of the decision problem, in particular the reference point that is used to compare potential decision outcomes to available decision options. Gómez-Mejía et al. (2007) argue that the pursuit of SEW by family owners influences the reference point against which family-firm owners compare the outcomes of their strategic decisions. Family owners are argued to be loss averse with regard to their SEW – a loss of it would imply negative consequences for the family such as a loss of intimacy with the firm and a loss of social status in the community in which they live. This particular type of loss aversion influences the family firm's risk behavior in a way that it makes them more risk willing and risk averse at the same time. To avoid losses of SEW, family firms are more willing than other firms to accept performance hazard risks. This type of risk refers to the possibility to financially underperform, e.g., in comparison to the firm's past performance or to peers, and in the worst case to the risk of organizational failure. The acceptance of performance hazard risk by family firms may create a paradox situation in which they accept a higher risk of firm failure (which would also imply a total loss of SEW) to prevent a loss of SEW. By contrast, family firms are less likely to accept venturing risks, i.e., risks associated with the search for alternative routines and opportunities (Bowman, 1982; Fiegenbaum & Thomas, 1988). Using R&D spending as a proxy for investments in innovation, empirical studies have shown that family firms avoid venturing risks (Block, 2012; Munari, Oriani, & Sobrero, 2010). An explorative search strategy can lead to unexpected outcomes and increases the variance in performance (March, 1991). The outcome is often highly uncertain and skewed in nature (Scherer & Harhoff, 2000). Family firms, preventing the SEW of its owners, strive to avoid uncertain and risky projects as these threaten the firm's independence and further increase the probability of firm failure.

Yet, noneconomic measures of performance are relevant not only to family firms but to entrepreneurs more generally. As Gimeno et al. (1997) have shown, entrepreneurs persist with underperforming firms for reasons other than financial gain. Other studies on the motivations of entrepreneurs have also shown that most entrepreneurs are motivated by factors other than economic return in whether to start a new venture at all as well as in deciding on the kinds of new ventures they start (Amit & MacCrimmon, 2001; Baum & Locke, 2004; Gabrielsson & Politis, 2011; Hessels, Van Gelderen, & Thurik, 2008). The rise of social entrepreneurship provides further evidence for the role of SEW in entrepreneurship, albeit composed of a very different set of ingredients from what is being discussed in the family business literature (Hemingway & Maclagan, 2004; Short, Moss, & Lumpkin, 2009; Townsend & Hart, 2008).

In fact, there is a wide variety of possible ingredients, ranging from personal aspirations, family and social values, and stewardship behaviors toward others and the zeal to reform society and combat climate change that can all constitute non-economic motivations or SEW that matter to entrepreneurs and their stakeholders within and outside of family firms. Given this range, and given the dependent variable that is the focus of this chapter, we may need to partition SEW as conceptualized within family firms into factors that facilitate and hinder the use of effectual logic. A recent article by Zellweger and Dehlen (2011: 4) helps us begin this task by partitioning SEW into family-centered and other-centered factors, the former operating at the level of the family and the latter at the level of the firm:

> At the family level, these goals include: pride in the firm, family status in the community, entrepreneurial tradition, social support among friends, harmony among family members (Chrisman, Chua, Pearson, & Barnett, 2010). Furthermore, family-centered nonfinancial goals shape the identity claims of the family (Berrone et al., 2010). At the firm level, nonfinancial goals include: responsible employee practices, trusting relationships with suppliers and customers, environmental actions, corporate social performance, support for local community, and the like (Gomez-Mejia et al., 2007; Zellweger & Nason, 2008). These firm-level nonfinancial goals are centered on nonfamily stakeholders and are meant to be illustrative rather than exhaustive.

Each of these firm level other-centered values is necessary for effectual entrepreneurs to build stronger stakeholder networks using the crazy quilt principle. Therefore, in our theorizing concerning these, we may want to begin by identifying a minimal subset of SEW variables, call it effectual SEW (or ESEW for short) that enable and facilitate the use of the crazy quilt principle. As shown in Figure 1.2, ESEW may contain items from both family-centered and other-centered SEW, but with modifications on the family-centered factors so that they are applicable to nonfamily stakeholders as well. In other words, ESEW is more outward-facing and directed toward committed self-selected stakeholders, irrespective of whether they are family members or not. We chose four elements to be part of ESEW:

- intelligent altruism;
- responsible practices toward all stakeholders;
- trusting relationships with all committed stakeholders;
- stewardship toward all committed stakeholders.

We did not want to include all the elements listed under other-centered SEW because while they may be desirable from a normative standpoint, they are not strictly necessary for a minimal set that will enable effectuators to create effective corridors through which stakeholders can self-select themselves into the venture creation process. Let us briefly examine why the four we selected may be necessary to constitute a minimal set.

As argued in Sarasvathy (2008) intelligent altruism is key to the effectual process for several reasons. Intelligent altruism is the idea that most humans are neither entirely selfish nor entirely altruistic, but have developed judgments about when to be one or the other (Thompson, 1998). Moreover, biological and social evolution has ensured that most humans are not only biased toward

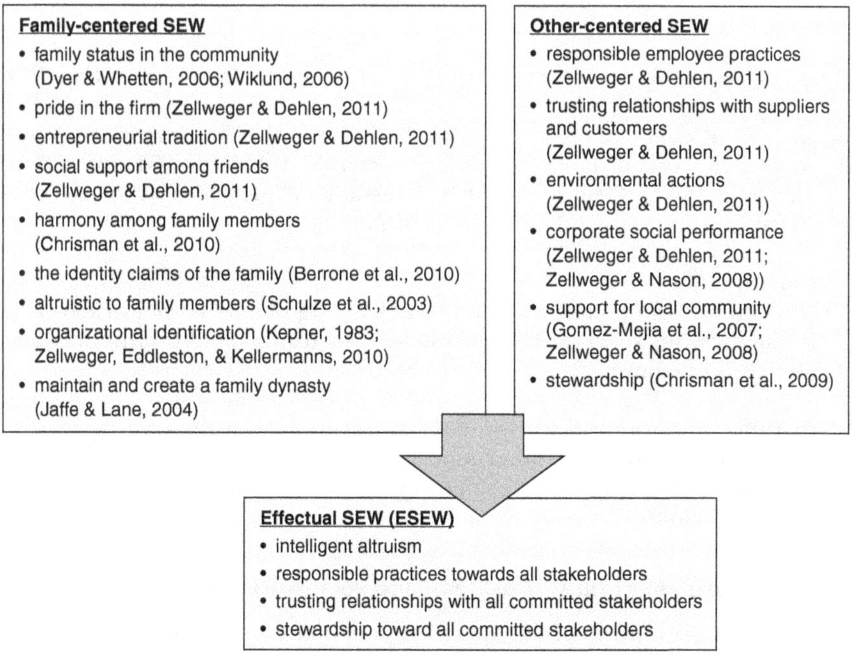

Family-centered SEW

- family status in the community (Dyer & Whetten, 2006; Wiklund, 2006)
- pride in the firm (Zellweger & Dehlen, 2011)
- entrepreneurial tradition (Zellweger & Dehlen, 2011)
- social support among friends (Zellweger & Dehlen, 2011)
- harmony among family members (Chrisman et al., 2010)
- the identity claims of the family (Berrone et al., 2010)
- altruistic to family members (Schulze et al., 2003)
- organizational identification (Kepner, 1983; Zellweger, Eddleston, & Kellermanns, 2010)
- maintain and create a family dynasty (Jaffe & Lane, 2004)

Other-centered SEW

- responsible employee practices (Zellweger & Dehlen, 2011)
- trusting relationships with suppliers and customers (Zellweger & Dehlen, 2011)
- environmental actions (Zellweger & Dehlen, 2011)
- corporate social performance (Zellweger & Dehlen, 2011; Zellweger & Nason, 2008))
- support for local community (Gomez-Mejia et al., 2007; Zellweger & Nason, 2008)
- stewardship (Chrisman et al., 2009)

Effectual SEW (ESEW)

- intelligent altruism
- responsible practices towards all stakeholders
- trusting relationships with all committed stakeholders
- stewardship toward all committed stakeholders

Figure 1.2 Defining minimal ESEW as a modified subset of SEW.

altruism in appropriate situations; they are also more likely to induce others to be so whenever they behave in an altruistic manner (Simon, 1993). Intelligent altruism does not entail continual self-sacrifice or other heroic behaviors. It can consist of simple understanding of when and how to give and take advice and provide small measures of help at affordable loss levels to oneself and to listen, sympathize, and empathize when needed. This type of altruistic behavior and a reasonably good judgment about when to be altruistic and when to take care of one's own self-interest whether at the level of the person or the firm or the community one is crucial to attracting stakeholders who will freely make commitments to a new venture operating in conditions of multiple and high uncertainties.

Similarly, without responsible practices and trust, stakeholders will most likely not want to commit anything of value, especially ahead of proved success in a new venture. Nor will any profitable long-run relationships be sustainable without responsible practices and trust between stakeholders. Stewardship behaviors go hand in hand with all three of the above elements of ESEW. Without stewardship, agency problems between stakeholders are likely to develop and fester, resulting in reduced levels of organizational identification and commitment over time, both of which may undermine the new venture from even coming to be, let alone surviving and thriving.

Based on our definition of ESEW above, we can develop the following propositions about the relationship between ESEW and the use of effectual logic.

Proposition 5:
Entrepreneurs and their firms, whether family owned or not, are more likely to use effectual logic in general, and the crazy quilt principle in particular, if they invest in and nurture ESEW.

Additionally, we know from previous work on effectuation that when used effectively, effectual logic has two positive impacts on performance. At the venture level, the use of effectual logic increases the likelihood of innovative outcomes and reduces the costs of failure, irrespective of the probability of failure (Dew, Sarasathy, et al., 2009; Read et al., 2009; Sarasvathy, 2001, 2008; Wiltbank et al., 2009). That leads us to the following proposition.

Proposition 6:
Ceteris paribus, the higher the level of ESEW, the better the performance of the family firm; specifically, performance in terms of innovativeness and lower costs of failure.

Note that this proposition does not make any claims about the positive or negative performance impacts of other aspects or types of SEW. Nor does it make any claims on positive firm performance in general – only in terms of innovativeness and cost of failure.

Conclusion: bringing family, business, and society together

At the heart of entrepreneurial expertise appears to be a method of stitching together co-operative networks of inter-subjective relationships that evoke the feel of a family or a community more than that of either an authoritarian organization (hierarchy) headed by a Williamsonian opportunist or an efficient machine plowing its way through a hostile competitive landscape (market). But for that method to work, people do need to be able to express their individuality and bring their idiosyncratic preferences and abilities to bear on the choice to self-select into particular ventures and markets. In other words, enduring ventures need to be open to anyone who is willing to commit real resources to co-create a shared future, irrespective of whether they are family members or not. Maybe the way ahead would be for family businesses to learn to be effectual so they can expand their membership through committed stakeholders while ensuring overlaps in core values even if there are significant differences in aspirations and preferences for particular operationalizations of those core values. And for all firms to treat their stakeholders more like our best ideals of a good family.

References

Agrawal, A., & Nagarajan, N. J. (1990). Corporate capital structure, agency costs, and ownership control: The case of all-equity firms. *Journal of Finance, 45*(4), 1325–1331.

Amit, R., & MacCrimmon, K. R. (2001). Does money matter? Wealth attainment as the motive for initiating growth-oriented technology ventures. *Journal of Business Venturing, 16*(2), 119.

Anderson, R. C., & Reeb, D. M. (2003). Founding-family ownership and firm performance: Evidence from the S&P 500. *Journal of Finance, 58*(3), 1301–1328.

Anderson, R. C., & Reeb, D. M. (2004). Board composition: Balancing family influence in S&P 500 firms. *Administrative Science Quarterly, 49*(2), 209–237.

Atkinson, L., & Galaskiewicz, J. (1988). Stock ownership and company contributions to charity. *Administrative Science Quarterly, 33*(1), 82–100.

Baker, T., & Nelson, R. E. (2005). Creating something from nothing: Resource construction through entrepreneurial bricolage. *Administrative Science Quarterly, 50*(3), 329.

Baker, T., Miner, A. S., & Eesley, D. T. (2003). Improvising firms: Bricolage, account giving and improvisational competencies in the founding process 1. *Research Policy, 32*(2), 255–276.

Bammens, Y., Voordeckers, W., & Van Gils, A. (2008). Boards of directors in family firms: A generational perspective. *Small Business Economics, 31*(2), 163–180.

Baum, J. R., & Locke, E. A. (2004). The relationship of entrepreneurial traits, skill, and motivation to subsequent venture growth. *Journal of Applied Psychology, 89*(4), 587–598.

Bennedsen, M., Nielsen, K., Pérez-González, F., & Wolfenzon, D. (2005). Inside the family firm: The role of families in succession decisions and performance. *Quarterly Journal of Economics, 122*(2), 647–691.

Berrone, P., Cruz, C., Gomez-Mejia, L. R., & Larraza-Kintana, M. (2010). Socioemotional wealth and corporate responses to institutional pressures: Do family-controlled firms pollute less? *Administrative Science Quarterly, 55*(1), 82–113.

Block, J. H. (2012). R&D investments in family and founder firms: An agency perspective. *Journal of Business Venturing, 27*(2), 248–265.

Bopaiah, C. (1998). Availability of credit to family businesses. *Small Business Economics, 11*(1), 75.

Bowman, E. H. (1982). Risk seeking by troubled firms. *Sloan Management Review, 23*(4), 33–42.

Brettel, M., Mauer, R., Engelen, A., & Kupper, D. (2011). Corporate effectuation: Entrepreneurial action and its impact on R&D project performance. *Journal of Business Venturing, 27*(2), 167–184.

Chaganti, R., & Damanpour, F. (1991). Institutional ownership, capital structure, and firm performance. *Strategic Management Journal, 12*(7), 479–491.

Chaganti, R., & Schneer, J. A. (1994). A study of the impact of owner's mode of entry on venture performance and management patterns. *Journal of Business Venturing, 9*(3), 243–260.

Chandler, G. N., DeTienne, D. R., McKelvie, A., & Mumford, T. V. (2011). Causation and effectuation processes: A validation study. *Journal of Business Venturing, 26*(3), 375–390.

Chen, H. L., & Hsu, W. T. (2009). Family ownership, board independence, and R&D investment. *Family Business Review, 22*(4), 347.

Chiles, T. H., Bluedorn, A. C., & Gupta, V. K. (2007). Beyond creative destruction and entrepreneurial discovery: A radical Austrian approach to entrepreneurship. *Organization Studies, 28*(4), 467.

Chiles, T. H., Gupta, V. K., & Bluedorn, A. C. (2008). On Lachmannian and effectual entrepreneurship: A rejoinder to Sarasvathy and Dew (2008). *Studies, 29*(2), 247–253.

Chrisman, J. J., Chua, J. H., & Kellermanns, F. (2009). Priorities, resource stocks, and performance in family and nonfamily firms. *Entrepreneurship: Theory and Practice, 33*(3), 739–760.

Chrisman, J. J., Chua, J. H., Kellermanns, F. W., & Chang, E. P. C. (2007). Are family managers agents or stewards? An exploratory study in privately held family firms. *Journal of Business Research, 60*(10), 1030–1038.

Chrisman, J. J., Chua, J. H., & Steier, L. (2005). Sources and consequences of distinctive familiness: An introduction. *Entrepreneurship: Theory and Practice, 29*(3), 237–247.

Chua, J. H., Chrisman, J. J., Kellermanns, F., & Wu, Z. (2011). Family involvement and new venture debt financing. *Journal of Business Venturing, 26*(4), 472–488.

Chua, J. H., Chrisman, J. J., & Sharma, P. (1999). Defining the family business by behavior. *Entrepreneurship: Theory and Practice, 23*, 19–40.

Cruz, C., Justo, R., & De Castro, J. O. (2012). Does family employment enhance MSEs performance? Integrating socioemotional wealth and family embeddedness perspectives. *Journal of Business Venturing, 27*(1), 62–76.

Davis, J. H., Allen, M. R., & Hayes, H. D. (2010). Is blood thicker than water? A study of stewardship perceptions in family business. *Entrepreneurship: Theory and Practice, 34*(6), 1093–1116.

Davis, P. S., & Harveston, P. D. (1998). The influence of family on the family business succession process: A multi-generational perspective. *Entrepreneurship: Theory and Practice, 22*(3), 31.

Dawson, A. (2011). Private equity investment decisions in family firms: The role of human resources and agency costs. *Journal of Business Venturing, 26*(2), 189–199.

Déniz, M. d. l. C. D., & Suárez, M. K. C. (2005). Corporate social responsibility and family business in Spain. *Journal of Business Ethics, 56*(1), 27–41.

Dew, N. (2009). Serendipity in entrepreneurship. *Organization Studies*, 30(7),735–753.

Dew, N., Read, S., Sarasvathy, S. D., & Wiltbank, R. (2009). Effectual versus predictive logics in entrepreneurial decision-making: Differences between experts and novices. *Journal of Business Venturing, 24*(4), 287–309.

Dew, N., Sarasvathy, S., Read, S., & Wiltbank, R. (2009). Affordable loss: Behavioral economic aspects of the plunge decision. *Strategic Entrepreneurship Journal, 3*(2), 105–126.

Dew, N., Sarasvathy, S. D., & Venkataraman, S. (2004). The economic implications of exaptation. *Journal of Evolutionary Economics, 14*(1), 69–84.

Diwisch, D., Voithofer, P., & Weiss, C. (2009). Succession and firm growth: Results from a non-parametric matching approach. *Small Business Economics, 32*(1), 45–56.

Dyer, G. W., & Whetten, D. A. (2006). Family firms and social responsibility: Preliminary evidence from the S&P 500. *Entrepreneurship: Theory and Practice, 30*(6), 785–802.

Eddleston, K. A., & Kellermanns, F. W. (2007). Destructive and productive family relationships: A stewardship theory perspective. *Journal of Business Venturing, 22*(4), 545–565.

Endres, A. M., & Woods, C. R. (2010). Schumpeter's "conduct model of the dynamic entrepreneur": Scope and distinctiveness. *Journal of Evolutionary Economics, 20*(4), 583–607.

Ensley, M. D., & Pearson, A. W. (2005). An exploratory comparison of the behavioral dynamics of top management teams in family and nonfamily new ventures: Cohesion, conflict, potency, and consensus. *Entrepreneurship: Theory and Practice, 29*(3), 267–284.

Ericsson, K. A., & Simon, H. A. (1993). *Protocol analysis: Verbal reports as data (rev. ed.)*. Cambridge, MA: MIT Press.

Fiegenbaum, A., & Thomas, H. (1988). Attitudes toward risk and the risk-return paradox: Prospect theory explanations. *Academy of Management Journal, 31*(1), 85–106.

Fiegener, M. K., Brown, B. M., Dreux Iv, D. R., & Dennis Jr, W. J. (2000). CEO stakes and board composition in small private firms. *Entrepreneurship: Theory and Practice, 24*(4), 5.

Fischer, E., & Reuber, A. R. (2011). Social interaction via new social media: (How) can interactions on Twitter affect effectual thinking and behavior? *Journal of Business Venturing, 26*(1), 1–18.

Gabrielsson, J. (2007). Correlates of board empowerment in small companies. *Entrepreneurship: Theory and Practice, 31*(5), 687–711.

Gabrielsson, J., & Politis, D. (2011). Career motives and entrepreneurial decision-making: Examining preferences for causal and effectual logics in the early stage of new ventures. *Small Business Economics, 36*(3), 281–298.

Gallo, M. A., Tapies, J., & Cappuyns, K. (2004). Comparison of family and nonfamily business: Financial logic and personal preferences. *Family Business Review, 17*(4), 303–318.

Gimeno, J., Folta, T. B., Cooper, A. C., & Woo, C. Y. (1997). Survival of the fittest? Entrepreneurial human capital and the persistence of underperforming firms. *Administrative Science Quarterly, 42*(4), 750–783.

Goel, S., & Karri, R. (2006). Entrepreneurs, effectual logic, and over-trust. *Entrepreneurship: Theory and Practice,* 30(4), 477–493.

Gómez-Mejía, L. R., Haynes, K. T., Núñez-Nickel, M., Jacobson, K. J. L., & Moyano-Fuentes, J. (2007). Socioemotional wealth and business risks in family-controlled firms: Evidence from Spanish olive oil mills. *Administrative Science Quarterly, 52*(1), 106–137.

Gomez-Mejia, L. R., Larraza-Kintana, M., & Makri, M. (2003). The determinants of executive compensation in family-controlled public corporations. *Academy of Management Journal, 46*(2), 226–237.

Gomez-Mejia, L. R., Nuñez-Nickel, M., & Gutierrez, I. (2001). The role of family ties in agency contracts. *Academy of Management Journal, 44*(1), 81–95.

Habbershon, T. G., Williams, M., & MacMillan, I. C. (2003). A unified systems perspective of family firm performance. *Journal of Business Venturing, 18*(4), 451–465.

Harmeling, S. S., Sarasvathy, S. D., & Freeman, R. E. (2009). Related debates in ethics and entrepreneurship: Values, opportunities, and contingency. *Journal of Business Ethics, 84*(3), 341–365.

Harris, D., Martinez, J. I., & Ward, J. L. (1994). Is strategy different for the family-owned business? *Family Business Review, 7*(2), 159–174.

Hayward, M. L. A., Forster, W. R., Sarasvathy, S. D., & Fredrickson, B. L. (2009). Beyond hubris: How highly confident entrepreneurs rebound to venture again. *Journal of Business Venturing, 25*(6), 569–578.

Hemingway, C. A., & Maclagan, P. W. (2004). Managers' personal values as drivers of corporate social responsibility. *Journal of Business Ethics, 50*(1), 33–44.

Hessels, J., Van Gelderen, M., & Thurik, R. (2008). Entrepreneurial aspirations, motivations, and their drivers. *Small Business Economics, 31*(3), 323–339.

Jaffe, D. T., & Lane, S. H. (2004). Sustaining a family dynasty: Key issues facing complex multigenerational business and investment owning families. *Family Business Review, 17*(1), 81–98.

James, W. (1948). What pragmatism means. *Essays in Pragmatism,* 141–158.

Jones, C. D., Makri, M., & Gomez-Mejia, L. R. (2008). Affiliate directors and perceived risk bearing in publicly traded, family-controlled firms: The case of diversification. *Entrepreneurship: Theory and Practice, 32*(6), 1007–1026.

Kahneman, D., & Tversky, A. (1979). Prospect theory: An analysis of decision under risk. *Econometrica: Journal of the Econometric Society, 47*(2), 263–291.

Kellermanns, F. W., & Eddleston, K. A. (2006). Corporate entrepreneurship in family firms: A family perspective. *Entrepreneurship: Theory and Practice, 30*(6), 809–830.

Kepner, E. (1983). The family and the firm: A coevolutionary perspective. *Organizational Dynamics, 12*(1), 57–70.

La Porta, R., Lopez-de-Silanes, F., & Shleifer, A. (1999). Corporate ownership around the world. *Journal of Finance, 54*(2), 471–517.

Lee, M. S., & Rogoff, E. G. (1996). Research note: Comparison of small businesses with family participation versus small businesses without family participation: An investigation of differences in goals, attitudes, and family/business conflict. *Family Business Review, 9*(4), 423.

Mahto, R. V., Davis, P. S., Pearce Ii, J. A., & Robinson Jr, R. B. (2010). Satisfaction with firm performance in family businesses. *Entrepreneurship: Theory and Practice, 34*(5), 985–1001.

March, J. G. (1991). Exploration and exploitation in organizational learning. *Organization Science, 2*(1), 71–87.

Miller, D., & Le Breton-Miller, I. (2005). *Managing for the long run: Lessons in competitive advantage from great family businesses.* Cambridge, MA: Harvard Business Press.

Miller, D., & Le Breton-Miller, I. (2006). Family governance and firm performance: Agency, stewardship, and capabilities. *Family Business Review, 19*(1), 73–87.

Miller, D., Le Breton-Miller, I., & Lester, R. H. (2010). Family ownership and acquisition behavior in publicly-traded companies. *Strategic Management Journal, 31*(2), 201–223.

Mishra, C. S., & McConaughy, D. L. (1999). Founding family control and capital structure: The risk of loss of control and the aversion to debt. *Entrepreneurship: Theory and Practice, 23*(4), 53–64.

Morck, R. (2000). Introduction to *Concentrated Corporate Ownership.* Chicago, IL: University of Chicago Press.

Morck, R., & Yeung, B. (2003). Agency problems in large family business groups. *Entrepreneurship: Theory and Practice, 27*(4), 367–382.

Morck, R., Wolfenzon, D., & Yeung, B. (2005). Corporate governance, economic entrenchment, and growth. *Journal of Economic Literature, 43*, 655–720.

Munari, F., Oriani, R., & Sobrero, M. (2010). The effects of owner identity and external governance systems on R&D investments: A study of Western European firms. *Research Policy, 39*(8), 1093–1104.

Olson, P. D., Zuiker, V. S., Danes, S. M., Stafford, K., Heck, R. K. Z., & Duncan, K. A. (2003). The impact of the family and the business on family business sustainability. *Journal of Business Venturing, 18*(5), 639–666.

Palmer, D., Friedland, R., Jennings, P. D., & Powers, M. E. (1987). The economics and politics of structure: The multidivisional form and the large U.S. corporation. *Administrative Science Quarterly, 32*(1), 25–48.

Read, S., Dew, N., Sarasvathy, S. D., Song, M., & Wiltbank, R. (2009). Marketing under uncertainty: The logic of an effectual approach. *Journal of Marketing, 73*(3), 1–18.

Read, S., Song, M., & Smit, W. (2009). A meta-analytic review of effectuation and venture performance. *Journal of Business Venturing, 24*(6), 573–587.

Romano, C. A., Tanewski, G. A., & Smyrnios, K. X. (2001). Capital structure decision making: A model for family business. *Journal of Business Venturing, 16*(3), 285–310.

Sarasvathy, S. D. (2001). Causation and effectuation: Toward a theoretical shift from economic inevitability to entrepreneurial contingency. *Academy of Management Review, 26*(2), 243–263.

Sarasvathy, S. D. (2008). *Effectuation: Elements of entrepreneurial expertise.* Cheltenham, UK: Edward Elgar Publishing.

Sarasvathy, S. D., & Dew, N. (2005). New market creation through transformation. *Journal of Evolutionary Economics, 15*(5), 533–565.

Sarasvathy, S. D., & Dew, N. (2008). Effectuation and over trust: Debating Goel and Karri. *Entrepreneurship: Theory and Practice, 32*(4), 727–737.

Sarasvathy, S. D., & Venkataraman, S. (2011). Entrepreneurship as method: Open questions for an entrepreneurial future. *Entrepreneurship: Theory and Practice, 35*(1), 113–135.

Scherer, F. M., & Harhoff, D. (2000). Policy implications for a world with skew-distributed returns to innovation. *Research Policy, 29*, 559–566.

Schulze, W. S., Lubatkin, M. H., & Dino, R. N. (2003a). Exploring the agency consequences of ownership dispersion among the directors of private family firms. *Academy of Management Journal, 46*(2), 179–194.

Schulze, W. S., Lubatkin, M. H., & Dino, R. N. (2003b). Toward a theory of agency and altruism in family firms. *Journal of Business Venturing, 18*(4), 473–490.

Schulze, W. S., Lubatkin, M. H., Dino, R. N., & Buchholtz, A. K. (2001). Agency relationships in family firms: Theory and evidence. *Organization Science, 12*(2), 99–116.

Sharma, P., Chrisman, J. J., & Chua, J. H. (2003). Predictors of satisfaction with the succession process in family firms. *Journal of Business Venturing, 18*(5), 667–687.

Shepherd, D. A., & Zacharakis, A. (2000). Structuring family business succession: An analysis of the future leader's decision making. *Entrepreneurship: Theory and Practice, 24*(4), 25.

Short, J. C., Moss, T. W., & Lumpkin, G. T. (2009). Research in social entrepreneurship: Past contributions and future opportunities. *Strategic Entrepreneurship Journal, 3*, 181–194.

Simon, H. A. (1990). A mechanism for social selection and successful altruism. *Science, 250*(4988), 1665.

Simon, H. A. (1991). Organizations and markets. *Journal of Economic Perspectives, 5*(2), 25–44.

Simon, H. A. (1993). Altruism and economics. *American Economic Review, 83*(2), 156.

Simon, H. A. (1996). *The sciences of the artificial.* Cambridge, MA: MIT Press.

Sirmon, D. G., Arregle, J.-L., Hitt, M. A., & Webb, J. W. (2008). The role of family influence in firms' strategic responses to threat of imitation. *Entrepreneurship: Theory and Practice, 32*(6), 979–998.

Stavrou, E., Kassinis, G., & Filotheou, A. (2007). Downsizing and stakeholder orientation among the Fortune 500: Does family ownership matter? *Journal of Business Ethics, 72*(2), 149–162.

Steijvers, T., Voordeckers, W., & Vanhoof, K. (2010). Collateral, relationship lending and family firms. *Small Business Economics, 34*(3), 243–259.

Thompson, W. E. (1998). *A new look at social cogniton in groups: A special issue of basic and applied social psychology.* Mahwah, NJ: Lawrence Erlbaum Associates, Inc.

Thomsen, S., & Pedersen, T. (2000). Ownership structure and economic performance in the largest European companies. *Strategic Management Journal, 21*(6), 689–705.

Townsend, D. M., & Hart, T. A. (2008). Perceived institutional ambiguity and the choice of organizational form in social entrepreneurial ventures. *Entrepreneurship: Theory and Practice, 32*(4), 685–700.

Uhlaner, L., Floren, R., & Geerlings, J. (2007). Owner commitment and relational governance in the privately-held firm: An empirical study. *Small Business Economics, 29*(3), 275–293.

Venkataraman, S., Sarasvathy, S. D., Dew, N., & Forster, W. (2012). Whither the promise: Moving forward with entrepreneurship as a science of the artificial. *Academy of Management Review, 37*(1), 21–33.

Villalonga, B., & Amit, R. (2005). How do family ownership, control and management affect firm value? *Journal of Financial Economics, 80*, 385–417.

Villalonga, B., & Amit, R. (2010). Family control of firms and industries. *Financial Management, 39*(3), 863–904.

Westhead, P., & Cowling, M. (1998). Family firm research: The need for a methodological rethink. *Entrepreneurship: Theory and Practice, 23*(1), 31–56.

Westhead, P., & Howorth, C. (2007). "Types" of private family firms: An exploratory conceptual and empirical analysis. *Entrepreneurship and Regional Development, 19*(5), 405–431.

Wiklund, J. (2006). Commentary: "Family firms and social responsibility: Preliminary evidence from the S&P 500". *Entrepreneurship: Theory and Practice, 30*(6), 803–808.

Wiltbank, R., Read, S., Dew, N., & Sarasvathy, S. D. (2009). Prediction and control under uncertainty: Outcomes in angel investing. *Journal of Business Venturing, 24*(2), 116–133.

Wiseman, R. M., & Gomez-Mejia, L. R. (1998). A behavioral agency model of managerial risk taking. *Academy of Management Review, 23*(1), 133–153.

Zahra, S. A., Hayton, J. C., Neubaum, D. O., Dibrell, C., & Craig, J. (2008). Culture of family commitment and strategic flexibility: The moderating effect of stewardship. *Entrepreneurship: Theory and Practice, 32*(6), 1035–1054.

Zahra, S. A., Hayton, J. C., & Salvato, C. (2004). Entrepreneurship in family vs. nonfamily firms: A resource-based analysis of the effect of organizational culture. *Entrepreneurship: Theory and Practice, 28*(4), 363–381.

Zellweger, T. M., & Dehlen, T. (2011). Value is in the eye of the owner: Affect infusion and socioemotional wealth among family firm owners. *Family Business Review*, 1–18.

Zellweger, T. M., & Nason, R. S. (2008). A stakeholder perspective on family firm performance. *Family Business Review, 21*(3), 203–216.

Zellweger, T. M., Eddleston, K. A., & Kellermanns, F. W. (2010). Exploring the concept of familiness: Introducing family firm identity. *Journal of Family Business Strategy, 1*(1), 54–63.

Zellweger, T. M., Nason, R. S., Nordqvist, M., & Brush, C. G. (2013). Why do family firms strive for nonfinancial goals? An organizational identity perspective. *Entrepreneurship: Theory and Practice, 37*(2), 229–248.

2 Corporate Family Entrepreneurship: the seven circumstances[1]

Salvatore Sciascia and Cristina Bettinelli

Introduction

The present chapter is devoted to the concept of *Corporate Family Entrepreneurship* (CFE) and aims at reviewing past literature and trying to propose where research should go in such a field of studies.

CFE is a concept that stands at the interface between family business studies and corporate entrepreneurship research, a conceptual crossing representing an interesting research area for scholars of both fields (Chrisman, Chua, & Sharma, 2005; Hoy, 2006; Lumpkin, Brigham, & Moss, 2010). Research efforts are called because of a twofold justification: on the one hand, the importance of family businesses in the global economy (La Porta, Lopez-de-Silanes, & Shleifer, 1999); on the other hand, the empirical evidence of the effects of corporate entrepreneurship on firm performance (e.g., Rauch, Wiklund, Lumpkin, & Frese, 2009; Zahra, 1991), organizational learning (e.g., Dess, Ireland, Zahra, Floyd, Janney, & Lane, 2003), and industries' growth and development (e.g., Audretsch & Thurik, 2003).

Although recent efforts have been made to review extant knowledge on the topic (McKelvie, McKenny, Lumpkin, & Short, 2014) we continue here the debate by exploring this topic from a different perspective. Specifically, the approach that we use is based on Hermagoras' method of the "seven Ws" (see Figure 2.1). Hermagoras of Temnos was an ancient Greek rhetorician who lived in the first century BC and developed the method of dividing a topic into its seven circumstances: who, what, when, where, why, in what way, by what means. In each of the seven Ws we will try to report the published literature and propose new avenues for future research.

Our effort will be of help for readers interested to know more about Family Entrepreneurship in the corporate context. In particular, we offer an updated review of articles via a rhetorical method that ensures thoroughness in the coverage of CFE. The chapter addresses the definitional issue (what), the levels of analysis in CFE (who), the reasons why CFE is developed (why), how CFE is developed, meaning in what way and by what means CFE is carried out, the role of time in CFE (when) and the role of industrial and geographical context (where).

The papers that we review originated from the following literature collection strategy. We searched a number of databases (EconLit, Business Source Premier; Psychology and Behavioral Sciences Collection; Library, Information Science & Technology Abstracts; MLA International Bibliography; MLA Directory of Periodicals; Humanities International Complete; SocINDEX; JSTOR;

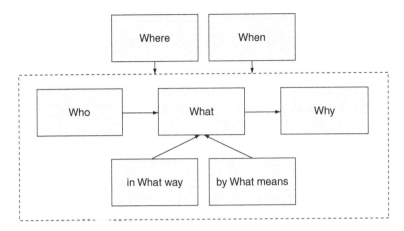

Figure 2.1 Our model for approaching CFE – authors' re-elaboration based on Hermagoras'
7 Ws.

and Web of Knowledge) for articles that explicitly mentioned "corporate entrepreneurship," "entrepreneurial orientation," "intrapreneurship," "strategic
renewal," "organizational renewal," "innovation," "new business venturing,"
"strategic entrepreneurship," "corporate venturing," or "internal ventures," in
the *title, abstract,* or *keywords* without placing boundaries on time period (the
search ended on September 30, 2013). We requested that the abstract must
also contain one of the following: "family firm," "family business," or "family
enterprise" and/or common derivations (e.g., "family businesses"). This search
yielded *123* relevant articles. From this list we eliminated *71* non-academic
articles, teaching cases, and those with only weak ties to corporate entrepreneurship and family business. To ensure that articles of relevance not using
specified keywords were included we performed a focused/manual search and
added *31* papers.

This resulted in a total of 83 articles, 53 of them were empirically based: they are listed
and classified in the Appendix to this chapter (the search ended on September
30, 2013: the search of empirical papers on CFE was closed on this date to respect
the submission deadlines of the call for this edited book). Hereafter we offer a
review by mainly considering the empirical efforts that have been made up to
now and the potential research agenda that could emerge.[2]

What

In the context of the present study, we adopt a wide definition of Corporate
Entrepreneurship referring both to the firm-level entrepreneurial content
(Sharma & Chrisman, 1999) and the firm-level entrepreneurial process
(Lumpkin & Dess, 1996; Miller, 1983; Zahra, 1991). The former refers to Corporate Entrepreneurship in a strict sense, i.e., corporate venturing, innovation, and
strategic renewal (Sharma & Chrisman, 1999). In particular, corporate venturing
refers to organizational creation and can be either external (when results in the
creation of ventures residing outside the existing organizational domain, as

spin-offs, joint ventures, and venture capital initiatives), or internal (when the new venture resides within existing organization); innovation is defined as the introduction of something new to the marketplace; strategic renewal is the "organizational renewal involving major strategic and/or structural changes" (Sharma & Chrisman, 1999:21). The latter refers to entrepreneurial orientation and its components: innovativeness, proactiveness, risk-taking, autonomy and competitive aggressiveness (Lumpkin & Dess, 1996; Miller, 1983; Zahra, 1991).

Similarly, we adopt a wide definition of family business, i.e., a company characterized by a considerable involvement of the family, in political, cultural, or generational terms (Astrachan, Klein, & Smyrnios, 2002). *Thus, the field of CFE studies firm-level entrepreneurial content and process when a family is considerably involved in the established organization* (see Figure 2.2).

Numerous papers (*21* out of 53) focused on firm-level entrepreneurial processes and explicitly on *entrepreneurial orientation.* In this case, it is interesting to note that the Miller (1983) scale was the most frequently used (eight out of 21 papers) even if a number of alternative scales and variations of them has flourished.

Many more papers focused instead on firm-level entrepreneurial content (*24* out of 53). Several papers (15) focused on *innovation* and in particular on the effects of the family (e.g., family involvement, family ownership, family features) on innovation *activities* and *attitudes.* The most underrepresented themes are corporate venturing and strategic renewal. Only five papers considered *corporate venturing* in family firms. In this case, the main focus has been on internal corporate venturing's role in revitalizing and achieving family firms' competitiveness (e.g., Au, Chiang, Birtch, & Ding, 2013), and on how family firms differ from nonfamily firms when corporate venturing activities occur (Greidanus & Mark, 2012; Wong, Chang, & Chen, 2010).

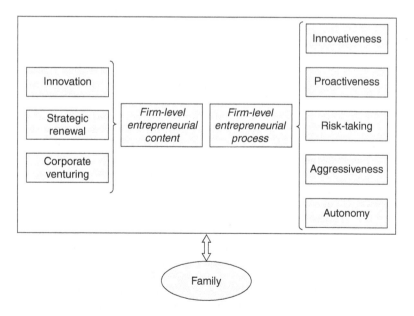

Figure 2.2 Corporate Family Entrepreneurship (source: authors' re-elaboration based on Sharma & Chrisman, 1999 and Lumpkin & Dess, 1996).

We could find four papers on *strategic renewal*: in particular, Scholes and colleagues considered family owners' exit and subsequent strategic change (Scholes, Wright, Westhead, & Bruining, 2010), while Salvato, Chirico, and Sharma (2010) considered the factors that influence exit from the founder's business and subsequent entrepreneurial renewal in a generational family firm. Last, Hall, Melin, and Nordqvist (2001) and Barresi, Coppolino and Marisca (2012) focused on the antecedents of organizational change.

The remaining *eight* papers proposed a focus on other *Corporate Entrepreneurship-related aspects* such as entrepreneurial risk-taking (Huybrechts, Voordeckers, & Lybaert, 2013; Memili, Eddleston, Kellermanns, Zellweger, & Barnett, 2010; Zahra, 2005), family EO (Zellweger, Nason, & Nordqvist, 2012), entrepreneurial intensity (Pistrui, Welsch, Wintermantel, Liao, & Pohl, 2000), organizational ambidexterity (Stubner, Blarr, Brands, & Wulf, 2012), search breadth (Classen, Van Gils, Bammens, & Carree, 2012), and portfolio entrepreneurship (Sieger, Zellweger, Nason, & Clinton, 2011). Moreover, the majority of the papers (39 out of 53) considered family characteristics as an antecedent of Corporate Entrepreneurship. Up until now, the family has been seen either as an antecedent or as the context of Corporate Entrepreneurship rather than being studied as the entity influenced by Corporate Entrepreneurship (Marchisio, Mazzola, Sciascia, Miles, & Astrachan, 2010).

To sum up, although much has been done, there is still room for more research on external corporate venturing (i.e., spin-off), strategic renewal, and the effects of Corporate Entrepreneurship on the family system.

Who

The possible levels of analysis for CFE refers to the firm, the family, and the individual. We analyzed the papers in our sample by considering their main focus and their main level of analysis. The majority of the papers has analyzed data mainly at the family firm level (*37*), but some papers adopted a multi-level approach: *seven* papers considered all the three possible levels, while the rest has either focused on family and firms (*six*) or on individuals and firms (*three*). The papers that focused on all the three levels of analysis have used qualitative methods (with only one exception). Qualitative approaches indeed are well suited in new research contexts. In such cases indeed, some theory-building is needed (e.g., Moog, Mirabella, & Schlepphorst, 2011), and the aim is to consider simultaneously many complexities that often quantitative data are not able to gauge (e.g., Marchisio et al., 2010; Salvato et al., 2010; Zellweger & Sieger, 2012). One exception is offered by the paper by Danes and colleagues, where the authors were able to orchestrate different sources to offer a quantitative analysis that considers dynamics at a firm, an individual, and a family level. In particular, the authors found several moderation effects of individual features on the resource transfers between the family and the business (Danes, Stafford, & Loy, 2007).

At the firm level, research that compares family firms with nonfamily firms has not been able to converge on univocal results. One explanation is that the family may be involved at very different organizational levels, with different effects. Dimensions that could be considered are ownership (e.g., extent, dispersion, activeness), board of directors and TMT (e.g., extent and number of generations involved), CEO and workforce (e.g., Cruz & Nordqvist, 2012; Kellermanns, Eddleston, Barnett, & Pearson, 2008). Additionally, extant family business literature suggests that the effects of these forms of family involvement on CFE may change on the basis of a number of additional features. These features comprise the generation in charge that has specific resource needs (Cruz & Nordqvist, 2012; Gedajlovic, Carney, Chrisman, & Kellermanns, 2012), the social context that shapes identity (Miller & Le Breton-Miller, 2011; Shepherd & Haynie, 2009), the contingent time orientation, and the satisfaction for current performance (Bergfeld & Weber, 2011; Chrisman & Patel, 2012). In addition, the effects of family involvement on CFE may be non-linear (Sciascia, Mazzola, & Chirico, 2013b) therefore requiring appropriate models to gauge them. A first conclusion is that the phenomenon is so complex that we are called to start *adopting multiple theories to grasp it while abandoning the family firms versus nonfamily firms dichotomy.*

Research *at the family level* is scant and proposes that different types of families (especially in terms of relationships and communication) may produce different effects on firm-level entrepreneurship. In particular, family cohesiveness promotes learning and Corporate Entrepreneurship broadly defined (Zahra, 2012) while conversation and moderate pluralism in family communication promotes firm innovativeness (Sciascia, Clinton, Nason, James, & Rivera-Algarin, 2013a).

The shift toward the family level of investigation was invited by Zellweger and colleagues (2012) who proposed the concept of *Family Entrepreneurial Orientation.* The authors theorize and validate a construct that taps into the family-level mindset to engage in entrepreneurial behaviors. They define family entrepreneurial orientation as the "attitudes and mindsets of families to engage in entrepreneurial activity" (Zellweger et al., 2012: 143). This new concept goes beyond the one suggested by Martin and Lumpkin (2003), who introduced the notion of family orientation as an alternative to entrepreneurial orientation. Zellweger and colleagues (2012) did not oppose family orientation to entrepreneurial orientation but considered how individual and organizational aspects of firm-level entrepreneurship may be contextualized by taking into account also family dynamics. *We believe that the new family orientation construct introduced by Zellweger and colleagues could foster the debate and be used for new and more fine-grained empirical research on CFE.*

At the individual level, research is a greenfield. There is a need to study how individuals and their characteristics (gender, age, generation, education, commitment) may affect CFE and vice versa. Some first efforts have been made by Moog and colleagues (2011) who have considered how orientations at an individual level affect family firms' behaviors. The authors have found that the personal orientations and motivations of owners (at the individual level) do strongly affect the orientation, actions, and movements of the companies. Interestingly, the authors found that individual EO in family firms is mixed with the orientations of the family (*family orientation*) and that it is difficult to consider them separately (Moog et al., 2011). Other interesting contributions are offered by the papers of Pistrui and colleagues and the paper of Toledano and colleagues. The former explored (by focusing mainly on the individual level of analysis) sociocultural forces, family dynamics, personality characteristics, and environmental perceptions of Eastern and Western Germany entrepreneurs (Pistrui et al., 2000). The latter explored how networking activities among individuals can foster Corporate Entrepreneurship within established family firms (Toledano, Urbano, & Bernadich, 2010).

The line of research that considers CFE by focusing on the individual level of analysis could help families to identify who to give the leadership in the entrepreneurial processes. At the same time, entrepreneurial activities could be considered as tools to test the capabilities and commitment of a successor, to select it, to increase his/her experience.

Why

Prior research seems to be based on the assumption that CFE is basically developed in order to increase firm performance (in terms of growth and/or profit). The assumption is based on the fact that research is mostly done at the firm level.

The effectiveness of CFE

CFE processes are effective when they positively influence firm performance. Although prior research focused on family involvement as an antecedent of corporate entrepreneurship, research recently started to explore if *family involvement mediates or moderates* the corporate entrepreneurship–*performance relationship*. For example, Kellermans and colleagues found that the relationship between generational involvement and employment growth is fully mediated by entrepreneurial behavior in family firms (Kellermanns et al., 2008). Memili and colleagues also found that family-related constructs such as high family expectations of the firm leader promote a family firm image and risk-taking, with benefits on firm performance (Memili et al., 2010). Chirico and colleagues found that generational involvement makes corporate entrepreneurship effective if coupled with a participative strategic management (Chirico, Sirmon, Sciascia, & Mazzola, 2011). Moreover, Kellermans and colleagues (2012) found that the benefits of innovativeness depend on generational ownership dispersion: the highest performance is realized when innovativeness is high and ownership is concentrated in the hands of a single generation (Kellermanns, Eddleston, Sarathy, & Murphy, 2012). *More can be done to explore the effectiveness of CFE. In particular, CFE could be studied in terms of activities, via qualitative research, to guide families toward processes that can increase the competitiveness of controlled firms.*

There is also abundant family business literature on conflicts that may be extended to the process of CFE. In particular, while fresh theoretical frameworks have been offered that include explanations of how conflicts may affect CFE (Sciascia et al., 2013a; Shepherd & Haynie, 2009), empirical work on these themes may be deepened. Indeed, family involvement may stimulate both task-related constructive conflicts and destructive relationship conflicts that may affect the CFE–performance relationship.

We should recognize the possibility that CFE is developed not only to reach firm goals but also to satisfy family needs. The latter may have monetary (dividends, job opportunities) and non-monetary nature (e.g., reputation, cohesiveness, identity, dynasty perpetuation) (Zellweger, Nason, Nordqvist, & Brush, 2011). For example, Au and colleagues explored how CFE (in this case external corporate venturing activities) could help the family perpetuate its entrepreneurial spirit from one generation to another. The authors described how a family firm could exploit the "familiness" resources embodied within the family and the enterprise to incubate the second generation. In particular, a succession plan nurturing external corporate venturing (spin-offs) by the second generation was developed in order to coach the second generation (Au et al., 2013). It would be interesting to study not only the reasons why CFE is developed, but also those reasons that prevent its development. For example, Miller and Le Breton Miller (2011) found that, in public firms, post-founder family owners and CEOs tend to assume identities as family nurturers, thereby limiting CFE and performance. The explanation is rooted in the fact that, since the post-founder family owners and CEOs are closely attached to family members in the firm, they tend to act as family nurturers and to focus on their responses to family demands (e.g., of family financial security, family reputation, and careers for family members). The authors explain how family members working in the family firm may share a common familial identity, reinforced by the roles they play (Cruz, Gómez-Mejia, & Becerra, 2010; Gómez-Mejía, Takács Haynes, Núñez-Nickel M., Jacobson, & Moyano-Fuentes, 2007) that may lead them to prioritize the above-mentioned family expectations since they will receive socioemotional satisfaction from doing so. Therefore, the disproportionate impact that family members may have on one another is one of the inhibitors of CFE. *Thus, research can be developed in order to better understand under what conditions CFE allows the satisfaction of non-economic needs – family needs included – and to explore the inhibitors of CFE.*

By what means

Entrepreneurship literature underlines the crucial role of *resources* in identifying and exploiting entrepreneurial opportunities. In this sense, CFE can be seen as a process in which family-influenced resources play a critical role. Among the most important family-influenced resources, the extant literature indicates human capital, social capital, survivability capital, and patient capital (Arregle, Hitt, Sirmon, & Very, 2007; Danes, Stafford, Haynes, & Amarapurkar, 2009; Sirmon & Hitt, 2003). A number of authors have considered also organizational culture as a resource that can affect CFE. Hall and colleagues (2001) explored how *organizational culture* affects a Corporate Entrepreneurship element such as radical change in family firms. They found that while some organizations' cultural patterns tend to preserve the traditional way of doing business (i.e., implicit and close cultures), others tend to facilitate entrepreneurial change (i.e., explicit and open cultures). Gudmundson, Tower, and Hartman (2003) found that an innovation supportive organizational culture is positively related to innovation in SMEs and that such a type of culture is more likely to emerge in family firms than nonfamily firms. Among the pioneers in exploring these aspects, Zahra and colleagues (2004) offered a focus on how organizational culture can be seen as a resource that family firms use to sustain CFE. The authors found that individualism has an inverted U-shaped effect on CFE, while external orientation, decentralization orientation, and long-term orientation positively affect CFE. Moreover, they found that these orientations are more likely to affect corporate entrepreneurship in family business rather than in nonfamily firms (Zahra, Hayton, & Salvato, 2004).

Chirico and Nordqvist (2010) considered *entrepreneurial orientation and paternalism* as typical family business cultures and found that they positively affect family inertia and negatively influence entrepreneurial actions, such as new market entry.

We believe that the approach suggested by Zellweger et al. (2012) can be extremely helpful: in order to take into account that family businesses are complex and dynamic systems, the scholars adopt a *paradox perspective* according to which family and business factors are not necessarily incompatible but can indeed be synergistic (Basco & Perez-Rodriguez, 2009; Stewart & Hitt, 2010; Zellweger & Nason, 2008). This perspective shifts the focus "from identifying the conditions under which organizations are more driven by certain factors to how firms engage in these competing factors simultaneously" (Zellweger et al. 2012: 145). This approach is coherent also with a growing "systemic" view that has been recently adopted (e.g., Basco & Perez-Rodriguez, 2009; Frank, Lueger, Nose, & Suchy, 2010; Habbershon, Williams, & MacMillan, 2003; Stewart & Hitt, 2010) and *could be extremely helpful in the analysis of how resource orchestration processes in family firms could hinder or foster CFE.*

Some steps have indeed already been recently taken in this direction. Eddleston, Kellermanns, and Sarathy (2008) found that a family resource such as reciprocal altruism positively affects performance. Interestingly, the authors also found that when the environment is rich in technological opportunities, a higher level of reciprocal altruism is associated with stronger family firm performance. Furthermore, Sieger and colleagues (2011) identified distinct resource categories and processes that are relevant for portfolio entrepreneurship and found that their importance varies across time. However, CFE seems to be valuable under certain circumstances. In particular, Chirico et al. (2011) find that CFE can be beneficial in family firms when synchronized with generational involvement and participative strategy. As previous research proposes, the influence of the family on firm resources could be either positive or negative. This opens to new opportunities *to study the conditions/contingencies that allow the family to increase the stock of available firm resources rather than eroding it. Another interesting research avenue may consider the effects of these resources on CFE.* Even if there is consensus on the fact that family resources are dynamic and therefore may change over time, the empirical literature has mainly used cross-sectional observations to explore how family firms' resources relate to CFE – with the notable exceptions of Hall et al. (2001) and Sieger et al. (2011). *Moving from a static to a dynamic view of the issue (both theoretically and empirically), it could be interesting to better understand how resource management for CFE works. Additional avenues of useful research refer to the exploration of how to foster effective processes of resource acquisition, accumulation, divestment, and combination in family firms.*

In what way

In this section we try to emphasize how CFE can take place (i.e., CFE processes) and the main elements that are related to CFE processes. This aspect of CFE includes the day-to-day activities and micro-processes of family firms' life which are deeply entrenched in family values, emotions, and the socio-psychological dimensions (Hall, Melin, & Nordqvist, 2006).

Internal vs. external CFE

CFE processes could be managed internally or externally. Extant literature clearly emphasizes the benefits of building and maintaining external network ties for family businesses, for example because of the access to family members' personal networks and because of the family's reputation (Arregle et al., 2007; Miller, Le Breton-Miller, & Scholnick, 2008; Salvato & Melin, 2008). Recently Classen and colleagues claimed that research on innovation in family firms until now has neglected externally oriented innovation cooperation. The authors focused on an aspect related to CFE, i.e., the number of different external sources or partner types firms rely upon to acquire resources for their innovative activities (i.e., search breadth). Specifically, they show that family SMEs have a lower search breadth than their nonfamily counterparts. The authors also found that the CEO's level of education and the top management team features (the presence of nonfamily members) positively affect the search breadth and that these two elements positively interact (Classen et al., 2012). *Research should be consequently advanced to understand how to promote external collaborations for CFE.*

Incremental vs. radical CFE

Similarly, *CFE could have radical or incremental nature.* The literature asserts that families are more oriented to develop *incremental innovation.* For example, Block and colleagues (2013) by studying the number of patent citations, show how family firms run the danger of producing only incremental rather than radical innovations, which can reduce their competitiveness. Specifically *founder-managed firms,* that are assumed to be more entrepreneurial, develop more radical innovation than other firms, while family-managed firms develop lower radical innovation because they tend to pursue socioemotional wealth for the family (Block, Miller, Jaskiewicz, & Spiegel, 2013). Sharma and Salvato (2011) propose that firms that concurrently engage in multiple levels of innovation (i.e., incremental, progressive, and radical) may enjoy sustainable performance advantages over time. *Research should consequently be advanced to understand how to promote different levels of innovation among family firms.*

Explorative vs. exploitative CFE

CFE can also have an exploitative or explorative nature and family firms vary in terms of success achieved over time when considering opportunity creation and exploitation (Sharma & Salvato, 2011). For example, the literature claims that "distinctive familiness" generated by enterprising families is one of the many resources that can be exploited for generating competitiveness and synergistic outcomes (Habbershon et al., 2003). *Understanding how family firms explore or exploit knowledge for CFE could be therefore useful.*

Another fruitful research avenue refers to organizational *ambidexterity* which is defined as "the ability of the organization to both efficiently exploit its existing competencies (via 'exploitation') and foster the innovativeness (via 'exploration')" (Patel, Messersmith, & Lepak, 2013:1420). *A better understanding of how the family influences organizational ambidexterity could open up new interesting ways to understand in what way CFE can be fostered.* A first attempt in this sense has been done by Stubner and colleagues: they show that family power and cultural alignment between family and firm interests lead to higher degrees of ambidexterity, that in turn is positively related to performance (Stubner et al., 2012). *We therefore believe that future investigation on process aspects could be related to the study of ambidexterity for CFE and to the understanding of what processes (explorative vs. exploitative) are more adequate for the family and the firm.*

When

The temporal dimension is also relevant in studying CFE. Firms, families, and individuals may live different phases of their own lifecycle, in which attitudes and capabilities toward entrepreneurship may vary significantly: *synchronizing these lifecycles is a challenge that requires research efforts* (Hoy, 2006). Additionally, as Miller (2011) noted with regards to entrepreneurship in general, *event-based aspects of context that include transformations in an industry or crises in a firm may be worthy of exploration.* Indeed, the term "time" evokes the current hard years of recession that developed economies are living: CFE is of great interest in this contingency and research should take into account the specificities of these years. An additional area of investigation that appears to be relevant is the exit from CFE experiences: exit is a phase of the entrepreneurial process that is as much relevant as the entry, especially for the family unit (Nordqvist & Melin, 2010). In the context of family business literature, the time dimension is strictly related to the generational issue. *According to the literature, a generational change at the firm leadership is a fertile context for CFE, but the issue deserves more attention* (Zellweger & Sieger, 2012). *Moreover, there is no agreement yet on the generational stage that is more conducive to effective Corporate Entrepreneurship, thus opening to additional research efforts.* Specifically, Beck, Janssens, Debruyne, and Lommelen (2011) found that later-generation family firms are associated with a lower level of innovation. With reference to public family firms, Miller and Le Breton Miller (2011) found a similar result by showing that firms with lone founder owners and CEOs exhibit higher levels of EO than those with post-founder family owners–CEOs. On the other hand, Casillas and Moreno (2010) found that EO positively influences growth only when family businesses reach the second generation, and that the moderating influence of generational involvement is related to the risk-taking dimension.

We call for further research that tries to delve into the role of generational stage in developing effective CFE.

Where

The above thoughts bring us to the issue of spatial context, which is considered to be one of the major factors influencing entrepreneurial process (Miller, 2011). We focus here on the geographic and industrial context used for the study of CFE. Among the articles analyzed, only five out of 53 have performed empirical analysis on more than one country (Beck et al., 2011; Chirico & Nordqvist, 2010; Classen et al., 2012; Sieger et al., 2011; Zellweger et al., 2012). With the exception of Pistrui et al. (2000) which discusses differences and similarities in entrepreneurial orientations and family forces between East and West German entrepreneurs, the role of the geographical context has never been explored in CFE.

In single country studies, the most used geographical contexts seem to be the North American (14), the Italian (six), the Spanish (five), the Swiss (five), and the German (four) ones. This clearly indicates that the majority of studies are still limited to North America and Europe while South America, Africa, Russia, and Asiatic countries (with the exception of Taiwan) remain quite underrepresented. This is surprising if we consider the economic relevance of family firms in these areas.

In view of the recent brilliant efforts that are being done in order to gather and analyze CFE worldwide through the STEP project (Nordqvist & Zellweger, 2010) we expect that many studies based on this international source of information will follow the existing ones not only to better understand CFE in single countries (Au et al., 2013; Salvato et al., 2010; Zellweger et al., 2012) but also to develop cross-country analyses (Sieger et al., 2011).

The exploration of the spatial dimension is relevant for cultural reasons. A useful way to categorize national cultures is the one proposed by Hofstede, Hofstede, and Minkow (2010). According to this classification, national cultures can be analyzed in terms of power distance (PD), individualism (IDV), masculinity (MAS), uncertainty avoidance (UAI), and long-term orientation (LTO). Power distance is defined as the extent to which the less powerful members of institutions and organizations within a country expect and accept that power is distributed unequally. Individualism is the preference for a loosely knit society in which individuals are expected to take care of themselves and their immediate families; masculinity refers to the preference for achievement, heroism, competitiveness, assertiveness, and material rewards; uncertainty avoidance refers to the extent to which the members of a culture feel threatened by ambiguous or unknown situations and try to avoid them; finally, the long-term orientation dimension deals with the extent to which a society shows a pragmatic future-oriented perspective rather than a conventional historical short-term point of view (Hofstede et al., 2010). According to Hofstede et al. (2010) all these elements make for a national culture that may affect organizational behaviors. Additionally, national laws, economies, and levels of institutional development may condition the nature of entrepreneurship (Johns, 2006; Miller, 2011). *Therefore the role of the spatial dimension is a greenfield for CFE studies: specifically, a deeper understanding of the types of national cultures, laws, and institutional elements associated to CFE could be very important to advance the research field.* A good example of how this cultural differences could turn into an exciting stream of research is based on the data represented in Figure 2.3. This shows that emerging economies such as China or Brazil are characterized by different cultures that may affect CFE both on the family side (e.g., differences in power distance and individualism) and the entrepreneurship side (e.g., differences in uncertainty avoidance and long-term orientation). Other interesting future investigations refer to CFE in *multi-cultural families* – that are increasing in number and size (Li, 2009). Family dynamics could be very different from those arising in mono-cultural families, therefore CFE may be influenced in a peculiar way.

Beside a real space, there is also an industrial space for CFE that refers to the *sectors* where to develop entrepreneurial activities. Among the empirical papers that we reviewed, the majority of them (39) based their analysis on multiple

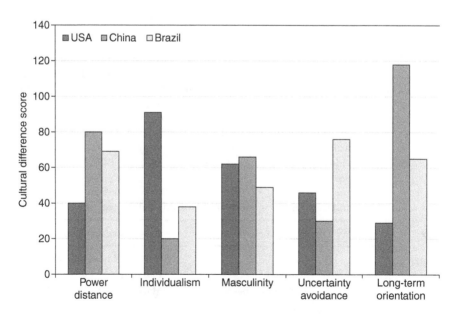

Figure 2.3 Cultural differences between United States, China, and Brazil (source: authors' elaboration, based on http://geert-hofstede.com/united-states.html).

industries, five considered the manufacturing sector in general, one the high-tech industries, and the rest focused on specific sectors such as food and beverage (two), steel and metal (two), textile, chemical, and health.[3] Even if some papers included moderating variables such as environmental dynamism in their model (e.g., Casillas, Moreno, & Barbero, 2011) or measured the perception of technological opportunities (Kellermanns & Eddleston, 2006) specific papers that consider how industry characteristics affect CFE were not found. *Therefore we join Miller's (2011) claim that it would be important to understand which industrial structures enhance entrepreneurial behaviors and we call for additional efforts for the specific case of CFE.* Such context-based studies could be of great interest to scholars and practitioners alike. As shown in Table 2.1, CFE may have specificities, for example, depending on the technological level of the industry of reference, given that critical knowledge and learning processes considerably differ in low- and medium-tech industries compared to high-tech industries (Robertson, Smith, & von Tunzelmann, 2009).

Conclusions

This chapter offered a review of the literature on CFE. We have tried to explore the empirical research that stands at the interface between family business studies and corporate entrepreneurship research by using Hermagoras' method of the "seven Ws" (who, what, when, where, why, in what way, by what means). From our analysis of 53 empirical journal papers published up until September 2013, some elements have emerged.

First, with regards to the different aspects of CFE (i.e., What) we have noticed that future research should explore more in detail two aspects of entrepreneurial content, namely, external corporate venturing activities and strategic renewal. Additionally, the family has been mainly seen in the past either as an antecedent or as the context of CFE: it would be interesting to explore the effects of Corporate Entrepreneurship on the family system.

Second, in terms of different possible levels of analysis that have been used in the past (i.e., Who) it emerged that scholars have mainly studied CFE at the firm level while multi-level approaches are less frequent but growing. The phenomenon is so multifaceted that we suggest to adopt multiple theoretical approaches in order to grasp it. Moreover, a more accentuated integration of different disciplines (e.g., psychology, sociology, history) may contribute to the development of a deeper understanding of CFE. Additionally, CFE may be a useful situation where families may identify the next generation leader, train him/her, and test

Table 2.1 Knowledge and learning in high-tech and low- and medium-tech industries

Industry	High-tech	Low- and medium-tech
Learning	R&D	Informal knowledge diffusion
Critical knowledge	Scientific	Practical
	Technology based	Market based
	Explicit	Tacit

Source: authors' elaboration.

his/her capabilities: thus, the individual level of analysis represent a fruitful field of future research.

Third, with regards to the reasons why CFE is developed (i.e., Why), extant literature seems to assume that CFE increases firm performance. Future research could offer a better understanding of CFE effectiveness and on the factors that affect it. We also suggest delving more into this topic and shedding some light on *why* in some cases CFE is inhibited and on the ways by which non-economic needs (e.g., family needs) are satisfied thanks to CFE.

Fourth, when we considered the role of resources for CFE (i.e., by What means) it emerged that a better understanding of how resource orchestration processes in family firms could hinder or foster CFE could be useful. Specifically, there is a need for a clearer definition of the conditions/contingencies that allow the family to develop (rather than corrode) the firm stock of resources. Moreover, future research may offer a better understanding of the family resources' effects on CFE. We believe that, through a shift from a static to a dynamic investigative perspective, it could be interesting to explore how resource management for CFE works. This could help us also understand how to foster effective processes of resource acquisition, accumulation, divestment, and combination in family firms.

Fifth, in terms of how CFE can take place (i.e., in What way), more empirical research is needed to comprehend how family involvement may foster constructive and or destructive conflicts and how these conflicts affect the relationship between CFE and performance. A better understanding of how to promote external collaborations, how to exploit or explore knowledge, and how to develop ambidexterity *for* CFE, could be also useful, to the benefit of families *and* firms.

Sixth, the temporal dimension (i.e., When) represents a potential for a future research stream that takes into account how time affects CFE. Specifically, research that considers how the family, the firm, and the individual lifecycles may (or may not) be synchronized through CFE activities could be useful. This review also indicates that future research may delve more into the role of generational stage in developing effective CFE, into event-based aspects of context such as industries' transformations or downturns, and into the exit from CFE experiences.

Seventh, also the spatial and industrial dimensions (i.e., Where) are a greenfield for CFE studies. On the one hand, a grasp of the types of national cultures, laws, and institutional elements associated to CFE could be very useful. On the other hand, an exploration of which industrial structures enhance or reduce CFE would also be important.

All the research suggestions above can be useful for scholars of both the family business and the entrepreneurship fields. Nevertheless, our review has some limitations. First of all, it is based exclusively on empirical papers published in academic journals, therefore it only marginally takes into account all the very good theoretical contributions on the topic and the material published in books or in other forms. In addition, this chapter lacks a systematic analysis of the theoretical approaches that have been adopted to study CFE. Moreover, although the method of the seven circumstances is useful to differentiate and deepen concepts and issues, we recognize that in some cases some conceptual overlaps remained.

Within this chapter we have tried to organize and analyze the existent empirical research on an increasingly relevant topic such as CFE. Notwithstanding the numerous limitations of our contribution we hope that our efforts can be useful for our readers to understand what CFE is and where research efforts should be oriented.

Appendix

Table 2.A.1 Empirical articles on corporate family entrepreneurship

Article	Method	What	Who (main level of analysis and type of firms)	By what means (X if resources are explicitly considered)	In what way	Where (sector)	Where (geography)
Au, Chiang, Birch, & Ding (2013)	Qualitative (case study)	Corporate venturing (external)	Individual, family, firm. Small-medium Hong-Kong based manufacturing sector STEP	–	–	Manufacturing	China
Barresi, Coppolino, & Marisca (2012)	Qualitative (case study)	Strategic change	Firm. Small medium private held hospital	–	–	Health	Italy
Beck, Janssens, Debruyne, & Lommelen (2011)	Quantitative (survey)	Innovation	Firm. Small (mean 28.55 employees)	–	–	Multiple industries	Belgium and the Netherlands
Bergfeld & Weber (2011)	Qualitative (interviews)	Innovativeness (behaviors)	Family, firm. 10 large firms founded pre-1913	–	–	Multiple industries	Germany
Block, Miller, Jaskiewicz, & Spiegel (2013)	Quantitative (archive)	Innovation (patent counts and patent citations)	Firm. Listed (multiple industries)	–	X	Multiple industries	USA
Carrasco-Hernández & Jiménez-Jiménez (2013)	Quantitative (survey)	Innovation	Firm. Small medium (20–250 employees)	X	–	Multiple industries	Spain
Casillas & Moreno (2010)	Quantitative (survey)	Entrepreneurial orientation (Lumpkin, 1998; Lumpkin & Dess, 2001: innovativeness, risk-taking, proactiveness, competitive aggressiveness, and autonomy)	Firm. Small firms (mostly fewer than 25 employees)	–	–	Multiple industries	Spain

Study	Method	Construct	Level & firm size		Industry	Country
Casillas, Moreno, & Barbero (2010)	Quantitative (survey)	Entrepreneurial orientation (Lumpkin, 1998; Lumpkin & Dess, 2001: innovativeness, risk-taking, proactiveness)	Firm. Small firms (mostly fewer than 25 employees)	–	Multiple industries	Spain
Casillas, Moreno & Barbero (2011)	Quantitative (survey)	Entrepreneurial orientation (Miller's 1983 items)	Firm. Small firms (mostly fewer than 25 employees)	–	Multiple industries	Spain
Chang, Wu, & Wong (2010)	Quantitative (event study)	Innovation	Firm. Public companies	–	Multiple industries	Taiwan
Chirico & Nordqvist (2010)	Qualitative (multiple case studies)	Entrepreneurial orientation (innovativeness, proactiveness, risk-taking – no scales) and entrepreneurial performance (product-line extension; product diversification; expansion to new markets; adoption of new technology, investments)	Firm. Established firms	X	Beverage industry	Switzerland, Italy
Chirico, Sirmon, Sciascia & Mazzola (2011)	Quantitative (survey)	Entrepreneurial orientation (Miller's 1983 items)	Firm. Small medium (92 mean employees)	X	Multiple industries	Switzerland
Classen, Van Gils, Bammens, & Carree (2012)	Quantitative (survey)	Search breadth: number of external partners or search channels that firms rely upon in their innovative activities	Firm. Small medium (between 10 and 250 employees, mean 48.27)	X	Manufacturing	Belgium and the Netherlands
Craig & Dibrell (2006)	Quantitative (survey)	Innovation	Firm. SME	–	Multiple industries	USA
Craig & Moores (2006)	Quantitative (survey)	Innovation	Firm. SME (mean 150 employees)	–	Multiple industries	Australia
Cruz & Nordqvist (2011)	Quantitative (survey)	Entrepreneurial orientation (Miller's 1983 items)	Firm. SME (mean employees 54)	–	Multiple industries	Spain
Danes, Stafford, & Loy (2007)	Quantitative (survey)	Innovation	Individual, family, firm. SME (mean 6, max. 250 employees)	–	Multiple industries	USA

continued

Table 2.A.1 Continued

Article	Method	What	Who (main level of analysis and type of firms)	By what means (X if resources are explicitly considered)	In what way	Where (sector)	Where (geography)
Eddleston, Kellermanns, & Sarathy (2008)	Quantitative (survey)	Innovation	Family, firm. SME (mean 97 employees)	X	–	Not presented but suppose multiple industries	USA
Eddleston, Kellermanns, & Zellweger (2012)	Quantitative (survey)	Entrepreneurial orientation defined as innovation, competitive aggressiveness, and proactiveness (based on a selection of items presented in Barringer & Bluedorn, 1999)	Firm. Small medium (mean 341 employees)	X	–	Multiple industries	Switzerland
Greidanus & Mark (2012)	Qualitative (case studies)	Corporate venturing (internal)	Individual, firm. Small medium (8–250)	–	–	Multiple industries	Not presented
Gudmundson, Tower, & Hartman (2003)	Quantitative (survey)	Innovation	Firm. SME (fewer than 250 mean not reported)	X	–	Multiple industries	USA
Gurrieri (2008)	Quantitative (survey)	Innovation	Firm. Small (details not available)	X	–	Textile	Italy
Hall, Melin, & Nordqvist (2001)	Qualitative (two longitudinal case studies)	Organizational renewal (radical change)	Family, firm. Medium sized (values not presented)	X	–	Manufacturing	Sweden
Huybrechts, Voordeckers, & Lybaert (2013)	Quantitative (survey)	Entrepreneurial risk-taking (measured as "performance variability")	Firm. Small medium (59 mean employees)	–	–	Multiple industries	Belgium
Kellermanns & Eddelston (2006)	Quantitative (survey)	Entrepreneurial orientation (Miller's 1983 items)	Firm. Small firms (mean 97 employees)	–	–	Not presented but suppose multiple industries	USA

Author (Year)	Method	Construct	Level / Firm type			Industry	Country
Kellermanns, Eddleston, Barnett, & Pearson (2008)	Quantitative (survey)	Entrepreneurial orientation (Miller's 1983 items)	Firm. Small firms	–	–	Not presented but suppose multiple industries	USA
Kellermanns, Eddleston, Sarathy, & Murphy (2012)	Quantitative (survey)	Innovativeness (based on Miller 1983)	Family, Firm. Small firms (mean 93 employees)	–	–	Not presented but suppose multiple industries	USA
Liang, Li, Yang, Lin, & Zheng (2013)	Quantitative (archive)	Innovation performance (patenting frequency)	Firm. Listed high-tech	–	–	High-tech	China
Marchisio, Mazzola, Sciascia, Miles, & Astrachan (2010)	Qualitative (three in-depth case studies)	Corporate venturing	Individual, family, firm. Chemical manufacturing, varying size from 300–2300 employees	X	–	Chemical	Italy
Memili, Eddleston, Kellermanns, Zellweger, & Barnett (2010)	Quantitative (survey)	Entrepreneurial risk-taking (as a mediator)	Family, firm. Type of firm not presented	X	–	Multiple industries	Switzerland
Miller & Le Breton-Miller (2011)	Quantitative (archive)	Entrepreneurial orientation (authors scale)	Firm. Listed (multiple industries)	–	–	Multiple industries	USA
Moog, Mirabella, & Schlepphorst (2011)	Qualitative (case studies)	Entrepreneurial orientation (authors scale)	Individual, family, firm. 3 small businesses	–	–	Multiple industries	Germany
Naldi, Nordqvist, Sjöberg, & Wiklund (2007)	Quantitative (survey)	Entrepreneurial orientation (innovativeness, proactiveness, risk-taking based on 9 items proposed by Covin & Slevin, 1989)	Firm. SMEs	–	–	Multiple industries	Sweden
Pistrui, Welsch, Wintermantel, Liao, & Pohl (2000)	Quantitative (survey)	Entrepreneurial intensity	Individual, firm. Small firms (mostly fewer than 50 employees)	–	–	Not presented but suppose multiple industries	Germany

continued

Table 2.A.1 Continued

Article	Method	What	Who (main level of analysis and type of firms)	By what means (X if resources are explicitly considered)	In what way	Where (sector)	Where (geography)
Pittino & Visintin (2009)	Quantitative (structured interview)	Innovation (product, process, business model)	Firm. Small (30–150 employees)	–	–	Multiple industries	Italy
Pittino, Visintin, Bau, & Mazzurana (2013)	Quantitative (survey)	Innovation strategies and technology sourcing alliances	Firm. Small medium (average 26 employees)	X	–	Multiple industries	Italy
Salvato, Chirico, & Sharma (2010)	Qualitative (historical case study)	Organizational renewal (strategic change via exit)	Individual, family, firm. Large steel firm (Falck)	X	–	Steel	Italy
Scholes, Wright, Westhead, & Bruining (2010)	Quantitative (survey)	Organizational renewal (strategic change)	Firm. Small and private (mean 271 employees), multiple industries	–	–	Multiple industries	UK
Sciascia, Mazzola, & Chirico (2013b)	Quantitative (survey)	Entrepreneurial orientation (Miller's 1983 items)	Firm. Small medium (92 mean employees)	–	–	Multiple industries	Switzerland
Short, Payne, Brigham, Lumpkin, & Broberg (2009)	Qualitative (content analysis)	Entrepreneurial orientation (Lumpkin & Dess, 1996 definition: autonomy, competitive aggressiveness, innovativeness, proactiveness, and risk-taking)	Firm. S&P 500 (public companies)	–	–	Multiple industries	USA
Sieger, Zellweger, Nason, & Clinton (2011)	Qualitative (multiple case studies)	New ventures (family portfolio)	Individual, family, firm. Large (mean 2225 employees)	X	–	Multiple industries	Ireland, France, Chile, Guatemala
Stubner, Blarr, Brands, & Wulf (2012)	Quantitative (survey)	Organizational ambidexterity	Firm. Small (average size 24 employees)	X	–	Not presented but suppose multiple industries	Germany

Reference	Method	Concept	Level / firm			Industry / sector	Country
Toledano, Urbano, & Bernadich (2010)	Qualitative (two comparative case studies)	Corporate venturing, innovation	Individual, firm. Small firms	X	–	Metal sector	Spain
Tsao & Lien (2013)	Quantitative (archive)	Innovation	Firm. Listed	–	–	Multiple industries	Taiwan
Wagner (2010)	Quantitative (secondary)	Innovation	Firm. S&P 500	–	–	Multiple industries	USA
Weismeier-Sammer (2011)	Quantitative (survey)	Entrepreneurial orientation (Miller's 1983 items)	Firm. Small firms (mean 18 employees)	–	–	Food and beverage industry	Austria
Wong, Chang, & Chen (2010)	Quantitative (event study)	Corporate venturing	Firm. Public companies, multiple industries	–	–	Multiple industries	Taiwan
Yordanova (2011)	Quantitative (survey)	Entrepreneurial orientation (innovativeness, proactiveness, risk-taking based on 9 items proposed by Covin & Slevin, 1989)	Firm. Mainly small medium private firms	–	–	Multiple industries	Bulgaria
Zahra (2005)	Quantitative (survey)	Entrepreneurial risk-taking	Firm. Small and large (mean 890 employees)	–	–	Manufacturing	USA
Zahra (2012)	Quantitative (survey)	EO (Miller & Le Breton-Miller, 2005; Zahra 1996, 2003, 2008)	Firm. Small and large (mean 15,136 employees)	X	–	Multiple industries	USA
Zahra, Hayton, & Salvato (2004)	Quantitative (survey)	Entrepreneurial orientation (Miller's 1983 items)	Firm. Small (mean 76 employees), manufacturing	X	–	Manufacturing	USA
Zellweger & Sieger (2012)	Qualitative (case studies)	Entrepreneurial orientation (authors' scale)	Individual, family, firm. Medium sized (175–2000 employees) STEP	–	–	Multiple industries	Switzerland
Zellweger, Nason, & Nordqvist (2012)	Quantitative (survey)	FAMILY entrepreneurial orientation	Family, firm. Medium (mean 491 employees) sector not specified	X	–	Not presented	(Mainly Northern America, but also Latin America, Europe, Africa, Asia

Notes

1 The present chapter is based on two speeches on the topic given by Salvatore Sciascia at EM Lyon (first Corporate Entrepreneurship Workshop, June 2011; fifth ELab Symposium on Family Entrepreneurship, June 2013) further developed by Cristina Bettinelli.
2 We use Hermagoras' 7Ws as an organizing framework and, as such, some papers could be categorized in multiple frames. When papers could be dual categorized, we elected, for the sake of parsimony, to go allocate them to what we agreed was the dominant category.
3 The classification is based on the data retrieved from the papers and from the authors when possibile (not all papers were categorizable).

References

Arregle, J. L., Hitt, M. A., Sirmon, D. G., & Very, P. 2007. The development of organizational social capital: Attributes of family firms. *Journal of Management Studies*, 44(1): 73–95.

Astrachan, J. H., Klein, S. B., & Smyrnios, K. X. 2002. The F-PEC scale of family influence: A proposal for solving the family business definition problem. *Family Business Review*, 15(1): 45–58.

Au, K., Chiang, F., Birtch, T., & Ding, Z. 2013. Incubating the next generation to venture: The case of a family business in Hong Kong. *Asia Pacific Journal of Management*, 30: 749–767.

Audretsch, D. B. & Thurik, A. R. 2003. Entrepreneurship, industry evolution and economic growth. *Advances in Austrian Economics*, 6: 39–56.

Barresi, G., Coppolino, R., & Marisca, C. 2012. Criticalities of ICT implementation: The case of a family firm operating in the Italian health-care sector. *International Journal of Technology Management and Sustainable Development*, 11: 177–189.

Barringer, B. R. & Bluedorn, A. C. 1999. The relationship between corporate entrepreneurship and strategic management. *Strategic Management Journal*, 20(5): 421–444.

Basco, R. & Perez-Rodriguez, M. J. 2009. Studying the family enterprise holistically evidence for integrated family and business systems. *Family Business Review*, 22(1): 82–95.

Beck, L., Janssens, W., Debruyne, M., & Lommelen, T. 2011. A study of the relationships between generation, market orientation, and innovation in family firms. *Family Business Review*, 24: 252–272.

Bergfeld, M.-M. H. & Weber, F.-M. 2011. Dynasties of innovation: Highly performing German family firms and the owners' role for innovation. *International Journal of Entrepreneurship and Innovation Management*, 13(1): 80–94.

Block, J., Miller, D., Jaskiewicz, P., & Spiegel, F. 2013. Economic and technological importance of innovations in large family and founder firms an analysis of patent data. *Family Business Review*, 26(2): 180–199.

Carrasco-Hernández, A. & Jiménez-Jiménez, D. 2013. Can family firms innovate? Sharing internal knowledge from a social capital perspective. *Electronic Journal of Knowledge Management*, 11(1): 30–37.

Casillas, J. C. & Moreno, A. M. 2010. The relationship between entrepreneurial orientation and growth: The moderating role of family involvement. *Entrepreneurship and Regional Development*, 22(3–4): 265–291.

Casillas, J. C., Moreno, A. M., & Barbero, J. L. 2011. Entrepreneurial orientation of family firms: Family and environmental dimensions. *Journal of Family Business Strategy*, 2(2): 90–100.

Chang, S. C., Wu, W. Y., & Wong, Y. J. 2010. Family control and stock market reactions to innovation announcements. *British Journal of Management*, 21(1): 152–170.

Chirico, F. & Nordqvist, M. 2010. Dynamic capabilities and trans-generational value creation in family firms: The role of organizational culture. *International Small Business Journal*, 28: 487–504.

Chirico, F., Sirmon, D. G., Sciascia, S., & Mazzola, P. 2011. Resource orchestration in family firms: Investigating how entrepreneurial orientation, generational involvement, and participative strategy affect performance. *Strategic Entrepreneurship Journal*, 5(4): 307–326.

Chrisman, J. J. & Patel, P. C. 2012. Variations in R&D investments of family and nonfamily firms: Behavioral agency and myopic loss aversion perspectives. *Academy of Management Journal*, 55(4): 976–997.

Chrisman, J. J., Chua, J. H., & Sharma, P. 2005. Trends and directions in the development of a strategic management theory of the family firm. *Entrepreneurship: Theory and Practice*, 29(5): 555–576.

Classen, N., Van Gils, A., Bammens, Y., & Carree, M. 2012. Accessing resources from innovation partners: The search breadth of family SMEs. *Journal of Small Business Management*, 50(2): 191–215.

Covin, J. G. & Slevin, D. P. (1989). Strategic management of small firms in hostile and benign environments. *Strategic Management Journal*, 10(1): 75–87.

Craig, J. & Dibrell, C. 2006. The natural environment, innovation, and firm performance: A comparative study. *Family Business Review*, 19(4): 275–288.

Craig, J. B. & Moores, K. 2006. A 10-year longitudinal investigation of strategy, systems, and environment on innovation in family firms. *Family Business Review*, 19(1): 1–10.

Cruz, C. & Nordqvist, M. 2012. Entrepreneurial orientation in family firms: A generational perspective. *Small Business Economics*, 38: 33–49.

Cruz, C. C., Gómez-Mejia, L. R., & Becerra, M. 2010. Perceptions of benevolence and the design of agency contracts: CEO-TMT relationships in family firms. *Academy of Management Journal*, 53(1): 69–89.

Danes, S. M., Stafford, K., & Loy, J. T.-C. 2007. Family business performance: The effects of gender and management. *Journal of Business Research*, 60(10): 1058–1069.

Danes, S. M., Stafford, K., Haynes, G., & Amarapurkar, S. S. 2009. Family capital of family firms bridging human, social, and financial capital. *Family Business Review*, 22(3): 199–215.

Dess, G. G., Ireland, R. D., Zahra, S. A., Floyd, S. W., Janney, J. J., & Lane, P. J. 2003. Emerging issues in corporate entrepreneurship. *Journal of Management*, 29(3): 351–378.

Eddleston, K. A., Kellermanns, F. W., & Sarathy, R. 2008. Resource configuration in family firms: Linking resources, strategic planning and technological opportunities to performance. *Journal of Management Studies*, 45(1): 26–50.

Eddleston, K. A., Kellermanns, F. W., & Zellweger, T. M. 2012. Exploring the entrepreneurial behavior of family firms: Does the stewardship perspective explain differences? *Entrepreneurship: Theory and Practice*, 36(2): 347–367.

Frank, H., Lueger, M., Nose, L., & Suchy, D. 2010. The concept of "familiness": Literature review and systems theory-based reflections. *Journal of Family Business Strategy*, 1(3): 119–130.

Gedajlovic, E., Carney, M., Chrisman, J. J., & Kellermanns, F. W. 2012. The adolescence of family firm research taking stock and planning for the future. *Journal of Management*, 38(4): 1010–1037.

Gómez-Mejía, L. R., Takács Haynes, K., Núñez-Nickel, M., Jacobson, K. J. L., & Moyano-Fuentes, J. 2007. Socioemotional wealth and business risks in family-controlled firms: Evidence from Spanish olive oil mills. *Administrative Science Quarterly*, 52(1): 106–137.

Greidanus, N. S. & Mark, S. 2012. An exploration of internal corporate venturing goals in family firms. *Journal of Small Business and Entrepreneurship*, 25: 169–183.

Gudmundson, D., Tower, C. B., & Hartman, E. A. 2003. Innovation in small businesses: Culture and ownership structure do matter. *Journal of Developmental Entrepreneurship*, 8: 1, World Scientific Publishing Company.

Gurrieri, A. R. 2008. Knowledge network dissemination in a family-firm sector. *Journal of Socio-Economics*, 37(6): 2380–2389.

Habbershon, T. G., Williams, M., & MacMillan, I. C. 2003. A unified systems perspective of family firm performance. *Journal of Business Venturing*, 18(4): 451–465.

Hall, A., Melin, L., & Nordqvist, M. 2001. Entrepreneurship as radical change in the family business: Exploring the role of cultural patterns. *Family Business Review*, 14(3): 193–208.

Hall, A., Melin, L., & Nordqvist, M. 2006. Understanding strategizing in the family business context. In P. Poutziouris, K. Smyrnios, & S. Klein (Eds.), *Handbook of research on family business* (Vol. 14, pp. 253–268). Cheltenham, UK: Edward Elgar Publishing.

Hofstede, G., Hofstede, G., & Minkow, M. 2010. *Cultures and organizations: Software for the mind* (3rd ed.). New York: McGraw-Hill.

Hoy, F. 2006. The complicating factor of life cycles in corporate venturing. *Entrepreneurship: Theory and Practice*, 30: 831–836.

Huybrechts, J., Voordeckers, W., & Lybaert, N. 2013. Entrepreneurial risk taking of private family firms: The influence of a nonfamily CEO and the moderating effect of CEO tenure. *Family Business Review*, 26(2): 161–179.

Johns, G. 2006. The essential impact of context on organizational behavior. *Academy of Management Review*, 31(2): 386–408.

Kellermanns, F. W. & Eddleston, K. A. (2006). Corporate entrepreneurship in family firms: A family perspective. *Entrepreneurship: Theory and Practice*, 30(6): 809–830.

Kellermanns, F. W., Eddleston, K. A., Barnett, T., & Pearson, A. 2008. An exploratory study of family member characteristics and involvement: Effects on entrepreneurial behavior in the family firm. *Family Business Review*, 21(1): 1–14.

Kellermanns, F. W., Eddleston, K. A., Sarathy, R., & Murphy, F. 2012. Innovativeness in family firms: A family influence perspective. *Small Business Economics*, 38(1): 85–101.

La Porta, R., Lopez-de-Silanes, F., & Shleifer, A. 1999. Corporate ownership around the world. *Journal of Finance*, 54(2): 471–517.

Li, G. (Ed.). 2009. *Multicultural families, home literacies, and mainstream schooling (PB)*. Charlotte, NC: Information Age Pub Inc.

Liang, Q., Li, X., Yang, X., Lin, D., & Zheng, D. 2013. How does family involvement affect innovation in China? *Asia Pacific Journal of Management*, 30(3): 677–695.

Lumpkin, G. T. 1998. Do young firms have an entrepreneurial orientation? (Working paper). Salt Lake City: University of Utah.

Lumpkin, G. T. & Dess, G. G. 1996. Clarifying the entrepreneurial orientation construct and linking it to performance. *Academy of Management Review*, 21(1): 135–172.

Lumpkin, G. T. & Dess, G. G. 2001. Linking two dimensions of entrepreneurial orientation to firm performance: The moderating role of environment industry life cycle. *Journal of Business Venturing*, 16: 429–451.

Lumpkin, G. T., Brigham, K. H., & Moss, T. W. 2010. Long-term orientation: Implications for the entrepreneurial orientation and performance of family businesses. *Entrepreneurship and Regional Development*, 22: 241–264.

McKelvie, A., McKenny, A., Lumpkin, G., & Short, J. C. 2014. Corporate entrepreneurship in family businesses: Past contributions and future opportunities. In L. Melin, M. Nordqvist, & P. Sharma (Eds.), *SAGE handbook of family business* (pp. 340–363). London: Sage.

Marchisio, G., Mazzola, P., Sciascia, S., Miles, M., & Astrachan, J. 2010. Corporate venturing in family business: The effects on the family and its members. *Entrepreneurship and Regional Development*, 22: 349–377.

Martin, W. L. & Lumpkin, G. T. 2003. From entrepreneurial orientation to family orientation: Generational differences in the management of family businesses. In *Frontiers of entrepreneurship research: Proceedings of the 23rd annual Entrepreneurship Research Conference*, pp. 309–321.

Memili, E., Eddleston, K. A., Kellermanns, F. W., Zellweger, T. M., & Barnett, T. 2010. The critical path to family firm success through entrepreneurial risk taking and image. *Journal of Family Business Strategy*, 1(4): 200–209.

Miller, D. 1983. The correlates of entrepreneurship in three types of firms. *Management Science*, 29(7): 770–791.

Miller, D. 2011. Miller (1983) revisited: A reflection on EO research and some suggestions for the future. *Entrepreneurship: Theory and Practice*, 35(5): 873–894.

Miller, D. & Le Breton-Miller, I. 2005. *Managing for the long run: Lessons in competitive advantage from great family businesses*. Boston, MA: Harvard Business Press.

Miller, D. & Le Breton-Miller, I. 2011. Governance, social identity, and entrepreneurial orientation in closely held public companies. *Entrepreneurship: Theory and Practice*, 35: 1051–1076.

Miller, D., Le Breton-Miller, I., & Scholnick, B. 2008. Stewardship vs. stagnation: An empirical comparison of small family and non-family businesses. *Journal of Management Studies*, 45(1): 51–78.

Moog, P., Mirabella, D., & Schlepphorst, S. 2011. Owner orientations and strategies and their impact on family business. *International Journal of Entrepreneurship and Innovation Management*, 13(1): 95–112.

Naldi, L., Nordqvist, M., Sjöberg, K., & Wiklund, J. 2007. Entrepreneurial orientation, risk taking, and performance in family firms. *Family Business Review*, 20(1): 33–47.

Nordqvist, M. & Melin, L. 2010. Entrepreneurial families and family firms. *Entrepreneurship and Regional Development*, 22(3–4): 211–239.

Nordqvist, M. & Zellweger, T. 2010. *Transgenerational entrepreneurship: Exploring growth and performance in family firms across generations*. Cheltenham, UK: Edward Elgar Publishing.

Patel, P. C., Messersmith, J. G., & Lepak, D. P. 2013. Walking the tightrope: An assessment of the relationship between high-performance work systems and organizational ambidexterity. *Academy of Management Journal*, 56: 1420–1442.

Pistrui, D., Welsch, H. P., Wintermantel, O., Liao, J., & Pohl, H. 2000. Entrepreneurial orientation and family forces in the new Germany: Similarities and differences between East and West German entrepreneurs. *Family Business Review*, 13(3): 251–263.

Pittino, D., & Visintin, F. 2009. Innovation and strategic types of family SMEs: A test and extension of Miles and Snow's configurational model. *Journal of Enterprising Culture*, 17(3): 257–295.

Pittino, D., Visintin, F., Bau, M., & Mazzurana, P. 2013. Collaborative technology strategies and innovation in family firms. *International Journal of Entrepreneurship and Innovation Management*, 17(1): 8–27.

Rauch, A., Wiklund, J., Lumpkin, G. T., & Frese, M. 2009. Entrepreneurial orientation and business performance: An assessment of past research and suggestions for the future. *Entrepreneurship: Theory and Practice*, 33(3): 761–787.

Robertson, P., Smith, K., & von Tunzelmann, N. 2009. Innovation in low-and medium-technology industries. *Research Policy*, 38(3): 441–446.

Salvato, C. & Melin, L. 2008. Creating value across generations in family-controlled businesses: The role of family social capital. *Family Business Review*, 21(3): 259–276.

Salvato, C., Chirico, F., & Sharma, P. 2010. A farewell to the business: Championing exit and continuity in entrepreneurial family firms. *Entrepreneurship and Regional Development*, 22(3–4): 321–348.

Scholes, L., Wright, M., Westhead, P., & Bruining, H. 2010. Strategic changes in family firms post management buyout: Ownership and governance issues. *International Small Business Journal*, 28(5): 505–521.

Sciascia, S., Clinton, E., Nason, R. S., James, A. E., & Rivera-Algarin, J. O. 2013a. Family communication and innovativeness in family firms. *Family Relations*, 62: 429–442.

Sciascia, S., Mazzola, P., & Chirico, F. 2013b. Generational involvement in the top management team of family firms: Exploring nonlinear effects on entrepreneurial orientation. *Entrepreneurship: Theory and Practice*, 37: 69–85.

Sharma, P. & Chrisman, J. J. 1999. Toward a reconciliation of the definitional issues in the field of corporate entrepreneurship. *Entrepreneurship: Theory and Practice*, 23: 11–27.

Sharma, P. & Salvato, C. 2011. Commentary: Exploiting and exploring new opportunities over life cycle stages of family firms. *Entrepreneurship: Theory and Practice*, 35(6): 1199–1205.

Shepherd, D. & Haynie, J. M. 2009. Family business, identity conflict, and an expedited entrepreneurial process: A process of resolving identity conflict. *Entrepreneurship: Theory and Practice*, 33(6): 1245–1264.

Short, J. C., Payne, G. T., Brigham, K. H., Lumpkin, G. T., & Broberg, J. C. 2009. Family firms and entrepreneurial orientation in publicly traded firms: A comparative analysis of the S&P 500. *Family Business Review*, 22(1): 9–24.

Sieger, P., Zellweger, T., Nason, R. S., & Clinton, E. 2011. Portfolio entrepreneurship in family firms: A resource-based perspective. *Strategic Entrepreneurship Journal*, 5(4): 327–351.

Sirmon, D. G. & Hitt, M. A. 2003. Managing resources: Linking unique resources, management, and wealth creation in family firms. *Entrepreneurship: Theory and Practice*, 27(4): 339–358.

Stewart, A. & Hitt, M. A. 2010. The Yin and Yang of kinship and business: Complementary or contradictory forces? (And can we really say?). *Advances in Entrepreneurship, Firm Emergence and Growth*, 12: 243–276.

Stubner, S., Blarr, W. H., Brands, C., & Wulf, T. 2012. Organizational ambidexterity and family firm performance. *Journal of Small Business and Entrepreneurship*, 25(2): 217–229.

Toledano, N., Urbano, D., & Bernadich, M. 2010. Networks and corporate entrepreneurship, *Journal of Organizational Change Management*, 23: 396–412.

Tsao, S. M. & Lien, W. H. 2013. Family management and internationalization: The impact on firm performance and innovation. *Management International Review*, 53(2): 189–213.

Wagner, M. 2010. Corporate social performance and innovation with high social benefits: A quantitative analysis. *Journal of Business Ethics*, 94(4): 581–594.

Wong, Y. J., Chang, S. C., & Chen, L. Y. 2010. Does a family-controlled firm perform better in corporate venturing? *Corporate Governance: An International Review*, 18(3): 175–192.

Yordanova, D. I. 2011. Entrepreneurial orientation in family and non-family firms: evidence from Bulgaria. *International Journal of Economic Sciences and Applied Research*, 4(1): 185–203.

Zahra, S. A. 1991. Predictors and financial outcomes of corporate entrepreneurship: An exploratory study. *Journal of Business Venturing*, 6(4): 259–285.

Zahra, S. A. 1996. Goverance, ownership, and corporate entrepreneurship: The moderating impact of industry technological opportunities. *Academy of Management Journal*, 39(6): 1713–1735.

Zahra, S. A. 2003. International expansion of US manufacturing family businesses: The effect of ownership and involvement. *Journal of Business Venturing*, 18(4): 495–512.

Zahra, S. A. 2005. Entrepreneurial risk taking in family firms. *Family Business Review*, 18: 23–40.

Zahra, S. A. 2008. The virtuous cycle of discovery and creation of entrepreneurial opportunities. *Strategic Entrepreneurship Journal*, 2(3): 243–257.

Zahra, S. A. 2012. Organizational learning and entrepreneurship in family firms: Exploring the moderating effect of ownership and cohesion. *Small Business Economics*, 38(1): 51–65.

Zahra, S. A., Hayton, J. C., & Salvato, C. 2004. Entrepreneurship in family vs. non-family firms: A resource-based analysis of the effect of organizational culture. *Entrepreneurship: Theory and Practice*, 28(4): 363–381.

Zellweger, T. & Sieger, P. 2012. Entrepreneurial orientation in long-lived family firms. *Small Business Economics*, 38: 67–84.

Zellweger, T. M. & Nason, R. S. 2008. A stakeholder perspective on family firm performance. *Family Business Review*, 21(3): 203–216.

Zellweger, T. M., Nason, R. S., & Nordqvist, M. 2012. From longevity of firms to transgenerational entrepreneurship of families: Introducing family entrepreneurial orientation. *Family Business Review*, 25: 136–155.

Zellweger, T. M., Nason, R. S., Nordqvist, M., & Brush, C. G. 2011. Why do family firms strive for nonfinancial goals? An organizational identity perspective. *Entrepreneurship: Theory and Practice*, 37(2): 229–248.

3 Social Family Entrepreneurship

Social issues and stakeholder salience in small- and medium-sized family firms

Giovanna Campopiano, Alfredo De Massis, and Lucio Cassia

Introduction

Family businesses play a pivotal role in all European countries. This is particularly true in Italy, where a study conducted by Aidaf (Italian Association of Family Enterprises) and the Bank of Italy (2004) shows that family businesses represent 93 percent of the nation's companies and employ 98 percent of the workforce in manufacturing companies with fewer than 50 employees (European Commission, 2008). This evidence appears to be closely linked to the fact that family businesses are mostly small- and medium-sized enterprises (SMEs) and that they account for 99 percent of Italian firms (Istat, 2008).

Family firms are increasingly committing themselves to face and solve social issues, behaving as social entrepreneurs and involving their resources in philanthropic activities (Campopiano, De Massis, & Chirico, 2014). They are usually interested not only in the financial returns that are necessary for survival, but also in non-economic returns (Chrisman et al., 2012; Kotlar & De Massis, 2013), considered at times more relevant for the firm success and considered by family members when making strategic decisions (Short, Moss, & Lumpkin, 2009). Non-economic rationales that drive family firm decisions and activities lead to a socially responsible behavior and compliance with environmental and social standards (Berrone et al., 2010). There is in addition an increasing attention by practitioners to family firms' commitment toward philanthropy; and growing evidence of family firms that place emphasis on their role in the community, planning, and engaging in philanthropic activities (see, for example, the KPMG website section dedicated to philanthropy and family business). Family members consider their family's wealth, satisfaction, self-realization, image, and reputation as strongly tied to the business (Ward, 2004); they regard their business as a relevant entity of their own, within which they share common objectives (e.g., sustainability across generations) (Long & Mathews, 2011).

In some cases, these elements are exacerbated, and family firm entrepreneurs actually act as social entrepreneurs, as this behavior also allows them to have the family name positively linked to a business that is attentive to social issues in the community, and thus consistent with their objectives. Family owners indeed aim to strengthen the firm, its employees, and the relationships with all its stakeholders (Hoopes & Miller, 2006). Social entrepreneurship often overlaps with corporate social responsibility (CSR) as it refers to the accomplishment of social activities within the community where the firm is located. In particular, while social entrepreneurship relates especially to the entrepreneurial activity of a business aimed at achieving a social goal (Cukier, Trenholm, Carl, & Gekas,

2011), CSR is usually referred in the literature as the set of actions and practices accomplished by a firm in order to address any social issue to proactively "give back" to society (Carroll, 2000).

The focus on SMEs is important for several reasons. The first reason is that small firms have a number of specific characteristics that affect the key aspects of small business social responsibility (SBSR) (Lepoutre & Heene, 2006). In addition, empirical research on social entrepreneurship and corporate social responsibility in small businesses is limited in the number of studies (Thompson & Smith, 1991). According to Lepoutre and Heene (2006), in the literature there is, on the one hand, the idea that small businesses are socially responsible by nature; on the other, the presence of barriers, due to smaller firm size, is thought to constrain SMEs' ability to engage in social action.

It is therefore interesting to investigate what characterizes small- and medium-sized family firms in their behavior as social entrepreneurs. In particular, the aim is to link the underlying motivations of entrepreneurs to the salience of the stakeholders, whose claims the firm is called to respond. The chapter is thus organized as follows: the first section defines and reviews the social entrepreneurship and corporate social responsibility literatures, focusing especially on family firms' behavior; then a section is dedicated to developing the framework used for the analysis, as it is based on stakeholder theory and social identity theory. Methods and findings are then reported, and discussion and conclusions are finally drawn to close the chapter.

Social entrepreneurship and social issues in family firms: a review of the literature

Social entrepreneurship

Social entrepreneurship is defined as innovative, social value creating activity that can occur within or across the nonprofit, government, or business sectors (Austin, Stevenson, & Wei-Skillern, 2006). It involves the recognition, evaluation, and exploitation of opportunities that result in social value (Certo & Miller, 2008). In the business sector, in particular, social entrepreneurship means combining commercial enterprises with social impact (Letts, Brown, & Alvord, 2004). In this perspective, entrepreneurs have used business skills and knowledge to create firms that accomplish social purposes, and simultaneously are commercially viable (Emerson & Twersky, 1996). However, we still know very little about the opportunity recognition or identification processes of social entrepreneurs (Corner & Ho, 2010; Mair & Noboa, 2006). Since social value creation is about engaging with social problems and trying to generate solutions for these problems (Thompson, 2002), Hockerts (2006) states that opportunities to create social value surface through philanthropic activities, social activism, and through notions of self-help that engender systems enabling people to help themselves similar to the microfinance movement. Because social entrepreneurship is mission related, internal values and motivations largely guide the venture (Dees, 1998; Hemingway, 2005). For example, social entrepreneurs are often led by their passion to meet the needs of a population (Bornstein, 2004), or by their personal values (Drayton, 2002; Hemingway, 2005), charisma (Roper & Cheney, 2005), and leadership skills (Thompson, Alvy, & Lees, 2000). Social entrepreneurship opportunities are embedded in a social or community context (Robinson, 2006); moreover, whether among entrepreneurs there are some family members that have grown up within the business it is likely that they have broad interests that may include social and environmental benefits for their local community (Chell, 2007).

Corporate social responsibility

CSR is defined as a company's voluntary contribution to sustainable development which goes beyond legal requirements (Gamerschlag, Möller, & Verbeeten, 2011; Crane & Matten, 2007; De Bakker, Groenewegen, & Den Hond, 2005; Carroll, 1999, 2006). The topic has long been debated among scholars and the aforementioned definition is one of the most shared. A step forward has been done in analyzing in depth the components of CSR, identifying economic, legal, ethical, and discretionary responsibilities (Carroll, 1991). Moreover, an interesting point of view on the topic deals with the reinterpretation of the acronym CSR with "Company Stakeholder Responsibility," so that not only large corporations, but every company may engage in CSR, and that the primary objective for the firm is the satisfaction of its stakeholders' claims (Freeman, Velamuri, & Moriarty, 2006).

As regards literature on CSR in family business, a review of extant literature highlights the presence of few contributing studies (Fitzgerald et al., 2010). On the one hand there are papers that analyze family and firm characteristics in relation to socially responsible behavior of businesses (Niehm, Swinney, & Miller, 2008; De la Crus Deniz & Suarez, 2005; Uhlaner, Van Goor-Balk, & Masurel, 2004; Kilkenny, Nalbarte, & Besser, 1999); one of the most relevant insights is that a socially responsible business culture may emerge from the values and attitudes of the owning family. Other scholars focus on the impact of social and economic climate of a community on the performance of socially responsible processes by family businesses (Fitzgerald et al., 2010), consistently with the Sustainable Family Business Theory (SFBT), that recognizes the interplay between family businesses and their communities (Danes et al., 2008; Stafford et al., 1999).

Theoretical and empirical studies in the context of CSR have been conducted and results are sometimes contrasting. Moreover, in spite of the large amount of literature on the concept of CSR, there is no ultimate agreement on the reasons that lead a firm to embrace socially responsible initiatives (Campbell, 2007). In prior studies, the motivations driving individuals and firms to engage in socially responsible activities are essentially of two kinds: instrumental or normative. On the basis of the Motivation Theory developed in Psychology, according to which behaviors are explained by extrinsic and intrinsic motivations, where the latter may be split into normative and hedonistic motivations, firms pursue CSR strategies for four motivations: (i) defense of the reputation; (ii) justification of the cost benefits; (iii) integration with competitive strategies; and (iv) learning, innovation, and risk management (Zadek, 2000).

The focus on family businesses as object of the analysis may allow a deeper comprehension of the antecedents and behavior with respect to social issues because of the idiosyncratic characteristics of these firms, that can effectively affect their commitment as social entrepreneurs. The study aims, particularly, at investigating which are the prevailing motivations that family firms' owners and managers consider at the basis of their social activities, by gathering direct information on the socially responsible activities developed by small- and medium-sized family firms toward their stakeholders. A recent debate has focused on the approach of family firms toward social responsibility: on the one hand, some scholars assert that family firms are merely self-interested (Morck & Yeung, 2004); on the other hand, the attention is on the relevance of image and reputation for firms that have a strong organizational identity, as family firms do (Dyer & Whetten, 2006). It is thus interesting to understand to what extent the presence of the family at the helm may affect their social entrepreneurship attitude.

Theoretical foundation and research framework

This study is rooted in stakeholder theory and social identity theory. A stakeholder perspective has been adopted to develop the main part of the study. Stakeholders are all those individuals and constituencies that contribute, either voluntarily or involuntarily, to the firm's wealth (Post, Preston, & Sachs, 2002). According to Freeman (1984), considered the founder of stakeholder theory: "Stakeholder is a group or an individual that may affect or be affected by the corporate objectives achievement."

At the core of stakeholder theory is the idea that the long-term sustainability of a firm is dependent on the cooperation of numerous constituents, and not only on shareholders (Donaldson & Preston, 1995; Freeman, 1984), and extant research indicates that CSR initiatives are successful in generating returns to the company to the extent that they foster strong and enduring relationships with stakeholders (Waddock & Smith, 2000). It is no more enough to foster the sole interests of the shareholders of the firm; it is required for the companies' explicit and sustainable commitment towards their stakeholders.

Stakeholders with similar interests, expectations, and rights can be grouped in categories, such as employees, customers, shareholders, and so on. These groups can be in turn classified in two categories, primary and secondary stakeholders. Primary stakeholders are necessary for the company survival; indeed, whether the interests of a group of primary stakeholders were not met, the firm would be highly damaged. Instead, secondary stakeholders affect or are affected by the firm activities, but they are not engaged with it and are not so important for its survival (Clarkson, 1995; Freeman & Reed, 1983).

Scholars agree on the relevance and importance of stakeholders according to their salience – the degree to which managers give priority to competing stakeholder claims. To understand who and what really matters for the firm, it is essential to systematically assess the relationships, actual and potential, between stakeholders and managers, in terms of relative absence or presence of all or some of the stakeholder salience attributes: power, legitimacy, and urgency (Mitchell, Agle, & Wood, 1997). Power is an attribute that can be evaluated according to the kind of resources utilized to exercise it, coercive, utilitarian, or normative (Etzioni, 1964; Pfeffer, 1981). Legitimacy is the perception that a firm's actions are desirable and appropriate within a social system of norms, values, and beliefs (Suchman, 1995). Legitimacy and power are distinct attributes: they both can exist thus creating authority, defined as the legitimate use of power, but they can also exist independently (Mitchell, Agle, & Wood, 1997; Weber, 1947). Power and legitimacy as independent variables in the relationship between stakeholders and managers lead to a theory of the identification and salience of the stakeholders, but it does not catch the dynamics in the interactions between the actors involved. Urgency is a third and necessary attribute, defined as the degree to which stakeholder claims call for immediate attention. Therefore, an entity may also have a legitimate position or expectation, but, unless it either has the power to exercise its will or has expectations perceived urgent by the firm, it would not be salient enough for the firm's managers.

However, a critic has been moved to this kind of stakeholder classification and identification. The main drawback of the above-mentioned criteria is the firm-centric view of stakeholders, who are identified only in terms of their economic relevance to the firm (Dunfee, 2008). There is instead a perspective that provides a different way to identify stakeholders. According to social identity theory, people self-identify in groups as an expression of the social identity, and not simply because of the power, legitimacy, and urgency of their claims (Crane & Ruebottom, 2011). From this complementary perspective, identification is distinct from behavior, and therefore also stakeholder salience is differently conceptualized.

Social identification entails one's belongingness to a social category (Ashforth & Mael, 1989), to which she/he feels attached. The individual can benefit from this group membership in terms of emotional values associated with it. Moreover, identity salience is key and motivates attitudes and behavior (Lobel & St. Clair, 1992). A category salience depends on a set of elements. First, accessibility and fit with a situation (Oakes, 1987), that is the relative readiness of a certain category to be activated and then translated in reality for the individual who self-identifies with the group; these elements are specific to the identity, the individual, and the context. Second, connectedness is a relevant dimension, since a category characterized by many connections with others is more salient than those categories that are connected to few personal relationships (Stryker & Burke, 2000). Third, distinctiveness is a key factor affecting the inclination of individuals to identify with a specific group because a category that encompasses an observable and clear-cut difference is the most salient for those individuals who can thus share identity and social interactions (Mehra, Kilduff, & Brass, 1998).

It is worth underlining that self-identification with a category is relational and comparative (Tajfel & Turner, 1985), so that the extent to which an individual self-identifies is a matter of degree (Ashforth & Mael, 1989). In addition, individuals usually have multiple identities, but when there is an alignment of two or more identities, they feel to converge toward the focal entity (Sharma & Irving, 2005), thus resulting in their personification with the entity itself, in their belief in the entity's goals, and in their desire to contribute to the achievement of these goals.

As regards family business, many family members self-identify with their firms (Rosenblatt et al., 1985) and use the firms to place themselves in the communities in which they live and operate (McGivern, 1978).

Family business literature argued that family firms are characterized by distinctive features, such as their structure (Tsang, 2002), the relationships (Pearson, Carr, & Shaw, 2008), cognitions (Mitchell, Morse, & Sharma, 2003), decision-making process (Mitchell et al., 2009), and strategy (Sirmon & Hitt, 2003). More interesting, according to Mitchell et al. (2011), is that sources of power, legitimacy, and urgency apply to family involvement in business and are unique in the family context, consistent with the claim that family members and the family itself are stakeholders (De la Crus Deniz & Suarez, 2005). Mitchell and colleagues (2011) thus propose that: (i) family firms pursue family-centered non-economic (FCNE) goals (Chrisman, Chua, & Sharma, 2005; Janjuha-Jivraj & Spence, 2009; Sharma, Chrisman, & Chua, 1997) in order to create socioemotional wealth

(Gómez-Mejía et al., 2007); (ii) these goals are rooted in the relationships existing among family members (Long & Matthews, 2011; Pearson, Carr, & Shaw, 2008); (iii) FCNE goals and traditional goals of profitability and growth may be considered as synergic, though independent (Gomez-Mejia, Makri, & Kintana, 2010; Zellweger & Nason, 2008); and (iv) family firms are heterogeneous in the way they respond to stakeholders' claims and pressures (Melin & Nordqvist, 2007). In addition, family members, in accordance with the extent of their identification with the family and the business, may have different agendas and claims as stakeholders, so that it is important for decision makers to recognize this and mediate among the various goals of the people involved (Poza, Alfred, & Maheshwari, 1997).

The research framework

Rooted in the aforementioned theoretical background, we developed a research framework that let us analyze the linkage between motivations, socially responsible activities, and each stakeholder's claims (Campopiano, De Massis, & Cassia, 2012a). In particular, we referred to the internal stakeholders of the family firms considered, first because they are among the primary stakeholders and for them it is high the degree of identification with the firm, second because of the methodological difficulties encountered in gathering data from external stakeholders in person, especially as regards customers and suppliers. This framework was obtained through an appropriate elaboration of the stakeholder/responsibility matrix introduced by Carroll (1991), that creates a connection between each stakeholder and all socially responsible initiatives according to their kind (economic, legal, ethical, philanthropic).

In this study, each internal stakeholder is linked to the different socially responsible activities, as emerged in the case studies. In particular, CSR activities are previously divided according to the motivations, derived from Motivation Theory, that emerged as antecedents of their accomplishment. Moreover, on the basis of the three attributes that characterize stakeholder salience, the classification of internal stakeholders is as follows (Mitchell, Agle, & Wood, 1997): when power, legitimacy, and urgency are high they are definitive stakeholders, and all their claims are considered priority by the firm's management; they are dominant stakeholders when they are powerful and legitimate, so that they can influence the firm since they usually create within it a "dominant coalition" (Cyert & March, 1963); when they have legitimate and urgent claims, they are called dependent stakeholders, and since they have not enough power, the satisfaction of their claims depends on the protection by other more powerful stakeholders or by the guideline values of the firm's managers; finally, when power and urgency are high, they are dangerous stakeholders, since they are not legitimate and they could be coercive and violent.

It is therefore possible to identify a linkage between stakeholders' salience and socially responsible activities in order to clarify how the firm addresses each stakeholder's claims.

In summary, the proposed framework consists of a table, that, for each socially responsible activity undertaken firm, links the underlying motivations and the salience of stakeholders, whose claims the firm is called to respond.

This framework enabled us to address the following research questions: (i) What are the motivations that characterize the socially responsible activities of small- and medium-sized family firms? (ii) What is the link, if it exists, between the motivations leading family firms to behave as social entrepreneurs and their stakeholders' salience?

To the best knowledge of the authors, this is the first study aimed at investigating why family firms behave as social entrepreneurs, and whether the involvement of the family in the business actually affects their behavior as social entrepreneurs. Furthermore, according to the different motivations it is possible to understand if family firms are driven more by the willing to respect norms, to behave in a socially responsible manner because of the owner's personal desire and family's sensibility, to improve corporate reputation, or even to create a competitive advantage.

Methodology

Given the aim of the investigation, we adopted an exploratory approach and gathered empirical evidence through a multiple cases study (De Massis & Kotlar, 2014; Yin, 2003), in order both to examine each case in-depth and to identify contingency variables that distinguish each case from the other. We contacted small- and medium-sized family firms located in the Province of Bergamo, already involved in socially responsible activities. The Chamber of Commerce of the Province of Bergamo in 2010 compiled a list of firms according to their commitment to CSR, as witnessed from their good practices. Bergamo is an area rich of SMEs driven by families, usually operating in the manufacturing industry. To assess that sampled firms were SMEs, they have to fulfill the criteria of the SME definition of the European Commission as from January 2005: an enterprise qualifies as small- and medium-sized if its number of employees is between ten and 250, and it reports a total turnover between €2 million and €50 million. All the analyzed cases fulfill these criteria. As regards family involvement in the sampled firms, we defined a family firm as a firm owned and managed by a family or a small group of families in order to pursue the vision of the business and to be sustainable across generations (Chua, Chrisman, & Sharma, 1999). In order to check whether the companies under investigation were effectively family firms, we looked at all the three dimensions of the F-PEC scale (Klein, Astrachan, & Smyrnios, 2005), power, experience, and culture. The degree of intensity of these three dimensions characterizes a family business, since they are measured on a continuous scale that allows for different levels of involvement, effective and potential, of the family in the business. Power is associated with the degree of involvement of family members in ownership and management, thus we collected detailed information on the equity shares and management roles of the family members. As regards experience, we asked how many generations are involved in the management of the firm, and whether the founder is still at the helm. Finally, culture is the attribute that assesses the degree of overlap between family and corporate values, as well as the degree of commitment of family members to support managers to both pursue economic goals and ensure the development of mutual interrelationships between family, business, and environment. We therefore asked the family members whether they agree on a five-point Likert scale to specific sentences related for example to loyalty, values sharing, and pride.

After a first step of e-mailing and phone calls to explain the project, 30 percent of the contacted companies took part in the investigation, with a final number of four detailed case studies. We performed a semi-structured interview to multiple internal stakeholders for each case. In particular, we collected information from: (i) the family owner of the firm; (ii) another component of the family involved in the ownership and/or management of the company; and (iii) an employee of the considered firm. This multiple respondent approach has been already employed in family business research (e.g., Cassia, De Massis, & Pizzurno, 2011). The interviewees were initially asked personal data and their role within the firm. Then the semi-structured interview allowed them to talk openly about social responsibility and about the relationships with the stakeholders, with particular attention paid to the motivations that led them to behave as social entrepreneurs. This procedure for data collection helped enhance the reliability of the research (Yin, 2003). The interviewers' task was precisely to invite them to talk about experiences and personal opinions on the topic. All interviews were tape-recorded and transcribed; moreover, an abbreviated interview protocol is provided in the Appendix.

Data and information gathered through the case studies were manipulated before being analyzed. In particular, we applied the following techniques (Miles & Huberman, 1984): (i) data categorization, that is the decomposition and aggregation of information in order to highlight some characteristics (e.g., motivations leading to a specific CSR behavior) and to facilitate comparisons; (ii) data contextualization, that entails the analysis of contextual factors that may result in relevant relationships between events and circumstances. Indeed, once motivations were collected, for each case study we classified them according to the Motivation Theory previously presented. We were thus able to distinguish family firms according to their social entrepreneurship attitude. Then, we connected the emerged motivations to the socially responsible activities performed by the firms, as answered to the corresponding questions. In particular, to identify and categorize social responsible actions, we relied on a set of questions similar to those used to collect data in previous studies: it is asked whether the entrepreneurs know the definition of Corporate Social Responsibility, as it is spread through the *Green Book* in Italy: "A concept whereby companies integrate social and environmental concerns in their business operations and in their interaction with their stakeholders on a voluntary basis"; moreover, the interviewees have been asked for information on the relationships with employees, suppliers, customers, the community, and whether and how firms communicate their CSR practices (e.g., Campopiano, De Massis, & Cassia, 2012b; Campopiano & De Massis, 2015). Finally, we isolated the socially responsible activities performed toward the internal stakeholders and we identified the existent linkages between their salience and the motivations that led the firm to engage in those activities, following the framework previously presented.

Findings

In this section for each case study, on the basis of the methodology described above, we provide a brief description of the business activity, detailed information on the family involvement in the firm's ownership and management, on the motivations leading them to behave in a socially responsible way, and on internal stakeholders' salience, as emerged from the interviewed parties' words, reported as illustrative anecdotes.

First, some descriptive information on the firms involved in the analysis is shown in Table 3.1.

Table 3.1 Background information on the studied companies

Company	Size (no. of employees)	Year of foundation	Turnover (2009) (€ million)	Code of ethics	Social balance sheet
Gam Edit Srl	15	1948	1.6	No	No
Zanetti Arturo e C.	70	1964	18	No	No
Bellini Srl	22	1943	12	No	No
RoburSpA	220	1956	28	No	Yes

Gam Edit Srl is a family business traditionally in the printing works industry. Experience and knowledge of a craft that the family has developed for three generations allow it to grow, widening the production structure and the range of products. Today the business is focused on printing, stationery, and communication.

Family involvement is high, as emerged by the analysis of the three attributes of the F-PEC scale for Gam Edit Srl: the family owns 100 percent of the equity of the firm; three family members and an external manager participate in the Board of Directors. Father and daughter, the current CEO, are at the helm, the family business is right now at its third generation, proving that experience is high. The CEO's brother explicitly clarifies the importance of sharing goals in a few words: "Everyone in the family care about our company." All the dimensions used to evaluate the degree of family culture within the business present medium-high scores, with an average score equal to 4, as the family itself evaluated each dimension during the interview. The emphasis is especially on loyalty, care fate, and pride. However, the owner said she feels corporate and family reputations only partially related.

The rest of the interviews have shown that motivations characterizing the actions of the family are of the extrinsic type, i.e., linked to the achievement of the set goals by pursuing an ethical behavior. As declared by the CEO: "Nowadays, our CSR policy is especially focused on environment, and represents the real competitive advantage of our business." Deepening the level of analysis, it emerges that also normative motivations play a role, since the firm needs to fulfill some expected industrial requirements, as regards for example safety and cleanliness. We can conclude that Gam Edit Srl performs CSR activities pushed by motivations mainly attributable to the search for competitive advantage and compliance with the rules of the game. The approach toward internal stakeholders is related to ethical and moral concepts, indeed CSR activities may be counted as legal and ethical dimensions. As asserted by the third generation CEO:

> Sustainability, in an industry like this one, is a business opportunity with social implications, internal and external to the firm, close to my personal sensibility, but it creates also the conditions conducive to the development of the firm and to the presence on the market.

Stakeholder salience of owners, family members, and employees is included in the analysis: from the interview it emerges that family members have power, but their claims are not considered as urgent as those of owners and employees. It is clear from the words of an employee that their involvement in CSR activities is relevant:

We are periodically informed on the environmental policies adopted by the firm, since we are all called to operate according to specific procedures, and since we have internal and external audits. Moreover, we take part in courses, mainly related to CSR topics.

Zanetti Arturo e C. is a family business at its first generation, leader in the industry of environmental services management; with advanced equipment and qualified employees, it collects, moves, and retrieves and/or disposes of urban garbage and special dangerous and non-dangerous refuse. For 20 years it has been active in CSR, especially regarding environmental issues. It proves to evolve in synchrony not only with market needs but also with those of society and the planet.

Family power is high: the family owns 100 percent of the equity of the firm; the founder and other three family shareholders participate in the Board of Directors. Regarding experience, it is important to highlight that the father/founder of the business is preparing for the generational change. Business culture has been evaluated by the interviewees as important, especially in the dimensions of loyalty, care fate, pride, positive influence by the business, and shared values among family members, with an average score of 4.4.

From the analysis of the interviews it emerges that motivations are of an intrinsic type. "For 20 years we have been driven by the will to respect neighbors, institutions, consortia, and communities; it was and it is needful to operate in accordance with all that surrounds us," said the owner. In particular, motivations are hedonistic toward both the employees and the family itself. The firm considers CSR as pushed by motivations mainly attributable to an innate sensibility and an inner desire to be socially responsible. "I personally care about CSR issues and I try to pass on to my sons," the owner states, and adds "Corporate reputation is strongly linked to family reputation." His son's words show a strong commonality of thoughts: "At the moment we do not need to revise our CSR policies, they are in perfect harmony with my father's ideas." The industry, in addition, forces to pay attention to the company reputation and the founder does not omit that within the industry in which it operates CSR may be translated also in a source of competitive advantage: "Our certifications allow us to reach higher visibility and regard in bargaining with the main clients." Toward internal stakeholders, the approach to CSR is mainly related to emotions and moral concepts. We can identify this business with a socio-economic view of CSR activities, since Zanetti Arturo e C. reconciles profit maximization with social claims' satisfaction, able even to benefit from a better image and good relationships with its clients. Employees are even involved: "We take part in three training sessions per year on CSR activities." Finally, stakeholder salience of owners, family members, and employees has been studied: from the interview it emerges that family members have power, but their claims are not considered as urgent as those of owners and employees.

Bellini Srl is a family business in the industry of trade of oil derivatives since 1943. The experience in the oil sector is the strategic element that makes the firm an authoritative reference, letting it be not only a supplier but effectively a consulting and proactive partner. CSR is not formalized, but the ethical concepts that implies are the pillars on which the entrepreneur builds his activity.

As regards power, the Bellini family owns 92 percent of equity, and three of the family members constitute the Board of Directors. The second generation is driving the company, but the family is laying the groundwork for the generational change to the third one. As asserted by the CEO, CSR has been one of the most important and disruptive elements of the succession process from the first to the second generation:

> When I joined the company, I put CSR first. At the time, the company run by my father survived through means at the limit of the allowable. I instead was committed to pay taxes, respect laws, environment, people, and clients, mainly through trust in the relationships with them. My father did not understand it, and I must say that mine was a very strong generational transition.

Culture is considered an important dimension within the business, with an average score equal to 4.1. During the interview, the highest score has been attributed to dimensions like agreement with goals, loyalty, care fate, and orientation toward the attainment of long-term outcomes. "The company has my name and I feel it as mine," the son said.

Motivations to engage in CSR activities are of intrinsic type, they are mainly normative, related to morality, ethics, and compliance with laws; as asserted by the owner, business success is a consequence, not an antecedent: "Social responsibility is an ethical principle that translates in an advantage, both in economic and in social terms. It is a proper key to success." CSR activities in Bellini Srl regard, among others, the respect for environment. In accordance with this aspect, they decided to differentiate the product portfolio, thanks also to the research on vegetable-based lubricants. Attention to CSR has thus pushed innovation and created a competitive advantage based on innovative products.

The firm is active in creating social relationships with all stakeholders, especially the internal ones, in order to involve and motivate them. As explained by the CEO:

> A business is not the sum of each contribution, but it is much more: it is the job organization, coordinated on shared goals, that creates added value; but whether there is not attention paid to internal stakeholders' claims, it would be impossible to obtain that added value and we would not be competitive. Coordination, team stimulation and participation to business goals are essential; therefore, the responsible action towards stakeholders represent a key to be successful.

A positive feedback is also found in the words of the interviewed employee: "There is a high attention to our non-working and family issues, also thanks to the human relationship that is quite easy to obtain due to the small size of the firm."

Robur SpA is a medium-sized enterprise that invests in research, develops, and produces, totally in Italy, heating systems with high efficiency and low environmental impact. Technological innovation is the key to be competitive, with a deep belief in the opportunity to make profits without destroying the future, indeed trying to build it. Robur SpA has defined "7 pillars," i.e., seven core values of working experience of each person and of business ethics: Sharing, Education, Quality, Innovation, Service, Social Responsibility, Witness.

The family owns the firm totally. The founder and his wife participate in the Board of Directors. The family business is still at its first generation stage; the second generation is still involved, even if not all the members of the family are employed in the business: only two out of the five offspring work in the family business. Culture is a fundamental dimension and evaluated as really important by the interviewees, with an average score equal to 4.8 for the sub-dimensions evaluated by the interviewed family owner.

The family's activities in CSR are characterized by motivations of intrinsic type. They are hedonistic, related to feeling, will, social conscience, and ethics. The founder's wife, in this regard, asserts: "Among the most important things in my life I place family, love for the business, passion for people, commitment to continue to improve as a more responsible person." She is president of the ONLUS Foundation and coordinator of educational programs. Commitment to CSR is an increasing phenomenon: "Our social initiatives are always evolving, and involve various CSR scopes," says the CEO's wife.

With respect to the other case studies, the interviewees in Robur SpA pay particular attention to the urgency of each internal stakeholder's claims, that is in agreement with what the CEO states: "One of our strengths has been the intuition and belief that a community, even professional, bears fruit if well maintained, understood and enhanced. Our experience taught that positive relationships create quality and intelligence that become high productivity." And indeed many activities are accomplished toward employees, especially regarding health, safety, equal opportunities, and fair compensation.

In order to compare the major results, we provide a synoptic representation in Table 3.2.

Discussion

The findings of our case studies provide an amount of hints to be discussed in-depth. First, it emerged that motivations driving the socially responsible activities of small- and medium-sized family firms are mainly of an intrinsic type. Family owners' decisions as social entrepreneurs seem to depend on ethics and the feeling to do the right thing, but there are differences among them: on the one hand, a normative type of motivations prevails, weighing more the moral aspects; on the other hand, the hedonistic type triumphs when the interviewee explains

Table 3.2 Synoptic representation of the major results of the multiple case studies

Company	Motivations	Stakeholder/responsibilities	Stakeholder salience
Gam Edit Srl	Extrinsic Instrumental	Legal – ethical	Definitive family owners Dominant family members Dominant employees
Zanetti Arturo e C.	Intrinsic Hedonistic	Ethical	Definitive family owners Dominant family members Dominant employees
Bellini Srl	Intrinsic Normative	Ethical	Definitive family owners Dominant family members Dominant employees
Robur SpA	Intrinsic Hedonistic	Ethical – philanthropic	Definitive family owners Definitive family members Dominant employees

that she/he is driven especially by a social conscience and by her/his will to be socially responsible. Even if the sample size is small, the scene appears to be highly heterogeneous. Therefore, even as regards the orientation toward CSR, it is not possible to include all family firms into a homogeneous group (Melin & Nordqvist, 2007). The differences in the motivations are certainly due to the personal attitude of the owner to behave as a social entrepreneur, as straightforwardly expressed by the family CEO of Bellini Srl, or by the CEO's wife in Robur SpA. However, the presence of a family at the helm of the firm plays a crucial role in the relevance given to CSR. The importance of socially responsible activities is transmitted from generation to generation, as emerges from the words of the younger generation in Zanetti Arturo e C., that highlight the accordance of orientation toward CSR. This is consistent with the idea that family members, thanks to the existing relationships, share goals (Long & Matthews, 2011). Therefore, social responsible behavior becomes part of the family legacy and one of the pillars on which the family business is built: the family is motivated by a strong commitment to a set of shared values reflected in business (Aronoff, 2004). The agreement among family members on the decisions on CSR issues is moderated by the degree of self-identification in the family business. From the findings of this research, it emerges that the more family members feel attached to their firm and are aligned with its goals, the higher is the long-term orientation and commitment to behave as social entrepreneurs, thus supporting the relevance of understanding and perceiving the self-identification of each stakeholder, in order to understand her/his salience (Poza, Alfred, & Maheshwari, 1997).

As regards the link between motivations and the internal stakeholders' salience, it is worth highlighting that almost all family firms involved in the study recognize that family relatives have power, but their claims are not considered to be as urgent as the employees' ones. It emerges that the relationships with employees are crucial for all the family firms involved in the study. The employees' involvement and fair compensation is really relevant for the family firm, and it emerges that these relations are based more on normative commitments rather than driven only by financial goals, since their long-term orientation to performance lead them to be aware of the importance of human capital and thus not to sacrifice it for short-term returns (Stavrou, Kassinis, & Filotheou, 2007). Employees are fundamental assets, and family firms care about their training and their well-being. This is even consistent with those studies showing that downsizing is rarely considered in the family business context (e.g., Block, 2010). As regards, instead, family members, they reveal to be dominant stakeholders, since their claims have power and legitimacy, but no urgency. This finding needs to be discussed in light of the social identity concept: it is necessary that family members are all completely identified and aligned with their family business in order to develop a "dominant coalition," as stated by Cyert and March (1963). If one or more family members do not self-identify with the organization, a conflict situation can arise, where these family members, although involved in the firm's activities, are not satisfied since their claims are not fulfilled as they expect, or are considered of secondary importance at a certain time. This can result in a dangerous situation, with potential negative repercussions also on the commitment to CSR. Therefore, the awareness of the presence of more urgent stakeholders' claims, by the family members who are involved in the business, is a necessary condition, even if this means that they sometimes have to sacrifice for their firm's sake. Moreover, this situation can be accepted only if the goals are understood and effectively shared by all family members. It appears clear that this reasoning reinforces the importance of building a family legacy that is shared by family members and passed to younger generations. Family firms have thus an advantage by transmitting, from generation to generation, also the orientation to CSR as a set of values that pays back the business both in terms of reputation and in terms of sustainability in the long run, with high benefits for the family.

Conclusions, implications, and limitations

The multiple case study analysis of small- and medium-sized family businesses provides a number of insights on behavior of family firms as social entrepreneurs, and on the existing linkages between the motivations driving family owners and managers to behave as social entrepreneurs, and internal stakeholders' salience. The results thus showed a range of motivations, mainly of an intrinsic type, driving the firms' socially responsible activities: we attributed the differences to the personal attitude of the family owner, but we highlighted the relevance of the degree of self-identification of the family members in their firms, since a high self-identification with their organizations entails a strong commitment to the firm's goals, and therefore allows a continuous engagement in CSR. We also identified a common trait in the appointment of family members into the category of dominant stakeholders, that is they have power and legitimate, but not urgent, claims. This may be a source of tension if they do not self-identify with the organization.

However, more research is needed in this field, to draw more firmly grounded conclusions on the commitment of family firms to behave as social entrepreneurs.

The results of our research can have significant implications for academics, practitioners, and policy makers. First, this research may benefit both family business, social entrepreneurship, and CSR scholars by theoretically and empirically considering how family involvement in ownership and management affects the family firm's behavior toward social issues. The involvement of family stakeholders in the organization represents a distinctive characteristic of family enterprises (Zellweger & Nason, 2008), and our study shows that this factor plays an important role in explaining the behavior of family firms as social entrepreneurs. In particular, by borrowing some arguments from social identity theory, and by focusing on the family business context through multiple-respondent interviews, research on social entrepreneurship may be highly beneficial and an important contribution to stakeholder theory may be provided in dealing with the special characteristics of family firms. In particular, family businesses prove that social entrepreneurship and CSR have become extremely important and in many cases they are driven by valuable principles and initiatives; moreover this behavior has become part of the family culture that is shared and passed through generations. Family members are special stakeholders, because of their multiple role and strong identification with their business. The discussion above has shown that the findings from these cases are relevant and can contribute to stakeholder theory, since it exists a category of primary stakeholders whose claims may be of secondary importance: family members' salience is thus dependent on their role within the firm and their acceptance of the potential sacrifices they have to bear.

Second, this study represents a very important issue for managers working in small- and medium-sized family firms. They should carefully consider how family involvement in ownership and management of the organization that hired them could affect the effectiveness of good practices. Finally, the research may guide policy makers in their strategic decisions. Increasing attention has been paid to CSR initiatives in the design of public policies and, particularly, family firms, due to their huge presence (Astrachan & Shanker, 2003; Anderson & Reeb, 2003), are considered critical for favoring the development of economies across the world (Villalonga & Amit, 2009; La Porta et al., 1999). In this respect, the research achievements will be useful since they address some suggestions on how to build a system of supporting socially responsible initiatives tailored to the idiosyncratic characteristics of family firms. For instance, the findings of our study may support policy makers in decisions regarding the funding of CSR activities in the current business context.

However, there are a number of limitations to the generalizability of our research findings. First, results cannot be statistically generalized, because of the adopted methodology based on the analysis of a limited sample of case studies. A larger number of cases would allow gathering more information to further support the results. Moreover, the analysis with the presented framework in this study is limited to the internal stakeholders. It is indeed difficult to have the possibility to interview the external stakeholders of the firm, especially because by definition a firm's activity affects many external actors in the society. Moreover, it is difficult to have a secondary data source to compare family firms in their orientation to CSR and behavior as social entrepreneurs, because of the predominant organizational climate that is largely informal and unstructured, as proved by the absence of written codes of ethics and social balance sheets (see Table 3.1). This is consistent with those scholars asserting that stakeholder management in SMEs is not as formal as in large firms (Russo & Perrini, 2010), and this is even exacerbated when considering the accomplishment of social activities toward them (Maitland, 2002), as it is also shown in previous studies on large firms (Campopiano, Cassia, & De Massis, 2012).

Appendix

3.A.1 *Abbreviated interview protocol*

Family owner:
Are you married?
Is your husband/wife involved in the family business? Which is his/her role? Does he/she participate in CSR initiatives?
Who are the family members directly involved in the business? Which are their roles?
Are there any family members who are not involved in the family business?
Which generation is at the helm? Are you considering making a generational change?
Which are the common values, shared among family members?
When your commitment to CSR started?
Why? Is it more an inner desire or a necessity? Is there any particular motivation to accomplish CSR activities, e.g., ethics, image, effectiveness, stakeholders' satisfaction, relationship benefits, external pressures?
Do you hold institutional positions in civic, sports, or cultural associations?
Is your firm's reputation linked to your family's reputation?

Is there anyone in the firm who is in charge of CSR issues?
Which are the most critical stakeholders, among employees, family members, nonfamily managers?
Which are the most influential stakeholders?
Which are the CSR initiatives toward employees' protection? Is there any particular issue you face, e.g., safety, employees' health, equal opportunities, fair compensation, irregular work?
Are there any CSR activities toward family members?
Is CSR important for the success of your business? Is it possible to exploit CSR as a competitive advantage?

Family member:
Do you share the firm's mission and values?
Are you going to pursue the same aims?
Are you going to take care of the future of the business?
Are you proud of your business?
Are you willing to put in more effort than is usually required in order to help the firm to be successful?
Are you going to change the CSR activities, for example on different areas of interest? Why?
Does it exist a well-defined career path for you in the business?
Are there any incentives based on non-economic outcomes?
Are you involved in the CSR activities? Which is your role?
Do you hold institutional positions in civic, sports, or cultural associations?
Is there any particular motivation to accomplish CSR activities, e.g., ethics, image, effectiveness, stakeholders' satisfaction, relationship benefits, external pressures?
Which is the most significant CSR area of interest for your business?

Employee:
Which is your role in the business?
Is the level of compensation satisfactory?
Are benefits provided?
Does a well-defined career path exist for you in the business?
Are there any arrangements or facilities?
Are there policies to protect against all forms of discrimination both in the workplace and at the time of recruitment?
What about safety, health, racial integration, contracts?
Are there any incentives based on non-economic outcomes?
Is it possible to work from home or with flexible hours?
Is there any attention paid to non-working and family issues of the employees?
Are there mechanisms of control, coordination, and communication?
How are employees involved in CSR activities?

References

Anderson, R.C. & Reeb, D.M. (2003). Founding-family ownership and firm performance: evidence from the S&P 500. *Journal of Finance*, 58(3), 1301–1327.
Aronoff, C. (2004). Self-perpetuation family organization built on values: necessary condition for long-term family business survival. *Family Business Review*, 17, 55–59.
Ashforth, B.E. & Mael, F. (1989). Social identity theory and the organization. *Academy of Management Review*, 14(1), 20–39.

Astrachan, J.H. & Shanker, M.C. (2003). Family businesses' contribution to the U.S. economy: a closer look. *Family Business Review*, 16(3), 211–219.

Austin, J., Stevenson, H., & Wei-Skillern, J. (2006). Social and commercial entrepreneurship: same, different, or both? *Entrepreneurship: Theory and Practice*, 30(1), 1–22.

Bank of Italy (2004). Proprietà e controllo delle imprese italiane, Cosa è cambiato nel decennio 1993–2003. Milano.

Berrone, P., Cruz, C., Gomez-Mejia, L.R., & Larraza-Kintana, M. (2010). Socioemotional wealth and corporate responses to institutional pressures: do family-controlled firms pollute less? *Administrative Science Quarterly*, 55(1), 82–113.

Bhattacharya, C.B., Korschun, D., & Sen, S. (2008). Strengthening stakeholder–company relationships through mutually beneficial corporate social responsibility initiatives. *Journal of Business Ethics*, 85(2), 257–272.

Block, J. (2010). Family management, family ownership, and downsizing: evidence from S&P 500 firms. *Family Business Review*, 23(2), 109–130.

Bornstein, D. (2004). *How to Change the World: Social Entrepreneurs and the Power of New Ideas.* Oxford University Press, Oxford, UK.

Campbell, J.L. (2007). Why would corporations behave in socially responsible ways? An institutional theory of corporate social responsibility. *Academy of Management Review*, 32(3), 946–967.

Campopiano, G. & De Massis, A. (2015). Corporate social responsibility reporting: a content analysis in family and non-family firms. *Journal of Business Ethics*, 129(3), 511–534.

Campopiano, G., Cassia, L., & De Massis, A. (2012). Italy: the interplay between sustainability and family entrepreneurship: an Italian case-study. In Halkias D., Thurman P. (Eds.), *Entrepreneurship and Sustainability: Business Solutions for Poverty Alleviation from around the World,* Gower Publishers, Farnham, Surrey, UK, 155–167.

Campopiano, G., De Massis, A., & Cassia, L. (2012a). The relationship between motivations and actions in corporate social responsibility: an exploratory study. *International Journal of Business and Society*, 13(3), 391–425.

Campopiano, G., De Massis, A., & Cassia, L. (2012b). Corporate social responsibility: a survey among SMEs in Bergamo. *Procedia Social and Behavioral Sciences Journal*, 62, 325–341.

Campopiano, G., De Massis, A., & Chirico, F. (2014). Firm Philanthropy in Small-and Medium-Sized Family Firms. The Effects of Family Involvement in Ownership and Management. *Family Business Review*, 27(3), 244–258.

Carroll, A.B. (1991). The pyramid of corporate social responsibility: toward the moral management of organizational stakeholders. *Business Horizons*, 34(4), 39–48.

Carroll, A.B. (1999). Corporate social responsibility: evolution of a definitional construct. *Business and Society*, 38(3), 268–295.

Carroll, A.B. (2000). Ethical challenges for business in the new millennium: corporate social responsibility and models of management morality. *Business Ethics Quarterly*, 10(1), 33–42.

Carroll, A.B. (2006). Corporate social responsibility: a historical perspective. In: Epstein, M.J. & Hanson, K.O. (Eds.), *The Accountable Corporation: Corporate Social Responsibility*, 3rd ed., Praeger, Westport, CT, 3–30.

Cassia, L., De Massis, A., & Pizzurno, E. (2011). An exploratory investigation on NPD in small family businesses from northern Italy. *International Journal of Business, Management and Social Sciences*, 2(2), 1–14.

Certo, S.T. & Miller, T. (2008). Social entrepreneurship: key issues and concepts. *Business Horizons*, 51(4), 267–271.

Chell, E. (2007). Social enterprise and entrepreneurship towards a convergent theory of the entrepreneurial process. *International Small Business Journal*, 25(1), 5–26.

Chrisman, J., Chua, J.H., Pearson, A.W., & Barnett, T. (2012). Family involvement, family influence, and family-centered non-economic goals in small firms. *Entrepreneurship: Theory and Practice*, 36(2), 267–293.

88   *G. Campopiano et al.*

Chrisman, J.J., Chua, J.H., & Sharma, P. (2005). Trends and directions in the development of a strategic management theory of the family firm. *Entrepreneurship: Theory and Practice*, 29, 555–576.

Chua, J.H., Chrisman, J.J., & Sharma, P. (1999). Defining the family business by behavior. *Entrepreneurship: Theory and Practice, 23*, 19–40.

Clarkson, M.E. (1995). A stakeholder framework for analyzing and evaluating corporate social performance. *Academy of Management Review*, 20(1), 92–117.

Corner, P.D. & Ho, M. (2010). How opportunities develop in social entrepreneurship. *Entrepreneurship: Theory and Practice*, 34(4), 635–659.

Crane, A. & Matten, D. (2007). Editor's introduction. Corporate social responsibility as a field of scholarship. In Crane, A., Matten, D. (Eds.), *Corporate Social Responsibility, Vol. 1: Theories and Concepts of Corporate Social Responsibility*, Sage Publications, London, xvi–xxx.

Crane, A. & Ruebottom, T. (2011). Stakeholder theory and social identity: rethinking stakeholder identification. *Journal of Business Ethics*, 102, 77–87.

Cukier, W., Trenholm, S., Carl, D., & Gekas, G. (2011). Social entrepreneurship: a content analysis. *Journal of Strategic Innovation and Sustainability*, 7(1), 99–119.

Cyert, R.M. & March, J.G. (1963). *The Behavioral Theory of the Firm*. Prentice-Hall, Englewood Cliffs.

Danes, S.M., Lee, J., Stafford, K., & Heck, R.K.Z. (2008). The effects of ethnicity, families, and culture on entrepreneurial experience: an extension of sustainable family business theory. *Journal of Developmental Entrepreneurship*, 13(3), 229–268.

De Bakker, F., Groenewegen, P., & Den Hond, F. (2005). A bibliometric analysis of 30 years of research and theory on corporate social responsibility and corporate social performance. *Business and Society*, 44(3), 283–317.

De la Crus Deniz, M. & Cabrera Suarez, K. (2005). Corporate social responsibility and family business in Spain. *Journal of Business Ethics*, 56, 27–41.

De Massis, A. & Kotlar, J. (2014). The case study method in family business research: guidelines for qualitative scholarship. *Journal of Family Business Strategy*, 5(1), 15–29.

Dees, J.G. (1998). Enterprising nonprofits. *Harvard Business Review*, 76, 54–69.

Donaldson, T. & Preston, L.E. (1995). The stakeholder theory of the corporation: concepts, evidence, and implications. *Academy of Management Review*, 20(1), 65–91.

Drayton, W. (2002). The citizen sector: becoming as entrepreneurial and competitive as business. *California Management Review*, 44(3), 120–132.

Dunfee, T.W. (2008). Stakeholder theory: managing corporate social responsibility in a multiple actor context. In Crane, A., McWilliams, A., Matten, D., Moon, J., & Siegel, D. (Eds.), *Oxford Handbook of Corporate Social Responsibility*. Oxford University Press, Oxford, 346–362.

Dyer, W.G. & Whetten, D.A. (2006). Family firms and social responsibility: preliminary evidence from the S&P 500. *Entrepreneurship: Theory and Practice*, 30(6), 785–802.

Emerson, J. & Twersky, F. (1996). *New Social Entrepreneurs: The Success, Challenge and Lessons of Non-profit Enterprise Creation*. Roberts Foundation, Homeless Economic Development Fund, San Francisco, CA.

Etzioni, A. (1964). *Modern Organizations*. Prentice-Hall, Englewood Cliffs, NJ.

European Commission (2008). *Overview of Family Business Relevant Issues Contract. Final Report*. No. 30-CE-0164021/00-51, p. 44, available at http://ec.europa.eu/DocsRoom/documents/10389.

Fitzgerald, M.A., Haynes, G.W., Schrank, H.L., & Danes, S.M. (2010). Socially responsible processes of small family business owners: exploratory evidence from the national family business survey. *Journal of Small Business Management*, 48(4), 524–551.

Freeman, R.E. (1984). *Strategic Management: A Stakeholder Perspective*. Pitman/Ballinger, Boston, MA.

Freeman, R.E. & Reed, D.L. (1983). Stockholders and stakeholders: a new perspective in corporate governance. *California Management Review*, 25(3), 88–106.

Freeman, R.E., Velamuri, S.R., & Moriarty, B. (2006). *Company Stakeholder Responsibility: A New Approach to CSR*. Business Roundtable Institute for Corporate Ethics.

Gamerschlag, R., Möller, K., & Verbeeten, F. (2011). Determinants of voluntary CSR disclosure empirical evidence from Germany. *Review of Managerial Science*, 5(2), 233–262.

Gómez-Mejía, L.R., Haynes, K.T., Núñez-Nickel, M., Jacobson, K.J.L., & Moyano-Fuentes, J. (2007). Socioemotional wealth and business risks in family-controlled firms: evidence from Spanish olive oil mills. *Administrative Science Quarterly*, 52(1), 106–137.

Gomez-Mejia, L.R., Makri, M., & Kintana, M.L. (2010). Diversification decisions in family-controlled firms. *Journal of Management Studies*, 47(2), 223–252.

Hemingway, C.A. (2005). Personal values as a catalyst for corporate social entrepreneurship. *Journal of Business Ethics*, 60(3), 233–249.

Hockerts, K. (2006). Entrepreneurial opportunity in social purpose business ventures. In Mair, J., Robinson, J. & Hockerts, K. (Eds.), *Social Entrepreneurship*, Palgrave Macmillan, New York, 142–154.

Hoopes, D.G. & Miller, D. (2006). Owner preferences, competitive heterogeneity and strategic capabilities. *Family Business Review*, 19(2), 89–101.

Istat (2008). *Rapporto annuale: La Situazione nel paese nel 2008*, pp. 92–93, available at www3.istat.it/dati/catalogo/20090526_00/rapporto_annuale_2008.pdf.

Janjuha-Jivraj, S. & Spence, L.J. (2009). The nature of reciprocity in family firm succession. *International Small Business Journal*, 27, 702–719.

Kilkenny, M., Nalbarte, L., & Besser, T. (1999). Reciprocate "community support" and small town small business success. *Entrepreneurship and Regional Development*, 11, 231–246.

Klein, S.B., Astrachan, J.H., & Smyrnios, K.X. (2005). The F-PEC scale of family influence: construction, validation, and further implication for theory. *Entrepreneurship: Theory and Practice*, 29(3), 321–340.

Kotlar, J. & De Massis, A. (2013). Goal setting in family firms: goal diversity, social interactions, and collective commitment to family-centered goals. *Entrepreneurship: Theory and Practice*, 37(6), 1263–1288.

La Porta, R., Lopez-de-Silanes, F., Shleifer, A., & Vishny, R. (1999). Corporate ownership around the world. *Journal of Finance*, 54(2), 471–517.

Lepoutre, J. & Heene, A. (2006). Investigating the impact of firm size on small business social responsibility: a critical review. *Journal of Business Ethics*, 67, 257–273.

Letts, C.W., Brown, L.D., & Alvord, S.H. (2003). *Social Entrepreneurship: Leadership that Facilitates Societal Transformation – An Exploratory Study*. Center for Public Leadership Working Paper Series, available at http://hdl.handle.net/1721.1/55803.

Lobel, S.A. & St. Clair, L. (1992). Effects of family responsibilities, gender, and career identity salience. *Academy of Management Journal*, 35(5), 1057–1069.

Long, R.G. & Mathews, K.M. (2011). Ethics in the family firm: cohesion through reciprocity and exchange. *Business Ethics Quarterly*, 21, 287–308.

McGivern, C. (1978). The dynamics of management succession: a model of chief executive succession in the small family firm. *Management Decision*, 16(1), 32–42.

Mair, J. & Noboa, E. (2006). *Social Entrepreneurship and Social Transformation: An Exploratory Study*. University of Navarra-IESE Business School Working Paper Series, 955.

Maitland, A. (2002). Affordable responsibility: small suppliers. *Financial Times*, May 16, 14.

Mehra, A., Kilduff, M., & Brass, D.J. (1998). At the margins: a distinctiveness approach to the social identity and social networks of underrepresented groups. *Academy of Management Journal*, 41(4), 441–452.

Melin, L. & Nordqvist, M. (2007). The reflexive dynamics of institutionalization: the case of family business. *Strategic Organization*, 5, 321–333.

Miles, M.B. & Huberman, M. (1984). *Qualitative Data Analysis: A Sourcebook of New Methods*. London, Sage.

Mitchell, J.R., Hart, T.A., Valcea, S., & Townsend, D.M. (2009). Becoming the boss: discretion and postsuccession success in family firms. *Entrepreneurship: Theory and Practice*, 33(6), 1201–1218.

Mitchell, R.K., Agle, B.R., Chriman, J.J. & Spence, L.J. (2011). Toward a theory of stakeholder salience in family firms. *Business Ethics Quarterly*, 21(2), 235–255.

Mitchell, R.K., Agle, B.R., & Wood, D.J. (1997). Toward a theory of stakeholder identification and salience: defining the principle of who and what really counts. *Academy of Management Review*, 22, 853–886.

Mitchell, R.K., Morse, E.A., & Sharma, P. (2003). The transacting cognitions of nonfamily employees in the family businesses setting. *Journal of Business Venturing*, 18(4), 533–551.

Morck, R. & Yeung, B. (2004). Family control and the rent-seeking society. *Entrepreneurship: Theory and Practice*, 28(4), 391–409.

Niehm, L.S., Swinney, J., & Miller, N.J. (2008). Community social responsibility and its consequences for family business performance. *Journal of Small Business Management*, 46(3), 331–350.

Oakes, P. (1987). The salience of social categories. In Turner, J.C., Hogg, M., Oakes, P.J., Reicher, S.D., & Wetherell, M.S. (Eds.), *Rediscovering the Social Group: A Self-Categorization Theory*. Basil Blackwell, Oxford, 117–141.

Pearson, A.W., Carr, J.C., & Shaw, J.C. (2008). Toward a theory of familiness: a social capital perspective. *Entrepreneurship: Theory and Practice*, 32(6), 949–969.

Pfeffer, J. (1981). *Power in Organizations*. Pitman, Marshfield, MA.

Post, J., Preston, L., & Sachs, S. (2002). *Redefining the Corporation: Stakeholder Management and Organizational Wealth*, Stanford University Press, Stanford, CA.

Poza, E.J., Alfred, T., & Maheshwari, A. (1997). Stakeholder perceptions of culture and management practices in family and family firms: a preliminary report. *Family Business Review*, 10(2), 135–155.

Robinson, J. (2006). Navigating social and institutional barriers to markets: how social entrepreneurs identify and evaluate opportunities. In Mair, J., Robinson, J., & Hockerts, K. (Eds.), *Social Entrepreneurship*, Palgrave Macmillan, New York, 95–120.

Roper, J. & Cheney, G. (2005). The meanings of social entrepreneurship today. *Corporate Governance*, 5(3), 95–104.

Rosenblatt, P.C., De Mik, L., Anderson, R.M., & Johnson, P.A. (1985). *The Family in Business: Understanding and Dealing with the Challenges Entrepreneurial Families Face*. San Fransico, CA: Jossey-Bass Publishers.

Russo, A. & Perrini, F. (2010). Investigating stakeholder theory and social capital: CSR in large firms and SMEs. *Journal of Business Ethics*, 91, 207–221.

Sharma, P., Chrisman, J.J., & Chua, J.H. (1997). Strategic management of the family business: past research and future challenges. *Family Business Review*, 10, 1–35.

Sharma, P. & Irving, P.G. (2005). Four bases of family business successor commitment: antecedents and consequences. *Entrepreneurship: Theory and Practice*, 29(1), 13–33.

Short, J.C., Moss, T.W., & Lumpkin, G.T. (2009). Research in social entrepreneurship: past contributions and future opportunities. *Strategic Entrepreneurship Journal*, 3(2), 161–194.

Sirmon, D.G. & Hitt, M.A. (2003). Managing resources: linking unique resources, management, and wealth creation in family firms. *Entrepreneurship: Theory and Practice*, 27, 339–358.

Stafford, K., Duncan, K.A., Danes, S.M., & Winter, M. (1999). A research model of sustainable family businesses. *Family Business Review*, 12(3), 197–208.

Stavrou, E., Kassinis, G., & Filotheou, A. (2007). Downsizing and stakeholder orientation among the Fortune 500: does family ownership matter? *Journal of Business Ethics*, 72(2), 149–162.

Stryker, S. & Burke, P.J. (2000). The past, present, and future of an identity theory. *Social Psychology Quarterly*, 63(4), 284–297.

Suchman, M.C. (1995). Managing legitimacy: strategic and institutional approaches. *Academy of Management Review*, 20(3), 571–610.

Tajfel, H. & Turner, J.C. (1985). The social identity theory of intergroup behavior. In Worchel, S., & Austin, W.G. (Eds.), *Psychology of Intergroup Relations*, 2nd ed., Nelson-Hall, Chicago, IL, 7–24.

Thompson, J.L. (2002). The world of the social entrepreneur. *International Journal of Public Sector Management*, 15(5), 412–431.

Thompson, J.K. & Smith, H.L. (1991). Social responsibility and small business: suggestions for research. *Journal of Small Business Management*, 29, 30–44.

Thompson, J.K., Alvy, G., & Lees, A. (2000). Social entrepreneurship: a new look at the people and the potential. *Management Decision*, 38(5), 328–338.

Tsang, E.W.K. (2002). Learning from overseas venturing experience: the case of Chinese family businesses. *Journal of Business Venturing*, 17, 21–40.

Uhlaner, L., Van Goor-Balk, A., & Masurel, E. (2004). Family business and corporate social responsibility in a sample of Dutch firms. *Journal of Small Business and Enterprise Development*, 11, 186–194.

Villalonga, B. & Amit, R. (2006). How do family ownership, control and management affect firm value? *Journal of Financial Economics*, 80(2), 385–417.

Waddock, S. & Smith, N. (2000). Corporate responsibility audits: doing well by doing good. *Sloan Management Review*, 41, 75–83.

Ward, J. (2004). *Perpetuating the Family Business.* Family Enterprise Publishers, Marietta, GA.

Weber, M. (1947). *The Theory of Social and Economic Organization.* Free Press, New York.

Yin, R.K. (2003). *Case Study Research: Design and Methods.* Sage Publications, Thousand Oaks, CA.

Zadek, S. (2000). *Doing Good and Doing Well: Making the Business Case for Corporate Citizenship.* Research Report 1282-00-RR, The Conference Board, New York.

Zellweger, T.M. & Nason, R.S. (2008). A stakeholder perspective on family firm performance. *Family Business Review*, 21, 203–216.

4 Internal corporate venturing in multi-generational family enterprises

A conceptual model

Justin B. Craig, Robert Garrett, and Clay Dibrell

Internal corporate ventures (ICVs) are entrepreneurial initiatives that originate within a corporate structure and are intended from their inception as new businesses for the corporation (Sharma & Chrisman, 1999). By leveraging their resources in new business domains, firms practicing internal corporate venturing can benefit from increased growth (Thornhill & Amit, 2001; Tidd & Taurins, 1999), enhanced financial performance (Miles & Covin, 2002; Simon, Houghton, & Gurney, 1999), diversification (Sorrentino & Williams, 1995; Tidd & Taurins, 1999), the building of new competences (McGrath, 1995; Tidd & Taurins, 1999), and improved innovativeness (Day, 1994; Simon et al., 1999). Nonetheless, the history of ICV practice indicates that firms often fail in their attempts to create viable new businesses (Campbell, Birkinshaw, Morrison, & van Basten Batenburg, 2003).

The reasons why firms fail in their ICV efforts are often linked to venture mismanagement (Ginsberg & Hay, 1994). For example, ICVs are frequently targeted at business domains that are not well understood or where the parent company has no expertise (Zahra, Nielsen, & Bogner, 1999), unrealistic strategic objectives are established according to planning processes appropriate only for more established businesses (McGrath & MacMillan, 1995), parent companies exert too much or too little control over their ICVs (Thornhill & Amit, 2001), and parent companies often fail to protect ventures from outside interference as the ventures struggle in their nascence (Burgelman & Sayles, 1988). In spite of the challenges of internal corporate venturing, Burgelman and Valikangas (2005:29) articulated that it is "a strategic leadership imperative for top management to learn to better manage the ICV cycle" because of the strategic advantages they portend. Additionally, Guth and Ginsberg (1990:13) stated "research that contributes to increasing the frequency and success of corporate entrepreneurship will, in our view, be highly valued in the academic and practitioner communities."

Family enterprises represent a unique context to investigate internal corporate venturing strategies (Hoy, 2006). Family enterprises have been defined as firms that consist

> of the vision held for the firm by a family or a small group of families and the intention of the dominant condition to shape and pursue this vision, potentially across generations of the same family or group of families.
>
> (Chua, Chrisman, & Sharma, 1999:35)

This definition focuses on the attitudes of the various family members toward the future ownership and management of the business, attempting to transcend quantitative measures characteristic of other definitions. In line with Kelly, Athanassiou, and Crittenden (2000), the definition is grounded in the notion of family ownership and control along with the desire to pass on the entity to future generations. Family enterprises that desire to grow – whether for the objective of generating more profit or for offering greater employment opportunities for family members – face the same challenges as those confronted by large diversified firms attempting to venture (Brockhaus, 1994). However, there is comparatively little research that has attempted to examine venturing from the perspective of family enterprises (Kellermanns & Eddleston, 2006; Marchisio et al., 2010; Salvato, 2004; Ying-Juan, Shao-Chi, & Li-Yu, 2010; Zahra, Hayton, & Salvato, 2004). Drawing on stewardship theory, we contribute to this conversation by positioning stewardship climate as a positive enhancer of family enterprises' willingness to successfully engage in ICVs in order to sustain the multi-generational family. Specifically, we propose that stewardship climate will positively moderate the parent–venture relatedness to venture autonomy relationship.

With a particular contextual emphasis on established multi-generational family enterprises in this chapter, we suggest that the dynamics of family produce a very unique context to investigate what types of ICVs are pursued, how they are pursued, and how governance mechanisms need to be in place to ensure that there is a contribution to the transgenerational sustainability of the business. By firmly couching our arguments related to internal venturing in stewardship theory, this research provides a more complete picture of an unexplored aspect of entrepreneurship in the family firm.

This chapter is structured as follows. First, our theoretical setting is introduced through an overview of stewardship theory. When deciding how to frame our article, we elected to commit to stewardship theory, though acknowledge recent discussions related to the appropriateness of stewardship and agency perspectives being valid and having application under different circumstances (see, for example, Le Breton Miller, Miller, & Lester, 2011; Le Breton Miller, & Miller, 2009). We proceed to frame our arguments in extant family enterprise and internal corporate venturing literature. Propositions are distilled and included in our conceptual model before a discussion of the implications of our research closes the chapter.

Stewardship theory and stewardship climate

Stewardship theory allows "researchers to examine situations in which executives as stewards are motivated to act in the best interests of their principals" (Davis, Shoorman & Donaldson, 1997:24). Through this lens, stewards are positioned to gain higher long-term utility from pro-social and collectivistic behaviors than they would from economic, individualistic, and self-serving behaviors. From this perspective, for example, when faced with a decision to pursue an option for personal gain over one that would contribute to the larger stakeholder group, stewards will pursue the latter. In this situation, not only are the interests of principals protected, and advanced, but also the steward's own utility is maximized. As an extension, the personal beliefs of those charged with the leadership of the organization will not only guide their individual actions, but also steer them to design their organizations in such a way as to elicit stewardship behaviors from their employees. We consider this as a stewardship climate.

Though not explicitly framed as such, Davis et al.'s (1997) seminal steward-ship theory shares much with the organizational climate discourse. Specifically, both distinguish between individual (psychological) and situational (firm) factors. The combination of these factors refers to employees' shared perceptions or experiences of the policies, practices, and procedures of their workplace, along with an understanding of the behaviors that are expected and that are rewarded (Denison, 1996; Schneider, 1990). In our context, stewards can shape organizational climate by instituting policies and procedures that encourage the involvement and empowerment of the entire workforce, through open and trans-parent communication, by setting and abiding by standards of accountability, and through their own example. Stewardship climate, then, and the associated accountable behavior, is likely to occur when core values converge and an internal sense of responsibility is created (Dicke & Ott, 2002). Such a context promotes standard behavior, common work, and organization-related attitudes on the part of followers. A climate synonymous with the dimensions of steward-ship also engenders a shared belief among organizational members that leaders govern the organization by using appropriate forms of power and reward mecha-nisms. Finally, this would also suggest that promoting the well-being of the col-lective (i.e., work unit, team, organization) has priority over individual accomplishment and individual's economic interests. According to this reason-ing, then, the organizational climate in a stewardship theoretical frame reflects individual (psychological) factors that serve to shape and define contextual ele-ments within the organization.

Intrinsic motivation (Maslow, 1970; McClelland, 1975; McGregor, 1966), iden-tification with the organization (Porter, Steers, Mowday, & Boulian, 1974; Salan-cik & Meindl, 1984; Staw, McKechnie, & Puffer, 1983), and use of power are the three individual factors put forward by Davis et al. (1997) to define stewardship. Involvement orientation (Lawler, 1992), collectivist culture, and power distance (Hofstede, 1991), are the three key situational assumptions that define steward-ship, from a situational vantage.

There is growing interest in stewardship theory-grounded applications to be used as, for example, a complementary governance perspective to agency theory (e.g., Hernandez, 2012; Miller, Le Breton Miller & Scholnick, 2008; Wasserman, 2006). The interests of principals and agents can be aligned when the "stewards" of an organization are motivated through a combination of positive organiza-tional actions and cooperative interests which reside outside of personal wealth maximization (Wasserman, 2006). With a dual focus on the individual psycholog-ical behaviors of the steward and the situational contexts of the firm, stewardship theory describes the benefits organizations receive when their executives are motivated to act in the best interests of their principals (Davis et al., 1997; Miller & Le Breton Miller, 2006). It is therefore appropriate to develop our model, which explores entrepreneurial behavior, using this theoretical lens.

Family enterprise and entrepreneurial behavior

While this chapter touts the context of the family enterprise as a potentially fruit-ful domain for research on internal corporate venturing, it remains important to acknowledge here an ongoing debate in the literature regarding whether family enterprises behave entrepreneurially and demonstrate risk-taking behaviors or if they avoid taking risks and pursuing new entrepreneurial initiatives due to a preference to maintain the status quo (Johannisson, 2002; Nordqvist & Melin, 2010). Diversification presents a tremendous challenge for family firms, as the family's desire to maintain control of the organization collides with the wish to diversify the family's concentrated business risk (Jones, Makri, & Gomez-Mejia, 2008). Some of the literature on family enterprises shows that family firms have a tendency to become conservative, unable, or unwilling to take entrepreneurial risks (Dertouzos, Lester, & Solow, 1989). This rigidity may be, in part, due to the founders of family firms trying to build a lasting legacy and are wary of the perceived high risk of failure in entrepreneurial ventures (Morris, 1998), with the accompanying risk of destroying family wealth (Sharma, Chrisman, & Chua, 1997). Additionally, agency theory has been applied to the family firm to argue that family control inhibits firm growth because they are less likely to fund innovative ventures due to inefficient risk bearing, more likely to engage in managerial entrenchment, and more likely to seek wealth preservation through political lobbying (Carney, 2005; Fama & Jensen, 1983). Jones et al. (2008) state that family firms are reluctant to diversify, since this might lead to a loss of family control and the family may lack expertise in different markets. Since family CEOs typically stay on the job three to five times longer than nonfamily enterprise CEOs (Lansberg, 1999; Ward, 2004), they may take a farsighted long-term perspective that makes them hesitant to engage in risky expedients such as hazardous acquisitions or unrelated entrepreneurial initiatives, which could potentially produce great wealth for the family (Amihud & Lev, 1999; Le Breton-Miller & Miller, 2009b; Morck, Shleifer, & Vishny, 1990).

On the other hand, some researchers argue that the long-term nature of family firms' ownership allows them to create and invest in highly productive dedicated resources required for innovation and risk-taking (Dyer, 1996; Zahra et al., 2004). Furthermore, family firms uniquely possess kinship ties that are believed to have a positive effect on entrepreneurial opportunity recognition (Barney, Clark, & Alvarez, 2003). These opportunities are then pursued because owner-managers understand that the family firm's survival depends on leveraging new markets, creating new businesses, and increasing the distinctiveness of the firm's products (Hall, 2003; Lumpkin, Brigham, & Moss, 2010; Ward, 1987; Zahra, 2003; Zahra et al., 2004). Exploiting these opportunities to mitigate risk provides significant benefits to the family firm, since it reduces the volatility of earnings and thereby provides greater financial security to the family while potentially improving the chances of firm survival (Faccio, Lang, & Young, 2001).

While recent literature has attempted to resolve the debate through empirical examination of the antecedents to family enterprise corporate entrepreneurship (e.g., Kellermanns & Eddleston, 2006; Salvato, 2004), scholars and practitioners alike still know relatively little about *how* corporate entrepreneurship is conducted within a family enterprise and what unique attributes of family enterprises differentiate the conduct of entrepreneurial initiatives in this context from that of the large diversified firm.

Internal corporate venturing

Hitt, Nixon, Hoskisson, and Kochhar (1999) suggest that organizational context considerations (e.g., top management team support, organizational politics) have a significant influence on the performance of corporate entrepreneurship initiatives, of which ICVs are one manifestation. Unlike other new businesses, ICVs exist not only within an external competitive context but also within the organizational context of the corporate parent, and so they frequently find themselves interacting with the other parent-corporation subunits and managers (Garvin, 2002). In the case of an ICV, the ability to pursue a creative idea within the context of an existing organization – to mobilize resources in support of its development and to bring it to fruition – is invariably affected by features of the organizational context (Dobrev & Barnett, 2005). However, there is a paucity of research on the unique organizational context of a parent firm and the effect of that context on venturing strategies and subsequent ICV performance.

Prior research on internal corporate venturing has demonstrated the importance of parent–venture relatedness and venture autonomy on subsequent ICV performance. Tanriverdi and Venkatraman (2005) found that knowledge relatedness was positively correlated with performance in multi-business firms. Focusing specifically on the field of corporate venturing, Campbell et al. (2003) find that among the units they studied that were set up to develop significantly new businesses for the parent company (named "new leg" ventures by the authors, indicating little to no relatedness between the parent and the venture), none were successful. Sorrentino and Williams (1995), however, had previously found in their quantitative analysis no significant relationship between relatedness and ICV performance, leading them to postulate that perhaps the relationship between relatedness and performance is contingent on other venture-related considerations.

One such consideration is venture autonomy, or the amount of independence allowed to the venture by the parent company. Simon et al. (1999) argue that ventures pursuing newer, experimental markets require a great deal of freedom. Contrarily, ventures operating in relatively familiar domains for the parent firm may benefit from increased monitoring to avoid costly mistakes. Furthermore, the research of Kuratko et al. (2009) finds a significant positive correlation for the direct effect of venture planning autonomy on ICV performance. While the relationships of these two variables – parent–venture relatedness and venture autonomy – with subsequent ICV performance may be complex, previous research has indicated their importance and proximal effect on performance. Thus, the current conceptual examination's aim of understanding the effects of family enterprise governance considerations on venture relatedness and autonomy is an attempt to fill a knowledge void in the literature regarding these two constructs instrumentally important to ICV performance.

Development of propositions

We consider that the stewardship climate of family enterprises is composed of psychological and situational dimensions and the governance of the family enterprise to include family and business mechanisms. The conceptual development, reflected in Figure 4.1, explores the effects of these aspects of a family enterprise on what kinds of ICVs are pursued in terms of parent–venture relatedness and how those ventures are governed by the parent company.

Recall that stewardship theory has been offered as a complementary and alternative view of organizations where the interests of principals and agents can be aligned. Additionally, organizational climate refers to employees' shared perceptions or experiences of the policies, practices, and procedures of their workplace, along with an understanding of the behaviors that are expected and that

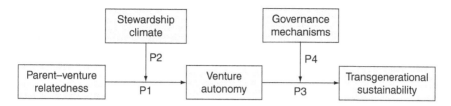

Figure 4.1 Conceptual model.

get rewarded (Denison, 1996; Schneider, 1990). In the context of ICVs, steward-ship theory permits scholars to further explain the possible role this strategy may have on family enterprises. Drawing on stewardship theoretical perspective in family firms (Craig & Dibrell, 2006; Miller & Le Breton-Miller, 2006), family enterprises will embrace ICVs, as it will enable them to extract resources from the organization's resource bundle from existing businesses owned by the family and from the family itself (Kellermans & Eddleston, 2006). Additionally, ICVs allow the steward-manager to more aptly align their goals with those of the family enterprise, as it keeps the steward engaged in the family enterprise instead of being concerned with the extraction of wealth from the family enterprise, which may put the survival of the family enterprise in jeopardy.

Parent–venture relatedness

The concept of relatedness has been explored within multi-business firms using a variety of dimensions of the construct of relatedness, for example: product relat-edness (Rumelt, 1974), manufacturing relatedness (St. John & Harrison, 1999), technological relatedness (Robins & Wiersema, 1995; Silverman, 1999), and mar-keting relatedness (Capron & Hulland, 1999). Relatedness as used in the research domain of internal corporate venturing has to do with the strategic fit between the parent and its ventures and is posited to benefit the venture by increasing venture access to the parent's resources (Sorrentino & Williams, 1995; Thornhill & Amit, 2000). For ICVs, which are typically early stage business experi-ments for the parent corporation (as opposed to mature businesses in a large diversified company), the most important resources possessed by the parent are product development and market knowledge resources because ICVs frequently operate in product-market domains adjacent to those of the firm's established businesses (Birkinshaw, van Basten Batenburg, & Murray, 2002; Hill & Birkin-shaw, 2008; Thornhill & Amit, 2001). Thus, the definition of parent–venture relatedness used in this manuscript focuses on product and market similarity between the parent and venture. More specifically, parent–venture relatedness is the extent to which the venture is similar to other businesses of the corporation in terms of the products/services offered and the markets targeted by the venture. This definition is consistent with Kurakto et al.'s (2009) conceptualiza-tion of market/product similarity between ICVs and their parents.

Sound venturing strategy dictates that parent companies typically venture in domains that are adjacent to the firm's core businesses (Birkinshaw et al., 2002). While this strategy attempts to minimize down-side risk, it also potentially limits up-side gain and growth. While family firms are initially based in innovative ideas, they often lose their entrepreneurial momentum after a few years (Salvato, 2004) and the CEOs begin to make more conservative decisions in order to minimize the risk of failure in their ventures and the risk of losing family wealth (Morris, 1998; Sharma et al., 1997). This loss of entrepreneurial momentum can translate into low amounts of corporate entrepreneurship (Kellermanns & Eddleston, 2006), and thus high degrees of relatedness in the ventures are pursued. Given this logic, we consider that those involved will leverage that which connects them and pursue ventures more similar than dissimilar.

Venture autonomy

Venture autonomy has been found to be among the strongest predictors of ICV success (Kurtako et al., 2009). Because ICVs seek to develop a whole new business specifically tailored to enter new and emerging markets (Block & MacMillan, 1993), they often require their own unique organizational structure, culture, and systems (Simon et al., 1999). Previous research has identified three primary types of autonomy important to ICVs (Kuratko et al., 2009). First, venture planning autonomy is the extent to which the venture's management is responsible for establishing goals, timetables, event milestones, and strategy for the venture; as opposed to corporate parent management having those responsibilities. Second, venture operations autonomy is the extent to which the venture's management team is responsible for the design of the venture's internal operations. Last, venture operations independence is based on the organizational positioning of the venture and is the extent to which the venture's operations are linked to those of the other businesses of the corporation.

Venture-level self-determination with regard to strategic management decisions like goal selection, strategy formulation, and performance criterion establishment may be positive for venture performance because venture-level management often has the best knowledge of how to strategically lead their business, while parent-level management may have less complete, accurate, or timely information (Kuratko et al., 2009). However, this logic applies best only when the knowledge of parent-level managers is not applicable to the ICV, such as when the ICV is sufficiently unrelated to the parent's businesses. When the venture is related to the parent's businesses, it is reasonable that the parent will possess adequate and appropriate knowledge and expertise to gainfully participate in the venture's strategic decisions. Thus, related ICVs will manifest lower levels of venture autonomy, while unrelated ICVs will manifest higher levels of venture autonomy.

P1: *Parent–venture relatedness is negatively associated with venture autonomy.*

As subsequent generations get involved in the business, typically, the need for growth and diversification becomes more necessary in order to support a larger number of people in the family enterprise (Poza, 1988). Indeed, family enterprises owned and managed by multiple generations must rejuvenate and reinvent themselves, if they are to maintain the same level of financial performance of the previous generation (Jaffe & Lane, 2004). Usually, subsequent generations in family enterprises tend to push for new ways of doing things (Kepner, 1991; Moores & Barrett, 2002), including creating new products and services and reaching new markets (Sharma et al., 1997).

An emphasis on intrinsic rewards such as opportunities for growth, achievement, affiliation, and self-actualization are examples of individual climate aspects of stewardship behaviors. The extrinsic versus intrinsic focus is a major distinction between stewardship and agency theories, with the steward's motives coordinated with the objectives of the principals, or, in the context of this chapter, the family. Following this reasoning, a steward has a greater proclivity to identify with the firm, and, therefore, the steward sees the firm as an extension of themselves. In contrast, the agent, in the accepted principal–agent framework, often does not share this same affinity toward their organization. More specifically, stewards benefit when they demonstrate commitment to making a significant contribution to their firm's mission, financial performance, and survivability, more so than their personal economic self-interest (Davis et al., 1997). We argue that when incumbents and offspring are mutually accountable, their goals and motivations are aligned, and, applying this logic to the ICV-venture autonomy relationship, propose the following.

P2: *The negative association between parent–venture relatedness and venture autonomy is positively moderated by stewardship climate.*

Transgenerational sustainability

Increasingly scholars are debating the role of non-financial metrics in the overall, current, and future performance of organizations. This conversation is not new as, for example, Lumpkin and Dess (1996) in their seminal work recommended that factors such as overall satisfaction and non-financial goals of the owners warranted greater consideration when evaluating performance. These authors singled out privately held firms as being particularly dictated by non-financial influences. Not surprisingly, due to the general tacit nature, unlike financial performance, monitoring the influence of non-financial indicators is more challenging to ascertain, and generalize due to the wide variance across organizations.

In the family enterprise context, up until relatively recently, non-economic motivations were assumed but not empirically, or even conceptually, understood (Gomez-Mejia et al., 2011). Due to the influence of the family and the long-term orientation of the business, family firms are considered to pay closer attention to matters related to non-financiality, manifested in such activities as maintaining family harmony (Eddleston & Kellermans, 2007), leveraging family brand (Craig, Dibrell, & Davis, 2008), and considering mentoring and learning activities to better position family members for opportunities to contribute to the family and the business (Moores & Barrett, 2002). When considered under the banner of altruism, without commercial foundations, these goals can incur costs, which adversely affect firm performance (Schultze, Lubatkin & Dino, 2002).

An appropriate way to address the issue of the preferred way to consider economic versus non-economic motivations is to categorize family businesses as either family first or business first (Basco & Perez Rodriguez, 2009). Managing the "business versus family" paradox is problematic as the two systems are independent and interdependent (Ward, 2004). For example, greater profitability (financial indicators) often transcends into enhancing the family reputation (non-financial indicators) and in meeting important family goals (non-financial indicator). Positive changes in the financial position of the business are manifest in positive changes in the financial position of the family. Thus, any assessment of the sustainable performance of the family enterprise must include an assessment of the expectations of the family. Generating that symbiotic relationship by alignment of interest between the firm and the family encourages the exploration of innovative ideas that stimulate growth and improves performance (Zahra, 2005).

> **P3:** *Venture autonomy is positively related to transgenerational sustainability.*

Governance mechanisms

The growing body of family enterprise literature has begun to explain how family enterprises may extend the underlying assumptions of traditional governance and management theories (Basco & Perez Rodriguez, 2011; Carney, 2005; Corbetta & Salvato, 2004; Mustakallio, Autio, & Zahra, 2002; Sharma & Nordqvist, 2013). There is potential for power ambiguity within the family system when multiple generations are involved, particularly during leadership transition. When it is not clear or obvious with whom authority and responsibility for strategic direction rests, governance mechanisms need to be in place to ensure clarity for stakeholders. Specific issues that can occur that make it unclear where authority rests include when family members are elevated to management positions for which they are not qualified; family members who, though not in operating or ownership positions, attempt to influence crucial business decisions; and philosophical divergence between generations over the strategic direction of the business (Kets de Vries, 1996; Schultze et al., 2002).

To address complex governance issues in family enterprise, research supports the introduction of monitoring initiatives including the use of outside experts. There is evidence in the broader management literature that engaging outside-the-firm experts is beneficial (Robinson, 1982; Sartain, 1998). Expert outsiders have been viewed as an externalized form of management and knowledge intermediaries (Fincham & Clark, 2002). As such, firms engaging expert outsiders are "a buyer of a knowledge service" (Werr & Styhre, 2003:47). Expert outsiders create value in organizations by generating objective information (Basco & Perez Rodriguez, 2011). Because their relationships are independent from day-to-day operational issues, outsiders are able to view organizational problems objectively and remain separate from internal power struggles, hidden agendas, and the like (Kubr, 1996; Kyrö, 1995). Expert outsiders "offer the potential advantage of being experienced observers and analysts without the related disadvantage of being locked into defending previously established positions or ways of thinking" (Gattiker & Larwood, 1985:120). However, leadership's position is not undermined as the expert outsider is viewed as an advisor, leaving the leadership with the responsibility for critical examination of recommendations and the use of advice (Kubr, 1996).

Many studies have supported the notion that strategic planning processes and the resulting strategies of family enterprises significantly differ conceptually from the processes and strategies of nonfamily firms (see for example, Gudmunson et al., 1999; Harris, Martinez & Ward, 1994; Ward, 1987). Strategic planning is critical for family enterprises as a way of reducing agency influences, for providing a framework for reconciling family and business issues and for promoting open and shared decision making (Ward, 1987). The empirical research examining the strategies pursued by or the strategic orientations of, family-owned and managed firms is limited and has provided conflicting results (Gudmonson et al., 1999). Family enterprise CEOs have been found to rate strategic planning less significant in successor preparation than nonfamily enterprise CEOs. Habbershon and Williams (1999) introduced three process interventions (i.e., strategic planning, family governance, and business governance) as being important to sustaining advantage through familiness. Recently, scholars (for example, Basco, 2013; Basco & Perez Rodriguez, 2009, 2011) have begun to more finely examine the contribution of family governance to business success. Governance forums such as the family meeting, family council, shareholder's assembly, board of directors, and top management teams are increasingly being introduced to ensure independence of thought and accountability in the business and communication and education for the family (Craig & Moores, 2015). Paralleling this is an increased interest by scholars leading to a better understanding of the role and characteristics of governance structures (e.g., see Gersick & Feliu, 2014; Goel, Jussila, & Ikäheimonen, 2014; Hoy & Sharma, 2010). In the context of this research, we suggest that such family and business governance mechanisms are a moderator in the development of family enterprise sustainability.

P4: *The positive relationship between venture autonomy and transgenerational sustainability is positively moderated by family and business governance mechanisms.*

Conclusion

The conceptual development presented in this manuscript provides new insight into factors that determine which ventures are pursued within a business and how they are pursued. By focusing on distinguishing features of the unique context of the family enterprise, the propositions explore how the relatedness of ICVs undertaken by the family firm may change as new generations begin to participate in the ownership and control of the firm.

The concepts presented have potentially important implications for scholars and practitioners. First, the types of ICVs pursued by firms may have as much to do with the personalities and personal wishes involved as they do with any formal planning or opportunity recognition process. Second, family firms wishing to venture into either related or unrelated business domains may encourage or discourage next generation participation in the family firm accordingly. Third, care perhaps should be taken when allowing a CEO to get involved in the management of an unrelated venture; these ventures may do better if they are left as autonomous units rather than being subject to parent-level management.

Our modeled arguments suggest that ICV-related decisions in multigenerational family enterprises are influenced by the development of an organizational climate with hallmarks identifiable with stewardship theoretical concepts. In such organizational climates (1) individuals from incumbent and next generations are aligned with a common purpose, and (2) this alignment contributes to the organization functioning in alignment with the owning family's current and future expectations. Additionally, transgenerational sustainability will be enhanced when complemented by monitoring systems afforded by the transparency and accountability afforded by business and family governance.

Future research should consider testing similar conceptual models to the one presented via empirical analysis. While difficult to access, such data may provide a wealth of information on the corporate venturing process, especially as it is present within family firms. Given their contribution to all economies, understanding the nature of entrepreneurial behavior in family firms is a timely topic that merits further consideration.

References

Ahimud, Y., & Lev, B. (1999). Does corporate ownership structure affect corporate diversification? *Strategic Management Journal*, 20, 1063–1069.

Barney, J. B., Clark, D., & Alvarez, S. (2003). Where does entrepreneurship come from? Network models of opportunity recognition and resource acquisition with application to the family firm. Paper presented at the Theories of the Family Enterprise Conference, University of Pennsylvania, Philadelphia (December).

Basco, R. (2013). The family's effect on family firm performance: A model testing the demographic and essence approaches. *Journal of Family Business Strategy*, 4(1), 42–66.

Basco, R., & Perez Rodriguez, M. J. (2009). Studying the family enterprise holistically. *Family Business Review*, 22(1), 82–95.

Basco, R., & Perez Rodriguez, M. J. (2011). Ideal types of family business management: Horizontal fit between family and business decisions and the relationship with family business performance. *Journal of Family Business Strategy*, 2(3), 151–165.

Birkinshaw, J., van Basten Batenburg, R., & Murray, G. (2002). Venturing to succeed. *Business Strategy Review*, 13(3), 10–17.

Block, Z., & MacMillan, I. (1993). *Corporate venturing: Creating new businesses within the firm.* Boston, MA: Harvard Business School Press.

Breton-Miller, I. L., & Miller, D. (2006). Why do some family businesses out-compete? Governance, long-term orientations, and sustainable capability, *Entrepreneurship: Theory and Practice*, 30(6), 731–746.

Brockhaus, R. H. (1994). Entrepreneurship and family business research: Comparisons, critique and lessons. *Entrepreneurship: Theory and Practice*, 19(1), 25–38.

Burgelman, R. A., & Sayles, L. R. (1988). *Inside corporate innovation: Strategy, structure and managerial skill.* New York: The Free Press.

Burgelman, R., & Valikangas, L. (2005). Managing internal corporate venturing cycles. *Sloan Management Review*, 46(4), 26–34.

Campbell, A., Birkinshaw, J., Morrison, A., & van Basten Batenburg, R. (2003). The future of corporate venturing. *Sloan Management Review*, 45(1), 30–37.

Capron, L., & Hulland, J. (1999). Redeployment of brands, sales forces, and general marketing management expertise following horizontal acquisitions: A resource-based view. *Journal of Marketing*, 63(2), 41–54.

Carney, M. (2005). Corporate governance and competitive advantage in family-controlled firms. *Entrepreneurship: Theory and Practice*, 29(3), 249–265.

Chrisman, J. J., Chua, J. H., & Sharma, P. (2003). *Current trends and future directions in family business management studies: Toward a theory of the family firm* (Cole Whiteman Paper Series).

Chua, J. H., Chrisman, J. J., & Sharma, P. (1999). Defining the family business by behaviour. *Entrepreneurship: Theory and Practice*, 23(4), 19–39.

Clark, T., & Fincham, R. (Eds.) (2002). Critical consulting: New perspectives on the management advice industry. Blackwell, Oxford.

Corbetta, G. and Salvato, C. A. (2004). The board of directors in family firms: One size fits all? *Family Business Review*, 17(2), 119–134.

Craig, J. B., & Dibrell, C. (2006). The natural environment, innovation, and firm performance: A comparative study. *Family Business Review*, 19(4), 275–288.

Craig, J. B., & Moores, K. (2015). Appreciating the nature of the family business difference: The A-GES Framework. In Scott L. Newbert (Ed.), *Small business in a global economy: Creating and managing successful organizations*, 2 vols. Santa Barbara, CA: Praeger.

Craig, J. B., Dibrell, C., & Davis, P. S. (2008). Leveraging family-based brand identity to enhance firm competitiveness and performance. *Journal of Small Business Management*, 46(3), 351–371.

Davis, J. H., Schoorman, F. D., & Donaldson, L. (1997). Toward a stewardship theory of management. *Academy of Management Review*, 22(1), 20–47.

Day, D. (1994). Raising radicals: Different processes for championing innovative corporate ventures. *Organization Science*, 5(2), 148–172.

Denison, D. (1996). What is the difference between organizational culture and organizational climate? A native's point of view on a decade of paradigm wars. *Academy of Management Review*, 21: 610–654.

Dertouzos, M. L., Lester, R. K., & Solow, R. M. (1989). *Made in America: Regaining the productive edge*. Cambridge, MA: MIT Press.

Dicke, L. A., & Ott, J. S. (2002). A test: Can stewardship theory serve as a second conceptual foundation for accountability methods in contracted human services? *International Journal of Public Administration*, 25(4), 463–487.

Dobrev, S. D., & Barnett, W. P. (2005). Organizational roles and transition to entrepreneurship. *Academy of Management Journal*, 48(3), 433–449.

Dyer, J. H. (1996). Does governance matter? Keiretsu alliances and asset specificity as sources of Japanese competitive advantage. *Organization Science*, 7, 649–666.

Eddleston, K. A., & Kellermanns, F. W. (2007). Destructive and productive family relationships: A stewardship theory perspective. *Journal of Business Venturing*, 22(4), 545–565.

Faccio, M., Lang, L. H., & Young, L. (2001). Dividends and expropriation. *American Economic Review*, 91(1), 54–80.

Fama, E. F., & Jensen, M. C. (1983). Separation of ownership and control. *Journal of Law and Economics*, 26, 301–326.

Fincham, R., & Clark. T. (2002). Introduction: The emergence of critical perspectives on consulting. In T. Clark & R. Fincham (Eds.), *Critical consulting: New perspectives on the management advice industry*, Oxford: Blackwell.

Garvin, D. A. (2002). A note on corporate venturing and new business creation. *Harvard Business Review*, 1–20.

Gattiker, U. E., & Larwood, L. (1985). Why do clients employ management consultants? *Consultation*, 4(1), 119–129.

Gersick, K. E., & Feliu, N. (2014). Governing the family enterprise: Practices, performance, and research. In L. Melin, M. Nordqvist, & P. Sharma (Eds.), *SAGE handbook of family business*. Thousand Oaks, CA: Sage.

Ginsberg, A., & Hay, M. (1994). Confronting the challenges of corporate entrepreneurship: Guidelines for venture managers. *European Management Journal*, 12(4), 382–389.

Goel, S., Jussila, I., & Ikäheimonen, T. (2014). Governance in family firms: A review and research agenda. In L. Melin, M. Nordqvist, & P. Sharma (Eds.), *SAGE handbook of family business*. Thousand Oaks, CA: Sage.

Gomez-Mejia, L. R., Cruz, C. Berrone, P., & De Castro, J. (2011). The bind that ties: Socioemotional wealth preservation in family firms. *Academy of Management Annals*, 5(1), 653–707.

Gudmundson, D., Hartman, E., Burk Tower, C., & Kaye, K. (1999). Strategic orientation: Differences between family and nonfamily firms. *Family Business Review*, 12(1), 27–39.

Guth, W. D., & Ginsberg, A. (1990). Guest editors' introduction: Corporate entrepreneurship. *Strategic Management Journal*, 11, 5–15.

Habbershon, T. G., & Williams, M. L. (1999). A resource-based framework for assessing the strategic advantages of family firms. *Family Business Review*, X11(1), 1–26.

Hall, A. (2003). Strategizing in the context of genuine relations. PhD Dissertation, Jonkoping International Business School, Sweden.

Harris, D., Martinez, J. I., & Ward, J. L. (1994). Is strategy different for the family-owned business? *Family Business Review*, 7(2), 159–174.

Hernandez, M. (2012). Toward an understanding of the psychology of stewardship. *Academy of Management Review*, 37(2), 172–193.

Hill, S. A., & Birkinshaw, J. (2008). Strategy-organization configurations in corporate venturing units: Impact on performance and survival. *Journal of Business Venturing*, 23(4), 423–444.

Hitt, M. A., Nixon, R. D., Hoskisson, R. E., & Kochhar, R. (1999). Corporate entrepreneurship and cross-functional fertilization: Activation process and disintegration of a new product design team. *Entrepreneurship: Theory and Practice*, 23(3), 145–167.

Hofstede, G. (1991). *Cultures and organizations: Software of the mind.* London: McGraw-Hill.

Hoy, F. (2006). The complicating factor of life cycles in corporate venturing. *Entrepreneurship: Theory and Practice*, 30, 831–836.

Hoy, F., & Sharma, P. (2010). *Entrepreneurial family firms.* Prentice Hall Entrepreneurship Series edited by M. Morris and D. Ireland. Upper Saddle River, NJ: Pearson Prentice Hall.

Jaffe, L. R., & Lane, S. H. (2004). Sustaining a family dynasty: Keys issues facing complex multigenerational business- and investment-owning families. *Family Business Review*, 69, 85–98.

Johannisson, B. (2002). Energizing entrepreneurship: Ideological tensions in the medium-sized family business. In D. Fletcher (Ed.), *Understanding the small family business.* London: Routledge.

Jones, C. D., Makri, M., & Gomez-Mejia, L. R. (2008). Affiliate directors and perceived risk bearing in publicly traded, family-controlled firms: The case of diversification. *Entrepreneurship: Theory and Practice*, 32(6), 1007–1026.

Kellermanns, F. W., & Eddleston, K. A. (2006). Corporate entrepreneurship in family firms: A family perspective. *Entrepreneurship: Theory and Practice*, 30(6), 809–830.

Kelly, L. M., Athanassiou, N., & Crittenden, W. F. (2000). Founder centrality and strategic behavior in the family-owned firm. *Entrepreneurship: Theory and Practice*, 25(2), 27–42.

Kepner, E. (1991). The family and the firm: A coevolutionary perspective. *Family Business Review*, 4, 445–461.

Kets De Vries, M. (1996). *Family business: Human dilemmas in the family firm.* London: Thomson Business Press.

Kubr, M. (1996). *Management consulting: A guide to the profession.* Geneva: International Labor Organization.

Kuratko, D. F., Covin, J. G., & Garrett, R. P. (2009). Corporate venturing: insights from actual performance. *Business Horizons*, 52(5), 459–467.

Kyrö, P. (1995). The management consulting industry described by using the concept of "profession." Doctoral thesis, Faculty of Education, University of Helsinki.

Lansberg, I. (1999). *Succeeding generations: Realizing the dream of families in business.* Boston, MA: Harvard Business School Press.

Lawler, E. E. (1992). *The ultimate advantage.* San Francisco, CA: Jossey-Bass.

Le Breton-Miller, I., & Miller, D. (2009a). Goal tolerance, outside investors, and family firm governance. *Entrepreneurship: Theory and Practice*, 33(6), 1193–1198.

Le Breton-Miller, I. & Miller, D. (2009b). Agency vs. stewardship in public family firms: A social embeddedness reconciliation. *Entrepreneurship: Theory and Practice*, 33(6), 1169–1191.

Le Breton-Miller, I., Miller, D., & Lester, R. H. (2011). Stewardship or agency: A social embeddedness reconciliation of conduct and performance in public family businesses. *Organization Science*, 22(3), 704–721.

Lumpkin, G. T., & Dess, G. G. (1996). Clarifying the entrepreneurial orientation construct and linking it to performance. *Academy of Management Review*, 21(1), 135–172.

Lumpkin G. T., Brigham K. H., & Moss, T. W. (2010). Long-term orientation: Implications for the entrepreneurial orientation and performance of family businesses. *Entrepreneurship and Regional Development*, 22(3–4), 241–264.

McClelland, D. C. (1975). *Power: The inner experience.* New York: Irvington.

McGrath, R. G. (1995). Advantage from adversity: Learning from disappointment in internal corporate ventures. *Journal of Business Venturing*, 10(2), 121–142.

McGrath, R. G., & MacMillan, I. C. (1995). Discovery-driven planning. *Harvard Business Review*, 73(4), 4–12.

McGregor, D. (1966). *Leadership and motivation.* Cambridge, MA: MIT Press.

Marchisio, G., Mazzola, P., Sciascia, S., Miles, M., & Astrachan, J. (2010). Corporate venturing in family business: The effects on the family and its members. *Entrepreneurship and Regional Development*, 22(3), 349–361.

Maslow, A. H. (1970) *Motivation and personality.* New York: Harper & Row.

Miles, M. P., & Covin, J. G. (2002). Exploring the practice of corporate venturing: Some common forms and their organizational implications. *Entrepreneurship: Theory and Practice*, 26(3), 21–40.

Miller, D., & Le Breton-Miller, I. (2006). Family governance and firm performance: Agency, stewardship, and capabilities. *Family Business Review*, 14(1), 73–87.

Miller, D., Le Breton-Miller, I., & Scholnick, B. (2008). Stewardship vs. stagnation: An empirical comparison of small family and non-family businesses. *Journal of Management Studies*, 45(1), 51–78.

Moores K., & Barrett, M. (2002) *Learning family business: Paradoxes and pathways.* Aldershot, UK: Ashgate. Reprinted (2010) Gold Coast: Bond University Press.

Morck, R., Shleifer, A., & Vishny, R. (1990). Do managerial objectives drive bad acquisitions? *Journal of Finance*, 45, 31–48.

Morris, M. H. (1998). *Entrepreneurial intensity.* Westport, CT: Quorum Books.

Muskatallio, M., Autio, E., & Zahra, S. (2002). Relational and contractual governance in family firms: Effects on strategic decision making. *Family Business Review*, 15(3), 205–222.

Nordqvist, M., & Melin, L. (2010). Entrepreneurial families and family firms. *Entrepreneurship and Regional Development*, 22(3–4), 211–239.

Porter, L. W., Steers, R. M., Mowday, R. T., & Boulian, P. V. (1974). Organizational commitment, job satisfaction, and turnover among psychiatric technicians. *Journal of Applied Psychology*, 5, 803–609.

Poza, E. J. (1988). Managerial practices that support interpreneurship and continued growth. *Family Business Review*, 1(4), 339–360.

Robins, J. A., & Wiersema, M. F. (1995). A resource-based approach to the multibusiness firm: Empirical analysis of portfolio interrelationships and corporate financial performance. *Strategic Management Journal*, 16(4), 277–299.

Robinson, R. B. Jr. (1982). The importance of "outsiders" in small firm strategic planning. *Academy of Management Journal*, 25, 80–93.

Rumelt, R. P. (1974). *Strategy, structure, and economic performance.* Cambridge, MA: Harvard University Press.

Salancik, G. R., & Meindl, J. R. (1984). Corporate attributions as strategic illusions of management control. *Administrative Science Quarterly*, 29, 238–254.

Salvato, C. (2004). Predictors of entrepreneurship in family firms. *Journal of Private Equity*, 7(3), 68–76.

Sartain, L. (1998). Why and how Southwest Airlines uses consultants. *Journal of Management Consulting*, 10(2), 12–17.

Schneider, B. (Ed.). (1990). *Organizational climate and culture* (1st ed.). San Francisco, CA: Jossey-Bass.

Schultze, W. S., Lubatkin, M., & Dino, R. N. (2002). Altruism, agency, and the competitiveness of family firms. *Managerial and Decision Economics*, 23, 247–259.

Schwass, J. (2005). *Wise growth strategies in leading family businesses.* New York: Palgrave.

Sharma, P., & Chrisman, J. J. (1999). Toward a reconciliation of the definitional issues in the field of corporate entrepreneurship. *Entrepreneurship: Theory and Practice*, 23(3), 11–27.

Sharma, P., & Nordqvist, M. (2013). Understanding the reasons for and consequences of varied family involvement in business: A configuration approach. In K. Smyrnios, P. Poutziouris, & S. Goel (Eds.), *Handbook of research on family businesses*, 2nd ed. Cheltenham, UK and Brookfield: Edward Elgar Publishing.

Sharma, P., Chrisman, J. J., & Chua, J. H. (1997). Strategic management of the family business: Past research and future challenges. *Family Business Review*, 10(1), 1–35.

Silverman, B. S. (1999). Technological resources and the direction of corporate diversification: Toward an integration of the resource-based view and transaction cost economics. *Management Science*, 45(8), 1109–1124.

Simon, M., Houghton, S. M., & Gurney, J. (1999). Succeeding at internal corporate venturing: Roles needed to balance autonomy and control. *Journal of Applied Management Studies*, 8(2), 145–158.

Sorrentino, M., & Williams, M. L. (1995). Relatedness and corporate venturing: Does it really matter? *Journal of Business Venturing*, 10, 59–73.

Staw, B. M., McKechnie, P. I., & Puffer, S. M. (1983). The justification of organizational performance. *Administrative Science Quarterly*, 28, 582–600.

St. John, C. H. S., & Harrison, J. S. (1999). Manufacturing-based relatedness, synergy, and coordination. *Strategic Management Journal*, 20(2), 129–145.

Tanriverdi, H., & Venkatraman, N. (2005). Knowledge relatedness and the performance of multibusiness firms. *Strategic Management Journal*, 26, 97–119.

Thornhill, S., & Amit, R. (2001). A dynamic perspective of internal fit in corporate venturing. *Journal of Business Venturing*, 16(1), 25–50.

Tidd, J., & Taurins, S. (1999). Learn or leverage? Strategic diversification and organizational learning through corporate venturing. *Creativity and Innovation Management*, 8(2), 122–129.

Ward, J. L. (1987). *Keeping the family business healthy: How to plan for continuous growth, profitability, and family leadership*. San Francisco, CA: Jossey Bass.

Ward, J. L. (2004). *Perpetuating the family business: 50 lessons learned from long-lasting, successful families in business*. New York: Palgrave Macmillan.

Wasserman, N. (2006). Stewards, agents, and the founder discount: Executive compensation in new ventures. *Academy of Management Journal*, 49(5), 960–976.

Werr, A., & Styhre, A. (2003). Management consultants – Friend or foe? Understanding the ambiguous client–consultant relationship. *International Studies of Management and Organization*, 32(4), 43–66.

Ying-Jiuan Wong, Shao-Chi Chang, & Li-Yu Chen. (2010). Does a family-controlled firm perform better in corporate venturing?. *Corporate Governance: An International Review*, 18(3), 175–184.

Zahra, S. A. (2003). International expansion of U.S. manufacturing family businesses: The effect of ownership and involvement. *Journal of Business Venturing*, 18(4), 495–512.

Zahra, S. A. (2005). Entrepreneurial risk taking in family firms. *Family Business Review*, 18(1), 23–40.

Zahra, S. A., Nielsen, A. P., & Bogner, W. C. (1999). Corporate entrepreneurship, knowledge, and competence development. *Entrepreneurship: Theory and Practice*, 23(3), 169–189.

Zahra, S. A., Hayton, J. C., & Salvato, C. (2004). Entrepreneurship in family vs. non-family firms: A resource-based analysis of the effect of organizational culture. *Entrepreneurship: Theory and Practice*, 28(4), 363–381.

Conclusion to Part I

Giovanna Dossena

The chapters of this first part each explore specific questions and contribute to building knowledge at the junction of the fields of family business and entrepreneurship. As the literature review in the Introduction to this book shows, this overlap is the focus of much of the previous research, but, until now, many aspects of entrepreneurship have been neglected in the family business literature.

Collectively, the contributions of these works expand the scope of research at the junction of these fields because the variety of views of entrepreneurial that can be called upon has been expanded. The contribution of Sarasvathy and colleagues demonstrates how the effectual framework can be useful to understand entrepreneurial behaviors of family businesses. Organizational entrepreneurship is developed in two ways: the seven circumstances and the model of Internal Corporate Venturing – each address very useful canvases for further research. Finally, although it is well known that family businesses are more socially responsible than other forms of organizations, the contribution of Campopiano and colleagues offers a view of Social Family Entrepreneurship upon which others can build.

In addition to the specific suggestions for further research detailed in each chapter, here we note the main common points which deserve more attention:

- the perceived need of family control in the family businesses or its spin offs and its consequences;
- the types and dynamics of the relationships between family and nonfamily shareholders, as well as the evolution over time of the distribution of shares among these two categories;
- the inclination and interest of external stakeholders for inclusion in family business's social responsible initiatives;
- the interactions between different generations involved in the family business, more specifically related to the degree of management autonomy and the capacity to generate new initiatives in the business context, more or less apt to support debate between generations;
- the influence of life cycle stages on the firm's capacity to react to environmental contingencies and to favor entrepreneurial initiatives.

In the same manner that multiplying the prisms of entrepreneurship expand our understanding of Family Entrepreneurship, varying the ways in which "family" is conceptualized influences in a significant manner how we understand family business. In Part II, research at the intersection of family and family business, we integrate as a fundamental assumption that more and more families are of variable geometry, triggered by changes in society, but also tracing back to different cultural and social models. What is consistent, though, is that the interpersonal relationships which are built within a social group represent one of the strongest influences to individual entrepreneurial capacity and inclination.

Part II

Intersection family business and family

5 The process of identity construction in the family business

A discursive psychology perspective

Richard T. Harrison and Claire M. Leitch

We argue for a revised conception of identity in Family Entrepreneurship research, drawing on the individual level identity theory dominant in entrepreneurship, that transcends the distinction between (sociology based) role identity theory and (social psychology based) social identity theory. Accordingly, we highlight the need to incorporate multi-level research into identity studies, in this case through the enmeshment of individual, family and organisational identities. In organisation and management scholarship, research into individual identity and organisational identity has developed as largely separate domains. Entrepreneurial identity research has tended to collapse these levels of analysis into one by assuming that the individual entrepreneur and the organization they create are one and the same. A focus on Family Entrepreneurship requires a formal analysis of identity and identity formation at the level of the individual, the family and the organisation, and of the interactive dynamics among them. In developing a framework for future research on identity and identity formation in the family business that is sensitive to the interplay of self, family and business, we build on recent discussions of the construct of familiness which has been identified as the 'unique, inseparable, and synergistic resource and capabilities arising from family involvement and interactions'. In addressing the implications of familiness for our understanding of identity, engaging with different discourses can help highlight the taken-for-granted assumptions in identity research and, thus, open up new avenues of research, stimulate new questions and help generate new insights for Family Entrepreneurship. Specifically, we develop a framework for Family Entrepreneurship identity research that draws on insights from the field of discursive psychology to examine identity positioning in the family business. As a theory of human action, discursive psychology sits within a social constructionist school of thought on identity. This views identity as something we do, not something we have and emphasises the need to study it as an inter-subjective, relational, back-and-forth social interaction, notably through the discursive devices used as linguistic building blocks in the construction of identity positions.

In summary, therefore, we make three arguments in this chapter as the basis for a new approach to the study of identity in Family Entrepreneurship. First, ontologically we reconceptualise identity not as an entity or essence which we 'are' but as identity-as-process which we 'do', created, presented and re-presented through talk-in-action in situational and social interactions. Second, epistemologically we move beyond identity and identity categories as variables used to explain or account for variations to replace this with a focus on how, when and to what effect identity categories are invoked in particular interactions. Third, methodologically we outline a discursive psychology perspective as the basis for further research, which embodies both our ontological and methodological positions in a broadly social constructionist tradition and gives due place to the primacy of talk-in-interaction as the basis for analysis by engaged reflexive researchers.

Introduction

This chapter proposes an approach to the study of the process of emergence of identity in Family Entrepreneurship, drawing on recent developments in organization studies. As Langley and Tsoukas (2010: 14) have recently argued, 'some of the most intriguing ideas in Process Organization Studies are emerging from research that takes categories and concepts that are usually considered as stable, and questions their underlying stability'. Their specific example is 'identity', a concept that has been problematised in recent work (Gioia and Patvardhan, 2012). Indeed, they point out that the term 'identity work' has been adopted to reflect the way in which individuals discursively and interactively relate to construct their identities.

From a Family Entrepreneurship viewpoint this stimulates a reconsideration of identity and identity construction, which has only comparatively recently become the focus of significant attention in entrepreneurship more generally (Fauchart and Gruber, 2011; Navis and Glynn, 2011). With limited exceptions (Zellweger, Eddleston and Kellermanns, 2010), and despite a long tradition of research on family identity (Cigoli and Scabini, 2006) in sociology and psychology, this attention has not extended to the study of the family business. Much of the research on identity in entrepreneurship has been empirical, employing a number of concepts (among them, role identity theory, social identity theory, structural identity theory, narrative and discourse analysis) to explore its role and impact, addressing the questions 'what is entrepreneurial identity?' and 'how do we measure entrepreneurial identity?' From a process entrepreneurial studies perspective we argue that the focus of research should shift to ask questions of 'how is entrepreneurial identity formed?' and 'how do we develop, change and transform entrepreneurial identity?' Given the expansion of research into family business as a distinctive organisational form (Pérez Rodriguez and Basco, 2011) we suggest that the Family Entrepreneurship domain is a particularly fruitful one for theory development and empirical application. Specifically, Family Entrepreneurship offers a context for the study of certain kinds of organisational phenomena (Steier, 2003) that can contribute to the development of management and entrepreneurial theory more generally as well as to a theory of the family firm per se (Chrisman, Kellermanns, Chan and Liano, 2010; Zahra, Hayton and Salvato, 2004).

Following Powell and Baker (2013) we argue for a revised conception of identity in Family Entrepreneurship research, drawing on the individual level identity theory dominant in entrepreneurship, that transcends the distinction between (sociology based) role identity theory and (social psychology based) social identity theory. Accordingly, we highlight the need to incorporate multi-level research (Rousseau 1985; Hitt, Beamish, Jackson and Mathieu, 2007) into identity studies, in this case through the enmeshment of individual, family and organisational identities. In organisation and management scholarship, research into individual identity and organisational identity has developed as largely separate domains. Entrepreneurial identity research has tended to collapse these levels of analysis into one by assuming that the individual entrepreneur and the organisation they create are one and the same. A focus on Family Entrepreneurship requires a formal analysis of identity and identity formation at the level of the individual, the family and the organisation, and of the interactive dynamics among them. In so doing we build on recent discussions of the construct of familiness which has been identified as the 'unique, inseparable, and synergistic resource and capabilities arising from family involvement and interactions' (Zellweger *et al.*, 2010: 54).

In addressing the implications of familiness for our understanding of identity, engaging with different discourses can help highlight the taken-for-granted assumptions in identity research and, thus, open up new avenues of research, stimulate new questions and help generate new insights for Family Entrepreneurship. Specifically, we develop a framework for Family Entrepreneurship identity research that draws on insights from the field of discursive psychology to examine identity positioning in the family business. As a theory of human action, discursive psychology sits within a social constructionist school of thought on identity. This views identity as something we do, not something we have (Shotter, 2010) and emphasises the need to study it as an inter-subjective, relational, back-and-forth social interaction (Mueller and Whittle, 2012), notably through the discursive devices used as linguistic building blocks in the construction of identity positions.

The dynamics of family and business

The family and the business

Despite the volume of research being undertaken, family business studies are still characterised by a stereotypical approach in which limited attention is paid to the familial domain (Stewart and Hitt, 2011), where 'family is treated as a "black box"' (Cread, 2000: 346). In other words, kinship has been employed as means to dichotomise samples into family and nonfamily firms. The use of 'family' as a variable is, however, a coarse-grained differentiator that is predicated on an assumption of homogeneity. This is reflected in an approach to research that views the family and the firm as discrete domains (Figure 5.1) in which the primary interest is on the influence of the family on the firm and, to a lesser extent, on the implications of the firm for the family. This traditional approach has not adequately addressed the complexities of the relationships, dynamics and interconnectedness between the family and the business: 'the managerial and family processes by which family firms can achieve their optimal mix requires fine-grained research to identify and understand them' (Stewart and Hitt, 2011: 76).

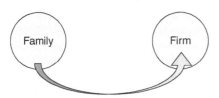

Figure 5.1 Family–firm interaction: the traditional view.

In other words, 'in a family firm, the family and business do not exist as distinct entities, but, instead are enmeshed with one another creating a complex, interactive web of relationships encompassing both the family and the firm' (Pearson, Carr and Shaw, 2008: 955) (Figure 5.2). From this perspective, family and business are not discrete; neither are they coterminous as there are elements of the business that are separate from the family and vice versa, and 'the creation of a family business does not guarantee the development of a family point of view' (Sorenson, Goodpaster, Hedberg and Yu, 2009: 250). It is, of course, a matter of empirical test to determine the extent of both the overlap between family and business and the degree of symmetry in terms of the proportion of the 'family' and the 'business' enmeshed in the relationship. What is of interest, and the challenge for Family Entrepreneurship research, is to understand the extent and content of the overlap.

Family orientation and familiness

Among the approaches adopted to deal with this enmeshment is the concept of family orientation to capture the otherwise problematic essence and distinctiveness of a family firm (Lumpkin, Martin and Vaughn, 2008). Family orientation refers to the values, intention and involvement of family in which an individual's orientation to the family and not the business differentiates family businesses from non-family businesses. Lumpkin *et al.* (2008: 130) suggest that in understanding how the family relates to the business we need to understand how individual members relate to the family, given that for most individuals the family is a primary source of identity and belonging, impacted by loyalty, security, safety, protection, legacy, trust and interdependency. This requires us to address the 'competing self-interests of individuals who occupy constituent positions somewhere in the ownership, family and business subsystems' (Dunn, 1999: 42) (Figure 5.3). This raises an important question over the choice of an appropriate level of analysis for Family Entrepreneurship research. Conventionally, research has taken the firm implicitly or explicitly as the unit of analysis, but it is increasingly clear that a comprehensive analysis of the phenomenon requires multi-level research (Rousseau, 1985; Hitt *et al.*, 2007) in which due attention is given to the individual, the family and the business and to the diverse pattern of interactions among these.

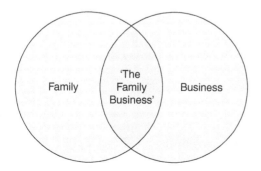

Figure 5.2 Dualist representation of the 'family business'.

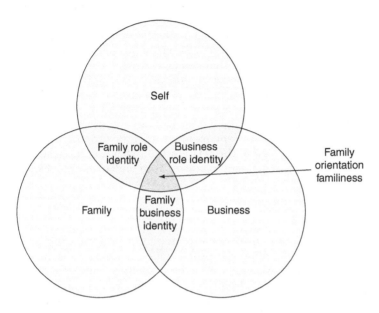

Figure 5.3 Unified systems view of identity in Family Entrepreneurship.

If Figure 5.2 represents the dualist approach to maintaining strong boundaries between the domains of family and business, in order to avoid spillovers between the two, Figure 5.3 illustrates a unified systems approach, in which family business is considered to be a meta-system of family, business and individual members (Knapp, Smith, Kreiner, Sundaramurthy and Barton, 2013). In seeking to understand this meta-system there is a growing stream of research on the construct of familiness as a representation of the uniqueness of the family firm as an organisational form. Originally grounded in the Resource-Based View (RBV) of the firm, Habbershorn and Williams (1999: 11) define it as 'the unique bundle of resources a particular firm has because of the systems interaction between the family, its individual members and the business'. Subsequently, they shifted focus from a purely RBV perspective to incorporate systems thinking in which familiness was defined as 'the idiosyncratic firm level bundle of resources and capabilities resulting from the systems interactions' (Habbershorn, Williams and MacMillian, 2003: 451).

Central to the familiness construct is the idea of a family business social system, where the focus is on how systemic interactions of the family unit (history, traditions and life cycle), business entity (strategy and structures to generate wealth) and individual family members (interests, skills, life stage of family owners/managers) are linked to performance outcomes. As such, there is an emphasis on enterprising families, transgenerational wealth creation and an attempt to explain differences between family and non-family firms and variations in behaviours (how does the family contribute to firm success?). For Chrisman, Chua and Zahra (2003: 468) familiness is understood as 'the resources and capabilities related to family involvement and interactions'. It is becoming clear that while family management of firms does not lead to clear performance improvements the role of owner-family members as internal monitors is the missing link in the ownership control and performance debate of family firms (Audretsch, Hülsbeck and Lehman, 2013).

The construct of familiness is in its infancy but has already been applied in a range of theoretical contexts in addition to its RBV and systems origins (Table 5.1). It is believed to be unique to the family business domain (Pearson *et al.*, 2008) and although typically taking the firm as the unit of analysis, is capable of being applied broadly at different levels. However, current expositions of familiness do not include a temporal element, notably an account of the extent to which it transfers intergenerationally, nor do they address the dynamics of the formation and representation of familiness. For Family Entrepreneurship, where the unit of analysis extends beyond just the business, the absence of a temporal and intergenerational dimension to familiness provides a fruitful area for further research. Given that the idea of familiness is obscure (Zellweger *et al.*, 2010) and that elements or components of it as a multi-dimensional construct have not yet been identified (Pearson *et al.*, 2008)

> what is needed is a complementary extension to the components of involvement and essence approaches that distinguishes when the family is a substantive part of the firm, versus merely a symbolic or supportive element that is not integrated into firm behaviour or the organisation's culture.
>
> (Zellweger *et al.*, 2010: 56)

Identity and Family Entrepreneurship

Given this emphasis in recent research on the interaction between and the dynamics of overlapping family and business systems, organisational identity as a key differentiator of and basis for competitive advantage for family firms has been identified as a valuable perspective (Zellweger *et al.*, 2010). As 'family identity is unique it is therefore impossible to completely copy it' (Sundaramurthy and Kreiner, 2008: 416). In other words, identity differentiates one organisation from another in the eyes of organisational members and other stakeholders (Scott and Lane, 2000). As originally articulated by Albert and Whetton (1985) organisational identity theory focuses on the central, distinctive and enduring features of an organisation to address the 'who are we as an organization?' question. In this, identity is viewed as a dynamic set of processes by which organisational identity is continually and socially constructed through the ongoing interchange between internal and external understanding of the organisation held by all organisational stakeholders (Hatch and Schultz, 2002). Organisational identity is therefore both a process of sense giving and sense making (Zellweger *et al.*, 2010), a cognitive framework for the interpretation and meaning of the work practices of organisational members (Nag, Corley and Gioia, 2007). This is the way by which they develop a shared understanding of the inner processes of the organisation and how this affects the behaviour of these individuals and the strategy of the organisation (Ravasi and Schultz, 2006).

When applied to the family firm, the development of organisational identity takes places through the overlapping of family and business systems and is reflected in the degree of involvement and influence which the family exercises (Zellweger *et al.*, 2010). It is, therefore, tied to family members' sense of

Table 5.1 Examples of familiness research

Research study	Theoretical viewpoints	Research conclusions
Chrisman, Chua and Zahara (2003)	Systems theory	The resources and capabilities related to family involvement and interactions
Craig and Moores (2005)	Evolutionary theory	Familiness described as a 'core essence' of family firms and integrate the concept into strategic balanced scorecard approach
Ensley and Pearson (2005)	Top management team and social capital theory	Group dynamics of family firms are defined by interactions of the top management team; familiness is positively related to group dynamics
Habbershorn and Williams (1999)	Resource-based view of the firm (RBV)	The unique bundle of resources a particular firm has because of the systems interaction between the family, its individual members and the business
Habbershorn, Williams and MacMillan (2003)	Systems theory	The idiosyncratic firm level bundle of resources and capabilities resulting from the systems interactions
Hayton (2006)	RBV of the firm and systems theory	Familiness is related to successful or unsuccessful HR practices for family versus nonfamily firms
Lester and Canella (2006)	Social capital theory	Interorganisational familiness as reflected in the broad linkages that create and support family firms
Pearson, Carr and Shaw (2008)	Social capital theory	Examines the development of familiness from a social capital theory and offers a theory of familiness by identifying unique behavioural and social resources and antecedents and outcomes
Ram and Holiday (1993)	Family sociology	Familiness represents the social relationships of the family, reflected in the flexibility and constraints created within the workplace
Tokarczk, Hansen, Green and Down (2007)	RBV of the firm	Qualitative study which links familiness as a competitive advantage through improved market orientation
Zellweger, Eddleston and Kellermans (2010)	Organisational identity theory	Organisational identity dimension of familiness reflects how family defines and views the firms which can facilitate performance advantages

Source: adapted from Pearson *et al.* (2008: 951).

self-worth and self-esteem; their perception that the firm is an extension of themselves; the building of common ground; the concept of the family extending beyond the family, leading to stewardship behaviours; the impact on brand and reputation; and the creation and allocation of internal and external resources. Given that there is variability in the degree to which family firms may choose to integrate family into organisational identity, there is a longstanding debate in family business research on how to manage the domains of family and business (Knapp *et al.*, 2013). On the one hand, the dual domains perspective sees a relatively static, macro-level boundary between the family and the business. On the other hand, the unified systems approach adopts a more dynamic and micro-level perspective on the relationship as a continuous and circular process. However, neither perspective illuminates how individuals manage boundaries, prompting Knapp *et al.* (2013) to examine how individuals use identity work tactics to create and manage their individual and organisational identities.

This identification of organisational identity theory as the basis for a new research direction in Family Entrepreneurship raises two sets of issues: the relationship between individual and organisational identity; and, the enduring versus dynamic perspective on identity. First, as Powell and Baker (2013) have argued, identity research in entrepreneurship has tended to conflate individual and organisational identity by implicitly or explicitly viewing the business as an extension of the entrepreneur. It has also adopted either a sociology based, role identity theory or a psychology based, social identity theory perspective. They suggest that progress can only be made by transcending and uniting these and by differentiating between the levels of analysis represented by the entrepreneur and the business. For Shepherd and Haynie (2009), who draw on the literature on social identity, this conflation between organisational and individual identity is an issue in family business research. They contend, therefore, that there is a need to go beyond the separate notions of family identity and business identity which are subsumed in a meta-identity, 'a structure we define as family-business meta-identity ... [which] represents the structure through which conflict at the intersection of family and business is resolved' (p. 1246).

Second, this emphasis on organisational identity capturing the most central, distinctive and enduring features of the business (Zellweger *et al.*, 2010; Whetton and Mackey, 2002) and on family-business meta-identity as a structure that accounts for aspects of performance and behaviour (Shepherd and Haynie, 2009) is at odds with more recent considerations of identity as dynamic, in flux and relational (Knapp *et al.*, 2013). Less entity than process, it is conversations and relationships that form and shape identity in an 'on-going dialogue as organizational members and leaders construct identity in the face of changing demands, situations and mindsets' (Knapp *et al.*, 2013: 4). Given that process organisational theorists have been urging researchers to place more emphasis on the process of organising rather than examining an organisation as an entity (Langley, 1999; Van de Ven and Poole, 1995), to see as it were, organisation as an emergent property of change rather than change as a property of organisation (Tsoukas and Chia, 2002), 'might we gain richer insights by studying identity as a process and flow rather than a thing?' (Gioia, Patvardhan, Hamilton and Corley, 2013). This shift from identity as an enduring entity to identity as process and flow does not, however, imply that identity is constructed and reconstructed every day to the extent that it becomes impossible to talk about it in any meaningful sense. Indeed, as Gioia *et al.* (2013) point out if there was not some sense of lasting or stable element to the 'who are we as an individual/organization?' questions it would be difficult to claim we were talking about identity at all. Identity, from a process perspective, does change but often presents the appearance of not changing, not least because 'identity labels can remain stable even as their meanings become malleable' (Gioia *et al.*, 2013: 168; Gioia, Schultz and Corley, 2000). Understanding the nature of this change has implications for understanding how we become who we are as individual, family and business. As such, this has ramifications beyond just the business level of analysis as this provides the macro-setting for individual, group and team endeavours and establishes the micro-foundations of meta-institutions. In the remainder of this chapter we outline one potentially fruitful approach to the process analysis of identity in Family Entrepreneurship and set out some principles for empirical research on this theme.

Discursive psychology and the concept of identity

The discursive psychology 'revolution'

Over the last 25 years discursive psychology has offered an 'alternative way of conceiving the mutual relationship between people, practices and institutions … [which focuses on] the contingent, flexible ways in which people construct, debate, and contest individual and collective meanings in the world' (Augoustinos and Tileagǎ, 2012: 406). As an examination of social psychology's foundational assumptions, and a challenge in particular to the cognitivist basis of these (Edwards, 2012; Potter, 2012a, 2012b), including a challenge to the 'psychologising' of social identity theory (Hepburn and Potter 1993), discursive psychology focuses on the constitutive relationship between the use of language and social action. Specifically, it studies systematically and in detail how 'individuals produce, debate, resist and implicate versions of worlds, minds, persons and social relationships' (Augoustinos and Tileagǎ, 2012: 406; Edwards, 2003). In their review, Wiggins and Potter (2007) argue that discursive psychology investigates people living their lives through interaction in everyday and institutional settings. It starts not with a technical focus on mental processes, neural events or behavioural outcomes that underlie interaction, but with the categories, constructions and orientations that are displayed situationally in a particular interaction. Discursive psychology emphasises discourse as the primary arena for action, understanding and intersubjectivity by people who are inherently social and relational.

One of the key contributions of the original discussions of discursive psychology (Potter and Wetherell, 1987) was to outline an alternative methodological approach to the more common reliance on experiments and questionnaires. This drew on a range of ideas, including conversation analytic research, post-structuralism in the Foucauldian tradition and from Barthes and Derrida, and from the work of Wittgenstein and the linguistic philosophers (Wiggins and Potter, 2007: 74). What linked these diverse strands together was a major focus on discourse, as archetypically represented in talk and texts created in the process of interaction. This focus has three main features. First, discourse is both constructed, comprising linguistic building blocks that are used to present particular versions of the world, and constructive in the sense that versions of the world are a product of the talk itself. In other words, there is a focus on the way in which representations are constructed, construed and oriented to action. Second, discourse is action oriented. In particular, there is a fundamental concern with understanding the ways in which discourse is oriented to actions within particular settings. Third, discourse is situated within specific contexts, both institutionally (for example, a family business, a school classroom, a domestic mealtime) and rhetorically (within a particular argumentative framework). Accordingly, underlying the whole discursive psychology approach is a general caution about attempts to develop explanations of conduct based on the cognition of individuals.

A discursive psychology perspective on identity

As we have seen above the idea that identity is socially constructed in an ongoing process of formation and re-formation is now widely accepted in organisation studies. More recent attempts to develop a discursive psychology perspective on it views identity – 'who we are?' – as something that we do, developed through our interaction with the social world around us rather than as something we have as a predefined, unified, self-contained entity (Mueller and Whittle, 2012). As such, it is a fragmented, fragile and fluid construct that is worked upon in the intersubjective, relational, back-and-forth flow of social interaction (Shotter, 2010).

This poses a challenge for us as researchers in the social sciences in general and in the analysis of identity in Family Entrepreneurship in particular. As Gergen (2010) has argued, if science (in the sense of disciplined, systematic inquiry) presumes a world constituted by stable entities (families, businesses, identities) then it is possible to envision that science being dedicated to the progressive illumination of its subject matter, developing cumulative knowledge that enables increasingly accurate predictions based on general laws. This of course implies and relies on maintaining a clear separation between the observer and that being observed. However, as we move from an entity based perspective to a process orientation, the boundaries of these 'entities' become increasingly indistinct and fluid, and the boundary between subject and object, 'entity' and observer, itself becomes blurred as reflexivity rather than independence characterises the research process. Rather than the scientist standing as an observer of an independent world they can be seen as participants within the broader processes that constitute social and cultural life. This has implications for our choice of research methodology, to which we return below. It also has implications for how we approach the elucidation of the increasingly indeterminate boundariness of the focus of our research, and it is to this that we turn in the context of identity in Family Entrepreneurship.

Discursive psychology, identity and Family Entrepreneurship

In developing a relational, processual and discursive understanding of identity (Gergen, 2010), and in so doing bringing a dynamic, processual lens to bear on an apparently static concept (Mueller and Whittle, 2012), the concept of identity work emphasises that identity is created and represented in the process of social interaction as people engage in the ongoing 'forming, repairing, maintaining, strengthening or revising the [identities] constructions that are productive of a precarious sense of coherence and distinctiveness' (Alvesson and Willmott, 2002: 626). In this context the discursive psychology perspective provides a framework for mapping the micro-linguistic moves through which this identity work is undertaken and, as such, it is a way to practise or implement a process orientation (Mueller and Whittle, 2012). This is consistent with recent arguments that discourse analysis as the exploration of the socially produced ideas and objects that comprise the social world represents an important basis for allowing entrepreneurship researchers to move beyond the taken-for-granted in generating new knowledge (Achtenhagen and Welter, 2007; Ahl, 2007; Salignac, 2012). In other words, discourses play an important role in producing social realities, including entrepreneurial identities, activities and perceptions (Phillips and Hardy, 2002), realities that are maintained through the relationships among discourse, text and action. In this section we set out the six core tenets of discursive psychology perspective on identity and discuss their implications for Family Entrepreneurship research (Table 5.2).

First, as a situated social process the primary focus for identity research in Family Entrepreneurship is not on identity per se, where much of the research to date has been concentrated, but on the identity claims and counter claims that are made in everyday talk and/or interaction. This rejects essentialist approaches to identity in favour of more emergent, processual notions. As such, ascribed or espoused identities can be treated as a membership category (Widdicombe, 1998) that is used in talk and interaction to differentiate oneself from others. The implication of this is that Family Entrepreneurship necessarily involves the study of the multiple identity claims that are developed through the process of collective sensemaking and sensegiving in dynamic interaction with others. The starting point for research, therefore, is the recognition that we are indeed studying multiple identity claims that are situationally and socially constructed in the process of presenting and re-presenting the self in interaction with others. Ontologically, this points to a very different focus for our research as compared to identity as a boundary defined object in Gergen's (2010) terms as represented, for example, in attempts to construct a family-business meta-identity structure (Shepherd and Haynie, 2009).

Second, discursive psychology is predicated on the argument that identity categories, including family, business and the like, should not or cannot be used to explain social behaviour and outcomes, such as business performance, innovation effectiveness or investment fund raising, for example. Rather, the focus is on how identity and identity categories are deployed by members themselves. The emphasis, therefore, is on how individuals use identity categories and identity work to achieve social meaning, action or order instead of trying to establish whether someone actually 'had' a particular identity or what 'having' that identity made them feel or do. For Family Entrepreneurship this represents an epistemological shift from the use of identity categories, such as 'being a family business', as an explanatory variable to an interest in the social meaning, action or order that this usage represents. In other words, identities such as family, business owner (along with others including age, gender, nationality, parental and marital status) are not necessarily and always a defining aspect of one's identity, but instead are dependent on what members themselves deem to be situationally and socially relevant. To be specific, identity constructs such as family orientation or familiness are not central or enduring characteristics and our research agenda, from this perspective, should move to understanding whatever it is that participants do evoke and how they use it (Edwards, 1998).

Third, as identities are negotiated in the process of interaction this is an unfolding and ongoing process. Identity in the complex enmeshment of the individual family firm is not an entity. Identities are negotiated or constructed through talk-in-interaction, and identity positions are employed interactionally to display identity to others within the context of specific interactions. Accordingly, during the interaction process identity claims and positions can be altered or refined, contested or recast. There is, thus, no necessary cognitive correlation between the identity category itself and the self-concept held by the individual. Identity in Family Entrepreneurship is not a fixed essence but something that changes in the process of interaction with others, whether this is in everyday taken-for-granted contexts or within institutional settings, including 'the business' or 'the family'. It is no surprise, therefore, that a number of studies have suggested that a proportion of respondents in businesses meeting the research definition of a 'family business' do not see that as part of their own espoused identity, and that in similar fashion a proportion of respondents in businesses that do not meet the classification of 'family business' do nevertheless see themselves as family businesses (for examples see the review by Zellweger *et al.*, 2010). The issue here is not one of the correctness or otherwise of our definitions and classifications as researchers, nor is it one of the accuracy or otherwise of the identities being represented (where the identification of identity conflict rather relies on the acceptance of a correspondence theory of truth). Instead, the question is one of how and why these identities have been constructed, for what purposes and in the context of what interactions. The answers to these questions require very different methodologies to address them effectively.

Fourth, in this enactment of identity positions the discursive psychology perspective highlights the role of identity in the performance of social actions. In the Family Entrepreneurship context this is seen in the manner in which the multiple identities as individual, family member and organisation member play out. For example, the justification of a business decision in the interests of the family represents the enactment of a family rather than a manager identity and will be associated with the performance of different social actions involving the conduct of the business (Miller and Le Breton-Miller, 2011). To give a simple illustration: a discourse interaction of the form 'as your line manager/CEO I would like you to do…' is rather different from that invoked by the 'as your father (or, in the interests of the family) I would like you to do…', in that the former invokes notions of power, hierarchy and authority in the business while the latter invokes issues of familial responsibility (in which, of course, different conceptions and dynamics of power and hierarchy play out). The meanings and social actions which follow from these two interactions may well be different. They also differ according to the situational context if, for instance, the interaction takes place on Monday afternoon on the business premises or over Sunday lunch at the family residence. Given that identity is a process of construction through interaction, Family Entrepreneurship research will benefit from extending the range of situational domains included in research designs.

Fifth, in contrast to much of the current research in Family Entrepreneurship, which seeks to define or delineate an identity proposition around the notion of the family business, familiness or some meta-theoretical family-business identity, the argument that identity is always in process within and across the individual,

Table 5.2 Discursive psychology, identity and Family Entrepreneurship

Central tenet of DP perspective	Implications for studying identity in/of organisations	Implications for Family Entrepreneurship research
Identity should be studied as part of social situations	Identity is not something that we simply 'bring to' interactions, it is something which we build and refine during social interaction. For example, what type of person we are seen as could change when we are faced with counter-narratives about 'who we are' told during organisational story-telling.	Identity should be studied situationally and socially as identity claims and counter-claims are made in everyday talk. In other words, identity stands as a membership category (Widdicombe, 1998: 52) that is used to differentiate oneself from others. These membership categories may be family, organisation or individual roles and attributes – Family Entrepreneurship necessarily involves the study of the multiple identity claims that are developed through the process of collective sensemaking and sensegiving (Kroezen and Heugens, 2012; Whetten and Mackey, 2002; Ravasi and Schultz, 2006), rather than constructing an assumed unified meta-identity (Shepherd and Haynie, 2009).
Identity categories should not be used to explain behaviour or outcomes – the focus should be on how, when and to what effect identity categories are invoked	Identity is not something that analysts need to know about because it explains something else. For example, knowing whether a speaker is a 'woman' or 'man' or 'manager' or 'employee', is not used to explain why they are behaving in a particular way, in a cause and effect manner. Instead, the focus is on which identities are being made relevant by the participants themselves. For example, if two people orient towards each other as 'managers' or as 'mates' it is likely to make a difference to the interaction and meaning-making.	How do identity categories (such as 'being family') achieve social meaning, action or order, as different identity positions can be adopted in different situations to perform different actions (Mueller and Whittle, 2012: 150).
Identity should be understood as an ongoing, unfolding process	Identity is not a fixed 'essence', rather it changes as we interact with others. For example, we may need to refine or defend our presentation of self if it comes up against challenges or counter-constructions in workplace conversations.	Identity – as family business or in the context of Family Entrepreneurship – is not an entity. Rather, identities are negotiated or constructed through talk-in-interaction where identity positions are employed interactionally to display identity to others within the context of specific interactions (Gergen, 1992; Benwell and Stokoe, 2006; Antaki and Widdicombe, 1998).

Identity-talk acts as a form of social action – it does things	Claims to having a particular identity make a difference because they perform social actions. For example, if someone says 'as your manager I would like you to do this', the identity category 'manager' performs the action of instruction through appealing to higher authority, whereas 'as your friend…' acts as a form of persuasion through appeal to the obligations of friendship.	Enacting identity positions permits the performance of social actions such as justifying business decisions 'in the interests of the family'. In the family business context enactment of a family, rather than, for example, a manager identity, will be associated with the performance of different social actions involving the conduct of the business.
Identity positions or claims can be flexible, varying according to the social and interactional context, including the possibility of contradiction	Identity is not a fixed entity that we bring to situations, but can vary according to different situations. For example, a speaker could emphasise being a woman in one context but emphasise her role as a manager in another encounter. Within the same stretch of interactions contradictory identity positions could be claimed, as participants use different repertoires to present themselves.	Given that identity is always in process, within and across the individual, family and firm levels, inconsistency and contradiction are to be expected. Analysis, therefore, should focus not on the resolution of contradictions but on how these inconsistencies are managed in specific situations and interactions.
Apparently 'factual' descriptions can also perform identity work	Descriptions of the 'world out there' are material for studying identity because they act to present the speaker in particular ways. For example, a speaker who appeals to descriptions of the economic context or changing customer preferences to justify the need for organisational change also presents him/herself as someone who is neutral and rational, without a personal axe to grind or vested interest in the change.	In both the specific context of a research study and in the more general process of interaction, apparently neutral descriptions of events (for example, an account of the business history of the family or a description of a particular course of action) do themselves bring about and articulate particular identity positions for the speaker, those spoken about and those participating in this talk-in-interaction.

Source: adapted from Mueller and Whittle (2012: 152).

family and firm levels, means that inconsistency and contradiction are to be expected. This reinforces the argument that identity is not a fixed essence or entity to be invoked in a cause–effect explanation of particular behaviours and outcomes. It suggests that instead of seeking to resolve multiple identity representations (or conflicts), Family Entrepreneurship research should recognise that identity claims can be flexible, varying according to the social and interactional context. Analytically, the focus should be not on the resolution of contradictions and inconsistencies but on understanding how these are managed and to what effect in specific situations and interactions.

Sixth, much of this discussion of the nature of identity and identity work from a discursive psychology perspective is located within a broader social constructionist approach. However, as Mueller and Whittle (2012: 153) have argued, discursive psychology 'expands the remit of identity research by examining how apparently "neutral" descriptions of events bring about certain identity positions for the speaker and for those spoken about'. This points to the way in which the so-called 'facts of the matter' get incorporated through discourse into the construction of a story about 'what happened'. They go on to argue that such descriptions involve recalling memories, making connections and advancing explanations, but they are also implicated in establishing identities as they influence the dispositions, attitudes, motives, temperament and values of those involved. As research into the multiple identities in Family Entrepreneurship will demonstrate, competing descriptions of events (for example, an account of the history of the business or of the family or the recollection of a particular decision or course of action) can provide the fulcrum for our questioning of the idea of identity itself as a personal possession or stable entity.

Methodological implications and challenges

This focus on identity as process raises a methodological challenge. If identity is not an entity which individuals, families and firms possess then 'how do we study it?' and 'how do we draw boundaries around such a dynamic construction?' For Gioia and Patvardhan (2012) methodological guidelines can be drawn from the expanding body of process research, where the concern is to unravel issues of how relationships and patterns among variables emerge, rather than attempting to answer questions of what the character of these relationships is. For identity research in Family Entrepreneurship this approach

> would translate to engagement with our phenomenon – not so much in terms of identifying what the core, distinctive, and 'enduring' attributes of an individual or organization are, but in pursuing how such an identity is negotiated, constructed, reconstructed, 'sustained' and projected backward and forward.
>
> (2012: 56)

Methodologically this raises three questions which Family Entrepreneurship scholars will need to address. First, how should we approach our subject of study? From a process studies viewpoint a comprehensive investigation of identity should capture both the admittedly partial, snapshot quality of identity and the motion-picture quality that details the processes of patterning and construction that constitute those snapshots. Second, what research strategies should be chosen to study identity as process? Here it appears that researchers are spoilt for choice: process research has been undertaken using grounded theory, analytic induction, ethnography and so on (Gioia and Patvardhan, 2012), and Langley (1999) has argued for the adoption of multiple strategies including grounding strategies (for example, grounded theory), organising strategies (for example, narrative and visual mapping) and replicating strategies (for example, synthetic research studies) that allow for both exploratory and explanatory research. As we will show below, discursive psychology offers some distinctive methodological opportunities that extends those available to Family Entrepreneurship researchers adopting a process perspective. Third, what would a compelling identity-as-process study look like? At root, and irrespective of the particular research strategy chosen, good process studies tell a story. A compelling identity story in Family Entrepreneurship, as in identity research more generally, is likely to comprise the following four elements: an account of temporal sequences, identifying when and in what order process emerge; identification of the focal actors who constructed or performed identity work; presentation of an identifiable narrative voice representing the reflexive input of the observer or interpreter; and signalling other indicators of content and context, including reference to the historical and institutional backdrop in which identity emerges and is played out. This, of course, is potentially a Herculean task, dealing as it does with unfolding events, not discretely measurable entities, involving multiple levels of analysis in research contexts which require obtaining access to organisations and their members for long periods of time.

While for discursive psychology there are no hard and fast rules for discourse research (Wiggins and Potter, 2007), there are some emerging protocols that offer interesting opportunities for Family Entrepreneurship researchers. While early research in the area used open-ended interviews and ethnographic interviews as the principal data collection technique (rather than the more constraining questionnaire and semi-structured interview approaches), these have been criticised on the basis that as commonly used they elide many of the interactional features of the research setting by focusing on extracts from participants' responses, they lose the fine detail of the elements of talk that matter for participants, they import prior social science agendas in question construction and terminology, and they overlook the positioning of the talk of interviewer and interviewee which occurs in complex ways and on sometimes indistinct footing positions (Potter and Hepburn, 2005).

Increasingly, therefore, discursive psychology research has focused on naturalistic materials, that is, audio and visual observational records of what people actually do in the everyday settings where identity is negotiated. This focus has a number of strengths (Wiggins and Potter, 2007: 78–79). First, it avoids the imposition of the researcher's own categories or assumptions on to the data. Second, it situates research into the apparently messy realm of everyday life and in so doing does not divorce respondents' participation from the issues of agency and accountability that arise in the process of social interaction. Third, by studying respondents' practices in situ, it offers a highly practical approach to research that avoids the hermeneutic dilemma of trying to 'apply' findings from one setting, for example, interviews, to another, such as, family businesses. Fourth, as an observational methodology in real-world settings, this approach allows the research to be guided by issues that may not have been anticipated by the researcher. Finally, this approach captures life as it happens, and in sufficient detail to allow the researcher to analyse the complexity of apparently mundane, even everyday, situations. All of this has implications for data collection and analysis, which increasingly uses digitised audio and video to allow a fluid working with the materials and the capture of features of talk relevant to action and interaction as situated, practical and orderly (Table 5.3).

Conclusion

In this chapter, we have argued that process entrepreneurship studies have stimulated a reconsideration of the way in which we both conceptualise and how we study identity and identity work in Family Entrepreneurship. Specifically, we propose that a discursive psychology perspective with its emphasis on intersubjectivity and relational interaction through discourse can provide insights into the empirical application of identity and identity work. In researching these constructs in the domain of family businesses we should, therefore, focus less on entities and states (things as they are) and more on processes (by which things come into being). For Gergen (2010), this shift in focus from things in themselves to what may be viewed as a relational forming has major implications for how we conduct research.

We begin to confront the limitations of scholarly expression. As scholars we rely primarily on traditions of linguistic representation. However, a language of nouns and pronouns essentially presumes a world constituted by discrete entities.

Table 5.3 Methodological features of discursive psychology

- The central topic is discourse – talk and texts as parts of practices. This recognises the primacy of the social and relational nature of human life and starts with that analytically.
- It is interested in the most intimate and personal of psychological phenomena – in feeling and thinking, in embodiment and in the way social life is organised institutionally.
- Research questions typically focus on what people do in the settings that they live their lives, and may build on prior work or be stimulated by a collection of materials.
- The materials for study are usually digital audio and/or video recordings of people in particular locations, for example, workplaces, meetings, family get-togethers.
- It is generally distinctive amongst qualitative approaches in being a nuanced observational science avoiding the apparatus of open-ended or ethnographic interviews, experiments and questionnaires.
- The materials for study are transcribed using a system that captures features of interaction such as intonation and overlap that are significant for what is going on.
- Analysis will work with both recording and transcript.
- A typical study will build a collection of some phenomenon that will be the topic of more intensive analysis.
- Analysis will work with this collection and focus on both standard patterns and exceptional cases, which are used to develop and test ideas about what is going on in the material.
- Analysis will work with and be validated by the understandings of participants which are displayed in the unfolding interaction.
- The research write up is designed as far as possible to allow the reader to assess the validity of the analytic claims made about the materials.
- Such studies may contribute to a cumulative new picture of persons in relation; they may contribute to a range of applied questions; and they may address broader critical issues related to ideology and asymmetry.

Source: Wiggins and Potter (2008: 81); Edwards (2004); Hepburn and Potter (2003).

To employ the language is to construct just such a world. At the same time, such a vehicle of representation cannot easily be used to describe processes in continuous motion. One may articulate particular states or stages, but not the process in motion. A space is opened now for new and innovative orientations to theoretical intelligibility (Gergen, 2010: 58)

In responding to this challenge we have made three arguments in this chapter as the basis for a new approach to the study of identity in Family Entrepreneurship. First, ontologically we reconceptualise identity not as an entity or essence which we 'are' but as identity-as-process which we 'do', created, presented and re-presented through talk-in-action in situational and social interactions. Second, epistemologically we move beyond identity and identity categories as variables used to explain or account for variations to replace this with a focus on how, when and to what effect identity categories are invoked in particular interactions. Third, methodologically we outline a discursive psychology perspective as the basis for further research, which embodies both our ontological and methodological positions in a broadly social constructionist tradition and gives due place to the primacy of talk-in-interaction as the basis for analysis by engaged reflexive researchers.

As a micro-level approach to studying identity-in-interaction by focusing on the process of defining, constructing and refining our sense of 'who we are' through social interaction (Mueller and Whittle, 2012: 172), the discursive psychology approach focuses on understanding how attitudes, memories and emotions are handled through discourse in the creation of identity. Specifically, the discursive psychology perspective turns attention away from both the simplicities of role identification in identity theory and the narrow precepts of social identity theory, which 'psychologises' the underlying forces behind group identification while ignoring issues of power and discourse (Wetherell and Potter, 1992: ch. 2). We suggest that the familiness construct with its focus on the family business social system and the interactions of individual family members, the family and the business, provides a fruitful area for studying the dynamics of identity work from a multi-level, processual and discursive perspective. In turn, we regard identity construction in Family Entrepreneurship as a growing and productive area for the development of new theoretical and empirical knowledge not only for entrepreneurship but more broadly for Process Organization Studies.

References

Achtenhagen, L. and Welter, F. (2007) Media discourse in entrepreneurship research. In H. Neergaard and J. Parm Ulhoi (eds) *Handbook of Qualitative Research Methods in Entrepreneurship*, Cheltenham, UK: Edward Elgar, pp. 193–215.

Ahl, H. (2007) A Foucauldian framework for discourse analysis. In H. Neergaard and J. Parm Ulhøi (eds) *Handbook of Qualitative Research Methods in Entrepreneurship*, Cheltenham, UK: Edward Elgar, pp. 216–252.

Albert, S. and Whetton, D. A. (1985) Organizational identity. In L. L. Cummings and M. M. Staw (eds), *Research in Organizational Behavior*, vol. 17, Greenwich, CT: JAI Press, pp. 263–295.

Alvesson, M. and Willmott, H. (2002) Identity regulation as organizational control: Producing the appropriate individual, *Journal of Management Studies* 39 (5), 1125–1149.

Antaki, C. and Widdicombe, S. (1998) Identity as an achievement and as a tool. In C. Antaki and S. Widdicombe (eds) *Identities in Talk*, London: Sage Publications, pp. 1–14.

Audretsch, D. B., Hülsbeck, M. and Lehman, E. E. (2013) Families as active monitors of firm performance, *Journal of Family Business Strategy* 4 (2), 118–130.

Augoustinos, M. and Tileagă, C. (2012) Editorial: Twenty five years of discursive psychology, *British Journal of Social Psychology* 51, 405–412.

Benwell, B. and Stokoe, E. (2006) *Discourse and Identity*. Edinburgh, UK: Edinburgh University Press.

Chrisman, J. J., Chua, J. H. and Zahra, S. A. (2003) Creating wealth in family firms through managing resources: Comments and extensions, *Entrepreneurship: Theory and Practice* 27 (4), 359–365.

Chrisman, J. J., Kellermanns, F. W., Chan, K. C. and Liano, K. (2010) Intellectual foundations of current research in family business: An identification and review of 25 influential articles, *Family Business Review*, 23, 9–26.

Cigoli, V. and Scabini, E. (2006) *Family Identity: Ties, Symbols, and Transitions*, London: Routledge.

Craig, J. and Moores, K. (2005) Balanced scorecards do drive the strategic planning of family business, *Family Business Review* 18 (2), 105–122.

Cread, G. W. (2000) 'Family values' and domestic economies, *Annual Review of Anthropology* 29, 329–355.

Dunn, B. (1999) The family factor: The impact of family relationships dynamics on business-owning families during transitions. *Family Business Review* 12 (1), 41–60.

Edwards, D. (1998) The relevant thing about her: Social identity categories in use. In C. Antaki and S. Widdecombe (eds) *Identities in Talk*, London: Sage, pp. 15–33.

Edwards, D. (2003) Analyzing racial discourse: The discursive psychology of mindworld relationships. In H. van den Berg, M. Wetherall and H. Houtkoop-Steenstra (eds) *Analyzing Race Talk: Multidisciplinary Approaches to the Interview*, Cambridge, UK: Cambridge University Press, pp. 31–48.

Edwards, D. (2004) Discursive psychology. In K. Fitch and R. Sanders (eds) *Handbook of Language and Social Interaction*, Mahwah, NJ: Lawrence Erlbaum, pp. 257–273.

Edwards, D. (2012) Discursive and scientific psychology, *British Journal of Social Psychology* 51, 425–435.

Ensley, M. D. and Pearson, A. W. (2005) An exploratory comparison of the behavioural dynamics of top management teams in family and nonfamily new ventures: Cohesion, conflict, potency and consensus. *Entrepreneurship: Theory and Practice* 29, 267–284.

Fauchart, E. and Gruber, M. (2011) Darwinians, communitarians, and missionaries: The role of founder identity in entrepreneurship, *Academy of Management* 54 (5), 935–957.

Gergen, K. (1992) *The Saturated Self: Dilemmas of Identity in Contemporary Life*, New York: Basic Books.

Gergen, K. (2010) Co-constitution, causality and confluences: Organizing in a world without entities. In T. Hernes and S. Maitlis (eds) *Process, Sensemaking and Organizing*, Oxford: Oxford University Press, pp. 55–69.

Gioia, D. A. and Patvardhan, S. (2012) Identity as process and flow. In S. Maguire, M. Schultz, A. Langley and H. Tsoukas (eds) *Constructing Identity In and Around Organizations*, Vol. 33, Oxford: Oxford University Press, pp. 50–62.

Gioia, D. A., Patvardhan, S. D., Hamilton, A. L. and Corley, K. G. (2013) Organizational identity formation and change, *Academy of Management Annals* 7 (1), 123–193.

Gioia, D. A., Schultz, M. and Corley, K. G. (2000) Organizational identity, image and adaptive instability, *Academy of Management Review* 25 (1), 63–81.

Habbershorn, T. G. and Williams, M. (1999) A resource-based framework for assessing the strategic advantage of family firms, *Family Business Review* 12, 1–25.

Habbershorn, T. G., Williams, M. and MacMillan, I. (2003) A unified systems perspective of family firm performance, *Journal of Business Venturing* 18 (4), 451–465.

Hatch, M. J. and Schultz, M. S. (2002) The dynamics of organizational identity, *Human Relations* 55, 989–693.

Hayton, J. C. (2006, January) Explaining competitive advantage in family firms: The effectuation paradox, Presentation at the United States Association for Small Business and Entrepreneurship, Tuscon, AZ.

Hepburn, A. and Potter, J. (2003) Discourse analytic practice. In J. Seale, D. Silverman, J. Gubrium and G. Gobo (eds) *Qualitative Research Practice*, London: Sage, pp. 180–196.

Hitt, M. A., Beamish, P. W., Jackson, S. E. and Mathieu, J. E. (2007) Building theoretical and empirical bridges across levels: Multilevel research in management, *Academy of Management Journal* 50 (6), 1385–1399.

Knapp, J. R., Smith, B. R., Kreiner, G. E., Sundaramurthy, C. and Barton, S. L. (2013) Managing boundaries through identity work: The role of individual and organizational identity tactics. *Family Business Review* 26, 333–355.

Kroezen, J. J. and Heugens, P. P. M. A. R. (2012). Organizational identity formation: Processes of identity imprinting and enactment in the Dutch microbrewing landscape. In M. Schultz, S. Maguire, A. Langley and H. Tsoukas (eds) *Constructing Identity In and Around Organizations*, Oxford: Oxford University Press, pp. 89–127.

Langley, A. (1999) Strategies for theorizing from process data, *Academy of Management Review* 24 (2), 691–710.

Langley, A. and Tsoukas, H. (2010) Introducing perspectives on process organization studies. In T. Hernes and S. Maitlis (eds) *Process, Sensemaking, and Organizing: Perspectives on Process Organization Studies*, Oxford: Oxford University Press, pp. 1–26.

Lester, R. H. and Canella, A. A. (2006) Interorganizational familiness: How family firms use interlocking directions to build community-level social capital, *Entrepreneurship: Theory and Practice*, 30 (6), 755–776.

Lumpkin, G. T., Martin, W. and Vaughn, M. (2008) Family orientation: Individual-level influences on family firm outcomes, *Family Business Review* 21 (2), 127–138.

Miller, D. and Le Breton-Miller, I. (2011) Governance, social identity and entrepreneurial orientation in closely held public companies, *Entrepreneurship: Theory and Practice* 35 (5), 1051–1076.

Mueller, F. and Whittle, A. (2012) Villains, victims and the financial crisis: Positioning identities through descriptions. In M. Schultz, S. Maguire, A. Langley and H. Tsoukas (eds) *Constructing Identity In and Around Organisations*, Oxford: Oxford University Press, pp. 147–179.

Nag, R., Corley, K. G. and Gioia, D. A. (2007) The intersection of organizational identity, knowledge and practice: Attempting strategic change via knowledge grafting, *Academy of Management Journal* 50 (4), 821–847.

Navis, C. and Glynn, M. A. (2011) Legitimate distinctiveness and the entrepreneurial identity: Influence on investor judgments of new venture plausibility, *Academy of Management Review* 36 (3), 479–499.

Pearson, A. W., Carr, J. C. and Shaw, J. C. (2008) Toward a theory of familiness: A social capital perspective. *Entrepreneurship: Theory and Practice* 32 (6), 949–969.

Pérez Rodriguez, M. J. and Basco, R. (2011) The cognitive legitimacy of the family business field, *Family Business Review*, 24 (4), 322–342.

Phillips, N. and Hardy, C. (2002) *Discourse Analysis: Investigating Processes of Social Construction*, Qualitative Research Methods Series No. 50. London/Thousand Oaks, CA: Sage Production.

Potter, J. (2012a) Re-reading discourse and social psychology: Transforming social psychology, *British Journal of Social Psychology*, 51, 436–455.

Potter, J. (2012b) Discourse analysis and discursive psychology. In H. Cooper (Editor-in-chief), *APA Handbook of Research Methods in Psychology: Vol. 2. Quantitative, Qualitative, Neuropsychological and Biological.* Washington, DC: American Psychological Association Press, pp. 111–130.

Potter, J. and Hepburn, A. (2005) Qualitative interviews in psychology problems and possibilities, *Qualitative Research in Psychology* 2, 38–55.

Potter, J. and Wetherell, M. (1987) *Discourse and Social Psychology: Beyond Attitudes and Behaviour.* London: Sage Publications.

Powell, E. and Baker, T. (2013) The coat of many colours: A process model of entrepreneurial identity, Paper presented for 2013 Academy of Management Annual Meeting.

Ram, M. and Holliday, R. (1993) Relative merits: Family culture and kinship in small firms. *Sociology* 27 (4), 629–648.

Ravasi, D. and Schultz, M. (2006) Responding to organizational identity threats: Exploring the role of organizational culture. *Academy of Management Journal* 49 (3), 433–458.

Rousseau, D. M. (1985) Issues of level in organizational research: Multi-level and cross-level perspectives. In L. L. Cummings and B. Staw (eds) *Research in Organizational Behavior*, Vol. 7, Greenwich, CT: JAI Press, pp. 1–37.

Salignac, F. (2012) Discourse analysis. In R. Seymour (ed.) *Handbook of Research Methods on Social Entrepreneurship*, Cheltenham, UK: Edward Elgar, pp. XX

Scott, S. G. and Lane, V. R. (2000) A stakeholder approach to organizational identity, *Academy of Management Review* 25 (1), 43–62.

Shepherd, D. and Haynie, J. M. (2009) Family business, identity conflict and an expedited entrepreneurial process: A process of resolving identity conflict, *Entrepreneurship: Theory and Practice* 33 (6), 1245–1264.

Shotter, J. (2010) Adopting a process orientation … in practice: Chiasmic relations, language and embodiment in a living world. In T. Hernes and S. Maitlis (eds) *Process, Sensemaking and Organizing*, Oxford: Oxford University Press, pp. 70–101.

Sorenson, R. L., Goodpaster, K. E., Hedberg, P. R. and Yu, A. (2009) The family point of view, family social capital and firm performance: An exploratory test. *Family Business Review* 22 (3), 239–253.

Steier, L. (2003). Variants of agency contracts in family-financed ventures as a continuum of familial altruistic and market rationalities, *Journal of Business Venturing* 18 (5), 597–618.

Stewart, A. and Hitt, M. A. (2011) Why can't a family business be more like a nonfamily business? Modes of professionalization in family firms, *Family Business Review* 25 (1), 58–86.

Sundaramurthy, C. and Kreiner, G. E. (2008) Governing by managing identity boundaries: The case of family business. *Entrepreneurship: Theory and Practice* 32 (3), 415–436.

Tokarczyk, J., Hansen, E., Green, M. and Down, J. (2007) A resource-based view and market orientation theory examination of the role of 'familiness' in family business success, *Family Business Review* 20 (1), 17–31.

Tsoukas, H. and Chia, R. (2002) On organizational becoming: Rethinking organizational change, *Organization Science* 13 (5), 567–582.

Van de Ven, A. H. and Poole, M. S. (1995) Explaining development and change in organizations, *Academy of Management Review* 20 (3), 510–540.

Wetherell, M. and Potter, J. (1992) *Mapping the Language of Racism: Discourse and the Legitimation of Exploitation*. London: Harvester Wheatsheaf

Whetton, D. A. and Mackey, A. (2002) A social actor conception or organizational identity and its implications for the study of organizational reputation, *Business and Society* 41 (4), 393–414.

Widdicombe, S. (1998) But you don't class yourself: The interactional management of category membership and non-membership. In C. Antaki and S. Widdicombe (eds) *Identities in Talk*, London: Sage Publications, pp. 191–206.

Wiggins, S. and Potter, J. (2007) Discursive psychology. In C. Willig and W. Stainton-Rogers (eds) *The Sage Handbook of Qualitative Research in Psychology*, London: Sage Publications, pp. 73–90.

Zahara, S. A., Hayton, J. C. and Salvato, C. (2004) Entrepreneurship in family vs. nonfamily firms: A resource-based analysis of the effect of organizational culture, *Entrepreneurship: Theory and Practice* 28 (4), 363–381.

Zellweger, T. M., Eddleston, K. A. and Kellermanns, F. (2010) Exploring the concept of familiness: Introducing family firm identity. *Journal of Family Business Strategy* 1 (1), 54–63.

6 Keeping it in the family

Financial rewards in family firms

Sara Carter and Friederike Welter

Introduction

Entrepreneurs running family firms have considerable discretion in determining the form, the value and the timing of their financial rewards. The financial rewards of entrepreneurship include both direct financial rewards (i.e. drawings, net profit, shareholder dividends and equity sales), and a range of indirect rewards, including goods and services owned by the firm but used for personal and household consumption. The extraction of financial rewards may be adjusted to suit prevailing business conditions and the entrepreneur's personal requirements. Within family firms, the close, often inseparable, relationship between the entrepreneur and the firm suggests that decisions about financial rewards are seldom based entirely on business logic, but also take into account personal and family needs. For example, frugal entrepreneurs may typically extract notional drawings, but the amount may vary depending on personal needs and the affordability to the business. Similarly, the value and timing of more substantial financial rewards, such as dividends and profit, may be varied by the judicious entrepreneur to suit prevailing business conditions and personal needs, and to maximize personal and business advantage. Arguably, the ability to vary the form, value and timing of the financial rewards extracted from the business is a distinguishing feature of entrepreneurship.

Exploring financial rewards and their allocation illuminates a relatively unknown dimension of Family Entrepreneurship – how families influence value extraction from family-owned businesses and, conversely, how the business influences family life in terms of its consumption behaviour and relative lifestyle. Hence, the exploration of reward decisions in family firms focuses attention on the interaction between the family and the firm. Although previous studies have touched on financial rewards, focusing on issues such as the influence of different types of parental altruism on family firm governance, including good allowances (Lubatkin, Durand and Ling 2007), wealth creation in family firms (Chrisman, Chua and Zahra 2003; Sirmon and Hitt 2003), family firm performance and competitiveness (Le Breton-Miller and Miller 2006), and capital flows in family business (Pearson, Carr and Shaw 2008; Sharma 2008), to date there has been no direct consideration of personal financial rewards and the influences upon reward allocation decisions within family firms. In many respects this is not unexpected, as studies of non-family entrepreneurial firms have also shied away from measuring the personal financial rewards of entrepreneurship and the reward allocation decisions made by entrepreneurs. Furthermore, data on financial rewards may be lacking, especially where family firms are not publicly traded and do not have to announce their net profit or similar.

The aim of this conceptual chapter is to explore financial rewards in Family Entrepreneurship, and the influence of factors, specific to Family Entrepreneurship, that are likely to impact on the allocation of financial rewards. In so doing, it illuminates a relatively unknown dimension of family businesses – how families influence value extraction from family-owned businesses and, conversely, how the business influences family life in terms of its consumption behaviour and relative lifestyle. Unlike non-family firms where reward decisions are largely determined by business efficiencies, and bounded by rigid governance requirements, reward decisions in family firms are also influenced by family needs and desires and by emotional relationships within the family. Family firms are also likely to be characterized by reward allocation structures and processes that are negotiated between the business and the family, regardless of whether governance requirements apply also. Thus, this chapter draws attention to previously unexplored interactions between the family and the firm that impact on both family and business strategies, and the role of altruism and trust as key dimensions in the allocation of financial rewards.

As so little is understood about the financial rewards of entrepreneurship, the chapter starts by considering what these rewards are and the reasons why there has been so little interest in researching this topic. The chapter next considers the types of financial rewards available within family firms, providing a broad overview of the factors that may influence reward allocation in the family firm. Next, the allocation of financial rewards is theorized. Stewardship, altruism and trust are important influences on financial rewards within the family business, drawing attention to the contexts within which families determine financial rewards. The chapter concludes with an outlook, outlining perspectives for future research.

The financial rewards of entrepreneurship

This chapter focuses on the personal financial rewards of entrepreneurial action for the individual and their families. Although there is a great interest in both entrepreneurship and family business ownership, we know remarkably little about the financial rewards derived from entrepreneurial action. This lack of knowledge lies in stark contrast to the well-established research efforts and sophisticated theoretical insights developed within related research areas. Theoretical insights into the creation, derivation and appropriation of entrepreneurial rents within the context of the firm have been regularly advanced within academic research (Alvarez 2007; Alvarez and Barney 2004; Casson 2005; Foss and Klein 2005). Despite the developments seen within this related research area, the effects of firm-level value creation on the entrepreneur and the entrepreneurial family remain unexplored (Carter 2011).

The main explanation for the paucity of research exploring the financial rewards of entrepreneurship lies in the obvious methodological difficulties associated with this research area. Studying the financial rewards of entrepreneurship is complex and 'inconvenient' (Davidsson 2004), and raises four immediate methodological problems. First, the unit of analysis is ambiguous (Chandler and Lyon 2001; Davidsson and Wiklund 2001). A focus on the individual draws attention to the cash payments received (drawings, salary, dividends etc.) but fails to account for the wealth and assets nominally owned by the firm, while a focus on the firm measures profits and capital gain but fails to account for the relative earnings, consumption and lifestyle of the individual and their family. Second, the measures of financial rewards are not immediately obvious. Researchers have noted the inherent problems of using net profit or drawings as the standard measure of entrepreneurial 'wage' (Hamilton 2000), but more robust indicators which can account for various forms of capital gain have proven difficult to operationalize. Third, the financial rewards of entrepreneurship typically accrue over long periods of time and, in the case of family firms, may take more than a generation to reach fruition. Cross-sectional research designs are unlikely to accurately capture financial rewards which are unevenly spread over these periods; indeed, even the most conscientious longitudinal design would be challenged by these timescales. Finally, investigating the personal financial rewards of entrepreneurship requires the probing of extremely sensitive information, which makes data collection highly problematic.

The few empirical studies that have considered the financial rewards of entrepreneurship have focused on cross-sectional snapshots of entrepreneurial earnings or analyses of household wealth, with remarkably divergent results. Studies of entrepreneurial earnings typically calculate an hourly wage where the numerator is actual earnings and the denominator is self-reported working hours (Blanchflower 2004; Hamilton 2000; Parker 1997; Parker, Belghitar and Barmby 2005; Skinner, Stuttard, Beissel-Durrant and Jenkins 2002). Compared with other occupational groups, entrepreneurs have been found to have lower median earnings (Blanchflower 2004; Parker 1997; Parker, Belghitar and Barmby 2005) and lower earnings growth. These low earnings levels have been explained in two main ways. The compensating differential thesis emphasizes the non-pecuniary benefits of business ownership, citing factors such as individual autonomy and job satisfaction, as compensation for low pecuniary earnings (Blanchflower and Shadforth 2007; Hamilton 2000; Shane 2008). An alternative explanation that entrepreneurs under-report incomes, builds on popular perceptions that the living standards of the self-employed are substantially higher than their reported low incomes suggest, has led to attempts to quantify the scale of under-reporting and assess the comparative consumption capability of entrepreneurial households, which may access a variety of business related goods and services at relatively low or zero charge. Estimates suggest that the under-reporting of entrepreneurial earnings ranges between 28 and 40 per cent of the value of reported earnings (Cagetti and De Nardi 2006; Kesselman 1989), while the personal consumption of business-related goods has been estimated to increase the consumption capability of entrepreneurial households by 34 per cent above reported income levels (Bradbury 1996).

While studies of entrepreneurial incomes have highlighted the relatively low level of financial rewards, studies of wealthy households have found these are more likely to comprise entrepreneurs than employees (Cagetti and De Nardi 2006; Hurst and Lusardi 2004; Quadrini 2000). For example, the median net worth of business owners in the US is slightly higher than for the self-employed, but both groups tend to be richer than the population as a whole, whose median net worth is less than 30 per cent of that of entrepreneurs (Cagetti and De Nardi 2006). The greater wealth of entrepreneurial households has been explained by their accumulation and savings patterns (Bradford 2003; Cagetti and De Nardi 2006; Quadrini 2000). Entrepreneurial households are more likely than employee households to benefit from lump sum dividends, and typically have higher levels of savings, required both to offset earnings risks (Parker, Belghitar and Barmby 2005) and reduce the need for costly external finance (Gentry and Hubbard 2004; Hurst and Lusardi 2004; Nanda 2008).

Prior studies of earnings and household wealth provide partial insights into the financial rewards of entrepreneurship; however, perhaps their most important contribution is to highlight both the complexity of the issue and the need to consider the different forms of financial rewards over the life-course of the business and their impact on the entrepreneurial family's consumption and relative living standards (Carter 2011). A focus on the financial rewards of entrepreneurship immediately highlights the centrality of the entrepreneurial family as a key influence on reward decision-making. Indeed, it is clear that the financial rewards of entrepreneurship cannot be considered in isolation to the family. Contextualizing financial reward decisions within the entrepreneurial family takes account of both the permeability of the boundaries between the business and the family with regard to earnings, wealth, expenditure and consumption, and also the influence of the family with regard to reward decisions, for example, structuring a family business to take advantage of tax efficiencies (De Man, de Bruijn and Groeneveld 2008; Mulholland 1996; Ram 2001; Wheelock and Mariussen 1997).

Financial rewards in family firms

If the financial rewards of entrepreneurship have been found difficult to estimate, then the analysis of the financial rewards within family firms is likely to be even more problematic. It is well established that family involvement adds complexity to business ownership (Chrisman, Chua and Sharma 2005; Chrisman, Chua and Steier 2005, 2003), and there is little doubt that family ownership also adds complexity to the consideration of financial rewards. Family firms may be composed of multiple family members and multiple generations, and may also include non-family employees in both the accrual of wealth and the dispersal of financial rewards. The potentially large number of family stakeholders, family shareholders as well as family and non-family employees increases the number of individuals with a financial interest in the firm, and also extends the range of possible permutations that require consideration in financial reward decisions.

In addition to the larger pool of family and non-family actors with an interest in the firm's financial reward decisions, family firms have a set of specific motivations and dynamics with the potential to influence reward decisions, including a sense of stewardship and business longevity (Le Breton-Miller and Miller 2009; Mitchell, Hart, Valcea and Townsend 2009; Sirmon and Hitt 2003). Both have potential ramifications for financial reward decisions, as there may be a strong impetus to preserve or steward the wealth rather than disperse it (Mitchell, Hart, Valcea and Townsend 2009). Similarly, family firms may seek to balance the firm's economic goals of wealth creation and the family's emotional well-being evidenced by a sense of family harmony (Le Breton-Miller and Miller 2009; Le Breton-Miller, Miller and Steier 2004). Trade-offs such as these may have implications for financial reward decisions that are made within family firms.

Family firms are also typically characterized as containing an individual with controlling power. As Carney (2005: 255) argued 'The unification of ownership and control concentrates and incorporates organizational authority in the person of an owner-manager or family.' This characteristic ensures that within family firms, the individual with controlling power has the ability to not only make decisions about financial rewards, but also to retain the discretion to select the beneficiaries. The presence of information asymmetries suggests that it is possible for these decisions to be made discretely and indirectly through, for example, related party transactions. Hence, the main decision-maker within family firms has the ability to exploit ambiguities that occur as a consequence of information asymmetries and which provide opportunities to decide on the form, value and timing of rewards, and also to determine the beneficiaries of these financial rewards. Although governance mechanisms reduce the opportunities for this type of ambiguity, research has found that governance inefficiencies permit different types of altruistic behaviours by parent-owners, enabling parent-owners to transfer 'normal' and 'merit' goods to their children (Lubatkin, Durand and Ling 2007).

Additionally, family firms are often defined by the process of successor selection (Le Breton-Miller, Miller and Steier 2004; Miller, Steier and Le Breton-Miller 2003; Mitchell, Hart, Valcea and Townsend 2009; Sharma, Chrisman and Chua 2003; Sharma and Irving 2005). Succession in the family firm encompasses both the transfer of leadership and the transfer of stock, with financial reward implications for both the selected successor and any unselected candidates. Hence, competitiveness between successor generation members may creep into the succession process in even the best prepared families. A review of the succession research literature showed that even firms with a single heir apparent often seek to enlarge the pool of candidates to include the heir's siblings, other family members and non-family managers, as an interim measure until the heir is ready, and to build the firm's resilience in case of unforeseen circumstances. Where there are multiple siblings who may each be considered as potential successors, competition may be explicitly encouraged or inadvertently fostered by the parent CEO (the *King Lear* syndrome). The selection of one successor to the family firm potentially leaves other family members unselected, and requiring a degree of financial, as well as emotional, compensation. In these circumstances, family firms may make decisions about financial rewards that are based less on business rationality and equality of individual contribution, than on the influence of strong emotional pressures from family members. Personal financial gains and losses may impact directly on the successor generation, who may find the transfer of the firm's financial controls to a sibling to be uncomfortable, unfair and even threatening.

Given the specific dynamics of, and the complex sets of relationships that exist within family-owned businesses, the analysis of financial rewards in family firms may not be best focused on the sterile and relatively trivial search to estimate the value of entrepreneurial earnings – the dominant theme of the financial rewards research effort to date. Instead, a more fruitful line of enquiry may emerge from a consideration of some of the larger, more theoretically focused, issues that influence and underpin financial reward decisions within family firms.

Theorizing financial rewards in family firms

A consideration of the issues that may underpin financial reward allocation decisions in family firms immediately draws attention to two key theoretical perspectives, stewardship and agency, which can potentially shed light on the factors influencing financial rewards. These two perspectives have been used extensively within the family business literature where they have often been seen as providing competing and mutually exclusive explanations for economic behaviour in family firms (Le Breton-Miller and Miller 2009). While agency theory is often depicted as assuming the types of opportunistic and self-serving behaviours associated with utility maximizing *homo economicus* (Albanese, Dacin and Harris 1997; Jensen and Meckling 1976), stewardship theory, in contrast, assumes individual behaviour as collectivist and organizationally centred (Davis, Schoorman and Donaldson 1997).

The difference between the two perspectives essentially centres on the assumptions made by each perspective about individual motivation, sometimes conceptualized as 'models of man' (Corbetta and Salvato 2004; Davis, Schoorman and Donaldson 1997). Agency theory focuses attention on extrinsic motivations and rewards, suggesting a self-serving model of man, while stewardship theory focuses on higher order, intrinsic motivations associated with a self-actualizing model of man. While agency and stewardship theories have been typically seen as distinctive and competing, representing broader divisions between the subject domains of economics on the one hand and psychology and sociology on the other, there have been important attempts both to identify common ground (Albanese, Dacin and Harris 1997) and to broker an integration of the two perspectives (Le Breton-Miller and Miller 2009). In a response to Davis *et al.*'s (1997) seminal description of stewardship theory as an explicit alternative to agency theory, Albanese *et al.* (1997) suggest that stewardship is not inconsistent with agency theory if it is perceived as providing utility. Indeed, given the variations in utility functions of principals and agents, and the dynamic nature of the principal–agent relationship, 'today's "agent" may be tomorrow's "steward," or vice versa' (Albanese, Dacin and Harris 1997: 611).

Given the centrality of individual rewards within both agency and stewardship theories, and the extensive adoption of both approaches within the family firms' literature, it is rather paradoxical that there has been so little explicit analysis of financial rewards within family firms. It is to this that we now turn our attention. We will focus on stewardship perspectives on financial rewards, because within agency theory extrinsic rewards are explicitly financial and reward systems, which have been put into place to reduce or control conflicts of interests arising out of the self-interest of individuals. These reward systems 'represent the control mechanisms of agency theory' (Davis, Schoorman and Donaldson 1997: 28), comprising rewards with a quantifiable financial value recognized by the conflicting parties.

Research has identified stewardship as a key motivating factor in family firms, distinguishing family firms from non-family firms, and providing an important sense of longevity that may enable family firms to survive longer than other organizations (Corbetta and Salvato 2004; Mitchell, Hart, Valcea and Townsend 2009). Le Breton-Miller and Miller (2006) drew attention to the long-term orientations typically seen within family firms, identifying these as a key explanation for the competitive performance of family-controlled businesses, and associated with stewardship approaches. Stewardship approaches to management, cast as diametrically opposite to approaches that favour short-term, profit-maximizing goals, place emphasis on the importance of looking after the family firm in order to hand it on in good shape to the next generation (Corbetta and Salvato 2004; Miller and Le Breton-Miller 2006). Stewardship theory typically emphasizes the importance of intrinsic rewards as the key motivation of individuals who view their interests as aligned with those of the organization. Of course, it would be naive to assume that stewards forego financial rewards or that they fail to gain significant financial benefits from the organization. As Davis *et al.* (1997: 25) explain, stewards perceive that 'utility gained from pro-organizational behavior is higher than the utility that can be gained through opportunistic, self-serving behaviour'.

It may be speculated that the implications of stewardship behaviours on the financial reward decisions of family firms are twofold. First, as stewardship is specifically associated with a long-term orientation, one consequence of this may be to favour the retention of assets and wealth within the firm. In other words, in family firms where there is a strong stewardship ethos, wealth is stewarded, rather than realized in the form of personal financial gain within the family. It might well be the case that stewardship is more pronounced in established and older family firms, compared to new and young ones. Second, while the retention of wealth within the firm may be beneficial for the firm, it requires family members to make collective and individual sacrifices regarding their own personal financial rewards. This raises further questions, such as: Who makes the decision about the stewarding of wealth? When is the decision made? Is this decision made once or regularly revisited? To what extent are these decisions discussed within the family, and to what extent are family members' views taken into consideration in reward decisions? Why are some families prepared to sacrifice certainty and regularity with regard to their income, for the sake of long-term business growth from which they may not personally benefit? More broadly, how do families in business manage their expenditure and consumption given the uncertainty surrounding value extraction, and what are the potential effects of this on family relations?

Such questions draw attention to the central role of the family, their lifestyles and consumption behaviour, as key contributors to the family firm. The contribution of the family can be seen specifically in the development of the organizational culture and characteristics that often typify family firms. Recent work on non-economic wealth creation, for example, suggests that family firms prefer sustaining their socioemotional wealth to the disadvantage of their business performance: they accept performance risks (which consequently may lower their reward position) in order to minimize or avoid the loss of their socioemotional wealth (Gómez-Mejía, Haynes, Núñez-Nickel, Jacobson and Moyano-Fuentes 2007). Interestingly, stakeholder involvement allows them to enhance their socioemotional wealth as stakeholders because stakeholders often do not focus on monetary gains from the business (Cennamo, Berrone, Cruz and Gomez-Mejia 2012).

Carney (2005) drew attention to the notion of parsimony as a distinguishing characteristic of family firm governance, where the use of the family's own money introduces a propensity towards cost minimization and an abiding sense of prudence throughout the organization. This view chimes with popular perceptions of family firm owners, seen as possessing Weberian-type characteristics of hard work, frugality and thrift, and who thrive on the deferment of personal gratification. The ability of some families to adapt their consumption, in the form of direct expenditure, to suit the prevailing conditions, and draw on the family as a largely invisible and usually free provider of labour, has been a longstanding explanation for the competitive success of family-owned businesses. In this regard, Chayanov's theory of peasant economy provides a particularly apposite early description of the competitive advantage of family firms:

In conditions where capitalist farms would go bankrupt, peasant families could work longer hours, sell at lower prices, obtain no net surplus, and yet manage to carry on with their farming year after year. For these reasons, Chayanov concluded that the competitive power of peasant family farms versus large scale capitalist farms was much greater than had [previously] been foreseen.

(Thorner 1966: xviii)

While decisions regarding financial rewards are relatively straightforward in firms that are barely managing to survive and therefore have little material assets available for redistribution, decisions become more complex in firms that have experienced great success, particularly with regard to profitability and growth, and therefore have greater and more obvious wealth. Family firms with clear governance practices are likely to have resolved at least some aspects of reward decision-making through the introduction of specific remuneration policies. The presence of greater success and therefore greater wealth within the firm may, however, make financial reward decisions more problematic. In particular, a focus on stewardship by a long-serving CEO and dominant shareholder, may conflict with the aspirations of minority shareholders who may wish to see a greater personal return on their investments.

The long-term orientation associated with stewardship perspectives suggests that succession decisions may become an important factor in family firms that emphasize this approach. It is likely that the successor selection process has a substantial impact on financial reward allocation. It is possible to speculate on the likely influences of succession on financial reward decisions by looking at the examples of competitive succession both in very successful companies and those where the future is less certain. Within successful firms, the succession process may favour the chosen successor with the dominant ownership and control of the firm; however, non-succeeding siblings may expect to receive substantial financial rewards, in the form of capital assets such as houses or cars, in compensation both for the loss of the potential ownership of the firm and also the emotional consequences of non-selection. Where the inheritance of family firms brings obvious long-term prosperity to the successor, such compensation may be seen as appropriate and equitable, contributing to the management of good relations within the family. By contrast, within less prosperous firms the financial benefits of succession may be a great deal less certain. This is especially the case where the chosen successor also assumes the financial responsibility for maintaining the retiring generation of owners. In these circumstances, the rewards of being selected as the successor may be more emotionally than financially advantageous, and an iniquitous contrast to the commitment-free distribution of capital rewards given as compensation to non-successor siblings. Clearly, the effects of succession on reward decisions in family firms are likely to be complex and far reaching; however, these are relatively unexplored issues that require deeper levels of understanding in order to advance our understanding of the dynamics of family firms.

The embeddedness of financial rewards within the family (firm)

Recognizing that stewardship and agency approaches alone provide only a partial explanation of family firm behaviour (Corbetta and Salvato 2004; Davis, Schoorman and Donaldson 1997), Le Breton-Miller and Miller (2009) suggest that the two approaches may be united through a social embeddedness perspective that views actors as embedded within multiple social systems. This approach highlights the importance of viewing behaviour within its own specific contexts (Welter 2011), implying that owners more embedded within the business than within the family may exhibit the 'self-actualizing' behaviours associated with stewardship, while owners more embedded within the family than the business may demonstrate behaviours associated with the pursuit of 'self-serving' family interests (Le Breton-Miller and Miller 2009). In this regard, Corbetta and Salvato (2004) draw attention to internal family dynamics influencing family firm behaviour. In the context of financial rewards, the roles of trust and altruism are of particular interest, as they reflect elements of social embeddedness (Greenwood 2003).

Altruism and financial rewards

At a theoretical level, altruism is typically linked to agency perspectives (Karra, Tracey and Phillips 2006; Van den Berghe and Carchon 2003); however, altruism is not inconsistent with stewardship perspectives. The self-serving focus of agency theory does not exclude altruistic behaviour which underlies the trusting relations that are said to dominate in family firms and that result in relational contracts as a key assumption explaining differences between family and non-family firms. Indeed, it is perfectly conceivable that stewardship within family firms – typically exhibited through a long-term orientation and a desire to hand on the firm in better shape than was inherited, and organizationally centred and collectivist management behaviour – is underpinned and motivated by the owners' strong sense of altruism.

Monroe (1994: 862) defines altruism as 'behaviour intended to benefit another, even when doing so may risk or entail some risk to the welfare of the actor'. This has been picked up by the family firms' literature, where altruism has been viewed as a utility function connecting the welfare of one person to that of others (Karra, Tracey and Phillips 2006; Lubatkin, Durand and Ling 2007; Schulze, Lubatkin and Dino 2002, 2003b). Lubatkin *et al.* (2007: 1023) describe altruism as 'a particular kind of "self-other" relationship, representing the tendency of principals (the "self") to integrate interests of "others" into their decision processes and actions'. Most commonly, this is seen in family firms where the parents' welfare is inextricably linked to the welfare of their children and other family members. The presence of altruism has been proposed as a key difference between family and non-family firms (Van den Berghe and Carchon 2003). As Karra *et al.* (2006: 864) explain, parents demonstrate altruism towards their children not only because of the family bond 'but also because their own interests, and those of the business, would be damaged were they to act less benevolently'. Altruistic behaviour presents both advantages and disadvantages to family firms, particularly with regard to agency costs. On the one hand, altruism in family firms has been found to offer competitive advantages and improve performance (Chrisman, Chua and Litz 2004; Van den Berghe and Carchon 2003). On the other hand, preferential treatment of family members, free riding and biased views of family member competence have been shown to increase agency costs (Schulze, Lubatkin and Dino 2003b). In this regard, Lubatkin *et al.* (2007) identify five different types of parental altruism: principal-based, ideal-typic, family-oriented, paternalistic and psychosocial, with different influences on family firm governance. Karra *et al.* (2006) argued that the advantages to family firms are most pronounced when altruism is reciprocal and symmetrical (i.e. evenly exhibited by both parties); however, as firms mature and increase in size, loss of reciprocity may result in asymmetrical altruism and a concomitant increase in agency costs.

The notion of altruism may be highly influential in understanding reward decisions in the family firms. It may be expected that the parent generation of family firms exhibit benevolence to their children, though in the context of financial rewards there may be tensions with regard to the form this may take. On the one hand, the influence of altruism may be exhibited through regular and high value financial rewards to family members. On the other hand altruism may be exhibited through the long-term stewarding of financial rewards within the firm, with individuals sacrificing their own short-term personal rewards for the long-term good of the firm and the next generation of owner-management.

The presence of altruism, especially if it is accompanied by concentrated ownership and management as is typical of family firms, may influence reward decisions also in other ways. While the rewards of entrepreneurship have so far highlighted direct financial returns (drawings, profit-sharing, dividends etc.), other indirect financial returns may also occur. The concentration of ownership and management results in dominant and, within the context of the family firm, potentially omniscient CEOs with the capacity to control information about rewards, and the ability to choose other forms of financial rewards for specific family members. The presence of information asymmetries allows the possibility of family firm CEOs to engage in related party transactions with some family members, through consultancy fees etc., without the knowledge of other family members. Such asymmetric altruism that rewards some family members at the potential expense, and without the prior knowledge, of other family members undoubtedly occurs within some family firms. However, the extent to which asymmetric altruism is exhibited and the effects on both the firm and family relations is unknown.

While altruism is an important element within family firms, our understanding of the concept and, in particular, the myriad ways in which it impacts on family firms, has emerged relatively recently (Greenwood 2003; Lubatkin, Durand and Ling 2007; Lubatkin, Schulze, Ling and Dino 2005; Schulze, Lubatkin and Dino 2003a, 2003b; Steier 2003). The level of altruism that is present within a family firm, and the degree to which it is exhibited equally by both parental and successor generations is not easily measured. Neither is it certain that levels of altruism remain static and balanced over time, as firms mature and issues of growth and succession become more prominent (Karra, Tracey and Phillips 2006). In short, the concept of altruism poses measurement challenges to family firm researchers, but the inclusion of altruism as a key influence on financial reward decisions may be great in terms of the depth of insight the concept offers.

Trust and financial rewards

Trust is assumed to play a large role in family firms (Corbetta and Salvato 2004), although it is only recently that family business research has started to study its role for the family firm. Research has analysed the role of trust as a governance mechanism (Eddleston, Chrisman, Steier and Chua 2010) and as a strategic advantage for family firms (Fink 2010; Steier 2001). Related to this, Sundaramurthy (2008) theorized how to sustain trust within a family firm context. Succession relations between the owner(s) and their families are seen as trust based with the different actors that are involved assuming reciprocity over time (Janjuha-Jivraj and Spence 2009; Raskas 1998). Other studies have focused on challenges in building and repairing trust between CEOs and families (Mari 2010), or, through analysing board of directors, showed the decrease in trust over generations of family firms which went hand in hand with an increase in control (Bammens, Voordeckers and Van Gils 2008).

In relation to financial rewards, the concept of trust draws attention to the mechanisms of how the allocation of financial rewards is regulated and executed. Family firms are usually seen as 'high trust' organizations (Fukuyama 1996), which implies that governance is informal, less regulated and based on norms of reciprocity. While trust can result from kinship and family bonds, it also arises from positive expectations of others, including altruistic behaviour (Möllering 2006). Generally, trust is seen as lowering transaction costs and agency costs (Karra, Tracey and Phillips 2006), because trust, drawing on previous knowledge, or, as in the case of family firms, on group characteristics inherent in family kinship, substitutes for control mechanisms such as contracts (Möllering 2005). Trusting behaviour can resemble a 'calculated risk' (Williamson 1993), because the risks which are associated with the bestowed trust not being fulfilled are justified by the potential gains if trust is maintained. Trust also can involve variable degrees of goodwill, which is partly due to behavioural routines that facilitate decision-making, in view of limited individual information capabilities.

In a family firm context, firm–family relationships have been said to be characterized by a high level of personal trust, which allows financial rewards decisions to be made on an informal basis and as fits the respective situation, if not stipulated otherwise by legal regulations. In this regard, trust may substitute for more formal control mechanisms. Over time, as the business matures and intergenerational change occurs, trust can erode, because families might start feuding or become too distant in relation to the business or each other. This may have an impact on financial rewards in situations where trust becomes fragile or conflicts within the family result in distrust between family members (Steier 2001). In such situations, financial reward decisions will be less and less influenced by symmetric altruism and stewardship considerations. Asymmetric altruism would start to dominate with owners favouring some family members over others, which in turn will contribute to a downward spiral of trust-based relationships within the business and family. Consequently, this may contribute to increasing agency costs, resulting in the need for more formal control and regulation mechanisms with regard to financial rewards.

However, where trust remains strong and substitutes for control mechanisms within the business, it may negatively influence financial rewards in situations where owners 'over-trust' (Goel and Karri 2006), thus rejecting and overlooking the need for effective decision-making mechanisms in order to decide on financial rewards. This 'dark side of relational trust' (Zahra, Yavuz and Ucbasaran 2006) may also result in increasing transaction and agency costs, in particular where it goes hand in hand with asymmetric altruism, power relations or nepotism within the family which shape the discussions and negotiations as to who receives which types of financial rewards.

Outlook

Entrepreneurial families are distinctive in so far as they are able to make decisions about the form, value and timing of financial rewards, and negotiate consumption and expenditure at the household and business level. There has been little research attention devoted to reward decisions within entrepreneurial organizations, but it is likely that such reward decisions are complex, bounded both by the revenue-generating capacity of the business and the financial needs of the family. Within family firms, characterized by the presence of multiple family members, potentially multiple generations, and both family and non-family employees, reward decisions are likely to be even more complex and subject to influences that do not exist within non-family firms.

Previous studies have distinguished family firms by the long-term orientations associated with stewardship and the potential for imperfect family relations as a consequence of the succession process, and the presence of altruistic and trusting (or non-trusting) behaviour among family members. These dimensions of family firms are likely to have an important influence on short-term and long-term reward decisions, as has been discussed within this chapter. But, it is clearly erroneous to view family firms as a homogeneous group with similar attitudes towards financial rewards, and similar structures and processes governing reward allocation. Le Breton-Miller and Miller (2009: 1176) argue that within family firms, the 'relative applicability of the stewardship and agency perspectives will depend on how the firm and its key executives are embedded within the family'. Moreover, altruistic and trusting behaviours have been shown to be context-dependent, with different levels and types of altruism depending on the relative circumstances of benefactor and beneficiary (Khalil 2004) and variations in personal trust depending on previous experiences, knowledge and situational aspects (Welter and Smallbone 2006). In addition, firm-related factors are important, such as the stage of business development, enterprise size or, specifically related to family firms, the status of family ownership.

Salvato (2002) identifies three types of family firms, namely the founder-centred family firm, the sibling or cousin consortium with full family ownership and management, and the open family firm with a mixture of family and non-family ownership and management structures. In summarizing our discussion from the previous sections, we suggest that in each of these types of firms, financial rewards and their allocation are influenced by different configurations of altruism and trust, which in turn influence levels of stewardship or agency. In the founder-centred family firm, it may be assumed that levels of trust are high and symmetric altruism prevails, resulting in stewardship relations influencing financial reward decisions. In sibling/cousin consortiums levels of trust and altruism may have decreased, warranting the need for a shift from stewardship-based towards more agency-based relationships in deciding on financial rewards. Finally, in open family firms, levels of trust and altruism may be assumed to be lower in comparison to founder-centred firms, resulting in formal regulations and mechanisms for financial rewards. This approach highlights the importance of contextualizing financial rewards decisions within the family and the business, and suggests that in relation to financial rewards within family firms, stewardship and agency may be seen as a duality, with both simultaneously influencing types and allocation of financial rewards.

While this chapter has attempted to surface some of the theoretical issues associated with financial rewards in family firms, empirical studies may provide a more nuanced and insightful view. However, researching financial rewards brings profound methodological challenges. Not least among these is the need to determine the timescale over which to measure the financial rewards of family firms, and decisions about which actors to include in empirical investigation of reward allocation decisions. Is the unit of analysis contingent on a research focus upon the sources of income (who earns what?) which implies a view of multiple economic actors, or on the distribution of financial rewards (who gets what?) which implies a focus on the household as a single entity.

Further empirical challenges lie in differentiating reward decisions within family firms with clear and transparent governance regarding decision processes, and reward decisions in family firms with less sophisticated governance. To date, decision-making and negotiation processes around financial rewards in entrepreneurial families have received little attention. Although it is recommended that decisions about payments and beneficiaries within family firms are done so transparently and with full disclosure (ECODA, 2010), the presence of information asymmetries suggests that these decisions may be made discretely and indirectly through, for example, related party transactions. In this regard, it is clear that the main decision-maker within family firms has the ability to exploit ambiguities that occur as a consequence of information asymmetries accruing from concentrated ownership and control. Such ambiguities provide opportunities for the main decision-maker not only to decide on the form, value and timing of rewards, but also to determine the beneficiaries of these financial rewards, without necessarily either informing or gaining consent from other family stakeholders. While it may be assumed that governance mechanisms reduce the opportunities for this type of ambiguity, Lubatkin *et al.* (2007) argue that governance inefficiencies permit different types of altruistic behaviours by parent-owners, enabling parent-owners to transfer 'normal' and 'merit' goods to their children.

Financial rewards in entrepreneurial families show specific characteristics: they are uncertain with regard to volume and timing; they are negotiable between the firm and the family; they are invisible because they include both cash and goods/services that can be consumed; and they are indivisible because family and business budgets are closely interlinked even if commonly seen as separate entities. Guided by stewardship and agency costs, altruism and trust, this will impact on the mechanisms families use to decide on, negotiate and distribute financial rewards. Business earnings and sharing within the family need to be viewed together in order to fully understand the impact of family on business and vice versa.

Because of the unique characteristics of financial rewards in entrepreneurship and in particular in family firms, there is greater scope for household decision-making with regard to financial rewards; and our chapter has uncovered just the tip of an iceberg with interesting perspectives for future research. Interesting themes, for example, include the role and potential conflicts between business-related and family stakeholders in financial rewards decisions; the role of governance mechanisms in guiding reward decisions; identifying differences between entrepreneurial orientated and long-term orientated family firms in their reward decisions, and the potential need to educate and further professionalize family firms and enterprising families in relation to financial reward (decisions).

References

Albanese, R., M. T. Dacin and I. C. Harris (1997), 'Agents as stewards', *Academy of Management Review*, 22 (3), 609–611.

Alvarez, S. A. (2007), 'Entrepreneurial rents and the theory of the firm', *Journal of Business Venturing*, 22 (3), 427–442.

Alvarez, S. A. and J. B. Barney (2004), 'Organizing rent generation and appropriation: toward a theory of the entrepreneurial firm', *Journal of Business Venturing*, 19 (5), 621–635.

Bammens, Y., W. Voordeckers and A. Van Gils (2008), 'Boards of directors in family firms: a generational perspective', *Small Business Economics*, 31 (2), 163–180.

Blanchflower, D. G. (2004), *Self-Employment: More May Not Be Better*, Cambridge MA: National Bureau of Economic Research.

Blanchflower, D. G. and C. Shadforth (2007), 'Entrepreneurship in the UK', *Foundations and Trends in Entrepreneurship*, 3 (4), 257–264.

Bradbury, B. (1996), *Are the Low Income Self-Employed Poor?* Sydney: University of New South Wales.

Bradford, W. D. (2003), 'The wealth dynamics of entrepreneurship for black and white families in the US', *Review of Income and Wealth* (1), 89–116.

Cagetti, M. and M. De Nardi (2006), 'Entrepreneurship, frictions, and wealth', *Journal of Political Economy*, 114 (5), 835–870.

Carney, M. (2005), 'Corporate governance and competitive advantage in family-controlled firms', *Entrepreneurship: Theory and Practice*, 29 (3), 249–265.

Carter, S. (2011), 'The rewards of entrepreneurship: exploring the incomes, wealth, and economic well-being of entrepreneurial households', *Entrepreneurship: Theory and Practice*, 35 (1), 39–55.

Casson, M. (2005), 'Entrepreneurship and the theory of the firm', *Journal of Economic Behavior and Organization*, 58 (2), 327–348.

Cennamo, C., P. Berrone, C. Cruz and L. R. Gomez-Mejia (2012), 'Socioemotional wealth and proactive stakeholder engagement: why family-controlled firms care more about their stakeholders', *Entrepreneurship: Theory and Practice*, 36 (6), 1153–1173.

Chandler, G. N. and D. W. Lyon (2001), 'Issues of research design and construct measurement in entrepreneurship research: the past decade', *Entrepreneurship: Theory and Practice*, 25 (4), 101.

Chrisman, J. J., J. H. Chua and R. A. Litz (2004), 'Comparing the agency costs of family and non-family firms: conceptual issues and exploratory evidence', *Entrepreneurship: Theory and Practice*, 28 (4), 335–354.

Chrisman, J. J., J. H. Chua and P. Sharma (2005), 'Trends and directions in the development of a strategic management theory of the family firm', *Entrepreneurship: Theory and Practice*, 29 (5), 555–575.

Chrisman, J. J., J. H. Chua and L. Steier (2005), 'Sources and consequences of distinctive familiness: an introduction', *Entrepreneurship: Theory and Practice*, 29 (3), 237–247.

Chrisman, J. J., J. H. Chua and L. P. Steier (2003), 'An introduction to theories of family business', *Journal of Business Venturing*, 18 (4), 441–448.

Chrisman, J. J., J. H. Chua and S. A. Zahra (2003), 'Creating wealth in family firms through managing resources: comments and extensions', *Entrepreneurship: Theory and Practice*, 27 (4), 359–365.

Corbetta, G. and C. Salvato (2004), 'Self-serving or self-actualizing? Models of man and agency costs in different types of family firms: a commentary on "comparing the agency costs of family and non-family firms: conceptual issues and exploratory evidence"', *Entrepreneurship: Theory and Practice*, 28 (4), 355–362.

Davidsson, P. (2004), *Researching Entrepreneurship*, New York: Springer.

Davidsson, P. and J. Wiklund (2001), 'Levels of analysis in entrepreneurship research: current research practice and suggestions for the future', *Entrepreneurship: Theory and Practice*, 25 (4), 81.

Davis, J. H., F. D. Schoorman and L. Donaldson (1997), 'Toward a stewardship theory of management', *Academy of Management Review*, 22 (1), 20–47.

De Man, R., J. de Bruijn and S. Groeneveld (2008), 'What makes the home boundary porous? The influence of work characteristics on the permeability of the home domain', in C. Warhurst, D. R. Eikhof and A. Haunschild (eds), *Work Less, Live More? Critical Analysis of the Work-Life Boundary*, London: Palgrave.

ECODA (2010), *Corporate Governance Guidance and Principles for Unlisted Companies in Europe*, Brussels: European Confederation of Directors' Association (ECODA).

Eddleston, K. A., J. J. Chrisman, L. P. Steier and J. H. Chua (2010), 'Governance and trust in family firms: an introduction', *Entrepreneurship: Theory and Practice*, 34 (6), 1043–1056.

Fink, M. (2010), 'Trust-based cooperation relationships between SMEs: are family firms any different?' *International Journal of Entrepreneurial Venturing*, 1 (4), 382–397.

Foss, N. J. and P. G. Klein (2005), 'Entrepreneurship and the economic theory of the firm: any gains from trade?' University of Missouri-Columbia, Working Paper.

Fukuyama, F. (1996), *Trust: The Social Virtues and the Creation of Prosperity*, New York: Free Press, Penguin Books.

Gentry, W. M. and R. G. Hubbard (2004), 'Entrepreneurship and household saving', *Advances in Economic Analysis and Policy*, 4 (1), 1–55.

Goel, S. and R. Karri (2006), 'Entrepreneurs, effectual logic, and over-trust', *Entrepreneurship: Theory and Practice*, 30 (4), 477–493.

Gómez-Mejía, L. R., K. T. Haynes, M. Núñez-Nickel, K. J. L. Jacobson and J. Moyano-Fuentes (2007), 'Socioemotional wealth and business risks in family-controlled firms: evidence from Spanish olive oil mills', *Administrative Science Quarterly*, 52 (1), 106–137.

Greenwood, R. (2003), 'Commentary on: "toward a theory of agency and altruism in family firms"', *Journal of Business Venturing*, 18 (4), 491–494.

Hamilton, B. H. (2000), 'Does entrepreneurship pay? An empirical analysis of the returns to self-employment', *Journal of Political Economy*, 108 (3), 604–631.

Hurst, E. and A. Lusardi (2004), 'Liquidity constraints, household wealth, and entrepreneurship', *Journal of Political Economy*, 112 (2), 319–347.

Janjuha-Jivraj, S. and L. J. Spence (2009), 'The nature of reciprocity in family firm succession', *International Small Business Journal*, 27 (6), 702–719.

Jensen, M. C. and W. H. Meckling (1976), 'Theory of the firm: managerial behavior, agency costs and ownership structure', *Journal of Financial Economics*, 3 (4), 305–360.

Karra, N., P. Tracey and N. Phillips (2006), 'Altruism and agency in the family firm: exploring the role of family, kinship, and ethnicity', *Entrepreneurship: Theory and Practice*, 30 (6), 861–877.

Kesselman, J. R. (1989), 'Income tax evasion: an intersectoral analysis', *Journal of Public Economics*, 38 (2), 137–182.

Khalil, E. L. (2004), 'What is altruism?' *Journal of Economic Psychology*, 25 (1), 97–123.

Le Breton-Miller, I. and D. Miller (2006), 'Why do some family businesses out-compete? Governance, long-term orientations, and sustainable capability', *Entrepreneurship: Theory and Practice*, 30 (6), 731–746.

Le Breton-Miller, I. and D. Miller (2009), 'Agency vs. stewardship in public family firms: a social embeddedness reconciliation', *Entrepreneurship: Theory and Practice*, 33 (6), 1169–1191.

Le Breton-Miller, I., D. Miller and L. P. Steier (2004), 'Toward an integrative model of effective FOB succession', *Entrepreneurship: Theory and Practice*, 28 (4), 305–328.

Lubatkin, M. H., R. Durand and Y. Ling (2007), 'The missing lens in family firm governance theory: a self-other typology of parental altruism', *Journal of Business Research*, 60 (10), 1022–1029.

Lubatkin, M. H., W. S. Schulze, Y. Ling and R. N. Dino (2005), 'The effects of parental altruism on the governance of family-managed firms', *Journal of Organizational Behavior*, 26 (3), 313–330.

Mari, I. (2010), 'The dynamics of trust across cultures in family firms', in M. Saunders, D. Skinner, G. Dietz, N. Gillespie and R. J. Lewicki (eds), *Organizational Trust: A Cultural Perspective*, Cambridge: Cambridge University Press.

Miller, D. and I. Le Breton-Miller (2006), 'Family governance and firm performance: agency, stewardship, and capabilities', *Family Business Review*, 19 (1), 73–87.

Miller, D., L. Steier and I. Le Breton-Miller (2003), 'Lost in time: intergenerational succession, change, and failure in family business', *Journal of Business Venturing*, 18 (4), 513–531.

Mitchell, J. R., T. A. Hart, S. Valcea and D. M. Townsend (2009), 'Becoming the boss: discretion and postsuccession success in family firms', *Entrepreneurship: Theory and Practice*, 33 (6), 1201–1218.

Möllering, G. (2005), 'The trust/control duality: an integrative perspective on positive expectations of others', *International Sociology*, (20), 283–305.

Möllering, G. (2006), *Trust: Reason, Routine, Reflexivity*, Amsterdam: Elsevier.

Monroe, K. R. (1994), 'A fat lady in a corset: altruism and social theory', *American Journal of Political Science*, 38 (4), 861.

Mulholland, K. (1996), 'Gender, power and property relations within entrepreneurial wealthy families', *Gender, Work and Organization*, 3 (2), 78–102.

Nanda, R. (2008), *Cost of External Finance and Selection into Entrepreneurship*, Cambridge, MA: Harvard Business School.

Parker, S. C. (1997), 'The distribution of self-employment income in the United Kingdom, 1976–1991', *Economic Journal*, 107 (441), 455–466.

Parker, S. C., Y. Belghitar and T. Barmby (2005), 'Wage uncertainty and the labour supply of self-employed workers', *Economic Journal*, 115 (502), C190–C207.

Pearson, A. W., J. C. Carr and J. C. Shaw (2008), 'Toward a theory of familiness: a social capital perspective', *Entrepreneurship: Theory and Practice*, 32 (6), 949–969.

Quadrini, V. (2000), 'Entrepreneurship, saving, and mobility', *Review of Economic Dynamics*, 3, 1–40.

Ram, M. (2001), 'Family dynamics in a small consultancy firm: a case study', *Human Relations*, 54 (4), 395–418.

Raskas, D. F. (1998), *Familiarity Breeds Trust as well as Contempt . . . What about Familiarity? An Examination of Familial Involvement and Trust in Family Firms*, New York: Columbia University.

Salvato, C. (2002), *Antecedents of Entrepreneurship in Three Types of Family Firms*, Jönköping: Jönköping International Business School.

Schulze, W. S., M. H. Lubatkin and R. N. Dino (2002), 'Altruism, agency, and the competitiveness of family firms', *Managerial and Decision Economics*, 23 (4/5), 247–259.

Schulze, W. S., M. H. Lubatkin and R. N. Dino (2003a), 'Exploring the agency consequences of ownership dispersion among the directors of private family firms', *Academy of Management Journal*, 46 (2), 179–194.

Schulze, W. S., M. H. Lubatkin and R. N. Dino (2003b), 'Toward a theory of agency and altruism in family firms', *Journal of Business Venturing*, 18 (4), 473–490.

Shane, S. A. (2008), *The Illusions of Entrepreneurship: The Costly Myths that Entrepreneurs, Investors, and Policy Makers Live By*, New Haven, CT: Yale University Press.

Sharma, P. (2008), 'Commentary: familiness: capital stocks and flows between family and business', *Entrepreneurship: Theory and Practice*, 32 (6), 971–977.

Sharma, P. and P. G. Irving (2005), 'Four bases of family business successor commitment: antecedents and consequences', *Entrepreneurship: Theory and Practice*, 29 (1), 13–33.

Sharma, P., J. J. Chrisman and J. H. Chua (2003), 'Predictors of satisfaction with the succession process in family firms', *Journal of Business Venturing*, 18 (5), 667–687.

Sirmon, D. G. and M. A. Hitt (2003), 'Managing resources: linking unique resources, management, and wealth creation in family firms', *Entrepreneurship: Theory and Practice*, 27 (4), 339–358.

Skinner, C., N. Stuttard, G. Beissel-Durrant and J. Jenkins (2002), 'The measurement of low pay in the UK Labour Force Survey', *Oxford Bulletin of Economics and Statistics*, 64, 653–676.

Steier, L. (2001), 'Family firms, plural forms of governance, and the evolving role of trust', *Family Business Review*, 14 (4), 353–368.

Steier, L. (2003), 'Variants of agency contracts in family-financed ventures as a continuum of familial altruistic and market rationalities', *Journal of Business Venturing*, 18 (5), 597–618.

Sundaramurthy, C. (2008), 'Sustaining trust within family businesses', *Family Business Review*, 21 (1), 89–102.

Thorner, D. (1966), 'Chayanov's concept of peasant economy', in D. Thorner, B. Kerblay and R. E. F. Smith (eds), *A.V. Chayanov on the Theory of Peasant Economy*, Homewood, IL: Richard D. Irwin.

Van den Berghe, L. A. A. and S. Carchon (2003), 'Agency relations within the family business system: an exploratory approach', *Corporate Governance: An International Review*, 11 (3), 171–179.

Welter, F. (2011), 'Contextualizing entrepreneurship: conceptual challenges and ways forward', *Entrepreneurship: Theory and Practice*, 35 (1), 165–184.

Welter, F. and D. Smallbone (2006), 'Exploring the role of trust in entrepreneurial activity', *Entrepreneurship: Theory and Practice*, 30 (4), 465–475.

Wheelock, J. and Å. Mariussen (eds), (1997), *Households, Work and Economic Change: A Comparative Institutional Perspective*, Boston, MA: Kluwer.

Williamson, O. E. (1993), 'Calculativeness, trust, and economic organization', *Journal of Law and Economics*, 36 (1), 453–486.

Zahra, S. A., R. I. Yavuz and D. Ucbasaran (2006), 'How much do you trust me? The dark side of relational trust in new business creation in established companies', *Entrepreneurship: Theory and Practice*, 30 (4), 541–559.

7 Understanding entrepreneurial behaviors in family firms

Does the socioemotional wealth model explain differences?

Jonathan Bauweraerts and Olivier Colot

Introduction

Corporate entrepreneurship – i.e., the act of establishing new ventures or insti-gating innovation or renewal associated within an existing organization (Sharma & Chrisman, 2007) – has become a topic of great interest in the family business literature (e.g., Eddleston et al., 2012; Sciascia et al., 2013; Zahra, 2005). While several authors argue that family firms are supportive of corporate entrepreneur-ship (Aldrich & Cliff, 2003; Eddleston et al., 2008; Eddleston et al., 2012; Zahra, 2005), others underline that family businesses display specific features that undermine entrepreneurial activities (Allio, 2004; Gersick et al., 1997; Kelly et al., 2000; Miller et al., 2008). Indeed, corporate entrepreneurship can be stimulated by family members through their transgenerational business goals (Zahra, 2005), willingness to pass a sustainable company on to subsequent generations (Eddel-ston et al., 2008), or ability to respond to threat of imitability (Sirmon et al., 2008). Conversely, the involvement of entrenched family members in decision-making (Gómez-Mejía et al., 2001), the existence of a generational shadow (Davis & Harveston, 1999), paternalistic attitudes (Chirico et al., 2012), confining legacy (Kelly et al., 2000), and the fixation on successful past strategies (Upton et al., 2001) can mire the organization in traditions and conservatism so that entrepre-neurial activities are stifled.

These inconsistencies clearly illustrate that we are lacking understanding of the emergence of corporate entrepreneurship in the context of family firms (Nordqvist & Melin, 2010). An explanation for this could be that the lens of cor-porate entrepreneurship is not sufficiently applicable to family business research (Heck et al., 2008; Zachary et al., 2013). Indeed, corporate entrepreneurship uses the organization as unit of analysis when examining the emergence of entre-preneurial activities (Sharma & Chrisman, 2007). However, recent works indicate that a more complete understanding of the entrepreneurial phenomenon could be gained by shifting the focus from the family business to the family in business (Moores, 2009). In that sense, Discua Cruz et al. (2013, p. 21) propose and define the concept of intrafamily entrepreneurship as "entrepreneurship in the existing family businesses as well as new ventures". This concept is broader and captures the interwoven entrepreneurial activities of families in business (Discua Cruz et al., 2013).

In this chapter, we would argue that the socioemotional wealth (SEW) model (Gómez-Mejía et al., 2007) may explain the role of families in developing entre-preneurial activities so that our understanding of intrafamily entrepreneurship will be increased. Indeed, families in business may fulfill their socioemotional needs by launching new ventures that provide jobs to family members and enlarge the sphere of influence of the family (Gomez-Mejia, Cruz, et al., 2011). At the same time, business families are likely to avoid developing new activities through technological innovation or diversification due to the SEW losses induced by such entrepreneurial choices (Chrisman & Patel, 2012; Cruz & Justo, 2009; Gomez-Mejia et al., 2010). Accordingly, we suggest that the degree to which business families are concerned with the preservation of their SEW exerts an influence on the type of entrepreneurial activities adopted by families in business (Berrone et al., 2012).

Going a step further, this chapter also takes into account that SEW is a multidimensional construct. Indeed, Berrone et al. (2012) identified five dimensions to depict SEW: family control and influence over the company, identification of family members with the firm, binding social ties, emotional attachment of family members, and renewal of family bonds through dynastic succession (known by the acronym FIBER dimensions). Since family members may use different frames of reference according to their individual preferences (Berrone et al., 2012; Cennamo et al., 2012), we suggest that the various weights family principals place on each of the FIBER dimensions that composed SEW may explain the entrepreneurial activities of business families. In doing so, we will provide a first conceptual framework that considers the pursuit of different socioemotional needs as potential drivers or obstacles to intrafamily entrepreneurship.

This chapter makes several important contributions to the entrepreneurship literature in general and in the family business field in particular. First, by addressing the relationship between family intrapreneurship and the family goals and reference frame, we add to the research stream that examines the ability and the motives of business families to pursue entrepreneurial objectives (Discua Cruz et al., 2013). While the family business literature emphasizes the role of non-financial objectives in decision-making (e.g., Gómez-Mejía et al., 2007), it has been relatively silent about the influence of socioemotional needs on entrepreneurial activities (Berrone et al., 2012).

Second, we contribute to the family business literature by providing a more fine-grained analysis of intrafamily entrepreneurship. More specifically, we consider the heterogeneity among family entrepreneurs who can opt for different frames of reference in making entrepreneurial choices (Berrone et al., 2012). In line with Cennamo et al.'s (2012) theoretical paper, we argue that the various weights family principals place on FIBER dimensions affect decision-making, and more specifically the entrepreneurial choices of family entrepreneurs. As such, we endeavor to reconcile divergent opinions regarding the emergence of entrepreneurial behaviors in the context of family businesses.

Finally, by combining SEW and intrafamily entrepreneurship, we answer to the call for theory-based studies in this area (Berrone et al., 2012; Zachary et al., 2013). While prior research has investigated how entrepreneurship is affected by SEW aspects such as kinship ties (Aldrich & Cliff, 2003), the long-term nature of family firm's ownership (Zahra et al., 2004) or the desire to protect family wealth (Naldi et al., 2007), we strive to build a structured conceptual framework that integrates the importance dedicated to the construct of SEW and its dimensions in order to understand entrepreneurial activities of business families. By doing so, we provide new directions to guide future research in this field.

Theoretical background

From corporate entrepreneurship in family firms to intrafamily entrepreneurship

Over the past few years, numerous studies have investigated corporate entrepreneurship in family firms (e.g., Eddleston et al., 2012; Sciascia et al., 2013). This growing interest is not surprising as corporate entrepreneurship – i.e., the sum of a company's innovation, renewal, and venturing efforts (Sharma & Chrisman, 2007; Zahra, 1995) – contributes to increase profitability, obtain future incomes, successfully enter new markets, or configure resources efficiently in order to develop a competitive advantage (Kuratko et al., 2005). Indeed, product innovation, process innovation through research and development, the revitalization of business activities and the expansion of operations in existing and new markets are recognized to generate growth (Kuratko et al., 2005; Miller, 1983; Zahra, 1995, 1996).

Despite the importance of these entrepreneurial activities to the success and survival of family firms, they are not necessary inclined to engage in such operations (Kellermanns & Eddleston, 2006). Indeed, a large debate surrounds the firm-level entrepreneurial activities in the context of family firms. Whereas several scholars see family involvement as a driver of corporate entrepreneurship (Aldrich & Cliff, 2003; Eddleston et al., 2008; Zahra, 2005; Zahra et al., 2004), others claim that family businesses are stagnant, conservative, and resistant to change (Allio, 2004; Gersick et al., 1997; Miller et al., 2008). Indeed, some argue that the deep connections between family members and their transgenerational business goals stimulate the quest for growth (Eddleston et al., 2008), thereby resulting in a greater propensity to pursue risky projects (Zahra, 2005). In contrast, the willingness of family members to retain control over the organization can have different consequences such as the presence of a generational shadow (Davis & Harveston, 1999), the absence of an effective board of directors that brings new ideas (Miller & Le Breton-Miller, 2006), the entrenchment of ineffective family managers (Gomez-Mejia et al., 2001), and the lack of an adequate human capital (Hayton & Kelley, 2006), which results in stagnation and conservatism undermining corporate entrepreneurship (Allio, 2004; Miller et al., 2008).

The ambiguity of these results reveals that we are lacking understanding of the entrepreneurial phenomenon in the context of family firms. An explanation for this could be that most prior studies take the business as an unquestioned unit of analysis whereas many families often have a portfolio of interconnected businesses (Carney & Gedajlovic, 2002) and create teams of family members to launch new family businesses (Iacobucci & Rosa, 2010). Accordingly, entrepreneurship in family firms could be better understood by considering the family in business as scope of analysis rather than the continuity of only one family business (Moores, 2009). Consistent with that view, Discua Cruz et al. (2013, p. 21) propose the concept of intrafamily entrepreneurship which refers to "entrepreneurship in the existing family businesses as well as new ventures". Thus, this concept includes all entrepreneurial activities of families in business.

To deepen our knowledge of intrafamily entrepreneurship, the subsequent sections of this chapter will endeavor to understand how the pursuit of non-economic goals exerts an influence on the type of entrepreneurial activities pursued by business families. Indeed, family members have multiple objectives beyond financial ones (Zellweger et al., 2013). One of these is the preservation of their socioemotional endowment (Gómez-Mejía et al., 2007), which in the context of families in business may be the critical point of reference that shapes decision-making (Berrone et al., 2010; Gómez-Mejía et al., 2007, 2010). Expanding on this logic, we shall argue that SEW preservation will affect the way in which intrafamily entrepreneurship manifests in business families.

Socioemotional wealth and intrafamily entrepreneuship

In the literature, it is recognized that family firms present a unique setting which makes them different from other organizations (Gomez-Mejia, Cruz et al., 2011). In order to understand these differences, Gomez-Mejia et al. (2007) developed the socioemotional wealth (SEW) model which is an extension of the behavioral agency theory previously formulated by Wiseman and Gomez-Mejia (1998), and Gomez-Mejia et al. (2000). According to this theory, choices are made depending on the reference point of the organization's dominant principals. Decisions are taken by the principals in order to preserve their accumulated endowment in the business. In the family firm's context, it means that family principals will emphasize preserving SEW, i.e., the stock of affect-related value derived from the controlling position of a family in a particular firm (Berrone et al., 2012). Under that perspective, family principals analyze the influence of actions on their socioemotional endowment so that decisions are made to protect family principals from SEW losses (Gómez-Mejía et al., 2007).

Whereas the SEW model has been used to analyze strategic choices in family firms (e.g., Berrone et al., 2010; Chrisman & Patel, 2012; Gómez-Mejía et al., 2007), we argue that its scope could be extended to families in business. Indeed, a business family could be seen as a group of family principals who possess multiple companies from which they derive affective benefits from their controlling position. As such, it could be argued that business families are more likely to avoid SEW losses in all family businesses to preserve their accumulated SEW endowment. By using SEW as a frame of reference, families in business may thus opt for entrepreneurial choices that maximize their socioemotional utility (Berrone et al., 2012). In the following, we investigate the role of SEW preservation in explaining differences of entrepreneurial activities adopted by business families, thereby increasing our understanding of intrafamily entrepreneurship.

According to Gomez-Mejia, Cruz et al. (2011, p. 685), new venture creation may be a suitable strategy for families in business as "it helps the family to achieve the non-economic goals of providing jobs to an expanded family cadre and ensures continued family control by accommodating each new generation". Indeed, business families may want to provide jobs to as many family members as possible by launching a new venture or division within the firm (Miller et al., 2003) or by building portfolios of related business with family members filling key positions (Cruz et al., 2011). Additionally, SEW also encompasses other aspects that may contribute to venture creation. For instance, the strong concern of family members for transgenerational sustainability facilitates the development of a long-term orientation which is recognized to stimulate the exploitation of new opportunities (Lumpkin et al., 2010; Zahra et al., 2004). The importance dedicated to binding social ties allow family in business to count on a significant social capital that is likely to enhance corporate venturing (Anderson et al., 2005; Arrègle et al., 2007; Zahra, 2010). Other business families may emphasize the protection of the family reputation (Dyer & Whetten, 2006). In order to achieve this non-economic goal, they may be tempted to engage in new ventures that contribute to build up the reputation of the business and the family (Miller & Le Breton-Miller, 2006).

However, SEW preservation may restrict new ventures in family firms to core-related activities (Cruz et al., 2011). Indeed, SEW preservation can place a constraint on product and technological innovation (Gomez-Mejia, Hoskisson et al., 2011; Chrisman & Patel, 2012). In other words, it means that business families are likely to put their firms at risk by depriving them of an entrepreneurial posture that stimulates innovation and growth (Ahuja et al., 2008). Indeed, business families' aversion toward control losses may impede the creation and commercialization of disruptive innovations (De Massis et al., 2013) because they require ceding shares to external parties such as venture capitalist and institutional investors (Gomez-Mejia, Cruz et al., 2011). This strong concern about potential control losses may also complicate collaborative relationships with external partners when open innovation implies a restriction to the firm's control over the product's technological trajectory (Almirall & Casadesus-Masanell, 2010).

Moreover, due to the inherent complexity of innovation management, business families are likely to need managerial talent and expertise from outside the pool of family members in order to exploit new opportunities (De Massis et al., 2013). Again, the reluctance of family principals to relinquish control may prevent business families from hiring external managers with the required skills and experience (Carney, 2005). In sum, as the development of groundbreaking innovation may significantly modify how family firms are organized, and this is likely to threaten business families' traditional sphere of influence (Gomez-Mejia et al., 2010), it can be argued that families in business are more inclined to pursue incremental innovation with lower economic importance (Block et al., 2013).

Furthermore, continuing the firm legacy and tradition may make change difficult to incorporate in business families (Casson, 1999). As family members often act as stewards of their inheritance, they are more inclined to conserve and enhance the family dynasty without implementing substantives changes (Casson, 1999). Indeed, family members derive value from passing on the value of the enterprising family tradition and nostalgia (Sharma & Manikutty, 2005). Accordingly, strategic renewal may be limited because it engenders higher levels of anxiety among family members who are reluctant to experiment and introduce new routines and modus operandi (Gomez-Mejia, Hoskisson et al., 2011).

These elements clearly illustrate that the frame of reference used by business families is likely to affect the entrepreneurial posture of their family businesses. While creating new ventures could be driven by the pursuit of SEW objectives, it also appears that SEW preservation is likely to affect innovation and strategic renewal. Accordingly, it seems that SEW exerts an influence on the way in which intrafamily entrepreneurship would manifest. However, differences can be expected within business families as they may use different frames of reference in decision-making (Cennamo et al., 2012). To take into account the heterogeneity of business families, we propose that differences in the logic behind entrepreneurial activities can be attributed to the existence of different frames of reference among dominant family principals. Based on that, the subsequent sections of this chapter try to understand how the various weights that families place on each of the dimensions of SEW will affect the emergence of different types of intrafamily entrepreneurship.

FIBER dimensions and intrafamily entrepreneurship

Prior research has shown that the heterogeneity in family principals' reference frames may affect decision-making (Berrone et al., 2012; Cennamo et al., 2012). Based on that, we expect differences in entrepreneurial activities to be explained by the various weights business families place on each of the FIBER dimensions that composed SEW. Berrone et al. (2012) suggest that the construct of SEW is a set of dimensions which encompasses family control and influence, identification of family members with the firm, binding social ties, emotional attachment of family members, and renewal of family bonds to firm through dynastic succession. These dimensions have different weights according to the preferences of family principals (Berrone et al., 2012; Cennamo et al., 2012). For instance, some family principals may display greater concern for maintaining control over the organization whereas others may place a greater value on binding social ties. Based on that, we argue that using the individual dimension of SEW as reference point will offer a more fine-grained analysis of the emergence of different types of entrepreneurial activities in business families. Figure 7.1 provides an overview of our conceptual model.

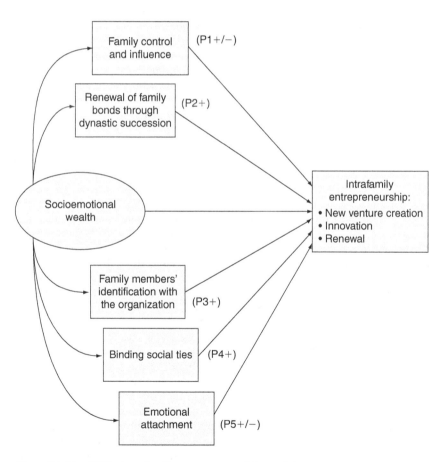

Figure 7.1 The SEW – intrafamily entrepreneurship model.

Family control and influence and intrafamily entrepreneurship

The first dimension is related to family control and influence. Indeed, a specific feature of business families is that family members exert control over strategic decisions (Chrisman et al., 2011; Chua et al., 1999; Klein et al., 2005). Control can be exerted directly through the position of CEO or chairman of the board, or indirectly through the appointment of top management team members in multiple family businesses. According to Berrone et al. (2012), the ability to exercise authority vested in family members finds its origins in a strong ownership position, an ascribed status, or personal charisma. Moreover, business families are used to exerting formal and informal control through the multiple roles they play in their companies (Carney, 2005; Mustakallio et al., 2002). In any case, the desire to perpetuate family control and influence is an integral dimension of SEW (Zellweger et al., 2013). It means that business families prefer to benefit from a continued direct or indirect control over their companies regardless of financial considerations (Gómez-Mejía et al., 2007).

By focusing on this reference point, business families may see entrepreneurship as a way to provide jobs to their extended family through venture creation (Gomez-Mejia, Cruz et al., 2011). However, the greater value placed on maintaining family influence reduces the propensity of business families to engage in diversification and innovation strategies (Chrisman & Patel, 2012; Gomez-Mejia et al., 2010). Indeed, family principals are less inclined to add new products to the firm's offerings and enter new markets since such entrepreneurial activities create new routines and procedures that are likely to threaten family influence (Gomez-Mejia et al., 2010). Accordingly, it could be argued that business families are more prone to launch new ventures in existing markets and core-related activities.

Furthermore, the reluctance of business families to relinquish control is more likely to constrain innovation (Gomez-Mejia, Cruz et al., 2011). While product and process innovation often induce greater complexity and specialization, this strong concern for family control can prevent the organization from drawing on expertize from outside the pool of family members (Carney, 2005). Indeed, a direct consequence of keeping decision-making in the hands of the family is that managers are hired within the owning family even if they tend to lack quality and experience (Carney, 2005), thus limiting the availability of skilled employees which are needed to develop innovative processes and products (Carney et al., 2015). Moreover, financing innovation often means ceding shares to external parties, such as venture capitalists or institutional investors (Astrachan & McConaughy, 2001; Zahra, 1996). Since issuing new stocks means that family principals can less closely monitor how the firm is managed, they are less likely to use such external funding (Mishra & McConaughy, 1999), thereby inducing lower levels of innovation (Chrisman & Patel, 2012; Gomez-Mejia, Hoskisson et al., 2011).

Besides, the less participative style of management resulting from the inclination of business families to keep control in the hands of the family prevents nonfamily employees from bringing new ideas and perspectives to the management team (Spinelli & Hunt, 2000). Hence, families in business adopting control preservation as frame of reference are less likely to incorporate nonfamily employees' ideas and perspectives in their strategic choices. This situation can be detrimental to the innovative process and strategic renewal since it is often organizational members acting outside the chain of command which generate these entrepreneurial activities (Burgelman, 1983). Indeed, autonomous individuals operating outside their usual works and routines represent an important source of creativity and initiative that positively contributes to entrepreneurial innovation and renewal (Burgelman & Sayles, 1986). Therefore, the reluctance of family principals to give up control is likely to deprive business families of skilled and autonomous human resources which are needed to pursue innovative opportunities (Green et al., 1999) and to revitalize the firm operations (Burgelman, 1983; Lumpkin et al., 2009).

All the above-mentioned arguments seem to indicate that business families who adopt the "family control and influence" dimensions of SEW will be more inclined to create new ventures in existing markets by developing core-related activities that do not require high levels of innovation and strategic renewal. Based on that, we propose:

> *Proposition 1: Business families that adopt the "family control and influence" dimension of SEW as the main frame of reference are more likely to engage in intrafamily entrepreneurship through new venture creation and low levels of strategic renewal and innovation.*

Family dynasty and intrafamily entrepreneurship

Another important point of reference is the willingness of family principals to pass a sustainable company on to subsequent generations (Berrone et al., 2012). Indeed, from the perspective of family owners, the firm is more than an asset and symbolizes the family's heritage and tradition (Casson, 1999). Consequently, transgenerational sustainability is viewed as an integral dimension of SEW (Berrone et al., 2012; Zellweger & Astrachan, 2008; Zellweger et al., 2012). That deep sense given to the organization has important implications for the time horizons in the decision-making process (Berrone et al., 2012). Indeed, family members consider the firm as a long-term family investment which has to be passed through next generations (e.g., Berrone et al., 2010; Kets de Vries, 1993; Miller & Le Breton-Miller, 2005; Miller et al., 2008; Sirmon & Hitt, 2003; Zellweger et al., 2012). As such, the renewal of family bonds through dynastic succession creates a generational investment strategy that generates patient capital (Sirmon & Hitt, 2003).

Based on these elements, it can be argued that business families in which a high value is placed on the perpetuation of the family dynasty are more likely to display a long-term orientation, i.e., a tendency to prioritize the long-range implications and impact of decisions and actions that come to fruition after an extended time period (Le Breton-Miller & Miller, 2006; Lumpkin et al., 2010). Accordingly, family members can put aside the pursuit of short-term goals in order to concentrate their efforts on the long-term well-being of their firms (Eddleston et al., 2012). Developing such a long-term orientation is often viewed as a driver of entrepreneurship (Eddleston et al., 2012; Lumpkin et al., 2010; Le Breton-Miller & Miller, 2011; Zahra et al., 2004). Indeed, adopting a long-term orientation allows families in business to exploit entrepreneurial opportunities which are rejected by their short-term oriented competitors (Zellweger, 2007). With the aim of pursuing long-term objectives that enhance firm survival, business families may also push the development of multiple new ventures in different projects as adopting such a strategy reduces risk in the product portfolios for next generations (Miller & Le Breton-Miller, 2005). Accordingly, launching new ventures could represent a suitable strategy for business families guided by dynastic succession.

Moreover, this strong concern for longevity is recognized to enhance R&D, the development of new product offerings, and the pursuit of new markets (Miller & Le Breton-Miller, 2005). In that sense, Lumpkin et al. (2010) suggest that the long-term orientation of family members fosters innovativeness and proactiveness in the marketplace. Families in business are also more inclined to commit the resources required for innovation and risk-taking (Zahra et al., 2004). The aim of transferring control of the business to the next generation of family members may also enhance strategic renewal. Indeed, the transgenerational family control intentions create an incentive to assiduously cope with new challenges in a way that ensures passing sustainable companies on to subsequent generations (Le Breton-Miller & Miller, 2006). As such, business families are more likely to be sensitive to strategic renewal because these types of entrepreneurial activities improve the firm's ability to overcome periods of turbulence and to face changing environments (Le Breton-Miller & Miller, 2011; Miller & Le Breton-Miller; 2005). Consequently, business families may consider strategic renewal as an imperative to ensure the firm's survival, and thus the perpetuation of the family dynasty. Based on these arguments, we suggest:

Proposition 2: Business families that adopt the "renewal of family bonds to the firm through dynastic succession" dimension of SEW as the main frame of reference are more likely to engage in intrafamily entrepreneurship through new venture creation, innovation, and renewal.

Identification of family members and intrafamily entrepreneurship

The third dimension refers to the close identification of family members with the organization. The intertwining of family and business is contended to create a unique identity within family firms (Berrone et al., 2010; Dyer & Whetten, 2006; Kepner, 1983; Sundaramurthy & Kreiner, 2008; Tagiuri & Davis, 1996). Indeed, family owner social status is strongly tied to organizational identity with the firm carrying the family's name (Tagiuri & Davis, 1996). Accordingly, family members avoid any threat to the firm's reputation since it can create a hazard to the individuals and the existence of the family itself (Dyer & Whetten, 2006). The perpetuation of family emblems is thus at the core of what a family firm identity represents (Littunen, 2003).

When identification acts as the main frame of reference for decision-making, business families are more likely to pursue business opportunities which do not jeopardize their long-standing image (Lumpkin & Brigham, 2011). This strong concern for the family image may make families in business care about the long-term prospects of their companies (Miller et al., 2008). Accordingly, they are more likely to act as stewards by privileging the firm's continuity (Miller & Le Breton-Miller, 2005) through the adoption of innovative and proactive behaviors with calculated risks (Corbetta & Salvato, 2004). As such, business families may be more inclined to build up the reputation of their businesses via long-term investments in innovation, R&D, new ventures, quality, and branding (Miller & Le Breton-Miller, 2006). By doing so, they allow family heirs to inherit very strong brands (Miller & Le Breton-Miller, 2005) while also enhancing the competitive profile of the firm (Zahra, 1996).

In addition to the importance dedicated to the firm's image, the strong identification of family members with the organization may foster the family-to-firm unity, i.e., "the bond a family has with the firm, embodying a sense of oneness and integration among family members and the firm" (Eddleston et al., 2012, p. 353). Family-to-firm unity is recognized to enhance the effectiveness of a participative governance structure (Steier, 2001) in such a way that the board of directors can encourage managers to revitalize firm activities (Zahra, 1996), thus preventing family firms from becoming rigid and stagnant due to the absence of multiple voices at the table (Sirmon et al., 2008). Indeed, the existence of heterogeneous points of view in the decision-making process fosters renewal and innovation (Talke et al., 2011). Furthermore, the sense of oneness between family members and the firm intensify their belief in the organization, thereby encouraging them to invest in innovative projects with longer term payoffs (Eddleston et al., 2012).

The strong identification of family members can also be reflected by a legacy corporate culture that makes recruitment more selective to facilitate the transfer of family values to employees (Arrègle et al., 2007). As such, families in business are more likely to treat nonfamily employees as members of their family, to indoctrinate them with family values and to invest in training in order to sustain their firms for the long run (Le Breton-Miller & Miller, 2011). By so doing, family principals benefit from loyal and knowledgeable employees who are capable of learning and renewal (Miller & Le Breton-Miller, 2005). All these arguments seem to indicate that the strong identification of family members with their firms enhances the emergence of intrafamily entrepreneurship in various forms. Therefore, we suggest:

Proposition 3: Business families that adopt the "identification of family members" dimension of SEW as the main frame of reference are more likely to engage in intrafamily entrepreneurship through new venture creation, innovation, and renewal.

Binding social ties and intrafamily entrepreneurship

This fourth dimension refers to family firms' ability to build social relationships with internal and external stakeholders (Berrone et al., 2012). A relevant framework to analyze the link between these relational factors and entrepreneurship is social capital (Gedajlovic et al., 2013). Indeed, it is commonly accepted that the social environment interplays with individuals and organizations to foster entrepreneurial activities (e.g., Corbett, 2007; Gedajlovic et al., 2013).

Social capital is an intangible resource that plays an important role in building mutual relationships between stakeholders (Adler & Kwon, 2002; Arrègle et al., 2007). Nahapiet and Ghoshal (1998, p. 243) define social capital as the "sum of actual and potential resources embedded within, available through, and derived from the network of relationships possessed by individuals or social units". In business families, social capital has two components: family and organizational social capital (Arrègle et al., 2007; Salvato & Melin, 2008; Zahra, 2010). Family social capital refers to the relationships and interactions among family members while organizational social capital is related to family firms' interactions, communications, and relationships with diverse external stakeholders (Zahra, 2010). In accordance with other scholars (Anderson et al., 2005; Arrègle et al., 2007; Rothaermel, 2001; Zahra, 2010), we argue that placing a greater value on developing social ties may stimulate entrepreneurial activities.

Although family social capital can be seen as a mean to enhance family members' satisfaction with family life (Bubolz, 2001), it is also considered a potential source of competitive advantage for family firms (Arrègle et al., 2007; Carney, 2005; Sirmon & Hitt, 2003). Arrègle et al. (2007) argue that family social capital contributes to the economic development of the firm. In line with this argument, interactions and relationships with family members have been shown to encourage and support entrepreneurship (Anderson et al., 2005). Indeed, family members often provide the needed capital and other resources such as access to markets, sources of supply, technology, and even new ideas (Sirmon & Hitt, 2003). Therefore, family members represent an important resource that supports the venture creation process (Greve & Salaff, 2003) and the entrepreneurial life of the firm through innovation and renewal (Anderson et al., 2005). Based on these elements, family social capital may be considered a driver of entrepreneurial activities within business families (Aldrich & Cliff, 2003; Chang et al., 2009).

Organizational social capital increases the availability of resources such as information, technology, knowledge, financial capital, distribution networks, and relationships with critical constituencies (Arrègle et al., 2007). This relational capital is a critical factor that fosters innovation (Rothaermel, 2001). In business families, the development of organizational social capital is enhanced by family members' external interactions (Arrègle et al., 2007) which are often intense and numerous (Yeung & Soh, 2000). Used in an appropriable way, organizational social capital may stimulate entrepreneurial initiatives in business families. Indeed, higher levels of organizational capital help family firms connect with other companies and acquire fresh knowledge that encourages innovation (Tsai & Ghoshal, 1998). In that sense, Zahra (2010) found that family firms can harvest their organizational social capital stock in order to invest in new ventures and to build profitable business relationships and alliances. Moreover, by developing closed ties with stakeholders, families in business can foster renewal as well as product and process innovation through the exchange of new ideas (Shipton et al., 2006). These arguments lead us to suggest:

Proposition 4: Business families that adopt the "binding social ties" dimension of SEW as the main frame of reference are more likely to engage in intrafamily entrepreneurship through new venture creation, innovation, and renewal.

Emotional attachment and intrafamily entrepreneurship

The last dimension refers to the role of emotions within business families. It is recognized that the intermingling of emotional factors arising from family involvement and business factors constitutes a distinctive attribute of family businesses (Tagiuri & Davis, 1996; Eddleston & Kellermanns, 2007). Indeed, in family firms, emotions can be attributed to both family (Carlock & Ward, 2001; Kepner, 1983) and business (Astrachan & Jaskiewicz, 2008; Zellweger & Astrachan, 2008) systems. Despite the relevance of emotions for SEW, little research has investigated how they influence the functioning of the family and the firm (Berrone et al., 2012). However, it is recognized that the wide range of emotions that family members experience influences the decision-making process (Baron, 2008), so that strategic decisions related to entrepreneurship may be affected (Labaki et al., 2013; Morris et al., 2010; Stanley, 2010).

According to Berrone et al. (2012), the emotional attachment of family principals to their firms enhances their sense of legacy. Indeed, the loss of their companies can be seen as a highly emotional event by family owners (Sharma & Manikutty, 2005). Consequently, transgenerational sustainability is often considered a central objective in families in business (Zellweger & Astrachan, 2008) and family principals view the company as a long-term family investment to be bequeathed to their heirs (Berrone et al., 2010). As such, business families provide patient capital (Sirmon & Hitt, 2003) and develop a long-term orientation (Lumpkin & Brigham, 2011) whose combination is likely to foster entrepreneurial activities (Lumpkin et al., 2010). Besides, other emotional aspects may foster entrepreneurship in business families. For instance, the joy at achieving the firm's goal and family harmony can enhance the development of stewardship behaviors that are recognized to drive entrepreneurship (Corbetta & Salvato, 2004; Eddleston et al., 2012). Trustworthiness arising from the strong kinship ties between family members encourages them to share sensitive and innovative ideas, thus fostering renewal and venture creation (Zahra et al., 2004).

However, positive emotions can also engender a lower inclination toward entrepreneurial risk-taking since individuals who are in a positive mood are less inclined to engage in risky projects (Isen et al., 1988). In that sense, Stanley (2010) suggests that family firms will display lower levels of risk-taking when they positively experience the start-up process. Stanley (2010) goes a step further by arguing that this early emotional experience can shape the future strategic posture of family firms. Indeed, historical events in the organization often explain why future strategic choices are made (Sydow et al., 2009). In line with this argument, it has been shown that family firms are more likely to become path-dependent than nonfamily firms (Priem & Cycyota, 2001). Accordingly, due to the transference of early emotional experiences to other family members who share similar experiences, knowledge, and perspectives, family firms may keep on avoiding entrepreneurial activities that induce greater levels of risk-taking and ruptures with past strategies (Stanley, 2010). As a result, positive emotions may have the potential to make business families less inclined to engage in corporate entrepreneurship through new venture creation, innovation, and renewal.

Families in business also experience negative emotions related to their affective experiences at the ownership level. For instance, family members may be confronted with negative emotions resulting from relationship conflicts (Davis & Harveston, 1999; Ling & Kellermanns, 2010) which are the most prominent form of family conflicts (Kellermanns & Eddleston, 2004). This type of conflict includes affective components such as annoyance, frustration, and irritation (Jehn & Mannix, 2001) and results in negative emotions like anger, resentment, and worry (Johnson & Ford, 2000). These negative emotions induce suspicion and resentment so that mutual understanding among individuals and goodwill decrease (Jehn, 1997). This situation can lead to a lack of consensus around organizational goals, thus obstructing collaborative exchange of different opinions (Michie et al., 2006). Hence, family firms are deprived of constructive debates around innovation and renewal (Talke et al., 2011) because criticism and differences in viewpoints are seen as personal attacks (Jehn, 1995) that impede the incorporation of fresh ideas (Gladstein, 1984). In this context, family managers are more likely to mire in narrow-thinking (Miller, 1993) and to encounter familiarity traps (Ahuja and Lampert, 2001), so that path-dependency is fostered (Priem & Cycyota, 2001). Therefore, entrepreneurial initiatives are stifled since family members rely on past strategies to cope with changes in the marketplace rather than identifying and exploiting new opportunities (Zahra, 2005).

Moreover, the hybrid identities of family and firm can cause identity clashes and role conflicts (Tompkins, 2010). Indeed, family members deal with competing identities, so that they constantly play different roles. This multiplicity of roles can induce emotional messiness, i.e., the simultaneous occurrence of negative and positive emotions in family firms, which can lead to positive and negative outcomes depending on how emotions are handled by family members (Brundin & Sharma, 2012). Brundin and Sharma (2012) suggest that, when family members have low levels of emotional intelligence in facing a messy situation, they are more likely to cause ruptures in family harmony, thereby depriving family firms of constructive debates around the entrepreneurial posture of the firm (Talke et al., 2011).

Based on these examples, we can see that emotions take several forms and may have different effects depending on the individuals who experienced them. Accordingly, it is impossible to posit a universal hypothesis regarding the influence of "emotional attachment" as main frame of reference on intrafamily entrepreneurship. This ambiguity leads us to suggest the following proposition which is deliberately more general.

Proposition 5: Adopting the "emotional attachment" dimension of SEW as the main frame of reference will positively or negatively affect the propensity of business families to engage in intrafamily entrepreneurship through new venture creation, innovation, and renewal.

Discussion and conclusion

Implications for research

In this chapter, we argue that the extent to which the controlling party values socioemotional needs explain why business families engage in different types of intrafamily entrepreneurship. Our research contributes to the entrepreneurship literature by taking into account the role of families in business and their underlying non-economic motives for understanding how entrepreneurial behaviors are shaped, an analytical angle largely unheeded so far in the literature.

By applying this way of thinking to the context of business families, our study suggests that, due to the preservation of the family's socioemotional wealth, family intrapreneurship would manifest in various ways. Recent studies are in line with our view (Chrisman & Patel, 2012; Gómez-Mejía et al., 2007; Gomez-Mejia et al., 2010; Gomez-Mejia, Cruz et al., 2011), suggesting that, due to SEW concerns, family firms are drastically different from other types of organizations when it comes to strategic issues. By meeting the need to build causal models (Sharma, 2004), our study contributes to the growing body of the literature that endeavors to understand entrepreneurship in family firms (Casillas & Moreno, 2010; Eddleston et al., 2012; Lumpkin et al., 2010; Sciascia et al., 2013). Moreover, we go beyond the dichotomization between family and nonfamily firms to investigate how the different reference frames of business families may influence entrepreneurial activities. Indeed, we suggest that intrafamily entrepreneurship may take different forms according to the dimension of SEW which is prioritized by business families. By considering the multidimensionality of SEW and the heterogeneity of family principals, we add to the family business literature which has ignored this issue for a long time (Berrone et al., 2012; Cennamo et al., 2012).

By investigating the effect of family principal's reference frame in shaping the entrepreneurial posture of business families, our study also emphasizes the role of family in entrepreneurial activities, thereby contributing to the Family Entrepreneurship literature (Heck et al., 2008). By extending the scope of SEW to families in business, we predict that the importance dedicated to family objectives will impact the propensity of business families to engage in intrafamily entrepreneurship. By so doing, this conceptual framework increases our understandings of Family Entrepreneurship (Zachary et al., 2013).

Implications for practice

Our study has an important practical implication for family owner-managers. With our competitive landscape becoming increasingly dynamic and uncertain (Hamel, 2000), a constant flow of entrepreneurial initiative is more than ever needed to face changes in the marketplace. In that sense, several scholars argue that family firms with a greater inclination toward entrepreneurship are more likely to create value in the long term (Casillas & Moreno, 2010; Lumpkin et al., 2010; Rauch et al., 2009) while family businesses characterized by conservatism and tradition would display lower levels of short- and long-term performance (Lumpkin et al., 2010). In this chapter, we suggest that the extent to which business families engage in intrafamily entrepreneurship depends on the importance they dedicate to SEW preservation. In particular, we suggest that families in business may emphasize certain socioemotional needs that are likely to affect intrafamily entrepreneurship in different ways. Whereas pursuing non-economic goals such as reputation building, transgenerational objectives, binding social-ties may foster entrepreneurial activities, greater concerns for maintaining family power and perpetuating traditions are likely to mire family businesses in conservatism and traditions. Therefore, the identification of the dominant SEW dimension(s) is an important point since the preservation of certain non-economic objectives can compromise the development of entrepreneurial behaviors, thereby impeding growth (Rauch et al., 2009). Although family members can maximize their immediate non-economic utility by preserving diverse socioemotional needs, they should be aware of their negative potential outcomes on the future of the company. Accordingly, it might be interesting to involve parties from outside the family in decision-making since they should bring rational voices that could make family principals sensitive to the detrimental effects of preserving certain socioemotional aspects.

Directions for future research and limitations

Our study offers several opportunities for researchers. One straightforward direction that could be followed is the empirical validation of our propositions. This represents a real challenge for scholars since the construct of SEW has not been empirically tested in a sufficient way (Berrone et al., 2012; Gomez-Mejia, Cruz et al., 2011). Although it is often argued that SEW is enhanced when family ownership increases (Berrone et al., 2010; Gómez-Mejía et al., 2007; Gomez-Mejia et al., 2010), Berrone et al. (2012) claim that this reasoning is reductionist since family ownership is unable to capture the entire spectrum of SEW. Recently, some scholars use four questions from the Strategic Orientations of Small and Medium-Sized Enterprises (STRATOS) questionnaire to measure SEW but they admit that more refinements are needed to propose a scale that integrates the complexity of SEW (Schepers et al., 2014; Vandekerkhof et al., 2015).

Furthermore, business families are heterogeneous entities. Therefore, future research should address how FIBER dimensions account for business families' heterogeneity, and how they affect decision-making in the definition of their entrepreneurial posture. By focusing on the individual dimensions of SEW to consider the different reference frames of business families, our study follows this direction but much remains to be done. For example, we have investigated the individual effect of each SEW dimension on the inclination of business families to engage in different types of intrafamily entrepreneurship. However, future research should determine whether SEW dimensions have an additive, conjunctive or disjunctive effect (Cennamo et al., 2012). Indeed, some family principals' socioemotional needs may overlap and lead to tradeoffs, thus impacting the decision-making process (Berrone et al., 2012). Accordingly, it would be of great interest to investigate the interactive effects of multiple FIBER dimensions on intrafamily entrepreneurship as the fact remains that each of these dimensions are fundamentally related to SEW as a second-order outcome (Berrone et al., 2012). For example, we could imagine that the interaction between dynastic goals and the identification of family members with the firm creates a favorable setting for entrepreneurial activities as both of these dimensions engender a long-term orientation that sustains entrepreneurial initiatives (Lumpkin et al., 2010).

However, business families can use antinomic reference frames. Indeed, business families are made up of various types of family principals whose SEW objectives can be different. For instance, a family member can privilege maintaining family control whereas another is more inclined to involve external stakeholders in decision-making. This could lead to intra-family conflicts that are recognized to cause disruptive effects on entrepreneurship (Kellermanns & Eddleston, 2004; Sciascia et al., 2013). Accordingly, future research should investigate which combinations of FIBER dimensions enhance and impede the development of intra-family entrepreneurship.

In this chapter, it is assumed that family principals and corporate entrepreneurs are the same person. This is more likely to be the case in the earlier stage of business families where the owner/founder is often the corporate entrepreneur. However, when business families grow, entrepreneurial initiatives may be taken by non-family members that do not necessarily possess the same SEW motivations as the family in business. While some of them can develop feelings of psychological ownership that make them become one with the business families and their SEW objectives (Pierce et al., 2001), others are less inclined to develop such feelings owing to their lack of power in the business families (Liu et al., 2012). As such, some non-family corporate entrepreneurs will share the SEW motivations of family principals and the others not. Therefore, it would be interesting to investigate how different types of nonfamily corporate entrepreneurs interact with family members to orientate the entrepreneurial activities of business families.

Another topic of interest would be to investigate the mechanisms through which SEW and its dimensions influence the process of intrafamily entrepreneurship, yet remains widely unstudied in family business research. Even though this chapter points out the importance of SEW and its dimensions on the emergence of different types of activities encompassed in the concept of intrafamily entrepreneurship (venture creation, innovation, and renewal), it does not focus on the process through which these activities emerge. Accordingly, it would be interesting to analyze how the pursuit of SEW objectives by business families affects the process of intrafamily entrepreneurship from opportunity recognition to opportunity exploitation.

Besides, another point that could be relevant to analyze is the existence of different contingency factors that are likely to affect the salience of SEW and its dimensions. Consistent with that view, it is argued that the importance given to SEW preservation and its dimensions evolve over time (Berrone et al., 2012). For instance, maintaining family control is more likely to represent a key reference point for family principals from first generation (Gómez-Mejía et al., 2007) while greater attention may be dedicated to the preservation of the family image by later generation family principals (Gomez-Mejia et al., 2003). It might also be relevant to analyze how environmental characteristics affect the entrepreneurial posture of business families through its influence on SEW. For instance, as environmental hostility creates a context in which only entrepreneurial firms flourish (Miller and Friesen, 1978), business families may be tempted to proactively engage in entrepreneurial activities because, without doing that, the future of their businesses and thus the socioemotional endowment of family members is threatened. Thus, it could be interesting to see which entrepreneurial strategies business families will pursue to meet their SEW objectives and ensure the future of their companies. Therefore, future research should address how SEW and its dimensions evolve over time and in different contexts, and how the evolution in reference frames affects the decision to pursue entrepreneurial activities.

To conclude, our study moves a step forward to understand how entrepreneurial activities take place in the context of family businesses. However, we can only capture a part of the relationship between SEW and intrafamily entrepreneurship. Although we theorized about the potential manifestation of several entrepreneurial activities that are encompassed in the concept of intrafamily entrepreneurship, we did not integrate all the components of intrafamily entrepreneurship. For instance, when analyzing venture creation, we did not differentiate between internal and external corporate venturing. This distinction should be an interesting topic for future research. Indeed, business families with a strong concern for preserving transgenerational family control could be more likely to choose for internal corporate venturing while family firms in which binding social ties represent the main reference point could opt for both internal and external corporate venturing. This research question is left for future developments.

Acknowledgments

We would like to thank Cristina Bettinelli and Salvatore Sciascia for their insightful comments and suggestions during the fifth E-LAB International Symposium on Family Entrepreneurship: A New Field of Research in June 2013.

References

Adler, P. S., & Kwon, S. W. (2002). Social capital: Prospects for a new concept. *Academy of Management Review*, 27(1), 17–40.

Ahuja, G., & Lampert, M. C. (2001). Entrepreneurship in the large corporation: A longitudinal study of how established firms create breakthrough inventions. *Strategic Management Journal*, 22(6–7), 521–543.

Ahuja, G., Lampert, C. M., & Tandon, V. (2008). Moving beyond Schumpeter: Management research on the determinants of technological innovation. *Academy of Management Annals*, 2(1), 1–98.

Aldrich, H. E., & Cliff, J. E. (2003). The pervasive effects of family on entrepreneurship: Toward a family embeddedness perspective. *Journal of Business Venturing*, 18(5), 507–525.

Allio, M. (2004). Family businesses: Their virtues, vices and strategic path. *Strategy and Leadership*, 32(4), 24–34.

Almirall, E., & Casadesus-Masanell, R. (2010). Open versus closed innovation: A model of discovery and divergence. *Academy of Management Review*, 35(1), 27–47.

Anderson, A. R., Jack, S. L., & Dodd, S. D. (2005). The role of family members in entrepreneurial networks: Beyond the boundaries of the family firm. *Family Business Review*, 18(2), 135–154.

Arrègle, J. L., Hitt, M. A., Sirmon, D. G., & Very, P. (2007). The development of organizational social capital: Attributes of family firms. *Journal of Management Studies*, 44(1), 73–95.

Astrachan, J. H., & Jaskiewicz, P. (2008). Emotional returns and emotional costs in privately held family businesses: Advancing traditional business valuation. *Family Business Review*, 21(2), 139–149.

Astrachan, J. H., & McConaughy, D. (2001). Venture capitalists and closely held IPOs: Lessons for family-controlled firms. *Family Business Review*, 14(4), 295–311.

Baron, R. A. (2008). The role of affect in the entrepreneurial process. *Academy of Management Review*, 33(2), 328–340.

Berrone, P., Cruz, C., & Gómez-Mejía, L.R. (2012). Socioemotional wealth in family firms: Theoretical dimensions, assessment approaches, and agenda for future research. *Family Business Review*, 25(3), 258–279.

Berrone, P., Cruz, C., Gomez-Mejia, L., & Larraza-Kintana, M. (2010). Socioemotional wealth and corporate responses to institutional pressures: Do family-controlled firms pollute less? *Administrative Science Quarterly*, 55(1), 82–113.

Block, J., Miller, D., Jaskiewicz, P., & Spiegel, F. (2013). Economic and technological importance of innovations in large family and founder firms an analysis of patent data. *Family Business Review*, 26(2), 180–199.

Brundin, E., & Sharma, P. (2012). Love, hate, and desire: The role of emotional messiness in the business family. In A. L. Carsrud & M. Brännback (Eds), *Understanding family businesses* (pp. 55–71). New York: Springer.

Bubolz, M. M. (2001). Family as source, user, and builder of social capital. *Journal of Socio-Economics*, 30(2), 129–131.

Burgelman, R. A. (1983). A process model of internal corporate venturing in the diversified major firm. *Administrative Science Quarterly*, 28(2), 223–244.

Burgelman, R. A. & Sayles, L. R. (1986). *Inside corporate innovation: Strategy, structure and managerial skills.* New York: Free Press.

Carlock, R. S., & Ward, J. L. (2001). *Strategic planning for the family business: Parallel planning to unify the family and business.* Palgrave Macmillan.

Carney, M. (2005). Corporate governance and competitive advantage in family-controlled firms. *Entrepreneurship: Theory and Practice,* 19(3), 249–265.

Carney, M., & Gedajlovic, E. (2002). The co-evolution of institutional environments and organizational strategies: The rise of family business groups in the ASEAN region. *Organization Studies,* 23(1), 1–29.

Carney, M., Van Essen, M., Gedajlovic, E. R., & Heugens, P. P. (2013). What do we know about private family firms? A meta-analytical review. *Entrepreneurship: Theory and Practice,* 39(3), 513–544.

Casillas, J. C., & Moreno, A. M. (2010). The relationship between entrepreneurial orientation and growth: The moderating role of family involvement. *Entrepreneurship and Regional Development,* 22(3–4), 265–291.

Casson, M. (1999). The economics of family firms. *Scandinavian Economic History Review,* 47(1), 10–23.

Cennamo, C., Berrone, P., Cruz, C., & Gomez-Mejia, L. R. (2012). Socioemotional wealth and proactive stakeholder engagement: Why family-controlled firms care more about their stakeholders. *Entrepreneurship: Theory and Practice,* 36(6), 1153–1173.

Chang, E. P., Memili, E., Chrisman, J. J., Kellermanns, F. W., & Chua, J. H. (2009). Family social capital, venture preparedness, and start-up decisions a study of hispanic entrepreneurs in New England. *Family Business Review,* 22(3), 279–292.

Chirico, F., Nordqvist, M., Colombo, G., & Mollona, E. (2012). Simulating dynamic capabilities and value creation in family firms: Is paternalism an "asset" or "liability"? *Family Business Review,* 25(3), 318–338.

Chrisman, J. J., & Patel, P. J. (2012). Variations in R&D investments of family and non-family firms: Behavioral agency and myopic loss aversion perspectives. *Academy of Management Journal,* 55(4), 976–997.

Chrisman, J. J., Chua, J. H., Pearson, A. W., & Barnett, T. (2011). Family involvement, family influence, and family centered non economic goals in small firms. *Entrepreneurship: Theory and Practice,* 36(2), 267–293.

Chua, J. H., Chrisman, J. J., & Sharma, P. (1999). Defining the family business by behavior. *Entrepreneurship: Theory and Practice,* 23(4), 19–39.

Corbett, A. C. (2007). Learning asymmetries and the discovery of entrepreneurial opportunities. *Journal of Business Venturing,* 22(1), 97–118.

Corbetta, G., & Salvato, C. (2004). Self-serving or self-actualizing? Models of man and agency costs in different types of family firms: A commentary on "comparing the agency costs of family and non-family firms: conceptual issues and exploratory evidence". *Entrepreneurship: Theory and Practice,* 28(4), 355–362.

Cruz, C., & Justo, R. (2009). Solving the paradox: A multifaceted approach to corporate entrepreneurship in family firms. *Frontiers of Entrepreneurship Research,* 29(14), 5.

Cruz, C., Justo, R., & Gomez-Mejia, L. (2011). *Solving the paradox: A multifaced approach to corporate entrepreneurship in family firms* (working paper). IE Business School.

Davis, P. S. & Harveston, P. D. (1999). In the founder's shadow: Conflict in the family firm. *Family Business Review,* 12(4), 311–323.

De Massis, A., Frattini, F., & Lichtenthaler, U. (2013). Research on technological innovation in family firms present debates and future directions. *Family Business Review,* 26(1), 10–31.

Discua Cruz, A., Howorth, C., & Hamilton, E. (2013). Intrafamily entrepreneurship: The formation and membership of family entrepreneurial teams. *Entrepreneurship: Theory and Practice,* 37(1), 17–46.

Dyer, W. G., & Whetten, D. A. (2006). Family firms and social responsibility: Preliminary evidence from the S&P500. *Entrepreneurship: Theory and Practice,* 30(6), 785–802.

Eddleston, K. A., & Kellermanns, F. W. (2007). Destructive and productive family relationships: A stewardship theory perspective. *Journal of Business Venturing,* 22(4), 545–565.

Eddleston, K. A., Kellermanns, F. W., & Sarathy, R. (2008). Resource configuration in family firms: Linking resources, strategic planning and environmental dynamism to performance. *Journal of Management Studies,* 45(1), 26–50.

Eddleston, K. A., Kellermanns, F. W., & Zellweger, T. M. (2012). Exploring the entrepreneurial behavior of family firms: Does the stewardship perspective explain differences? *Entrepreneurship: Theory and Practice*, 36(2), 347–367.

Gedajlovic, E., Honig, B., Moore, C. B., Payne, G. T., & Wright, M. (2013). Social capital and entrepreneurship: A schema and research agenda. *Entrepreneurship: Theory and Practice*, 37(3), 455–478.

Gersick, K. E., Davis, J. A., McCollom-Hampton, M., & Lansberg, I. (1997). *Generation to generation: Life cycles of the family business.* Boston, MA: Harvard Business School Press.

Gladstein, D. L. (1984). Groups in context: A model of task group effectiveness. *Administrative Science Quarterly*, 29(4), 499–517.

Gomez-Mejia, L. R., Cruz, C., Berrone, P., & de Castro, J. (2011). The bind that ties: Socioemotional wealth preservation in family firms. *Academy of Management Annals*, 5(1), 653–707.

Gómez-Mejía, L. R., Haynes, K. T., Núñez-Nickel, M., Jacobson, K. J. L., & Moyano-Fuentes, J. (2007). Socioemotional wealth and business risks in family-controlled firms: Evidence from Spanish olive oil mills. *Administrative Science Quarterly*, 52(1), 106–137.

Gomez-Mejia, L. R., Hoskisson, R. E., Makri, M., Sirmon, D. G., & Campbell, J. (2011). *Innovation and the preservation of socioemotional wealth in family controlled high technology firms.* Unpublished manuscript, Texas A&M University, College Station.

Gomez-Mejia, L. R., Larraza-Kintana, M., & Makri, M. (2003). The determinants of executive compensation in family-controlled public corporations. *Academy of Management Journal*, 46(2), 226–237.

Gomez-Mejia, L. R., Makri, M., & Larraza Kintana, M. (2010). Diversification decisions in family-controlled firms. *Journal of Management Studies*, 47(2), 223–252.

Gomez-Mejia, L. R., Nuñez-Nickel, M., & Gutierrez, I. (2001). The role of family ties in agency contracts. *Academy of Management Journal*, 44(1), 81–95.

Gomez-Mejia, L. R., Welbourne, T. M., & Wiseman, R. M. (2000). The role of risk sharing and risk taking under gainsharing. *Academy of Management Review*, 25(3), 492–507.

Green, P. G., Brush, C. G., & Hart, M. M. (1999). The corporate venture champion: A resource-based approach to role and process. *Entrepreneurship: Theory and Practice*, 23(3), 103–122.

Greve, A., & Salaff, J. W. (2003). Social networks and entrepreneurship. *Entrepreneurship: Theory and Practice*, 28(1), 1–22.

Hamel, G. (2000). *Leading the revolution.* Boston, MA: Harvard Business School Press.

Hayton, J. C. & Kelley, D. J. (2006). A competency-based framework for promoting corporate entrepreneurship. *Human Resource Management*, 45(3), 407–427.

Heck, R. K., Hoy, F., Poutziouris, P. Z., & Steier, L. P. (2008). Emerging paths of family entrepreneurship research. *Journal of Small Business Management*, 46(3), 317–330.

Iacobucci, D., & Rosa, P. (2010). The growth of business groups by habitual entrepreneurs: The role of entrepreneurial teams. *Entrepreneurship: Theory and Practice*, 34(2), 351–377.

Isen, A. M., Nygren, T. E., & Ashby, F. G. (1988). Influence of positive affect on the subjective utility of gains and losses: It is just not worth the risk. *Journal of Personality and Social Psychology*, 55(5), 710–717.

Jehn, K. A. (1995). A multimethod examination of the benefits and detriments of intragroup conflict. *Administrative Science Quarterly*, 40(2), 256–282.

Jehn, K. A. (1997). A quantitative analysis of conflict types and dimensions in organizational groups. *Administrative Science Quarterly*, 42(3), 530–558.

Jehn, K. A., & Mannix, E. A. (2001). The dynamic nature of conflict: A longitudinal study of intragroup conflict and group performance. *Academy of Management Journal*, 44(2), 238–251.

Johnson, C. & Ford, R. (2000). Emotional reactions to conflict: Do dependence and legitimacy matter? *Social Forces*, 79(1), 107–138.

Kellermanns, F. W., & Eddleston, K. (2004). Feuding families: When conflict does a family firm good. *Entrepreneurship: Theory and Practice*, 28(3), 209–228.

Kellermanns, F. W., & Eddleston, K. A. (2006). Corporate entrepreneurship in family firms: A family perspective. *Entrepreneurship: Theory and Practice*, 30(6), 809–830.

Kelly, L. M., Athanassiou, N., & Crittenden, W. F. (2000). Founder centrality and strategic behavior in the family-owned firm. *Entrepreneurship: Theory and Practice*, 25(2), 27–42.

Kepner, E. (1983). The family and the firm: A coevolutionary perspective. *Organizational Dynamics*, 12(1), 57–70.

Kets de Vries, M. F. R. (1993). The dynamics of family controlled firms: The good and the bad news. *Organizational Dynamics*, 21(3), 59–71.

Klein, S. B., Astrachan, J. H., & Smyrnios, K. X. (2005). The F-PEC scale of family influence: Construction, validation, and further implication for theory. *Entrepreneurship: Theory and Practice*, 29(3), 321–339.

Kuratko, D. F., Ireland, R. D., Covin, J. G., & Hornsby, J. S. (2005). A model of middle-level managers' entrepreneurial behavior. *Entrepreneurship: Theory and Practice*, 29(6), 699–716.

Labaki, R., Michael-Tsabari, N., & Zachary, R. (2013). Emotional dimensions in the family business: Towards a conceptualization. In K. Smyrnios, P. Poutziouris, & S. Goel (Eds.), *Handbook of research on family business* (pp. 734–763), 2nd ed. Elgar Publishing.

Le Breton-Miller, I., & Miller, D. (2006). Why do some family businesses out-compete? Governance, long-term orientations, and sustainable capability. *Entrepreneurship: Theory and Practice*, 30(6), 731–746.

Le Breton-Miller, I., & Miller, D. (2011). Commentary: Family firms and the advantage of multitemporality. *Entrepreneurship: Theory and Practice*, 35(6), 1171–1177.

Ling, Y., & Kellermanns, F. W. (2010). The effects of family firm specific sources of TMT diversity: The moderating role of information exchange frequency. *Journal of Management Studies*, 47(2), 322–344.

Littunen, H. (2003). Management capabilities and environmental characteristics in the critical operational phase of entrepreneurship: A comparison of Finnish family and non-family firms. *Family Business Review*, 16(3), 183–197.

Liu, J., Wang, H., Hui, C., & Lee, C. (2012). Psychological ownership: How having control matters. *Journal of Management Studies*, 49(5), 869–895.

Lumpkin, G. T., & Brigham, K. H. (2011). Long-term orientation and intertemporal choice in family firms. *Entrepreneurship: Theory and Practice*, 35(6), 1149–1169.

Lumpkin, G. T., Brigham, K. H., & Moss, T. W. (2010). Long-term orientation: Implications for the entrepreneurial orientation and performance of family businesses. *Entrepreneurship and Regional Development*, 22(3–4), 241–264.

Lumpkin, G. T., Cogliser, C. C., & Schneider, D. R. (2009). Understanding and measuring autonomy: An entrepreneurial orientation perspective. *Entrepreneurship: Theory and Practice*, 33(1), 47–69.

Michie, S., Dooley, R. S., & Fryxell, G. E. (2006). Unified diversity in top-level teams: Enhancing collaboration and quality in strategic decision making. *International Journal of Organizational Analysis*, 14(2), 130–149.

Miller, D. (1983). The correlates of entrepreneurship in three types of firms. *Management Science*, 29(7), 770–791.

Miller, D. (1993). The architecture of simplicity. *Academy of Management Review*, 18(1), 116–138.

Miller, D., & Friesen, P. H. (1978). Archetypes of strategy formulation. *Management Science*, 24(9), 921–933.

Miller, D., & Le Breton-Miller, I. (2005). *Managing for the long run*. Boston, MA: Harvard Business School Press.

Miller, D., & Le Breton-Miller, I. (2006). Family governance and family performance: Agency, stewardship, and capabilities. *Family Business Review*, 19(1), 73–87.

Miller, D., Le Breton-Miller, I., & Scholnick, B. (2008). Stewardship vs. stagnation: An empirical comparison of small family and non-family businesses. *Journal of Management Studies*, 45(1), 51–78.

Miller, D., Steier, L., & Le Breton-Miller, I. (2003). Lost in time: Intergenerational succession, change, and failure in family business. *Journal of Business Venturing*, 18(4), 513–531.

Mishra, C. S., & McConaughy, D. L. (1999). Founding family control and capital structure: The risk of loss of control and the aversion to debt. *Entrepreneurship: Theory and Practice*, 23(4), 53–64.

Moores, K. (2009). Paradigms and theory building in the domain of business families. *Family Business Review*, 22(2), 167–180.

Morris, M. H., Allen, J. A., Kuratko, D. F., & Brannon, D. (2010). Experiencing family business creation: Differences between founders, nonfamily managers, and founders of nonfamily firms. *Entrepreneurship: Theory and Practice*, 34(6), 1057–1083.

Mustakallio, M., Autio, E., & Zahra, S. A. (2002). Relational and contractual governance in family firms: Effects on strategic decision making. *Family Business Review*, 15(3), 205–222.

Nahapiet, J., & Ghoshal, S. (1998). Social capital, intellectual capital, and the organizational advantage. *Academy of Management Review*, 23(2), 242–266.

Naldi, L., Nordqvist, M., Sjöberg, K., & Wiklund, J. (2007). Entrepreneurial orientation, risk taking, and performance in family firms. *Family Business Review*, 20(1), 33–47.

Nordqvist, M., & Melin, L. (2010). Entrepreneurial families and family firms. *Entrepreneurship and Regional Development*, 22(3–4), 211–239.

Pierce, J. L., Kostova, T., & Dirks, K. T. (2001). Toward a theory of psychological ownership in organizations. *Academy of Management Review*, 26(2), 298–310.

Priem, R. L. & Cycyota, C. S. (2001). On strategic judgment. In M. A. Hitt, R. E. Freeman, & J. R. Harrison (Eds.), *Handbook of strategic management* (pp. 403–519). Oxford: Blackwell Publishing.

Rauch, A., Wiklund, J., Lumpkin, G. T., & Frese, M. (2009). Entrepreneurial orientation and business performance: An assessment of past research and suggestions for the future. *Entrepreneurship: Theory and Practice*, 33(3), 761–787.

Rothaermel, F. T. (2001). Incumbent's advantage through exploiting complementary assets via interfirm cooperation. *Strategic Management Journal*, 22(6–7), 687–699.

Salvato, C., & Melin, L. (2008). Creating value across generations in family-controlled businesses: The role of family social capital. *Family Business Review*, 21(3), 259–276.

Schepers, J., Voordeckers, W., Steijvers, T., & Laveren, E. (2014). The entrepreneurial orientation–performance relationship in private family firms: The moderating role of socioemotional wealth. *Small Business Economics*, 43(1), 39–55.

Sciascia, S., Mazzola, P., & Chirico, F. (2013). Generational involvement in the top management team of family firms: Exploring nonlinear effects on entrepreneurial orientation. *Entrepreneurship: Theory and Practice*, 37(1), 69–85.

Sharma, P. (2004). An overview of the field of family business studies: Current status and directions for the future. *Family Business Review*, 17(1), 1–36.

Sharma, P., & Chrisman, S. J. J. (2007). Toward a reconciliation of the definitional issues in the field of corporate entrepreneurship. In A. Cuervo, D. Ribeiro, & S. Roig (Eds.), *Entrepreneurship* (pp. 83–103). Berlin, Heidelberg: Springer.

Sharma, P., & Manikutty, S. (2005). Strategic divestments in family firms: Role of family structure and community culture. *Entrepreneurship: Theory and Practice*, 29(3), 293–311.

Shipton, H., West, M., Dawson, J., Birdi, K., & Patterson, M. (2006). HRM as a predictor of innovation. *Human Resource Management Journal*, 16(1), 3–27.

Sirmon, D. G., Arrègle, J.-L., Hitt, M. A., & Webb, J. W. (2008). The role of family influence in firms' strategic responses to threat of imitation. *Entrepreneurship: Theory and Practice*, 32(6), 979–998.

Sirmon, D. G., & Hitt, M. A. (2003). Managing resources: Linking unique resources, management, and wealth creation in family firms. *Entrepreneurship: Theory and Practice*, 27(4), 339–358.

Spinelli, S. J., & Hunt, J. (2000). *Leadership and entrepreneurial behavior in the next generation of self-described family owned businesses.* Paper presented at the BCERC, Babson College, USA.

Stanley, L. J. (2010). Emotions and family business creation: An extension and implications. *Entrepreneurship: Theory and Practice*, 34(6), 1085–1092.

Steier, L. (2001). Family firms, plural forms of governance, and the evolving role of trust. *Family Business Review*, 14(4), 353–367.

Sundaramurthy, C., & Kreiner, G. E. (2008). Governing by managing identity boundaries: The case of family businesses. *Entrepreneurship: Theory and Practice*, 32(3), 415–436.

Sydow, J., Schreyögg, G., & Koch, J. (2009). Organizational path dependence: Opening the black box. *Academy of Management Review*, 34(4), 689–709.

Tagiuri, R., & Davis, J. A. (1996). Bivalent attributes of the family firm. *Family Business Review*, 9(2), 199–208.

Talke, K., Salomo, S., & Kock, A. (2011). Top management team diversity and strategic innovation orientation: The relationship and consequences for innovativeness and performance. *Journal of Product Innovation Management*, 28(6), 819–832.

Tompkins, R. (2010). *The organizational identity of a family business: The role of hybrid identity in organizational events* (Unpublished doctoral dissertation). George Washington University, Washington, DC.

Tsai, W., & Ghoshal, S. (1998). Social capital and value creation: The role of intrafirm networks. *Academy of Management Journal*, 41(4), 464–476.

Upton, N., Teal, E. J., & Felan, J. T. (2001). Strategic and business planning practices of fast growth family firms. *Journal of Small Business Management*, 39(1), 60–72.

Vandekerkhof, P., Steijvers, T., Hendriks, W., & Voordeckers, W. (2015). The effect of organizational characteristics on the appointment of nonfamily managers in private family firms: The moderating role of socioemotional wealth. *Family Business Review*, 28(2), 104–122.

Wiseman, R. M., & Gomez-Mejia, L. R. (1998). A behavioral agency model of managerial risk taking. *Academy of Management Review*, 23(1), 133–153.

Yeung, H. W. C., & Soh, T. M. (2000). Corporate governance and the global reach of Chinese family firms in Singapore. *Seoul Journal of Economics*, 13(3), 301–334.

Zachary, R. K., Edward, G. R., & Phinisee, I. (2013). Defining and identifying family entrepreneurship: A new view of entrepreneurs. In M. Minniti (Ed.), *The Dynamics of entrepreneurship: Evidence from global entrepreneurship monitor data* (pp. 57–76). Oxford: Oxford University Press.

Zahra, S. A. (1995). Corporate entrepreneurship and financial performance: The case of management leveraged buyouts. *Journal of Business Venturing*, 10(3), 225–247.

Zahra, S. A. (1996). Governance, ownership, and corporate entrepreneurship: The moderating impact of industry technological opportunities. *Academy of Management Journal*, 39(6), 1713–1735.

Zahra, S. A. (2005). Entrepreneurial risk taking in family firms. *Family Business Review*, 18(1), 23–40.

Zahra, S. A. (2010). Harvesting family firms' organizational social capital: A relational perspective. *Journal of Management Studies*, 47(2), 345–366.

Zahra, S. A., Hayton, J. C., & Salvato, C. (2004). Entrepreneurship in family vs. non-family firms: A resource-based analysis of the effect of organizational culture. *Entrepreneurship: Theory and Practice*, 28(4), 363–381.

Zellweger, T. (2007). Time horizon, costs of equity capital, and generic investment strategies of firms. *Family Business Review*, 20(1), 1–15.

Zellweger, T. M., & Astrachan, J. H. (2008). On the emotional value of owning a firm. *Family Business Review*, 21(4), 347–363.

Zellweger, T. M., Kellermanns, F. W., Chrisman, J., & Chua, J. (2012). Family control and family firm valuation by family CEOs: The importance of intentions for transgenerational control. *Organization Science*, 23(3), 851–868.

Zellweger, T. M., Nason, R., Nordqvist, M., & Brush, C. (2013). Why do family firms strive for nonfinancial performance? *Entrepreneurship: Theory and Practice*, 37(2), 229–248.

8 Entrepreneurial family firms

A research note on their qualifying characteristics

Angelo Renoldi

Introduction: objectives

> In the US, 50 per cent of firms started today will be dead within five years, 25 per cent will last a decade and only 16 per cent will survive a generation. Family-owned businesses live twice as long, but not that long.
>
> (Steier & Davis, 2014)

In the US, and in many other developed countries, even the more prosperous and long-lived family firms are facing more aggressive competition than ever. As noted by family business scholars, in order to be able to survive successfully, family firms need to support growth, especially as the family firm ages (Eddleston, Kellermanns, Floyd, Crittenden, & Crittenden, 2013).

When the business concern – as almost always occurs at least in non-English contexts – has its driving force in one closed economic subject, identifiable in two or more people linked by family ties, then we have a family firm (Carlson & Frone, 2003; Dossena, 2009; Fattoum & Fayolle, 2009; Hoy, 2006; Hoy & Sharma, 2010). This definition is broad and stresses well how the family firm is an "abstract" concept or, better still, it is an extremely varied "logical category," due to the fact that the characteristic features distinguishing the individual entrepreneurs are extremely varied and even more so are the contexts (general; specific) in which they live and work. For example, even with the same character aspects, a family firm set up in Italy can assume different behavioral and performance patterns compared with those that would be manifested in South America.

The concept of family firm is by itself, substantially neutral and generic, unsuitable for expressing the complexity of the evolutionary path of enterprises, and lacks a distinctive meaning or the capacity to indicate how the entrepreneur's characteristics affect the way in which the firm is managed or its business model devised.

Starting with the recognition that the concept of family firm can have several meanings, the argument to be put forward in this contribution is that the family firm (as broadly defined above) can *evolve* in a virtuous way – to become an entrepreneurial family firm – or adopt a "neutral" configuration which could be described as an "owner's firm." This argument is in line with the main assumption of corporate entrepreneurship (CE) which is that it can serve to avoid decline and to revitalize a company that has entered a phase of decline (Hoy, 2006).

The aim of this contribution is to offer an analysis of some of the main factors that affect whether a family firm evolves virtuously to become entrepreneurial or not. Specifically, it is shown how this evolution, whether virtuous or neutral, depends on some of the entrepreneur's characteristics involving personality, socio-cultural aspects, but also on the environmental context and the strategic decisions that are taken.

A family can be classified as entrepreneurial when a balanced development between the economic objectives of the company and the expectations/aspirations of the members of the family is achieved in the long term (and hence value is created from generation to generation). As noted by Nordqvist and Melin (2010) entrepreneurial families both drive and constrain entrepreneurial activities and are one of the most important factors affecting both opportunity recognition and its exploitation aptitude, therefore, impacting on the possibility to grow a business out of it (Aldrich & Cliff, 2003). With this approach, family members are indeed responsible for managing the business in harmony or disharmony with a team of other family members (Heck & Trent, 1999). Therefore, different aspects of the entrepreneurial process are impacted by a family's access to, and management of, resources, such as financial, human, and social capital, as well as its specific norms, attitudes and values (Nordqvist & Melin, 2010; Rau, 2014). The main challenge remains transgenerational value creation (Zellweger, Nason, & Nordqvist, 2012).

Transgenerational value creation in family firms is far from easy, as evidenced by the high level of mortality of family businesses especially in correspondence with succession events (Chami, 2001), and requires that the family entrepreneurs have specific qualities. These include the ability to combine their business expertise with the ability to both nurture and assess family members' entrepreneurial skills (Habbershon & Williams, 1999).

It is evident both from the literature and from the direct observation of real-life cases, that transgenerational value creation requires, amongst others, activities aimed at planning how to manage human and intellectual resources of the family (i.e., internal human capital), with a dual purpose. First, to maintain both economic and socio-emotional satisfaction of those family members that have both the propensity and attitudes to take the baton and pursue entrepreneurial behaviors (Gomez-Mejia, Cruz, Berrone, & De Castro, 2011). Second, to establish an appropriate balance in terms of rewards, between these family members (i.e., those involved or designed to ensure the generational continuity of the family business) and those who, by choice or because of an evaluation of the entrepreneur, should be left out of the business and be considered as mere owners (Gersick, Davis, Hampton, & Lansberg, 1997).

If strategic planning is important, then the "internal human capital" of the family business is certainly none the less so. In fact, the entrepreneur at the head of the family firm has the sometimes difficult task of identifying his/her successor amongst the family members by considering who is the most likely to ensure continuity in the long term (survival) of the enterprise (Miller & Le Breton-Miller, 2005). Succession issues are a good example of how family firms differ from non-family firms. In both family and non-family firms, governance tools such as Nomination and Remuneration Committees can play a significant role during the succession process. However, in family firms, this process is even more complex as human and family dynamics interact and decision-making processes have to match rational and objective thinking with emotional and psychological issues related to the fact that the decisions will affect the family directly.

For some time in Economics (e.g., Schumpeter), the figure of the entrepreneur has been identified on the basis of two characteristic features: innovativeness and organizational capacity. These activities imply risk-taking (or uncertainty, as

Knight would say), given that the development-accomplishment of new ideas, of economic importance, implies a substantial market risk, while the organization involves responsibilities regarding finance and equity as well as reputation.

Family firms, therefore, can be considered as entrepreneurial when a dynamic balance is pursued between the challenges for economic growth and the internal human resources.

The aim of this contribution is to identify the levers that allow this balance to be found and to maintain the entrepreneurial spirit among family firms which also leads to competitiveness and growth.

Family firms and entrepreneurship

The complexity of the subject and the numerous different perspectives from which it must be analyzed require integrated and transversal skills and investigation methods involving above all economics, sociology, psychology, and even biology (Mclin, Nordqvist, & Sharma, 2014). In family firm literature we have been witnessing a revaluation of the role and figure of the entrepreneur, which, although present, does not have any equals in public companies. Together with the strictly economic profile of the phenomenon, it is essential to study additional elements such as the psychological and cultural characteristics that distinguish the entrepreneur, the relationships between this person and the other members of the family, the role, if any, of the latter in the firm, the characteristics of the decision-making process (as an individual or in a team), and the conflicts within the family and the repercussions on the management (Hoy & Sharma, 2010). By considering the above-mentioned questions, it is easy to deduce that the approach offered by the economic disciplines alone is not exhaustive. Indeed, the keys to an understanding of the family firms offered by economics, often consist of a "transposition" of theories with more general values that have arisen to interpret the phenomena of firms and even of the environment, such as the Life Circles Theory or the Agency Theory.

With regards to entrepreneurial family firms I now wish to delve into two of the main aspects that I argue are determinant in order to describe how family businesses can be classified as entrepreneurial family firms: (1) the family firms' life cycle and the relationships between the strategic management of the business and of the family's human capital; (2) the relationship between family firms' performance and the characteristics of family firms' managers.

With reference to the first, the family firms' life cycles entail different dynamics and complexities related to the fact that, in addition to the firm and the industry life cycle, the family's life cycle also has to be considered. An example of the consequences of such a complexity can be seen by considering how strategic planning and succession planning affect a family firm's growth. Eddeston and colleagues have found that the degree to which strategic planning and succession planning are associated with family firm growth depends on the generation managing the firm (Eddleston et al., 2013). Interestingly, according to the authors, neither form of planning confers much growth for second-generation firms. For third-and-beyond generation firms, the benefits of succession planning appear to reemerge. However, strategic planning is negatively associated with their level of growth.

Additionally, extant literature has widely shown that entrepreneurial activities require both a focus on innovation and the ability to recognize/seize opportunities, especially in a highly dynamic and "discontinuous" environment like the current ones (Kellermanns & Eddleston, 2006). Family firms – like any business – must overcome certain barriers. For family firms, those barriers are largely socio-psychological and may hinder the implementation of the processes that simultan-eously involve growth, generational takeovers, and the firm's survival in the long run (Gersick et al., 1997). Indeed, if the family firm does not grow, it becomes more difficult for the next generations to be motivated to take part in the family firms' entrepreneurial activities (Scherer, Adams, Carley, & Wiebe, 1989).

The removal of these barriers, as confirmed by Hoy (2006), takes place in the presence of certain conditions, in particular when the family's human capital has characteristics that would not fit in bureaucratic organizations and when the pro-pensity to change, seen as pro-active behavior toward innovation, is the common denominator of business management. Innovation, therefore, seems the solution that best allows a family firm to manage the risk of decline and it must be under-stood in the broadest sense, not only with reference to organizational aspects, but also in the perspective of the market (entry into new geographical areas) (Sharma, 2011). These factors – namely, the business, innovation (especially technology), the characteristics of the corporate staff, the age and educational level of both the founder and of the generation to which eventual succession is intended – describe a family firm's life cycles, whose stages are unlikely to be in harmony with each other (Gersick et al., 1997). It is important to note, however, that growth potential also largely depends on contextual variables. For example, research has shown that in the past Italian family firms have had difficulties in growing from small to medium enterprises and, therefore, have manifested a high degree of mortality. This difficulty was mainly related to socio-cultural habits that have led family firms mainly to finance themselves through bank debt (Scog-namiglio, 1987). Specifically, the main causes of these difficulties in achieving a larger scale are related to the growth-strategies adopted by Italian family busi-nesses which have relied heavily on bank debt and have systematically refused to "open" their equity to new shareholders. These strategies, however, have hin-dered the possibilities of survival and growth for Italian family. This helps to understand the reason why family firms often do not survive beyond the third generation (Chami, 2001). More precisely, it has been found that, as family firms get older, there is a reduction in the propensity to invest in projects that boost growth, with consequent negative effects on the survival rate of the family enter-prise (Miller, Le Breton-Miller, Lester, & Cannella, 2007; Miller, Le Breton-Miller, & Scholnick, 2008). I argue that, at the basis, there are psychological and behavioral components of the entrepreneur and his family as well: as accumu-lated wealth increases, the owner-family tends to experience a reduction in its risk appetite (although nowadays it is relatively resized thanks to Private Equity investments).

With reference to the second point, i.e., the relationship between family firms' performance and the characteristics of family firms' managers, empirical studies have shown that the issue is more complex and controversial than how it was originally described by Jensen and Mekling (1976) with the Agency Theory. If this theory comes to the conclusion that firms with high ownership concentration tend to perform better, the most recent contributions come, on the contrary, to more complex and contradictory conclusions which depend, in particular, on the type of entity that manages the enterprise (CEO). In this regard, Miller, Le Breton Miller, and Lester (2011) have shown that businesses run by the founder, are more entrepreneurial and characterized by growth-oriented strategies and have a good risk appetite and higher performance. At the other extreme, family businesses run by family members are characterized more by defensive/conservative strategies, averse to change, with weak economic performance. Additionally, no consensus exists at the moment on whether family firms outperform non-family firms and this is due to the fact that different definitions of family firms have been adopted and contextual variables may increase the already high level of complexity of this relationship (Villalonga & Amit, 2014).

To sum up, family firms' entrepreneurial behavior depends on a number of elements, of which the ones that seem to deserve more attention are the ability to consider simultaneously different types of life cycles while remaining innovative, and the consideration of the possible effects of family firms' managers' characteristics.

The entrepreneurial firm: the underlying factors

As a very brief summary, it could be argued that the entrepreneurial firm (Dew, Read, Sarasvathy, & Wiltbank, 2008; Nordqvist & Melin, 2010; Rogoff & Heck, 2003) is the "virtuous" evolution of the family firm; a firm that, at least according to profitability parameters, is able to persist over time (survive), and can evolve to reach large dimensions.

At the basis of this "virtuous" evolution, different influences may be listed, each of which can be demonstrated and they refer namely to the entrepreneur's characteristics. Hereafter, I briefly list and comment on the ones that seem to be the most relevant: long-term vision and value orientation, risk taking, the capacity to transform the idea into an innovative process (i.e., innovativeness), and the capacity to work in a team.

Long-term vision and value orientation

Orientation toward the dual long-term–value creation concept (Fruhan, 1979; Lumpkin, Brigham, & Moss, 2010; Rappaport, 1986; Stewart III, 1991), which is in itself absolutely coherent, is the one that best describes the figure of the entrepreneur. Additionally, within this long-term vision and value orientation approach of entrepreneurs some features emerge such as the fact that "ephemeral" activities (e.g., mere speculation) are excluded, while the principles of the *Stakeholder Theory* (Freeman & Velamuri, 2008) are included. In other words, the entrepreneurial firm is able to produce a benefit on the society-community which ennobles the figure of the "virtuous entrepreneur".

Risk taking

Long-term vision and value orientation also imply that entrepreneurial family firms, when organizing their innovation practices, take risks under two main conditions. First, the risk is *knowingly* taken, in other words it reflects the preliminary ascertainment of the level of efficacy of the innovation at the basis of the entrepreneurial project (Knight, 1971). Second, the risk is manageable. Amongst its various skills and capacities, the entrepreneurial firm also possesses one which more than consisting of the ability to minimize risk, refers to the ability to manage and control it in a proactive way (e.g., Memili, Eddleston, Kellermanns, Zellweger, & Barnett, 2010; Zahra, 2005). Therefore, given that risk is often associated with change and is a source of profit, the capacity to manage risk proactively in order to foster growth distinguishes entrepreneurial firms from other family firm configurations.

Innovativeness

Innovativeness refers, in a broad sense, to the capacity to transform the idea-invention into a process having innovation as its object. Entrepreneurial family firms possess two orders of skills, which are very exclusive and of high "value." First, especially in an initial phase (*start-up*) or during phases of profound renewal in its life cycle, they are capable of "seeing that which the others do not perceive" and translate the idea-invention into a feasible *business model*. However, what has just been described – on closer inspection – is not sufficient to qualify a firm as entrepreneurial. It is essential that the innovation activity becomes institutionalized in a process (Chen & Hsu, 2009; Dyer, Gregersen, & Christensen, 2008). This is important because it can transform the search for new ideas from a sporadic "phenomenon" (invention) to a systematic activity (innovation, understood also as a different combination of well-known elements); and it attenuates the auto-referential tendency of the entrepreneurial firm, because the process of innovation is associated with a tension within the whole company structure to find new know-how, in the awareness that the competition does not allow companies to benefit from "a favorable position" for very long.

The elements specified above also depend on a combination of characteristics which, in large part, lead back to, and overlap with, the psychological and behavioral sphere of the people forming the human capital of the entrepreneurial firm.

Without any claims to completeness, the "virtuous" entrepreneur presents elements such as ambition and need for achievement, dynamism and propensity for change, orientation toward the future, and consideration of himself and conviction of his own *vision* (e.g., Dossena, 2009; Stavrou, 1999) which can be supplemented, as facilitating factors, by the fact of belonging to a family of entrepreneurs or the availability of easily found resources (relationships; financial capital).

Investigation of these elements requires an interdisciplinary approach, particularly with regard to psychology and sociology for which research projects must be established in the field.

The capacity to work in a team

If the previous point concentrated essentially on the dimension of innovation, this one mainly concerns the relational component, in other words on an aspect of the organizational dimension (e.g., Rothaermel & Alexandre, 2009).

Even in its initial phase, the entrepreneurial family firm must behave as an open system which is willing to integrate skills and capacities in such a way that fruitful synergies emerge both in the short and in the long run (Clinton, Sciascia, Yadav, & Roche, 2013). More precisely, this "opening" must be directed on two levels, the endogenous and exogenous one.

The endogenous level refers to the tendency to coordinate and direct the human resources that exist in the entrepreneurial firm. This requisite may appear even too superfluous to be mentioned, if it were not for the fact that the family firm *tout court* is often characterized by an absolute "personalisation" of the firm, with marginal information systems and the absence of any integration of objectives or skills. On the contrary, as the entrepreneurial firm is orientated toward the long term, and toward value, it has to consider the importance of a systematic exploitation-enrichment of its human capital.

The exogenous level refers to the firm's willingness to avail itself of external *skills*, which can be provided by independent consultants called on to fill existing shortcomings or any that may arise during its development. Such an orientation, if well managed, allows the entrepreneurial firm to devise its own business model according to those long-term objectives creating value and progressive "depersonalization" which are a founding and distinctive characteristic of the firm.

I have described some of the most relevant features of the entrepreneur and explained how they allow an entrepreneurial family firm to grow. Long-term vision and value orientation lead to entrepreneurial decision-making which takes economic and social sustainability into consideration; while proactive risk management (instead of risk minimization) and innovativeness (that goes beyond the start-up phase to permeate the organization in a systematic way) both enable the growth objective to be achieved. Additionally, I have shown how the capacity to work in a team allows a better and more fruitful integration and exploitation of internal and external resources. I will now turn to the analysis of the main elements that, together with the entrepreneur's characteristics, may affect growth in family firms.

Competitive growth and entrepreneurial family firms

When family firms encompass the features that qualify them as entrepreneurial, they benefit from a considerable expected performance potential and *competitive advantage* and are able to catalyze the interest of strategic and financial investments (Wu, Chua, & Chrisman, 2007).

Having developed and possessing the incentives of value creation (e.g., innovation, in the widest sense of the term, dynamism, and internal and external relationships), the entrepreneurial firm possesses a large part (if not all) of the requisites to accomplish growth in size. *Sustainable growth is the highest merit that the family firm can benefit from* for two main reasons. First, the possibility of achieving a certain level of dimensional growth annually is a manifestation of the brilliance of the entrepreneur and the dynamism of the firm's organization (Eddleston et al., 2013; Kellermanns & Eddleston, 2006; Nordqvist & Zellweger, 2010). Additionally, it has been noted that although some firms are managed correctly and well positioned with regard to their product–market–technology mix, if they are not supported over time by adequate development and growth processes, they are clearly destined to a decline, which will be faster the more dynamic the context in which they operate (Dossena, 2009; Eddleston et al., 2013; Nordqvist & Zellweger, 2010).

Second, growth allows a virtuous circle to be activated concerning the use of financial resources which leads to the possibility of neutralizing *and mitigating* the risk that the small-sized family firm is unable to survive above a certain size threshold (Scognamiglio, 1987); and it also allows the best strategic inputs to be attracted, in other words intellectual capital and financial resources, without which it is impossible to proceed toward a consolidated development.

It is important to note that the topic outlined above is complex and entails an analysis of a group of investigation areas of unquestionable significance, areas that change as the family firm itself changes into an entrepreneurial firm and in accordance with the dimensional profile that it assumes. These areas concern *corporate governance* and the *different stages of growth.*

With regards to the former, the presence of an efficient system of governance (of the firm), for the individual firm but also for the economy as a whole, assumes distinctive characteristics and different levels of articulation if the firm is entrepreneurial. In fact by setting up an effective governance, the entrepreneurial family firm combines with its founding characteristics, i.e., long-term value orientation, risk-appetite, stabilization of the innovation process, work organization, the possibility of achieving more or less satisfactory levels of transparency/trust with regard to the *stakeholders* (Miller & Le Breton-Miller, 2011; Steier, Chrisman, & Chua, 2004; Villanueva & Sapienza, 2009). Indeed, a corporate governance system that is coherent with the entrepreneurial nature of the firm and graduated in relation to its dimensional significance, considers and develops around at least three tasks: reducing the cost of the capital, facilitating a more efficient use of the resources, and stimulating growth (e.g., Steier et al., 2004). The literature on Corporate Governance has focused mainly on the roles of the administrative body (e.g., Bettinelli, 2011; Chen & Hsu, 2009; Jensen & Meckling, 1976) and has been tackled in various important academic contributions, from the Agency Theory (Fama & Jensen, 1983; Wiseman & Gomez-Mejia, 1998), to the Stakeholder Theory (Freeman, 1994), to more recent, emerging approaches, such as the Team Production Theory which refers to the administrative body as a team with different skills (Kaufman & Englander, 2005). It is exactly in this latter perspective that it would be interesting to check the correlation that should be established in entrepreneurial family firms between their governance characteristics and growth, this topic also links up with the following one.

Finally, it is important to consider that growth tasks of entrepreneurial family firms, as the Life Cycles Theory stresses, can vary according to different stages. The entrepreneurial firm, even with its distinctiveness, does not constitute an exception. However, entrepreneurial family firms' life cycles may present distinctive characteristics. As Hoy notes: "to innovate and prosper, a family enterprise must contend with multiple life cycles, rarely synchronized, any one of which may be in a decline stage at any point in time" (2006: 831).

For example, as the author notes, the typical life cycle stages (i.e., birth, growth, maturity, and death/renewal) can also apply to entities relevant to the firm such as the founder, family members, key employees, the industry, and market segments. This means that entrepreneurial family firms, in order to be able to grow, need to incorporate different life-cycle models into strategic planning processes. This said, I conclude with a description of the growth stages that should guide entrepreneurial family firms. I do so by integrating the description offered by Bloch, Joseph, and Santi (2010) with the main arguments exposed in this chapter.

The start-up phase, also defined as the "initial development stage" represents the initial step, where the organizational scheme is simple and management control and performance measures are unlikely to be formalized. At this stage loose and informal control are adopted and lead to the creation of organic structures (Khandwalla, 1977).

Subsequently, during the functional-innovative phase, the entrepreneurial firm, although benefiting from the original idea, understands the importance of equipping itself with more structured R&D and innovation processes. The

original idea-invention has, in fact, provided the entrepreneurial firm with a competitive advantage that is not ephemeral, but is almost never such as to guarantee
a satisfying performance in the middle-term. In other words, the original idea-
invention of the technical–design phase represents, from the point of view of
strategy, a sort of *time to market value* (advantage of the *first mover*), the beneficial
effects of which are necessary to start up a continuous process of innovation,
capable of guaranteeing a competitive differential between the entrepreneurial
firm and other rival firms. A "mechanism" similar to *bridge sales* in the policies for
patenting innovations is set up. Consequently, the entrepreneurial firm endorses
professionalization and opens up to more articulated organizational arrangements (functional form, for example with a *product manager*), formalized control
systems, and structured performance analyses on economic-financial indicators
(ROI, capital intensity, degree of leverage).

Later we have the innovative-financial phase. This is the most highly developed
phase that removes the limits of the entrepreneurial firm anchored to the
previous stages. These limits concern the type of growth and the role of finance.

In the previous phases growth is often pursued by adapting the firm's structure according to traditional ways such as self-financing and bank debt. Innovative financial tools (such as private equity) have, in the previous phases, been
substantially absent, or at least marginal. Together with the consolidation of
innovation – risk management – team skills combination (the "real" component of the firm), the innovative-financial stage of the entrepreneurial firm
sees the development of finance as the lever to pursue growth for external
lines (acquisitions, mergers, agreements, joint ventures). Furthermore diversification processes can be set up, and ownership structures can be opened up
to a wider framework in which the industrial-strategic investors are joined by
financial investors who are able to provide capital according to the technical
forms, financial policy, and at a cost that is such as to make investments possible that would not otherwise be value creators. In such a context, an effective
and transparent corporate governance as well as formalized planning and
control systems acquire an importance while, in asserting the role of the financial function, the analysis of the company performance also avails itself of financial indicators (profit per share; *pay-off ratio*; P/E; rate of indebtedness; cash
flows).

Conclusions

The aim of this chapter is to support the argument that the entrepreneurial
nature of the family business is manifested in connection with certain requirements that should allow an ideal chain to be obtained: innovation – competitive
advantage-growth – value creation – survival.

The ways in which this argument could be further explored empirically are
different and complementary and could entail firm level, individual level, and
family level observations that go beyond economic measurements to include
socio-psychological parameters, such as those referred to the type of person who
runs the firm, the age of the latter, the relationship between firm–family, and
family.

The large number of research perspectives and the complexity of the relationships that may exist could imply the adoption of different methods with a specific
focus on each one of them that could then be integrated *post hoc.*

With reference to the Italian context and to my own experience, the aim of future research could be to examine the relationships that may exist among the following variables:

- investment in innovation and intangible assets (R&D activities and advertising investments, staff training costs, and patents);
- rate of growth in size (total revenue and dynamics over time);
- economic and strategic performance (ROI; placement according to Porter's model).

References

Aldrich, H. E. & Cliff, J. E. (2003) The pervasive effects of family on entrepreneurship: toward a family embeddedness perspective. *Journal of Business Venturing*, 18(5): 573–597.

Bettinelli, C. (2011) Boards of directors in family firms: an exploratory study of structure and group process. *Family Business Review*, 24(2): 151–169.

Bloch, A., Joseph, A., & Santi, M. (2010) Propelled into the future: managing family firm entrepreneurial growth despite generational breakthroughs within family life stage. In N. M. & T. M. Zellweger (Eds.), *Transgenerational Entrepreneurship: Exploring Growth and Performance in Family Firms Across Generations*. Edward Elgar Publishing, Cheltenham, UK: 142–166.

Carlson, D. S. & Frone, M. R. (2003) Relation of behavioral and psychological involvement to a new four-factor conceptualization of work-family interference. *Journal of Business and Psychology*, 17(4): 515–535.

Chami, R. (2001) What is different about family businesses? WP/01/70. Available at www. imf.org/external/pubs/ft/wp/2001/wp0170.pdf, accessed February 13, 2014.

Chen, H.-L. & Hsu, W.-T. (2009) Family ownership, board independence, and R&D investment. *Family Business Review*, 22(4): 347–362.

Clinton, E. A., Sciascia, S., Yadav, R., & Roche, F. (2013) Resource acquisition in family firms: the role of family-influenced human and social capital. *Entrepreneurship Research Journal*, 3(1): 44–61.

Dew, N., Read, S., Sarasvathy, S. D., & Wiltbank, R. (2008) Outlines of a behavioral theory of the entrepreneurial firm. *Journal of Economic Behavior and Organization*, 66(1): 37–59.

Dossena, G. (2009) *Entrepreneur and Enterprise: Lights and Shadows from the Italian Experience*. McGraw-Hill, Milan, Italy.

Dyer, J. H., Gregersen, H. B., & Christensen, C. (2008) Entrepreneur behaviors, opportunity recognition, and the origins of innovative ventures. *Strategic Entrepreneurship Journal*, 2(4): 317–338.

Eddleston, K. A., Kellermanns, F. W., Floyd, S. W., Crittenden, V. L., & Crittenden, W. F. (2013) Planning for growth: life stage differences in family firms. *Entrepreneurship: Theory and Practice*, 37(5): 1177–1202.

Fama, E. F. & Jensen, M. C. (1983) Separation of ownership and control. *Journal of Law and Economics*, 26(2): 301–325.

Fattoum, S. & Fayolle, A. (2009) Generational succession: examples from Tunisian family firms. *Journal of Enterprising Culture*, 17(2): 127–145.

Freeman, R. & Velamuri, S. R. (2008) A new approach to CSR: company stakeholder responsibility. *Available at SSRN 1186223*.

Freeman, R. E. (1994) The politics of stakeholder theory: some future directions. *Business Ethics Quarterly*, 4(4): 409–421.

Fruhan, W. E. (1979) *Financial Strategy: Studies in the Creation, Transfer, and Destruction of Shareholder Value*. RD Irwin, Homewood, IL.

Gersick, K. E., Davis, J. A., Hampton, M., & Lansberg, I. (1997) *Generation to Generation: Life Cycles of the Family Business*. Boston, MA: Harvard Business School Press.

Gomez-Mejia, L. R., Cruz, C., Berrone, P., & De Castro, J. (2011) The bind that ties: socio-emotional wealth preservation in family firms. *Academy of Management Annals*, 5(1): 653–707.

Habbershon, T. G. & Williams, M. L. (1999) A resource-based framework for assessing the strategic advantages of family firms. *Family Business Review*, 12(1): 1–25.

Heck, R. K. & Trent, E. S. (1999) The prevalence of family business from a household sample. *Family Business Review*, 12(3): 209–219.

Hoy, F. (2006). The complicating factor of life cycles in corporate venturing. *Entrepreneurship: Theory and Practice*, 30(6): 831–836.

Hoy, F. & Sharma, P. (2010) *Entrepreneurial Family Firms*. Prentice Hall, Englewood Cliffs, NJ.

Jensen, M. C. & Meckling, W. H. (1976) Theory of the firm: managerial behavior, agency costs and ownership structure. *Journal of Financial Economics*, 3(4): 305–360.

Kaufman, A. & Englander, E. (2005) A team production model of corporate governance. *Academy of Management Executive*, 19(3): 9–22.

Kellermanns, F. W. & Eddleston, K. A. (2006) Corporate entrepreneurship in family firms: a family perspective. *Entrepreneurship: Theory and Practice*, 30(6): 809–830.

Khandwalla, P. N. (1977) Some top management styles, their context and performance. *Organization and Administrative Sciences*, 7(4): 21–51.

Knight, F. H. (1971) *Risk, Uncertainty and Profit*. Courier Dover Publications, New York.

Lumpkin, G., Brigham, K. H., & Moss, T. W. (2010) Long-term orientation: implications for the entrepreneurial orientation and performance of family businesses. *Entrepreneurship and Regional Development*, 22(3–4): 241–264.

Melin, L., Nordqvist, M., & Sharma, P. (Eds.) (2014) *SAGE Handbook of Family Business*. Sage, London.

Memili, E., Eddleston, K. A., Kellermanns, F. W., Zellweger, T. M., & Barnett, T. (2010) The critical path to family firm success through entrepreneurial risk taking and image. *Journal of Family Business Strategy*, 1(4): 200–209.

Miller, D. & Le Breton-Miller, I. (2005) *Managing for the Long Run: Lessons in Competitive Advantage from Great Family Businesses*. Harvard Business Press, Boston, MA.

Miller, D. & Le Breton-Miller, I. (2011) Governance, social identity, and entrepreneurial orientation in closely held public companies. *Entrepreneurship: Theory and Practice*, 35(5): 1051–1076.

Miller, D., Le Breton-Miller, I., & Lester, R. H. (2011) Family and lone founder ownership and strategic behaviour: social context, identity, and institutional logics. *Journal of Management Studies*, 48(1): 1–25.

Miller, D., Le Breton-Miller, I., Lester, R. H., & Cannella, A. A. (2007) Are family firms really superior performers? *Journal of Corporate Finance*, 13: 829–858.

Miller, D., Le Breton-Miller, L., & Scholnick, B. (2008) Stewardship vs. stagnation: an empirical comparison of small family and non-family businesses. *Journal of Management Studies*, 45(1): 51–78.

Nordqvist, M. & Melin, L. (2010) Entrepreneurial families and family firms. *Entrepreneurship and Regional Development*, 22(3–4): 211–239.

Nordqvist, M. & Zellweger, T. M. (2010). *Transgenerational Entrepreneurship: Exploring Growth and Performance in Family Firms across Generations*. Edward Elgar Publishing, Cheltenham, UK.

Rappaport, A. (1986) *Creating Shareholder Value: The New Standard for Business Performance*. Free Press, New York.

Rau, S. (2014) Resource-based view of family firms. In L. Melin, M. Nordqvist, & P. Sharma (Eds.), *SAGE Handbook of Family Business*. Sage, London: 321–339.

Rogoff, E. G. & Heck, R. K. Z. (2003) Evolving research in entrepreneurship and family business: recognizing family as the oxygen that feeds the fire of entrepreneurship. *Journal of Business Venturing*, 18(5): 559–567.

Rothaermel, F. T. & Alexandre, M. T. (2009) Ambidexterity in technology sourcing: the moderating role of absorptive capacity. *Organization Science*, 20(4): 759–780.

Scherer, R. F., Adams, J. S., Carley, S., & Wiebe, F. A. (1989) Role model performance effects on development of entrepreneurial career preference. *Entrepreneurship: Theory and Practice*, 13: 53–81.

Scognamiglio, C. (1987) *Teoria e politica della finanza industriale* Il Mulino, Bologna, Italy.

Sharma, P. (2011) Strategic entrepreneurial behaviours in family businesses. *International Journal of Entrepreneurship and Innovation Management*, 13(1): 4–11.

Stavrou, E. T. (1999) Succession in family businesses: exploring the effects of demographic factors on offspring intentions to join and take over the business. *Journal of Small Business Management*, 37(3): 43–61.

Steier, L. P., Chrisman, J. J., & Chua, J. H. (2004) Entrepreneurial management and governance in family firms: an introduction. *Entrepreneurship: Theory and Practice*, 28(4): 295–303.

Steier, T. & Davis, J. A. (2014) Nasty, brutish, short: why businesses prosper then die at an ever faster pace. Available at www.cityam.com/article/1392004929/nasty-brutish-short-why-businesses-prosper-then-die-ever-faster-pace?utm_source=website&utm_medium=TD_opinion_right_col&utm_campaign=TD_opinion_right_col#sthash.MLPqR6i5.dpuf, accessed February 12, 2014.

Stewart III, G. B. (1991) *The EVA Management Guide: The Quest for Value*. Harper Business Publishers Inc., New York.

Villalonga, B. & Amit, R. (2014) Financial performance of family firms. In L. Melin, M. Nordqvist, & P. Sharma (Eds.), *SAGE Handbook of Family Business*. Sage, London: 157–178.

Villanueva, J. & Sapienza, H. J. (2009) Goal tolerance, outside investors, and family firm governance. *Entrepreneurship: Theory and Practice*, 33(6): 1193–1199.

Wiseman, R. M. & Gomez-Mejia, L. R. (1998) A behavioral agency model of managerial risk taking. *Academy of Management Review*, 23(1): 133–153.

Wu, Z., Chua, J. H., & Chrisman, J. J. (2007) Effects of family ownership and management on small business equity financing. *Journal of Business Venturing*, 22(6): 875–895.

Zahra, S. A. (2005) Entrepreneurial risk taking in family firms, *Family Business Review*, 18: 23–40.

Zellweger, T. M., Nason, R. S., & Nordqvist, M. (2012) From longevity of firms to transgenerational entrepreneurship of families introducing family entrepreneurial orientation. *Family Business Review*, 25(2): 136–155.

Conclusion to Part II

Giovanna Dossena

The chapters of this second part each explore specific questions and contribute to building knowledge at the junction of the fields of family and family business. As the literature review in the Introduction to this book shows, much of the extant literature focuses on how the family influences the business; there is a paucity of knowledge on the reverse causality. A second important point relates to the static and culturally specific definition of family: there is very little research on conceptualizations of family other than the nuclear family prevalent in the US until a decade ago.

The main contributions of this second part relate precisely to addressing these caveats. The framework enlightening how entrepreneurial identity, on the individual, family and organizational levels, is formed and evolves over time can support future research in entrepreneurship, family science and family business research. This work can be usefully expanded to questions such as how entrepreneurial identity influences preferred modes of entrepreneurial behaviors or actions. First elements of response to the question of family business' influence on families are offered in relation to the allocation of financial rewards. Future research can further explore the influence of trust and altruism on other firm factors which influence the family, such as work–family balance or even criteria which influence inclusion in the family. The chapter which extends the utilization of socio-emotional wealth to understanding a business family's entrepreneurial behaviors and its consequences on intrafamily entrepreneurship, as well as the influence of individual family members' SEW on intrafamily SEW can usefully support further research, in particular by diversifying the prisms of entrepreneurial behaviors as well as seeking reciprocal influences at the different levels (individual, family, family business) and mobilizing different conceptualizations of family to understand the relative strength of this framework.

In addition to the specific suggestions for further research detailed in each chapter, here we note the main common points which deserve more attention:

- the influence conceptualizations of family, which consider social and cultural specificities, and how they impact the family business;
- the differences in common law and civil law as to the rights and responsibilities of family members and how this influences entrepreneurial behaviors or exit strategies.

In this second part we comprehend that multiplying the conceptualizations of family, admitting an evolving identity and examining until now underexplored causal relationships expand our understanding of Family Entrepreneurship. In the Part III, research at the intersection of family and entrepreneurship, the collected chapters shed light on how the family influences entrepreneurship.

Part III

Intersection
entrepreneurship and family

9 Family context and new venture creation

Sharon M. Danes

Launching new business ventures creates extensive financial, time, and energy demands on resources of entrepreneurs and their families. Discrepancies between demands and resources that are used to meet those demands is a major component contributing to the liability of newness for venture-creating families (Danes & Morgan, 2004; Van Auken & Werbel, 2006). In fact, increasing evidence indicates that operating a small business creates more strain within families than other types of employment (Rahim, 1996; Jamal, 1997; Dolinsky & Caputo, 2003). Conceptual literature about venture creation has suggested that family support for the decision to start a new venture and communication about the new venture significantly influences successful formation and performance of those new ventures (Aldrich & Cliff, 2003; Van Auken & Werbel, 2006), but little empirical work has investigated this proposition. Both empirical analyses and theory about the decision context in new venture creation are this chapter's focus.

A significant part of an entrepreneur's immediate decision context is family, specifically interactions within the entrepreneurial couple relationship and resource flows between spouses to assist with the liability of newness of a new venture. In a decade review of marital stability research, Bradbury, Fincham, and Beach (2000) noted that many marital interaction scholars adhere to the position that meanings and implications of couple interactions and resource flows between them cannot be fully understood without consideration of the broader decision context in which those interactions occur. In the case of new venture creation, the couple relationship context impacts choices, opportunities, and challenges that entrepreneurs experience during venture creation in addition to the entrepreneur's business expertise (Dimov, 2007).

The availability of human and financial capital stocks, however, has been where the entrepreneurship discipline has focused. Although entrepreneurship research has examined the impact of social context on venture creation, it has done so without specific regard to the spousal relationship (Boden & Nucci, 2000; Carter et al., 2003; Gupta & York, 2008; Renzulli, Aldrich, & Moody, 2003). Metaphorically in the ocean of entrepreneurship, discounting the decision making processes of venture-creating couples is like traversing that ocean filled with icebergs. The dimensions of human and financial capital are vital to new venture viability, but these dimensions represent only the section of the iceberg that is above the water line. A huge section of the iceberg is hidden below the water line and that huge section represents the reciprocal influences of family on new venture and new venture on family. Discounting what is below the water line can be disastrous to entrepreneurial success because doing so ignores the social capital that creates resilience in entrepreneurs. "Family" is a structure but to understand its full impact, one must get beyond its structure to capture the processes that occur within that structure to combat the liability of newness of new venture creation.

Couples are the smallest decision making unit of the family science discipline, a discipline that has a long research history that can inform Family Entrepreneurship endeavors. The couple decision making context is ripe with a myriad of values, beliefs, expectations, goals, and emotions that must be traversed in moving toward mutually shared decisions. If entrepreneurs have a strong couple relationship as they create new ventures, that relationship strength can provide a reliable stock of resilience capacity that can be drawn upon to combat the liability of newness of new ventures (Danes, Matzek, & Werbel, 2010). Couple interactions are not only the foundation for such things as spousal commitment and support for the new venture, but, over time, solidarity or eroding of that relationship as the couple traverses the liabilities of newness can impact business achievements in the short term and business sustainability in the long term (Danes et al., 2010; Hall, 2005; Rogoff & Heck, 2003; Oughton & Wheelock, 2003; Van Auken & Werbel, 2006).

The study that serves as the foundation of this book chapter contributes to the literature in a number of ways. First of all, it is a longitudinal study capturing decision processes from prior to business launch to approximately one year after the business began operation. Second, the sample is composed of multi-informants with responses from entrepreneurs and their spouses within venture-creating couples. These multi-informants facilitate the collection of data across family and business systems and the collection of data about couple decision making and interaction processes. Third, the study is grounded in the Sustainable Family Business Theory (SFBT) allowing for conceptual development of such core concepts as copreneurial identity (Danes & Jang, 2013), conceptual precision in that individual and organizational effects are distinguished, and conceptual extensions in that not only are standard procedures considered in times of stability but exception routines (Stallings, 1998) are considered in times of change while creating a new venture. SFBT serves as the organizing guide to the chapter.

Theoretical underpinnings for studying Family Entrepreneurship

Conceptual grounding for any Family Entrepreneurship study requires a theory that acknowledges the heterogeneous nature of both families and firms. Those theories need to not only address structures and processes within both systems, but consider needed structures and processes both in times of stability and in times of change. The Sustainable Family Business Theory (SFBT; Figure 9.1) is inclusive of these characteristics (Stafford et al., 1999; Danes et al., 2008; Danes & Brewton, 2012). It controls for family and business structure while placing emphasis on the heterogeneity of family processes and links to family business processes and outcomes (Danes et al., 2007). Thus, with this theory, not only business heterogeneity is considered but the heterogeneity of families, as well.

Business sustainability over time is its primary outcome rather than such outcomes as revenue and profits because its main tenet is that sustainability is a function of both successful firm performance and healthy family functioning. Family capital stocks and flow processes of those family capital stocks are central to the

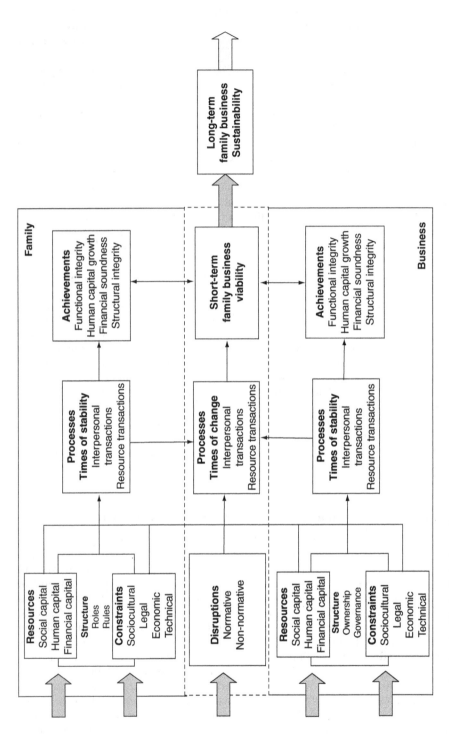

Figure 9.1 Sustainable family business theory.

theory. Family capital refers to stocks and flows of the total bundle of owning-family resources composed of human, financial, and social capital (Danes et al., 2009). SFBT assumes that firm and family systems are functional subsystems of the family business system and identifies parallel family capital resources and interpersonal and resource processes. SFBT also assumes that experiences in one system inform the other because of the focus on resource stocks and flows over time leading to short-term family and firm achievements and long-term family enterprise sustainability.

Most entrepreneurship research is based on theories whose focus is primarily on structures, roles, and rules. A major underlying assumption of these theories is that if structures are changed, processes will change accordingly in a way that might be observable. The same underlying assumption exists in most family theories. Family theories primarily focus on relationship dynamics among family members. Those dynamics are often based on such things as love and trust. SFBT is unique in that it aims to measure observable theoretical constructs.

The theory tracks accumulation of resources (human, social, and financial capital) and access and use of those capital stocks over time, including resource flows back and forth between family and firm. One major SFBT premise is that resource pattern use during times of stability creates adaptive capacity for challenges during times of planned change or unexpected internal and external disruptions. Owning-family adaptive capacity, when combined with its social capital, creates a type of resilience by facilitating resource transport across porous boundaries of the family and firm during change, while maintaining boundary integrity. Adaptive capacity is often what sustains the family enterprises when disruptions occur to either family or firm.

The theory also recognizes that there are standard operating procedures in times of stability and exception routines (Stallings, 1998) in times of change and/or disruption. Exception routines are mechanisms for addressing routines that need to be restored due to the social disorder caused by an internal or external disruption. Many theories used to study Family Entrepreneurship do not incorporate family members who are not owners or who do not work for pay in the business. SFBT assumes that all owning family members have an influence whether they work in the business or not. One of SFBT's unique characteristics is that it recognizes that there are some family processes that are within the family only and some business processes that are just within the business domain, but that there are other processes where resources are shared across boundaries at the intersection of the family and business systems. Two important assumptions of SFBT are that (a) an individual in either the family or business system may affect parts of both systems, and (b) the family or business system can die if the boundaries are too diffuse.

With SFBT as its foundation, this chapter utilizes a data set of entrepreneurs and their spouses who are starting a new business venture. Studying Family Entrepreneurship and venture creation is best investigated through multiple voices of those involved. The data set is longitudinal following venture-creating couples during the first couple of years of formation. The chapter takes the reader from spousal involvement before the business launch through development of a copreneurial identity and the goal congruence that emanates from that identity to its impact on new venture viability. The propositions of SFBT from its various segments will be integrated into the findings from the new venture data set.

New venture creation data set description

The study is a multidisciplinary research effort of two universities in the United States with investigator expertise in family science, entrepreneurship, and organizational behavior. Researchers partnered with Small Business Development Center (SBDC) directors in their respective states to obtain a sample of recently started business ventures. SBDCs are made up of a unique collaboration of the U.S. Small Business Administration, state and local governments, and private sector funding resources. SBDCs provide a wide array of technical assistance to small businesses and aspiring entrepreneurs supporting firm performance and sustainability. SBDCs provide services such as development of business plans, manufacturing assistance, financial packages, and procurement contracts.

Questionnaires were distributed to entrepreneurs and spouses and collected by the SBDCs from pre-venture counseling clients who had participated in at least five hours of start-up counseling. To ensure that we were sampling recently created businesses, two sample restriction questions started the questionnaire. First, we asked entrepreneurs to indicate if the business had started in the last year; second, we asked entrepreneurs if they had a spouse. Out of those that could be delivered, 41 percent were returned. The total sample was composed of 132 new ventures that were started in the last year. Of those businesses, 109 entrepreneurs were married and provided information from both entrepreneur and spouse. No differences were found in comparing the SBDC population who had received counseling and study sample by region of the state, gender, county, ethnic origin, NAICS (North American Industry Classification System) code, and the total counseling hours. In the second year of the study, questionnaires were sent only to entrepreneurs. In total, 94 entrepreneurs returned questionnaires for an 86 percent response rate.

Male entrepreneurs comprised 56 percent of the sample and 44 percent were female entrepreneurs. Industries represented varied. Table 9.1 indicates that distribution of the new ventures using NAICS codes; the industry categories with the largest numbers of new ventures were wholesale and retail trade (21 percent), other services (26 percent), and accommodation and food service (10 percent). Range of full-time work experience was from less than a year to 52 years with an average of 21 years. Industry work experience prior to venture creation ranged from less than a year to 50 years with an average of nine years.

Table 9.1 NAICS codes for new ventures

NAICS code	%
Agricultural	1
Construction	5
Manufacturing	8
Wholesale and retail trade	21
Finance and real estate	2
Professional, scientific, and technical	9
Education	1
Administration and support	5
Health care and social assistance	8
Arts, entertainment, and recreation	4
Accommodation and food service	10
Other services	26

Age of entrepreneurs ranged from 23 to 70 (mean was 42 years). Twelve percent had a high school degree or less, 45 percent had some college, 25 percent had an undergraduate degree, and 18 percent had a graduate degree. The majority of firms were home based (62 percent). Entrepreneurs worked, on average, about 46 hours a week in the new venture. However, entrepreneurs who already made a sale prior to study participation worked significantly more hours than those entrepreneurs whose ventures were still in incubation. Entrepreneurs who had already made a sale worked an average of 50 hours a week. Those in the incubation stage worked an average of 34 hours a week. Children lived at home in 59 percent of the cases. The distribution of ages of children living at home were as follows: 22 percent of the entrepreneurs had at least one child five years old or less living at home, 43 percent had at least one child between 6 and 17 years old living at home, and 8 percent with at least one adult child (18 years and older) living at home.

Early in the chapter, when delineating the nature of copreneurial interactions while creating a new venture, summaries of initial descriptive analyses and citations for that work are provided. More attention here will be spent on differences by gender of the entrepreneur and by timing of new venture breakeven points. Although structural equation modeling was used in analyses about goal congruence and copreneurial identity formation, citations are provided for those readers who want to explore the details about the complex analyses. What is presented in the chapter are results and discussion of the implications of those analyses.

According to SFBT, family capital resources are classified as a bundle of resources in the form of human, financial and social capital. Note that family capital resources are identical in the family and business systems (Figure 9.1). The only difference is that within the business system, nonfamily employee, manager, and leader capital is a part of the business structure in addition to that of family capital. Spouses of entrepreneurs can contribute family capital directly to the business by working in the business or indirectly by working outside the business providing income stability during the launching period and, in some cases, also providing health insurance for the family. Additionally, those spouses may provide social capital through commitment to the business and emotional or instrumental support to the entrepreneur. Both types of involvement can provide stability to the new venture (Danes & Olson, 2003; Liang, 2002).

There were some statistical differences in spousal capital contributed to the new business venture based on gender of the entrepreneur. Seven percent of spouses of entrepreneurs had neither direct nor indirect involvement in the business launch (Table 9.2). Eighteen percent worked in the business only. Thirty-seven percent of spouses worked outside the business in the marketplace only. And, 38 percent of spouses combined working both within the business and in the marketplace. More spouses of male entrepreneurs worked in the business only compared to their counterparts, whereas, more spouses of female entrepreneurs worked in the marketplace only.

Providing health insurance is an instrumental type of support for US venture-owning couples that creates resilience for the entrepreneur in that he/she does not have to concern themselves with that segment of family security as they initiate the new venture. Slightly over half (51 percent) of spouses working in the marketplace provided family health insurance. When that figure was broken down by entrepreneur's gender, 64 percent of spouses of female entrepreneurs

Table 9.2 Direct and indirect spousal involvement during new venture launch

	Total sample	Male entrepreneurs	Female entrepreneurs
Overall spousal involvement			
No involvement	7%	10%	4%
Work in business only	18%	**30%****	4%
Work in marketplace only	37%	22%	**54%****
Work in and outside business	38%	38%	38%
Spouse works outside business	74%	61%	**92%****
Provides health insurance	51%	35%	**64%***
Spousal average earnings	$32,756	$14,774	**$54,333****

Notes
* $p<0.10$.
** $p<0.05$; asterisk is placed at the higher bolded mean.

provided family health insurance through their marketplace employment compared to 35 percent of their counterparts. Spouses of female entrepreneurs who worked in the marketplace outside the business earned almost four times what the spouses of male entrepreneurs earned.

SFBT resources, structures, and constraints

Three SFBT propositions align with the SFBT segment about resources, structure, and constraints (Danes & Brewton, 2012):

a   Family capital (composed of human, social, and financial capital) from both family and business are inputs that can be used to solve problems of the collective interaction of family and business.
b   Capital can have simultaneous positive or negative effects on firm performance, depending on the circumstances.
c   Constraints impose limits on alternative capital, processes, and achievements available.

Family capital resource inputs to families and firms are inherently a stock concept which has characteristics of a reservoir that can be drawn upon. However, in SFBT, when drawn upon, the use of family capital is part of the processes of resource and interpersonal transactions. Understanding of family capital flows from the family to the firm is essential because Danes et al. (2009) found that access to and utilization of family social capital over time was more important for sustainability of a business venture than the family social capital level.

The dual empowering and constraining characteristics of family capital might be illustrated by family members working in the business. When couples start new business ventures, the family often provides the new venture with a steady supply of trustworthy human resources (Ward, 1997). Chrisman, Chua, and Steier (2002) stated that new ventures might not face the same liability of newness because of the labor provided by family members. In these formative years, the new venture benefits from family social capital in that it fosters commitment and a sense of identification with the founder's dream (Van Auken & Neeley, 2000; Van Auken, 2003; Winborg & Lanstrom, 2001). However, as the demands of a growing business expand, the human capital stock of the business may be eventually outstripped. Thus, constraints on families and their businesses limit resource use (Danes et al., 2008).

Couplehood: the foundational springboard for entrepreneurial ventures

Little attention has been given to the family social capital processes of entrepreneurship for venture-creating couples such as transferring trust capital from the couple relationship to development of support and commitment for the new venture. Based on the economic bonds of marriage, spouses become critical stakeholders in new venture creation providing resources to entrepreneurs as well as to the new ventures (Danes et al., 2010; Matzek, Gudmunson, & Danes, 2010; Steier & Greenwood, 2000). Although couples starting new business ventures commonly blend their personal and professional relationships (Muske et al., 2009), a lack of understanding of couple dynamics within the entrepreneurship discipline has led to a tendency to consider business-owning couples as a type of organizational team (Dyer, 2003; Kadis & McClendon, 1991).

This tendency has led to a faulty impression that these couples are a mere sum of individuals. Dimov (2007) states such an approach discounts the important stakeholder role of spouses in making entrepreneurial decisions and is a fundamental attribution error. Venture-creating couples are often portrayed as two independent individuals in a marital union having different or shared agendas in family and business. In fact, Davidsson and Honig (2003) suggested that simply having a spouse is an important resource for new venture owners. This view does not fully reflect uniquenesses of venture-creating couples that are different from business partners who are not in an intimate relationship. "Couplehood" defined as "the relationship between two committed individuals who share a sense of identity, commitment, and purpose" (McGovern, 2011) is a helpful concept in understanding the interactional history that creates a high level of trust between entrepreneur and spouse, an essential component of social capital. Couple-based trust is foundational for future endeavors such as creating a new venture.

Unlike other business partnerships that purposely select partners based on mutual business goals (Spekman et al., 1998), couples starting businesses build interactions around their new venture based on their existing couplehood (Sorenson, Goodpaster, & Hedberg, 2009). Reflecting this notion, venture-creating couples who have achieved couplehood consider their new venture as "our business" rather than "my business." An entrepreneur's decision to launch a new venture thus depends not only on opportunity analyses but also on how much an entrepreneur's spouse shares a common vision about firm goals, risks, and rewards (Van Auken & Werbel, 2006).

In this new venture creation study, spouses were asked about how the entrepreneurs had consulted and discussed business issues before the launch (Danes et al., 2010). The question stem read as follows: "Think back to before the business got started. How much do you agree or disagree with the following statements before the business was launched." Responses ranged from 1 (strongly disagree) to 5 (strongly agree).

Danes et al. (2010) reported the degree of various types of spousal consultation by the entrepreneur relative to the new venture prior to launch. Analyses of those queries were performed in that 2010 chapter for the entire venture-owning couple sample. Questions included willingness to financially invest in the new venture as well as such questions as to whether the spouse considered the new venture to be good for the family, knew the risks of the business, and whether they were familiar with the new venture business plan. One year later, actual spousal involvement in the business was obtained. By this time, the business was in operation long enough for actual spousal involvement patterns to be established whereas responses received prior to launch were more reflective of spousal intentions for business involvement.

These types of spousal consultation by the entrepreneur, however, emanate from the strength of the couple relationship. Thus, it is important to understand the spousal social capital context in which new venture creation evolves. A strong couple relationship provides a stock of resilience capacity composed of spousal resources from which entrepreneurs can draw (Danes et al., 2010). For the couple relationship strength question, entrepreneurs responded on a 5-point Likert scale from 1 (strongly disagree) to 5 (strongly agree) to "I have a deep sharing relationship with my spouse." About 39 percent of entrepreneurs reported having a very strong relationship (5 on the 5-point Likert scale) whereas 61 percent reported not having as strong a relationship (1–4 on the 5-point scale).

The process of drawing upon spousal resources creates a change in the spousal stock (either enhancement or reduction), that when added to the original level, becomes the current period's output, which will be input for the next time period (Danes et al., 2009). The connection between a strong couple relationship and spousal involvement prior to business launch is indicated in Table 9.3. Significant differences between couples who reported a very strong relationship (39 percent) and those who reported not having such a relationship (61 percent) were found.

Entrepreneurs who indicated that they had a very strong relationship had spouses who reported that they (a) were consulted more about their business ideas, (b) expressed more to the entrepreneur that the business was a good idea, (c) knew more about business risks, and (d) were more familiar with the business plan.

The garnering of spousal social capital early within the new venture creation process is demonstrated in the findings shown in Table 9.4. The effect of spousal consultation and involvement prior to the venture launch is investigated based on time to break even. Break-even point is a market indicator of new venture success. Entrepreneurs reporting higher spousal involvement levels before the launch reported shorter break-even points one year after launch. The break-even

Table 9.3 Spousal involvement prior to business launch and strong couple relationship

Spousal involvement indicator	Sample means	Not very strong relationship	Very strong relationship
Spouse was consulted more about ideas about business	3.76	3.58	**4.05****
Spouse expressed that new business was a good idea	4.18	4.00	**4.48****
Spouse was willing to co-sign a loan	4.10	4.03	4.21
Spouse considered business would be good for family	4.21	4.07	**4.43***
Spouse knew the risks of family business	4.18	4.15	4.24
Spouse was familiar with business plan	3.87	3.72	**4.12***

Notes
* $p<0.10$.
** $p<0.05$; asterisk is placed at the higher bolded mean.

Table 9.4 Effect of spousal consultation prior to business launch on break-even points

	Total sample		Male entrepreneur		Female entrepreneur	
	≤12 mos.	12 mos.	≤12 mos.	12 mos.	≤12 mos.	>12mos.
Told spouse new business was a good idea	**4.37***	3.94	4.28	4.15	**4.45***	3.67
Happy to co-sign a loan	**4.42***	3.91	4.39	4.15	**4.45***	3.60
Consider business will be good for family	**4.42***	3.97	4.28	4.15	**4.55***	3.73
Familiar with business plan	**4.03***	3.37	3.94	3.55	**4.10***	3.13
Had a lot of information about family business	**3.84***	3.26	3.83	3.60	**3.85***	2.80

Notes
* Statistically significant difference at $p<0.10$; asterisk is placed at the higher bolded mean.

point was lower for all the involvement questions; however, that effect might be overpowered by the half of the sample that were female entrepreneurs since that same effect was true for female entrepreneurs but not for male entrepreneurs.

A further indicator of whether entrepreneurs and spouses were "on the same page" about the business launch was their satisfaction with communication quality about the new venture (Harcourt, Richerson, & Wattier, 1991). Both entrepreneur and spouse were asked about communication quality on several dimensions of business operations. Those included satisfaction with communication about business objectives, future business plans, business strategy, business sales, business problems, and business finances. Entrepreneur and spouse were asked: "How satisfied or dissatisfied are you with the quality of communication from your spouse?" Responses ranged from 1 (very dissatisfied) to 5 (very satisfied). No significant differences were found between entrepreneur and spouse. After a year of operation, both entrepreneur and spouse were most satisfied with communication about business objectives and least satisfied about business finance communication. For all questions, spouses reported a higher satisfaction level than did entrepreneurs, although it was not statistically significant.

SFBT processes in times of stability

According to SFBT, resource transactions (e.g., utilization or transformation of social, human, or financial capital) and interpersonal transactions (e.g., commitment to the new venture or support to the entrepreneur) can facilitate or inhibit new venture sustainability. SFBT processes transform inputs into achievements in the short term and sustainability in the long term given structure and constraints. Short-term processes that entail capital flows result in transformed capital stocks that are available inputs for future time periods' processes. There are five SFBT propositions that relate to this segment of the theory:

a   The process of drawing upon family capital stock creates a change in that capital stock (either enhancement or reduction), that when added to the original level, becomes the current period's output, which will be input for the next time period.
b   Owning families manage both family and business system resources together to meet overlapping needs instead of each apart from the other.
c   The degree of overlap between family and business adjusts depending upon demands emanating from either internal or external demands.
d   Out of the overlap of family and business evolves a culture that assumes (either intentionally or unintentionally) some of the values, attitudes, and beliefs of the owning family.
e   Processes in the family and business are composed of interpersonal transactions and resource transactions that can be thought as routine or standard operating procedures.

The next set of findings illustrates the transformation of social capital stocks from the couple relationship (couplehood) into capital useable by entrepreneurs to accomplish short-term achievements within the new business venture. This transformation occurs at the interplay of family and firm systems. The transformation reflects values and beliefs of this venture-creating couple and becomes part of the standard operating procedures of the new venture. For instance, a strong value of respect for people's talents and opinions within the venture-creating couple may well play out in employee meetings where owners treat their employees' opinions with respect. An entrepreneur consulting his/her spouse about business issues even before the new venture began will most likely carry that approach into employee meetings.

Transforming spousal social capital from family to new venture

The couplehood of venture-creating couples grounded in the family system is closely related to the concept of copreneurs grounded in the business system. Copreneurs refers to business-owning couples having shared goals, dreams, and ideals about the new venture (Fitzgerald & Muske, 2002). Blenkinsopp and Owens (2010) argued that most new ventures are copreneurial with a varying extent of spousal involvement in the business. Spousal involvement in the business could be direct as when they work along with the entrepreneur in the new venture or they may contribute indirectly by providing emotional or financial support for the new venture. Regardless of the extent of spousal instrumental involvement in the business, the core of copreneurship is whether spouses share business and family goals as a couple (Van Auken & Werbel, 2006). This goal congruence is a critical dimension of copreneurship since the entrepreneur and spouse cannot pursue individual goals without considering their partners' goals (Gere et al., 2011) if they have a strong couplehood. New venture commitment is built from the shared goals and business vision that evolves out of a strong couplehood (Danes & Jang, 2013).

There are two distinct research streams about couples creating new ventures. One stream assumes conflict between husband and wife that impedes business success; in contrast, another stream assumes spousal and family support promoting success (Van Auken & Werbel, 2006). One reason two distinct streams of thought exist is that theoretical orientations have not allowed for the possibility of spousal resources having simultaneous positive and negative effects (resources being assets or liabilities). With strong "couplehood," a stock of resilience capacity composed of spousal resources exists from which entrepreneurs can draw (Danes et al., 2010). However, over time, spousal resources can contribute or detract from the liability of newness in venture creation before launch and continually thereafter (Danes et al., 2009).

The study spousal commitment measure represents moral commitment. Moral commitment may elicit a feeling of responsibility from the spouse leading to positive firm contributions such as personal sacrifice as well as feelings of burden and stress (Hall, 2005). Entrepreneurs reported on their spouses' firm commitment and spouses were asked to report on their own commitment. The scale was adapted from Penley and Gould (1988). Questions were modified to refer to the new venture. The question stem read as follows: "Please indicate how much you agree or disagree with the following statement regarding your spouses' feelings about the business" (Table 9.5). Responses ranged from 1 (strongly disagree) to 5 (strongly agree). High commitment levels were reported given by spouses and received by entrepreneurs.

Emotional support has enabling characteristics when it facilitates preservation of other valued resources (Hobfoll, 1989). For example, resources are preserved when entrepreneurs have a particularly hard day and over dinner, the entrepreneur and spouse problem-solve together resulting in motivation to tackle the

Table 9.5 Spousal commitment, social support, and business communication quality based on break-even points and gender of entrepreneur

	Total sample		Male entrepreneur		Female entrepreneur	
	≤12 mos.	>12 mos.	≤12 mos.	>12 mos.	≤12 mos.	>12 mos.
Spousal commitment						
Spouse dedicated to business goals	**4.34***	3.74	**4.33***	3.65	4.35	3.87
Spouse duty to support business goals	**4.34***	3.74	**4.33***	3.75	4.35	3.73
Spouse motivated by thoughts of greater personal rewards	**3.84***	3.26	**4.06***	3.35	3.65	3.13
Spouse gives effort when customers are loyal	3.76	3.29	**3.72***	3.00	3.80	3.67
Spouse feels personal responsibility to help achieve business goals	**4.39***	3.57	**4.44***	3.60	**4.35***	3.53
Spousal support						
Rely on spouse for emotional support	**4.00***	3.51	3.94	3.80	**4.05***	3.13
Go to spouse when feeling down about the business	**4.34***	3.80	4.33	4.20	**4.35***	3.27
Open about what we think about the business	**4.24***	3.63	4.33	3.80	**4.15***	3.40
Spouse sensitive to personal needs with running the business	**3.92***	3.46	4.11	3.75	**3.75***	3.07
Rely on advice of spouse	**3.80***	3.29	3.61	3.30	**3.95***	3.27
Most people are closer to spouse than I	1.79	**2.40***	2.00	2.35	1.60	**2.47***
Spouse does not understand the business so I consult others	2.05	**2.63***	2.11	2.55	2.00	**2.73***
Business communication quality						
Business objectives	**3.97***	3.23	**4.11***	3.30	**3.85***	3.13
Future business plans	**4.03***	3.20	**4.17***	3.35	**3.90***	3.00
Business strategies	**4.05***	3.26	**4.33***	3.35	**3.80***	3.13
Business finances	**3.82***	3.23	**4.06***	3.35	3.60	3.07
Business problems	**3.95***	3.31	**4.06***	3.40	3.85	3.20

Notes

* Statistically significant difference at $p<0.10$; asterisk is placed at the higher bolded mean.

problem the next day. However, because social support can have a stress contagion effect and has a time-limited effect (Hobfoll & Spielberger, 1992), if the problem persists for a long time, entrepreneurs could begin to feel that they are not meeting spousal expectations; spousal emotional support could then make entrepreneurs feel anxious that the business is not doing as well as expected. In that case, expression of emotional support drains the entrepreneur's energy rather than preserving energy, resulting in a constraining effect.

Emotional support represents a spouse's support for the entrepreneur's work role. Entrepreneurs and spouses were asked about their spouses' support for the business: "Please indicate how much you agree or disagree with the following statements" (Table 9.5). The responses ranged from 1 (strongly disagree) to 5 (strongly agree). These items were developed by Prodicano and Heller (1983). There were eight questions in this index. There were high amounts of emotional support given reported by spouses and received by entrepreneurs.

Spousal commitment and support indicators related to shorter break-even points

Although Danes et al. (2010) reported in frequencies of the entire sample of venture-creating couples that spouses reported giving statistically more commitment than entrepreneurs reported receiving and that there was agreement within the venture-creating couple on emotional support given and received, we do not know differences in commitment and emotional support by either gender of the entrepreneur or by length of break-even point. Table 9.5 depicts differences.

There were statistical differences between firms that broke even in 12 or fewer months and those that took more than 12 months to break even. The relationship for each spousal characteristic in Table 9.5 was one where the mean for the spousal indicator was higher when it took 12 or fewer months to break even. Thus, these indicators are described as having a positive impact on the break-even point. Spousal indicators are organized by conceptual labels of indexes that they represent in the literature. Groupings include spousal commitment, spousal support, and business communication quality.

Within analyses of the total sample, most questions of spousal commitment and support were statistically higher for those new ventures that broke even in less than one year. High quality communication with a spouse was significantly related to shorter break-even points. It appears that higher quality communication about business objectives, plans, strategies, finances, and problems helps the business break even within one year or less.

When investigating by entrepreneurs' gender, male entrepreneurs whose business broke even in less than one year had higher spousal commitment levels. The same findings were not true for female entrepreneurs except for the question, "Spouse feels personal responsibility to help achieve business goals."

For male entrepreneurs, there were no statistical differences based on break-even point for any of the spousal support questions. The opposite was true for female entrepreneurs. In most cases, expression of support helped the business break even in less than a year. However, for two questions about spousal closeness and whether the entrepreneur consulted with other than the spouse, the opposite was true. For most communication quality questions, with higher quality came a shorter break-even point. That was true for both male and female entrepreneurs.

SFBT processes in times of change

A unique contribution of SFBT is that it acknowledges that standard operating procedures used in normal times need to be adjusted in times of change. Launching a new business venture can be extremely demanding for many reasons (Prottas & Thompson, 2006). Most new ventures are privately owned with few to no employees (Astrachan & Shanker, 2003). Owners of these ventures typically work many hours (Lewin-Epstein & Yuchman-Yaar, 1991) and risk family financial assets in hopes of success (Astebro & Bernhardt, 2003; Basu & Parker, 2001; Haynes & Avery, 1996; Haynes et al., 1999). SFBT delineates five propositions that reflect the resource and interpersonal processes that occur during times of change:

a   Systems interact by exchanging capital (resources and constraints) at their boundaries during times of disruption and those resources can be tracked.
b   After disruptions, processes must be reconstructed to ensure sustainability over time.
c   Conflicts arise when there is a mismatch between demands and resources that can be used to meet those demands.
d   Patterns of resource and interpersonal transactions in firm and family systems during times of stability create a resilience capacity that serves as a foundation for addressing stresses during times of change and disruption.
e   Family and business are affected by environmental and structural change that can be normative and non-normative.

The primary family process of concern for new venture creation is work/family balance. In fact, Danes and Morgan (2004) found when surveying a nationally representative sample of family businesses that work/family balance was the highest tension producer and remained so over time (Danes, 2006). Work/family conflict indicators have to do with discrepancies between how entrepreneurs and spouses perceive work and family issues or differences in the preferences they hold. Work overload questions have to do with consequences that family members experience when work demands of entrepreneurs in terms of time and energy expended for business work spill into the family realm and begin to affect relationships there.

Major constraints (stressors) within venture-creating couples

Achieving and maintaining work/family balance may be especially difficult in the stressful conditions that are associated with launching a new venture (Van Auken & Werbel, 2006). Qualitative work has captured poignant descriptions of busy venture-creating couples' impressions of life imbalance, the personal cues in their lives that signaled a lack of balance, and their personal responses to "perceived breakdowns" (Stoner, Robin, & Russell-Chapin, 2005, p. 338). According to Stoner et al. (2005), dual CEO/manager couples indicated that imbalance was the result of "single-mindedness in the work domain" (p. 339); intense work involvement made life feel "horribly out of whack" (p. 337) and achieving balance seemed impossible for very long; and although some wanted to devote themselves exclusively to work, most wanted to maintain work/family balance but felt like they were "out of control" (p. 341). Inner emotional tension, moodiness, a myopic focus in life, frustration, anger, and physiological symptoms were all cues that life was out of balance. Ironically, most initially responded by trying to work harder – to work through job demands – but this was seldom a helpful response. Successful responses were based on stepping away, prioritizing, and redirecting work demands.

Work/family conflict refers to pressures experienced by entrepreneurs due to incompatible roles and the demands of those roles (Kopelman, Greenhaus, & Conolly, 1983). Both entrepreneurs and spouses were asked about their personal experience of work/family conflict using this stem: "Please indicate how much you agree or disagree with the following statements" (Table 9.6). The responses ranged from 1 (strongly disagree) to 5 (strongly agree). The items were developed by Kopelman et al. (1983). Because of the nature of the questions, a low score is a good thing and contributes to new venture viability.

Within the total sample, Table 9.6 indicates clearly that with higher work/family conflict, the breakeven point is extended beyond a year. However, when the sample is divided between male and female entrepreneurs, a different picture emerges. With female entrepreneurs, means for work/family conflict are higher in the greater than a year column and those means are statistically higher than for new ventures that broke even in less than a year. The only question for male entrepreneurs where there was a statistically higher work/family conflict among the break-even categories is for compatibility of spousal preference for family activities. For male entrepreneurs, when conflict was higher, that conflict extended the break-even time.

Time demands of a new venture are reflected in the measure of work overload. Respondents were asked about their personal experience of work overload: "Please indicate how much you agree or disagree with the following statements" (Table 9.6). The responses range from 1 (strongly disagree) to 5 (strongly agree). The items were developed by Kopelman, Greenhaus, and Connolly (1983). Because of the nature of the questions, a low score is a good thing and contributes to new venture viability.

For almost all work overload questions, the higher the work overload, the longer the new venture will take to break even when considering the entire sample of entrepreneurs. A clearer understanding emerges, however, when work overload issues are viewed by male and female entrepreneurs. For female entrepreneurs, when they personally are affected by work overload issues, the breakeven point is longer than a year. Comparatively, for male entrepreneurs, break-even points are extended when work overload issues affect their family relationships. For both genders, when work overload rises, break-even points for their new ventures are longer.

The findings in Table 9.6 indicate that work/family conflict and work overload issues within venture-creating couples extend break-even points in new ventures. The concerns of work/family conflict and work overload are ones that cross the porous boundaries between family and new business. The issues affect not only the family (spouse and children) but the entrepreneur, as well, in that there is spillover from the family system into the business system having short-term impacts on the family and entrepreneurs but also having long-term effects on new venture sustainability, if stressful conditions are not satisfactorily managed.

Table 9.6 Work/family conflict and work overload extends break-even points

	Total sample		Male entrepreneur		Female entrepreneur	
	≤12 mos.	>12 mos.	≤12 mos.	>12 mos.	≤12 mos.	>12 mos.
Work/family conflict						
Spouse and I differ about spending time alone	2.24	**2.83***	2.06	2.50	2.40	**3.27***
Spouse prefers that I do something else to earn money	1.74	**2.63***	1.83	2.45	1.65	**2.87***
Not compatible with spouse's preferences for family activities	1.58	**2.66***	1.61	2.50*	1.55	**2.87***
Work overload						
Come home too tired to do what I would like	2.63	**3.14***	2.78	3.00	2.50	**3.33***
Work takes away from my personal interests	2.61	**3.40***	2.72	3.25	2.50	**3.60***
Family dislikes my preoccupation with work while at home	2.16	**2.69***	2.17	2.45	2.15	**3.00***
Work too many hours in a day	2.55	**3.31***	2.50	3.15	2.60	**3.53***
Work often conflicts with family life	2.26	**3.03***	2.17	**3.05***	2.35	**3.00***
Work takes up time I like to spend with my family	2.68	**3.26***	2.72	**3.30***	2.65	3.20
Difficult to be the kind of spouse I want to be	2.18	**2.80***	1.89	**2.70***	2.45	2.93
Work is demanding, I'm irritable at home	2.63	2.86	2.33	**2.90***	2.90	2.80

Notes

* Statistically significant difference at *p*<0.10; asterisk is placed at the higher bolded mean.

Developing a copreneurial identity

Family social capital, particularly that of the spouse, can positively contribute to the resilience of the entrepreneur when the couple relationship is strong. That social capital is known to be the door to other human and financial capital that could be used to benefit the new venture. However, only a small understanding exists about the dynamics of how spousal social capital transforms other forms of capital that contributes productively to new venture viability. The development of copreneurial identity is one such way.

Entrepreneurial literature is filled with how entrepreneurs form their identity (Dimov, 2007). We know little, however, about how entrepreneurs and their spouses *mutually* form a collective, copreneurial identity. Fletcher (2010) studied ways in which venture creation was constructed between co-habiting couples in terms of both the "life making" (how couples established a work/family life while working together to create new venture viability) and "risk taking" (addressing the various challenges that starting a new business venture presents). Creating a copreneurial identity is the transformation of the social capital of couplehood into productive business capital.

Commitment to new venture goals by the entrepreneur's spouse is core to the formation of copreneurial identity (Danes & Jang, 2013). Understanding copreneurial identity formation is important because commitment links identity to behavior (Burke & Reitzes, 1991; Stets, 2006). In other words, commitment to the new venture by the entrepreneur's spouse is vital to that venture's viability in the short term. Entrepreneurial identity has been understood as an individual construct. Moving to the next phase of creating a collective, copreneurial identity involves a shared vision and investment involving each member of a couple. To progress to this next stage, it is not enough that each individual within the couple sees themselves as an entrepreneur; a collective cognition needs to form and the couple must become aware of the existence of the "us" in the copreneurial couple (Danes & Jang, 2013; Pierce & Jussila, 2010). That "we-ness" is a fundamental base of commitment to the new venture (Burke & Reitzs, 1991; Helmle, Seibold, & Afifi, 2011). Furthermore, couples with a mutual commitment to new venture goals have a substantial impact on its sustainability over time (Danes et al., 2010).

Mutual commitment cannot develop without satisfactory intra-couple communication concerning business objectives (Matzek et al., 2010). Starting a new business can be a continuous struggle of contradictions. Developing a collective cognition resulting in mutual commitment and a copreneurial identity requires continual communication between the entrepreneur and their spouse about business vision and goals (Danes & Jang, 2013; Van Auken and Werbel, 2006). Married couples already are steeped in a personal relationship that is connected through past interaction, communication, and decision making patterns. With new venture creation comes the need to negotiate and reconstruct a new type of relationship that is *both* personal and professional – a *copreneurial identity* (Helmle et al., 2011).

A mutual verification process between spouses is core to that reconstruction and is steeped in the venture-creating couple interaction and decision making processes. However, these processes are largely unseen patterns created, sustained, and modified through their couple relationship (Danes & Jang, 2013; Dyer & Dyer, 2009). These underlying couple patterns shape family life, determine family effectiveness, and are hypothesized to have reciprocal relationships with processes and outcomes of new venture creation; spousal resources are a family capital form that comes in a bundle of human, financial, and social capital resources (Danes et al., 2009). However, existing venture creation research has focused primarily on spousal human and financial resources within the total *family* capital bundle. Furthermore, this research has assumed that when spouses exist, their resources are used for the new venture's competitive advantage without actually measuring whether it was used (Danes et al., 2010).

Access to spousal resources by entrepreneurs depends, in part, on a spouse's commitment to new venture goals. That spousal commitment underlies the formation of a copreneurial identity, and that commitment and identity formation contributes to new venture stability (Burke & Stets, 1999). Cognitive moral commitment is of particular import because of its foundational roots being grounded in acceptance of and identification with new venture goals (Penley & Gould, 1988). Strong spousal commitment for new venture goals is a source of competitive advantage that facilitates business success (Danes et al., 2010). Inadequate commitment leads to diminished resources for the new venture both directly and indirectly (Werbel & Danes, 2010).

Spousal commitment influences entrepreneur's attitudes, resources, and motivation toward the firm, all of which fuel the entrepreneur's energy resources to facilitate firm success (Poza & Messer, 2001). Spousal commitment affects a spouse's willingness to deploy family-based resources for business support (Grote, 2003). However, spousal commitment is not an all-or-none phenomenon; rather, it is a continuum that changes over time or with circumstances either in the firm or family system. For example, in Kirkwood's (2009) spousal commitment study, female entrepreneurs tended to gain their spouse's commitment before starting the new venture whereas male entrepreneurs did not. With spousal commitment comes active support, such as spouses working in the new venture, or more passive emotional support such as the extent to which a spouse listens, offers ideas, or makes suggestions about the business with those actions positively influencing the quality of the entrepreneur's decision making.

Tensions and disagreements between entrepreneur and spouse are bound to arise in the stressful new venture creation context with its high work demands. However, Baxter (2004) posits that tensions can be negotiated through quality communication and those practices are reflective of past couple experiences. Helmle et al. (2011) posited that venture-creating couples experience most difficulty in the early stages of new venture creation because they are building and maintaining both the new business venture at the same time the couple is developing their copreneurial identity. Couple relationships are not static and a major change such as starting a new business requires reconstruction of a couple's communication processes (Matzek et al., 2010). Development of a copreneurial identity, then, is not only dependent on mutual commitment to new venture goals, but depends on quality communication about the venture's goals (Danes et al., 2010). Collective identities such as a copreneurial identity reside in relationships (Berscheid, 1994) so without mutual goal commitment and quality communication about goals, copreneurial identity cannot fully develop resulting in greater risks for new business sustainability.

The identity verification process has two parts; first is spousal input and feedback. That spousal feedback allows entrepreneurs to evaluate whether there is congruity between their identity standard and reflected appraisals of spousal commitment. The second part of the identity verification process is assessment of social interactions that occur within the role setting with regard to both entrepreneur and spouse identity standards. Identity standards are adjusted when they are not verified in their role setting (Burke & Stets, 1999). If there is congruity between a spouse's reflection of their commitment and entrepreneur's assessment of spouse's commitment, there will be more focused use of couple resources toward targeted business goals. Danes and Jang (2013) provide evidence that new venture creation is an iterative, interactive process between entrepreneurs and their immediate context, a big part of which is spousal interaction (Danes et al., 2010; Dimov, 2007). The next step is to investigate the enabling forces created through the total family capital flows of which entrepreneurs now have access due to this spousal commitment toward new venture goals.

The level of communication about business goals plays a role in the formation of a copreneurial identity (Danes & Jang, 2013). Communication, however, is socially constructed, which means that context (the couple relationship in this case) is vitally important (Danes et al., 2010). Communication between spouse and entrepreneur about new venture goals potentially has both advantages and disadvantages. And, because of this contextual orientation, there is no ideal amount of venture-related communication between entrepreneur and spouse that will lead to sustainability. Although sharing concerns about new venture issues may contribute to sustainability of a new venture and the couple relationship, excessive sharing may not be ideal for all couples (Vanlear, 1990). The appropriate and effective extent of communication about new venture goals depends on each couple's standards.

With regard to copreneurial identity formation, an important issue concerns deviations between entrepreneurs and spouses in assessment of spousal commitment to new venture goals (Danes & Jang, 2013). While there is variation across couples, entrepreneurs perceived less spousal commitment to new venture goals in the Danes and Jang (2013) study than reported by spouses. If left unmanaged, this situation could eventually undermine a new business venture as the entrepreneur perceives/needs more resource support than the spouse is willing to offer. However, with commitment to new venture goals by the spouse as well as the entrepreneur, a copreneurial identity evolves creating a resilience capacity that can be accessed during tough or hectic times within the new venture.

Achievements, short-term family business viability, and long-term sustainability

A core tenet of SFBT is that long-term sustainability is a function both of new venture success and of family functionality. However, SFBT also posits that achievements within family and business interact to create short-term new venture viability. This short-term venture viability is represented by the separate but related well-beings of family and business. That is because family and business are inextricably interconnected. One cannot achieve well-being in either system without reaching the well-being in the other system. Three SFBT propositions reflect these essential conditions.

a   Sustainability is a function of both business success and family functionality.
b   Owning families manage family and firm jointly to optimize achievements.
c   Family firms' outcomes include both short-term viability and long-term sustainability.

SFBT recognizes the multi-dimensionality of new venture sustainability. Financial and market measures have always been the gold standard in measuring business success. However non-pecuniary measures of new venture success provide more insight into the owners' commitment to or passion for the firm (Danes et al., 2008; Gimeno, 2005; Stanforth & Muske, 2001). The findings that follow reflect the importance of spousal goal congruence in its effect on new venture viability.

Copreneurial goal congruence and new venture viability

Copreneurial goal congruence (alignment of spousal goals) (Gere et al., 2011) reveals whether spouses are on the same page about their new venture goals. This goal congruence is grounded in the couple relationship rather than individuality (Jang & Danes, 2013; McGovern, 2011) in that the idea of "our new venture" evolves from their already established cognition of "we-ness" (Kaplan et al., 1995). A lack of couple goal congruence causes a critical stress for copreneurs (Nelton, 1986) and the disagreement on goals may result in destructive couple conflict (Van Auken & Weber, 2006). Copreneurs with couple goal congruence tend to contribute more to their new ventures, and, consequently, it boosts their business viability (Danes & Jang, 2013, Fitzgerald & Muske, 2002; Van Auken & Weber, 2006).

Spousal contribution is even stronger when spouses believe in the benefit of their business to family (Gersick et al., 1997). Gottman and Silver (1999) argue that couple goal congruence results in increasing communication between spouses. When couples share common goals, entrepreneurs can more easily discuss business vision, strategies, and decisions (Van Auken & Werbel, 2006). Hydock and Eckstein (2006) additionally state that a lack of couple goal congruence leads to miscommunication, and, subsequently, the inhibition of appropriate support exchange between entrepreneur and spouse.

The resilience capacity to tackle the liability of newness is built by interpersonal, interactive communication processes that serve as a buffer against stresses during new venture creation and during early years of business operation (Danes & Jang, 2013; Danes & Brewton, 2012). Just as shared goals are an indicator of current trust levels because they are a force that holds people together and motivates them to share what they know (Chow & Chan, 2008), the experience of future trust is determined by the content of behavioral exchanges between entrepreneur and spouse (Jones & George, 1998). For example, quality communication about business issues helps couples develop standard operating procedures for managing family and business (Jang & Danes, 2013). Doing so maintains the trust cycle between entrepreneur and spouse as they interact in cooperative ways; these continued positive interactions create future trusting beliefs (McKnight, Cummings, & Chervany, 1998). When the couple encounters disruptions, stored trust and standard operating procedures already established are then used to modify interpersonal transactions without causing chaos (Danes & Brewton, 2012), and, consequently, contributes toward new venture viability.

Venture-related communication enables copreneurs to share realistic expectations about the future of their new venture (Van Auken & Werbel, 2006). To plan the future, copreneurs need to share appropriate information concerning financial and strategic situations of the new venture (Ward, 1997). It is particularly crucial for copreneurs in the early stages of new venture creation to grasp the potential resource gain and loss of the new venture in reality (Danes et al.,

2010; Foley & Powell, 1997; Stewart & Danes, 2001). Furthermore, quality venture-related communication is critical for new venture performance (Nelton, 1986), copreneurial identity formation (Danes & Jang, 2013), work–family balance (Gudmunson et al., 2009), and mutual sustainability of the new venture, the couple, and family system (Jang & Danes, 2013; Matzek et al., 2010).

Moving from couple to family goal congruence

The findings that were just explained were about couple goal congruence; when "Family Entrepreneurship" includes more than one couple, however, goal congruence becomes more complex. If the multi-level complexity in "family" is not managed when attempting to create mutual goal attainment, the process becomes confounded and more conflictual than it needs to be. There are three steps to the progression of determining mutual family goals (Figure 9.2).

First, each individual needs to reflect on their own needs related to the goal to be decided upon. There are constraints that each gender faces at this juncture. Females need to determine their own view about the goal because they tend to consider what is important to their spouse or children instead of what is most critical for them; if females make that decision based on desires of someone else, they eventually experience dissatisfaction and tension leading eventually to feelings of resentment. Males need to consider how other family members besides themselves could potentially be affected by the various goal options; not considering other immediate family members could eventually lead to dissatisfaction and tension leading to feelings of lack of respect and importance. Once these individual goal reflections have been determined, it is only then that spouses of the couple should come together to attempt to attain consensus about goal reflections that they, as a couple within the family enterprise, should promote.

After each couple within the family enterprise has determined their view on the potential family enterprise goal, then all the family units involved can come

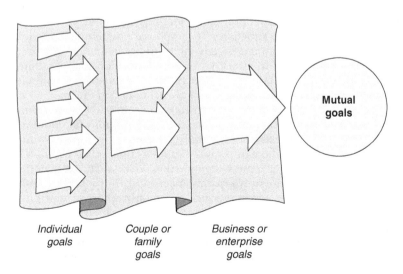

Individual goals   Couple or family goals   Business or enterprise goals

Figure 9.2 Three steps in mutual goal setting process.

together to work on mutual goal determination. If each of these steps does not occur, then individual goal uncertainty or individual couple disagreement about goals can confound the group or family decision making process. If this three-stage process is followed, it does not mean that there will be no conflict or tension, but it does reduce the potential for confounding of various levels of communication to become entangled such that the family enterprise decision process becomes immobilized.

This chapter presented longitudinal empirical findings from data of entre-preneurs and their spouses who were creating new business ventures. The pre-sentation of findings was grounded in the Sustainable Family Business Theory (Danes & Brewton, 2012). Metaphorically in the ocean of entrepreneurship con-taining icebergs, this chapter addressed the decision making processes of venture-creating couples that are positioned below the water line that conven-tional entrepreneurship research does not usually traverse.

Study findings indicated that strong couple relationships prior to business launch led to quality communication about new venture goals. Furthermore, this spousal social capital stock is the foundation for spousal commitment to new venture goals and emotional and instrumental support for entrepreneurs. Synergis-tic effects of spousal commitment for new venture goals and quality couple commu-nication about those goals forms a copreneurial identity and goal congruence that leads to shorter break-even points and greater venture viability over time.

The Sustainable Family Business Theory is a theory that has been empirically tested. Propositions of the theory were presented in the chapter; in fact, those propositions were the organizing guide for the chapter. SFBT acknowledges the heterogeneous nature of both businesses and families. The theory tracks accumu-lation of resources (human, social, and financial capital) and access and use of those capital stocks over time, including resource flows back and forth between family and firm. In the future, Family Entrepreneurship research must consider the role of family social capital in creating entrepreneurial resilience in addition to the conventional human and financial capital stock focus of past entrepre-neurial research.

More research is needed about copreneurial identity formation, the flow of spousal resources that occurs at varied levels of spousal commitment to new venture goals, communication about needs of entrepreneurs for resource support for the new venture, and its effect on the couple relationship over time. In addition, it is important to understand how couples assess spousal commit-ment about new venture goals. These suggestions are grounded in the main tenet of SFBT which states that viability of the new venture and sustainability over time is a function of both successful firm performance and healthy family functioning.

Future study is needed to investigate what underlies couple discrepancies and their consequences not only for the new venture but the couple relationship. It is also important to understand that spousal commitment is not a static concept; it changes over time. We need to identify circumstances in which spousal commit-ment is more or less resilient to adversity which commonly occurs in new busi-ness ventures. What actions can entrepreneurs take to increase spousal commitment?

Addressing such questions is important in building sustainability. Although Danes and Jang (2013) found that entrepreneur's assessment of spousal commit-ment was an important part of the identity verification of copreneurs, it is still unknown how spouse and entrepreneur exchange opinions about their identity standards. If couples don't communicate well, spouses may receive the wrong type of feedback leading to a stifling of spousal identity rather than messages that fertilize that identity. Future study is needed to explore associations between couple communication and spousal commitment in conceptual and methodological depth.

Copreneurial spouses are involved in their ventures to varying degrees and how each spouse contributes to the venture is unique to their individual set-up (Blenkinsopp & Owens, 2010). For some couples, both spouses are actively involved in business activities and have joint ownership from a legal standpoint. For others, the spouse might appear not to be involved in the business, but that spouse may significantly contribute to the venture through unofficial roles such as performing administration tasks, especially in the launching stage (Blenkinsopp & Owens, 2010). Similarly, the ideal extent of venture-related communication differs among copreneurs and depends on each couple's standards; while some couples enjoy talking about business issues at home, it may not be true for others (Helmle et al., 2011).

Copreneurs struggle in achieving well-being of family and firm simultaneously because success/failure of one system has an intrinsic influence on the other. Trust between entrepreneur and spouse is essential in tackling the liability of newness of new ventures. Positive expectations are a core indicator of trust (Jones & George, 1998) and they are mechanisms by which spouses and entrepreneurs continually evaluate ongoing quality of the trust experience. Expectations thus are a core aspect of new venture viability. Successful behavior exchanges are accompanied by positive expectations which help to cement the trust experience (Jones & George, 1998).

Thus, couplehood is an essential ingredient to combat the liability of newness of new venture creation. Business knowledge and experience and financial backing are critical to new venture viability, but this chapter has provided evidence that a strong couple relationship also provides a stock of existing resilience capacity that can be accessed, as well, to combat the liability of newness within new venture creation.

References

Aldrich, H., & Cliff, J. E. (2003). The pervasive effects of family on entrepreneurship: toward a family embeddedness perspective. *Journal of Business Venturing, 18,* 573–596.

Astebro, T., & Bernhardt, I. (2003). Launch-up financing, owner characteristics, and survival. *Journal of Economics and Business, 55,* 303–319.

Astrachan, J. H., & Shanker, M. C. (2003). Family businesses' contribution to the U.S. economy: a closer look. *Family Business Review, 16,* 211–219.

Basu, A., & Parker, S. C. (2001). Family finance and new business launch-ups. *Oxford Bulletin of Economics and Statistics, 63,* 333–358.

Baxter, L. (2004). Relationships as dialogue. *Personal Relationships, 11,* 1–22.

Berscheid, E. (1994). Interpersonal relationships. *Annual Review of Psychology, 4,* 29–79.

Blenkinsopp, J., & Owens, G. (2010). At the heart of things: the role of the "married" couple in entrepreneurship and family business. *International Journal of Entrepreneurial Behaviour and Research, 16,* 357–369.

Boden, R. J., & Nucci, A. R. (2000). On the survival prospects of men's and women's new business ventures. *Journal of Business Venturing, 15,* 347–362.

Bradbury, T. N., Fincham, F. D., & Beach, S. R. H. (2000). Research on the nature and determinants of marital satisfaction: a decade of research. *Journal of Marriage and the Family, 62*(4), 964–980.

Burke, P. J., & Reitzes, D. C. (1991). An identity theory approach to commitment. *Social Psychology Quarterly, 54*(3), 239–251.

Burke, P. J., & Stets, J. E. (1999). Trust and commitment through self-verification. *Social Psychology Quarterly, 62*(4), 347–366.

Carter, N. M., Gartner, W. B., Shaver, K. G., & Gatewood, E. J. (2003). The career reasons of nascent entrepreneurs. *Journal of Business Venturing, 18*, 13–39.

Chow, W. S., & Chan, L. S. (2008). Social network, social trust, and shared goals in organizational knowledge sharing. *Information and Management, 45*, 458–465.

Chrisman, J. J., Chua, J. H., & Steier, L. P. (2002). The influence of national culture and family involvement on entrepreneurial perceptions and performance at the state level. *Entrepreneurship: Theory and Practice, 26*(4), 113–129.

Danes, S. M. (2006). Tensions within family business-owning couples over time. *Stress, Trauma and Crisis, 9*(3–4), 227–246.

Danes, S. M., & Brewton, K. E. (2012). Follow the capital: benefits of tracking family capital across family and business systems (Ch. 14, pp. 227–250). In A. Carsrud & M. Brannback (Eds.), *Understanding Family Businesses: Undiscovered Approaches, Unique Perspectives, and Neglected Topics.* Springer, New York.

Danes, S. M., & Jang, J. (2013). Coprencurial identity development during new venture creation. *Journal of Family Business Management, 3*(1), 45–61.

Danes, S. M., & Morgan, E. A. (2004). Family business-owning couples: an EFT view into their unique conflict culture. *Contemporary Family Therapy, 26*(3), 241–260.

Danes, S. M., & Olson, P. D. (2003). Women's role involvement in family businesses, business tensions, and business success. *Family Business Review, 16* (1), 53–68.

Danes, S. M., Matzek, A. E., & Werbel, J. D. (2010). Spousal context during the venture creation process (pp. 113–162). In J. A. Katz & G. T. Lumpkin (Eds.), *Advances in Entrepreneurship, Firm Emergence and Growth*, Vol. 12. Emerald, New Milford, CT.

Danes, S. M., Lee, J., Stafford, K., & Heck, R. K. Z. (2008). The effects of ethnicity, families and culture on entrepreneurial experience: an extension of sustainable family business theory. Invited article for *Journal of Developmental Entrepreneurship, Special Issue* entitled Empirical Research on Ethnicity and Entrepreneurship in the U.S., *13*(3), 229–268.

Danes, S. M., Stafford, K., Haynes, G., & Amarapurkar, S. (2009). Family capital of family firms: bridging human, social, and financial capital. *Family Business Review, 22*(3), 199–215.

Danes, S. M., Stafford, K., & Loy, J. T. (2007). Family business performance: the effects of gender and management. *Journal of Business Research, 60*(10), 1058–1069.

Davidsson, P., & Honig, B. (2003). The role of social and human capital among nascent entrepreneurs. *Journal of Business Venturing, 18*, 301–331.

Dimov, D. (2007). Beyond the single-person, single-insight attribution in understanding entrepreneurial opportunities. *Entrepreneurship: Theory and Practice, 31*(5), 713–731.

Dolinksy, A. L., & Caputo, R. K. (2003). Health and female-self employment. *Journal of Small Business Management, 41*, 233–242.

Dyer, W. G. (2003). The family: the missing variable in organizational research. *Entrepreneurship: Theory and Practice, 27*(4), 401–416.

Dyer, W. G., Jr., & Dyer, W. J. (2009). Putting the family into family business research. *Family Business Review, 22*(3), 216–219.

Fitzgerald, M. A., & Muske, G. (2002). Copreneurs: an exploration and comparison to other family businesses. *Family Business Review, 15*, 1–16.

Fletcher, D. (2010). "Life-making or risk taking"? Co-preneurship and family business start-ups. *International Small Business Journal, 28*(5), 452–469.

Foley, S., & Powell, G. (1997). Reconceptualizing work-family conflict for business/marriage partners: a theoretical model. *Journal of Small Business Management, 35*, 36–47.

Gere, J., Schimmack, U., Pinkus, R. T., & Lockwood, P. (2011). The effects of romantic partners' goal congruence on affective well-being. *Journal of Research in Personality, 45*, 549–559.

Gersick, K., Davis, J., Hampton, M., & Lansberg, I. (1997). *Generation to Generation: Life Cycles of the Family Business.* Harvard Business School Press, Boston, MA.

Gimeno, A. (2005). Performance in the family business: a causal study of internal factors and variables. Doctoral Dissertation, ESADE Universitat Ramon Llull, Spain.

Gottman, J. M., & Silver, N. (1999). *The Seven Principles for Making Marriage Work.* Crown, New York.

Grote, J. (2003), Conflicting generations: a new theory of family business rivalry. *Family Business Review, 16,* 113–124.

Gudmunson, C. G., Danes, S. M., Werbel, J. D., & Loy, J. T. C. (2009). Spousal support and work/family balance in launching a family business. *Journal of Family Issues, 30,* 1098–1121.

Gupta, V. H., & York, A. S. (2008). Geographical and generational context effects of women's attitudes towards entrepreneurship. USASBE 2008 Proceedings. 1437–1455.

Hall, A. (2005). Beyond the legal: psychological ownership and responsibility in the family business. *FBN 16th Summit.*

Harcourt, J., Richerson, V., & Wattier, M. J. (1991). A national study of middle managers' assessment of organization communication quality. *Journal of Business Communication, 28*(4), 348–365.

Haynes, G. W., & Avery, R. J. (1996). Family businesses: can the family and the business finances be separated? Preliminary results. *Entrepreneurial and Small Business Finance, 5,* 61–74.

Haynes, G. W., Walker, R., Rowe, B. R., & Hong, G. S. (1999). The intermingling of business and family finances in family-owned businesses. *Family Business Review, 12,* 225–239.

Helmle, J. R., Seibold, D. R., & Afifi, T. D. (2011). Work and family in copreneurial family businesses (pp. 51–91). In C. T. Salmon (Ed.), *Communication Yearbook,* Vol. 35. Routledge, New York.

Hobfoll, S. E. (1989). Conservation of resources. *American Psychologist, 44*(3), 513–524.

Hobfoll, S. E., & Spielberger, C. D. (1992). Family stress: integrating theory and measurement. *Journal of Family Psychology, 6,* 99–112.

Hydock, R., & Eckstein, D. (2006). Help me help you: a systematic approach to goal support for couples. *Family Journal, 14,* 164–168.

Jamal, M. (1997). Job stress, satisfaction, and mental health: an empirical examination of self-employed and nonself-employed Canadians. *Journal of Small Business Management, 35,* 48–57.

Jang, J., & Danes, S. M. (2013). Are we on the same page? Copreneurial couple goal congruence and business viability. *Entrepreneurship Research Journal, 3*(4), 483–504.

Jones, G. R., & George, J. M. (1998). The experience and evolution of trust: implications for cooperation and teamwork. *Academy of Management Review, 23*(3), 531–546.

Kadis, L. B., & McClendon, R. (1991). A relationship perspective on the couple-owned business. *Family Business Review, 4*(4), 413–424.

Kaplan, L., Ade-Ridder, L., Hennon, C. B., Brubaker, E., & Brubaker, T. (1995). Preliminary typology of couplehood for community-dwelling wives: "I" versus "we". *International Journal of Aging and Human Development, 40,* 317–337.

Kirkwood, J. (2009). Spousal roles on motivations for entrepreneurship. *Journal of Family and Economic Issues, 30,* 372–385.

Kopelman, R., Greenhaus, J. H., & Connolly, T. F. (1983). A model of work, family, and interrole conflict: a construct validation study. *Organizational Behavior and Human Performance, 32,* 198–215.

Lewin-Epstein, N., & Yuchtman-Yaar, E. (1991). Health risks of self-employment. *Work and Occupations, 18,* 291–312.

Liang, C. (2002). My love and my business. *Academy of Entrepreneurship Journal, 8*(2), 53–77.

McGovern, J. (2011). Couple meaning-making and dementia: challenges to the deficit model. *Journal of Gerontological Social Work, 54,* 678–690.

McKnight, D. H., Cummings, L. L., & Chervany, N. L. (1998). Initial trust formation in new organizational relationships. *Academy of Management Review, 23*(3), 473–490.

Matzek, A. E., Gudmunson, C. G., & Danes, S. M. (2010). Spousal capital as a resource for couples starting a business. *Family Relations, 58,* 58–71.

Muske, G., Fitzgerald, M. A., Haynes, G., Black, M., Chin, L., MacClure, R., & Mashburn, A. (2009). The intermingling of family and business financial resources: understanding the copreneurial couple. *Journal of Financial Counseling and Planning, 20,* 27–47.

Nelton, S. (1986). *In Love and in Business: How Entrepreneurial Couples are changing the Rules of Business and Marriage.* Wiley, New York.

Olson, P. D., Zuiker, V. S., Danes, S. M., Stafford, K., Heck, R. K. Z., & Duncan, K. A. (2003). Impact of family and business on family business sustainability. *Journal of Business Venturing, 18*(5), 639–666.

Oughton, E., & Wheelock, J. (2003). A capabilities approach to sustainable household livelihoods. *Review of Social Economy, 61*(1), 1–22.

Penley, L. E., & Gould, S. (1988). Etzioni's model of organizational involvement. *Journal of Organizational Behavior, 9,* 43–59.

Pierce, J. L., & Jussila, I. (2010). Collective psychological ownership within the work and organizational context. *Journal of Organizational Behavior, 31*(6), 810–834.

Poza, E. J., & Messer, T. (2001). Spousal leadership and continuity in the family firm. *Family Business Review, 14,* 25–35.

Procidano, M. E., & Heller, K. (1983). Measures of perceived social support from friends and family: three validation studies. *American Journal of Community Psychology, 11,* 1–24.

Prottas, D. J., & Thompson, C. A. (2006). Stress, satisfaction, and the work-family interface: a comparison of self-employed business owners, independents, and organizational employees. *Journal of Occupational Health Psychology, 11,* 366–378.

Rahim, A. (1996). Stress, strain and their moderators: an empirical comparison of entrepreneurs and managers. *Journal of Small Business Management, 34,* 46–58.

Renzulli, L. A., Aldrich, H., & Moody, J. (2003). Family matters: gender, networks, and entrepreneurial outcomes. *Social Forces, 79*(2), 523–546.

Rogoff, E G., & Heck, R. K. Z. (2003). Evolving research in entrepreneurship and family business: recognizing family as the oxygen that feeds the fire of entrepreneurship. *Journal of Business Venturing, 18,* 559–566.

Sorenson, R. L., Goodpaster, K. E., & Hedberg, P. R. (2009). The family point of view, family social capital and firm performance. *Family Business Review, 22,* 239–253.

Spekman, R. E., Forbes, T. M., Isabella, L. A., & MacAvoy, T. C. (1998). Alliance management: a view from the past and a look to the future. *Journal of Management Studies, 35,* 747–772.

Stafford, K., Duncan, K. A., Danes, S. M., & Winter, M. (1999). A research model of sustainable family businesses. *Family Business Review, 12*(3), 197–208.

Stallings, R. (1998) Disaster and the theory of social order (pp. 127–145). In E. L. Quarantelli (Ed.), *What is a Disaster? Perspectives on the Question.* Routledge, New York.

Stanforth, N., & Muske, G. (2001). *An Exploration of Entrepreneurship.* Oklahoma State University Department of Design Housing and Merchandising, Stillwater, OK.

Steier, L., & Greenwood, R. (2000). Entrepreneurship and the evaluation of angel financial networks. *Organizational Studies, 21*(1), 163–192.

Stets, J. E. (2006). Identity theory (pp. 88–110). In P. J. Burke (Ed.), *Contemporary Social Psychological Theories.* Stanford University Press, Stanford, CA.

Stewart, C. C., & Danes, S. M. (2001). The relationship between inclusion and control in resort family business: a developmental approach to conflict. *Journal of Family and Economic Issues, 22,* 293–320.

Stoner, C. R., Robin, J., & Russell-Chapin, L. (2005). On the edge: perceptions and responses to life imbalance. *Business Horizons, 48,* 337–346.

Van Auken, J. (2003). An empirical investigation of bootstrap financing among small firms. *Journal of Small Business Strategy, 14*(2), 22–36.

Van Auken, J., & Neeley, L. (2000). Pre-launch preparations and the acquisition of capital. *Journal of Developmental Entrepreneurship, 5,* 169–182.

Van Auken, H. & Werbel, J. (2006). Family dynamic and family business financial performance: spousal commitment. *Family Business Review, 19,* 49–63.

Vanlear, C. A. (1990). Communication and marital satisfaction: social desirability and non-linearity. *Communication Research Reports, 7*(1), 38–44.

Ward, J. L. (1997). *Keeping the Family Business Healthy: How to Plan for Continuing Growth, Profitability, and Family Leadership.* Business Owner Resources, Marietta, GA.

Werbel, J. D., & Danes, S. M. (2010). Work family conflict in new business ventures: the moderating effect of spousal commitment to the new business venture. *Journal of Small Business Management, 48*(3), 421–440.

Winborg, J., & Landstrom, H. (2001). Financial bootstrapping in small business: examining small business managers' resource acquisition behaviors. *Journal of Business Venturing, 16*(3), 235–254.

10 The role of networking in the growth process of entrepreneurial family firms

Sarah Drakopoulou Dodd, Alistair Anderson and Sarah Jack

Introduction

In this chapter, we investigate the role of networks within the context of family firms. Our concern is how might networks support those family firms that look to engage in the process and practice of entrepreneurship. Our conceptual starting point is that networking provides structure, process and content for entrepreneurial firms (Hoang & Antoncic, 2003; Elfring & Hulsink, 2007; Slotte-Kock & Coviello, 2010). The social ties that form networks shape information, skills and knowledge availability, and perception of specific opportunities (Brüderl & Preisendörfer, 1998; Uzzi, 1997; Davidsson & Honig, 2003; Hite, 2005; Renzulli & Aldrich, 2005). Network relationships frame access to resources, customers and strategic partners, as well as configuring the entrepreneur's own perceived legitimacy. Networks may be especially important within the *familiness* of family business in that they provide external focal points to compare with the internalities of the family itself. The importance of networking holds true for venture creation, as well as for subsequent entrepreneurial developments of the enterprise. Moreover, ventures which survive start-up, and pursue growth, show signs of substantial evolution in their networking practices and relationships. In essence, then, the importance of external business–friend ties to venture growth is now well established. There is also evidence for the increasing strengthening of what begin as arms-length business ties, but transmute into rich, multiplex and complex relationships.

Family firms are characterized by the work/family dynamic and the relationship which this offers, which has been referred to as being unique (Drakopoulou Dodd et al., 2012). But the link to entrepreneurial theorizing has drifted as studies have tended to focus on structure, succession and business issues rather than process, practice and what drives their very existence and growth. This is a pity because by the very definition, a family firm is characterized by the special nature of the family relationship. Hence relationships outside the family should be interesting. Nonetheless, recent discussions have started to recognize that family firms can be entrepreneurial, especially in the ways in which they might grow and develop. However, much less is known about how the family might draw on networks and the impact these networks might have on if, and how, the family firm practices entrepreneurship and how venture growth might come about. The findings from the general entrepreneurship literature linking entrepreneurial venture growth and networking have thus far been so robust that it seems likely that this ought to be the case in family firms. Nevertheless, there are a number of contingencies which modify the nature of entrepreneurial networking, such as nationality (Dodd et al., 2002), ethnicity (Anderson & Lee, 2008), gender (Robson et al., 2008), class (Anderson & Miller, 2003), business sector, venture position in value-chain and – as noted already – stage of venture development (Anderson et al., 2010). Moreover, relational issues are likely to have a strong effect on the family firm's distinctive interconnections (Anderson et al., 2012). It thus seems feasible to propose that whilst networking will be as important for family firms as it is for other entrepreneurial ventures, some aspects of networking processes, structures and content may well be specific to the family firm context and influence how they engage with entrepreneurial process and practice.

We therefore pose the question, how do family firms who are engaged in the practice of entrepreneurship enhance, extend and evolve external network ties for venture growth? To address this question, we draw together theoretical developments from the family firm realm, and entrepreneurial networking theory, to analyze data from 12 family firms who were perceived to be acting entrepreneurially through the exploitation of new opportunities (Stevenson & Jarillo, 1990; Shane & Venkataraman, 2000). In doing so we investigate the ways in which these structures and processes interact to impact upon entrepreneurial growth. Three countries were selected for the fieldwork – Scotland, England and Greece – and both rural and urban contexts from each country were chosen. Family firms were purposefully chosen (Gartner & Birley, 2002; Pratt, 2009) who were identified as being (1) interesting at a theoretical level and (2) willing to share openly their experiences with the research team. Semi-structured interviews were carried out with 12 family firm entrepreneurs. Special attention was paid to issues relating to networking and growth. The constant comparative method (Jack et al., forthcoming) was utilized to analyze interview transcripts, with team members moving between data and theory in an iterative pattern until few new insights occurred.

Our findings identified interesting and important divergence in the patterns of networking enacted by family firm entrepreneurs during venture growth. For example, growth strategies for many of the family firms tended to be driven by resources available within the family–firm nexus. Market and technology evaluations took place through quite formal, "professional" mechanisms in many cases. The usage of weak-ties, which has come to be seen of diminished importance for non-family entrepreneurs, appeared more significant for family-firm growth. This has implications for the way we perceive networking within the context of the family firm and especially for the practice of entrepreneurship.

This chapter presents an overview of the academic literature pertinent to the research question, focusing especially on the growing body of work on entrepreneurial networking and growth, as well as attempting to unpick the complicated story of growth in the family firm. Next, the possible interactions between these two scholarly streams are discussed, to consider the specific nature of family firm networking during venture growth. The study's methodology is then recounted, followed by our findings. Finally, results are discussed in the light of extant conceptual and empirical contributions, and conclusions drawn.

Entrepreneurial networking, growth and the family firm

Entrepreneurial networking and growth

In the past decade scholars have attempted to examine the development of entrepreneurial networks over time, from pre-start up through establishment to venture growth. Whilst accepting that there are certainly other valuable approaches to studying entrepreneurial networking throughout the growth process (Jack et al., 2008; Anderson et al., 2010; Slotte Kock & Coviello, 2010), the life-cycle, staged model provides a helpful frame for considering these issues. Typically, such an approach focuses on three stages in the new venture's "life": pre-start; establishment and growth (see, for example, Jack et al., 2008, 128–129).

Considering first the pre-start phase, entrepreneurs dedicate a substantial amount of time to deploying existing social contacts, and identifying who key contacts may be to secure resources (Larson & Starr, 1993). Indeed, the very opportunity and resource perception which gives rise to the venture may derive largely from nascent entrepreneurs' close social ties (Hite, 2005). Existing social networks thus provide the main foundation for the venture (Lechner & Dowling, 2003), and are especially likely to include family, friends and business contacts from earlier employment (Anderson et al., 2010; Larson & Starr, 1993; Pages & Garmise, 2003; Ram, 2001). Family members in particular are often especially important and promote entrepreneurship, identify opportunities, offer practical assistance, provide specialized advice and act as sounding blocks. Former colleagues and customers offer a mid-level entry point for the new venture (Anderson et al., 2010). Much time is spent developing and maintaining these key contacts (Greve & Salaff, 2003), although there is also some evidence of new, instrumental ties being generated to meet specific start-up needs (Larson & Starr, 1993).

Such new ventures as survive the pre-start phase typically next enter a stage of venture establishment. Networks are both *deepened*, through the ongoing strengthening of existing ties, and also *broadened*, through the development of new network contacts. Ties which during start-up were essentially instrumental are often deepened, with social dimensions developing in economic ties, and potentially vice versa, as relationships become multiplex (Larson & Starr, 1993; Johannisson, 1995). In terms of broadening networks, Jack et al. (2008) find that entrepreneurs may recognize the need to shift the level, managerial position and status of their business contacts to a higher plane. They seem to achieve this by gathering a very wide pool of potential strong-tie contacts, with whom they share personal affinity, and who also appear to offer possible benefits to their firm. Greve and Salaff (2003) also find that during venture establishment more time is spent on network expansion. Technology entrepreneurs, in particular, have been shown to increase sales through the development of marketing networks during venture establishment, whilst also making the most of their technology base by leveraging co-opetition networks (Lechner & Dowling, 2003).

After establishment, ventures that have survived and thrived typically strive to attain substantial growth. This is the main focus of the current study, and hence will receive more detailed analysis than the two earlier stages (pre-start and establishment) reviewed above. One hallmark of entrepreneurial networking at the growth stage is that some aspects of strong-tie interaction may become routinized, or delegated to other people within the entrepreneur's venture (Larson & Starr, 1993; Jack et al., 2008). This provides the relational space for the entrepreneur to "trigger" the pool of latent ties developed during establishment, hunting for the ideas, opportunities and resources that will fuel their growth (Greve & Salaff, 2003; Jack et al., 2008). Similarly, Lechner and Dowling (2003) show that technology entrepreneurs often achieve venture growth by extending the co-opetition networks (activated during establishment) into through-going technological partnering.

Many scholars note that during the growth phase, it is probable that relational limits may be reached (Lechner & Dowling, 2003). Specific relational ties achieve their full multiplex complexity and richness during the growth stage, with strong emotional bonds, high levels of trust, elevated exchanges of information and resources, and well-integrated organizations (Larson & Starr, 1993). Entrepreneurs and their strong-ties may thus already be giving each other such an abundance of support that still more is not really possible. To grow further, an entrepreneur must find ways to move beyond what Hite and Hesterley (2001) perceptively call "identity-based strong tie networks", to avoid being held back by over-reliance on family and friends ties (Johannisson and Mønsted, 1997). Practices to overcome these relational constraints may include a more calculative approach to rationally choosing network partners (Hite & Hesterley, 2001); as well as continued development and deployment of ever-higher level strong-ties. Other approaches uncovered in studies of entrepreneurial growth networking include internalizing high-level strong-ties through the mechanism of board directorates. Entrepreneurs have also been found to build new strong-ties – often through a brokered connection – to explore specific new product, service and market development. Subsequently, growth is driven by the creation of product and service innovations in line with the articulated needs of these new strong-ties, and with the requisite resources extracted from the network, rather than being de facto held within the entrepreneurs' own venture. As this discussion has shown, in recent years a much clearer and quite consistent picture has emerged of the nature of entrepreneurial networking throughout various stages in a venture's life. What this has led to is an appreciation of the nature of networking during entrepreneurial growth. However, still relatively unexplored is the nature of networking of family firms and how this relates to entrepreneurial practice.

It is noteworthy that it is along social cultural lines that differences in entrepreneurial networking can most commonly be seen. Although broad universal patterns in entrepreneurial networking have been observed (Aldrich et al., 1989; Johannisson & Nilsson, 1989), national cultures have been found to shape social contexts and patterns and practices of networking in quite specific ways (Birley et al., 1991; Aldrich & Sakano, 1995; Staber & Aldrich, 1995; Greve, 1995; Dodd & Patra, 2002; Dodd et al., 2002; Mitchell & Co, 2004), suggesting various forms rather than being universal in character (Klyver & Terjesen, 2007, 3; Klyver et al., 2008, 333–335). For example, recent work has even gone so far as to suggest that German start-up networking patterns may vary very substantially indeed from other cultures (Witt et al., 2008). Other studies have indicated that gender (Aldrich et al., 1998), ethnicity (Ram, 1994), and indigeneity (Foley, 2008) may also influence some elements of entrepreneurial networking. This is not surprising since, as Curran and colleagues have argued, "networks are best seen as primarily cultural phenomena, that is as sets of meanings, norms and expectations usually linked with behavioural correlates of various kinds" (Curran et al., 1993). Since the family is one of humanity's most significant societal forms, we anticipate that for those engaged in entrepreneurial practices the influence of relational ties on venture growth in family firms is an interesting area to study.

Given the idiosyncratic nature of family firm relational matrices can we expect to see such extensive uses made of external strong ties during venture growth? Equally, since family firms of their very nature comprise "identity-based strong ties", how can they move beyond the constraints of relational limits to ties for growth? Before we explain how our empirical study explored such issues, it is important to consider the specific nature of growth within the family firm, and its specific facilitators and inhibitors.

The complicated story of growth in family firms

The foundation of the family firm is entrepreneurship (Chua et al., 2004). Many family firms act entrepreneurially through identifying and exploiting opportunities (Stevenson & Jarillo, 1990; Shane & Venkataraman, 2000), their behavior, strategies or practices (Short et al., 2009). Yet, little work has been carried out which really delves into the relationship between entrepreneurship and how it connects with family firms.

In a family firm, there are many complicated, diverse and ever changing interactions between the two key institutions of family and business venture. These complex interactions take place within a frame that appears simultaneously *both* to promote stability and conservatism, whilst *also* seeking entrepreneurial growth. Depending upon which is most likely to protect the socio-emotional wealth invested within their ventures, for example, business-owning families may enact either very risky, or, conversely, very risk-averse, strategic behaviors (Gómez-Meja et al., 2007). Matters are complicated still further, since within the same family firm factions may arise around the degree of individual identification with the family (Minchilli et al., 2010).

The tradition of stability associated with family firms may be characterized by a long-term strategic view, by firm-specific special skills and knowledge, by a passionate commitment to the venture and by an emphasis on the continuity of certain core values and norms (Chrisman et al., 2005; Habbershon et al., 2003; Habbershon & Williams, 1999; Miller & Le Breton-Miller, 2006; Shepherd & Zahra, 2003; Sirmon & Hitt, 2003; Tagiuri & Davis, 1996; Zahra, 2005; Zahra et al., 2004). Recent evidence has emerged that family firms are less likely to engage in diversification than non-family firms (Gómez-Meja et al., 2010). Miller et al. (2008) have argued that, if taken to extremes, this stewardship culture may turn into corporate stagnation, and inhibit growth very strongly indeed (see also Arregle et al., 2007). Such stagnation is often associated with a venture culture that prioritizes the needs and desires of the family, through kin-specific altruism (Lubatkin et al., 2005; Schulze et al., 2002).

On the other hand, and notwithstanding these forces toward stability and conservatism, family firms have also been found to have some specific drivers of organizational growth. Because ownership and managerial control are so concentrated, family firms may act quite rapidly, aggressively, flexibly and independently (Carney, 2005; Chrisman et al., 2009; 745; Miller & Le Breton-Miller, 2006). Innovation and entrepreneurship may also become enculturated within the family firm (Craig & Moores, 2006; Zahra et al., 2004), as key behavioral norms are developed and enhanced over several generations, and thus provide special resources to fuel family firm growth (Eddleston et al., 2008, 27).

In a recent examination of organization renewal within family firms, Drako-poulou Dodd and Theoharakis (2010) were able to conclude that certain family firms exhibit strong tendencies toward "morphing", which in turn generated substantial organizational growth. Their findings show that "founder CEOs, CEO growth aspiration, and succession planning facilitate morphing within the family firm ... whilst higher proportions of family employees curtails morphing".

Overall, then, it seems clear that some family firms develop a culture of innovation and organizational renewal which fuels venture growth. Making the most of their specific knowledge, skill, commitment, flexibility and rapidity, the enhanced performance of such firms may go some way toward explaining the continued success of the family firm sector (Chrisman et al., 2009).

Networking and growth in the family firm

As the literature reviewed above makes clear, most conceptualizations of growth issues within the family firm concentrate on the somewhat paradoxical dynamics of entrepreneurial culture and conservatism. Relatively little consideration has been given to the significance, or otherwise, of networking practices and processes for venture growth and how these support entrepreneurial practice within the family firm environment. Zahra (2010, 358) has shown that family firms leverage their organizational social capital to invest in newer ventures, thus accessing novel knowledge. Miller et al. (2008, 57) note that the networked cronyism of some large, established family firms with leading institutions (including government) may act to enhance conservatism and to inhibit entrepreneurship. Morck and Young (2003, 2004) have made similar arguments suggesting that successors may be more likely to seek growth through political rent-seeking, rather than through the pursuit of opportunities through entrepreneurship. If this is indeed so, then it suggests at least one possible growth strategy for family firms is indeed dependent upon social capital, albeit through the vehicle of political network ties.

An additional possibility for large family firms may be that their network position places them so as to be visible and attractive to other, potential growth partners. This visibility is enriched by a belief in the legitimacy of the venture as a family firm, which is seen to "guarantee" certain modes of business, values and strategies. These two elements – visibility and family firm legitimacy – combine to make the venture and its family members attractive business partners to other similar organizations, who then construct growth opportunity propositions which they present to the large family firm. Evidence for such practices has been found both by sociologists studying the Medici clan in medieval Florence (1993), as well as more recent work examining a large Irish waste management group (Clinton et al., 2010). Similarly, family firms can leverage their social capital to invest in new innovative firms, "in pursuit of new knowledge that can fuel innovation and entrepreneurship, thereby overcoming conservatism" (Zahra, 2010, 359).

Within the entrepreneurial context, ties to others have been argued to shape information, skills and knowledge and how specific opportunities might be perceived and exploited. Network relationships frame access to resources, customers and strategic partners, as well as configuring the entrepreneur's own perceived legitimacy. Critical to the early stages of the family firm are relationships and entrepreneurship. If networks are key for entrepreneurship (Hoang & Antoncic, 2003; Jack et al., 2008; Slotte Kock & Coviello, 2010), then we can expect those family firms engaged in entrepreneurship to be drawing on the networks in which they are embedded and to use these embedded ties as a mechanism to extend the activities of the firm. The personal and public worlds of the family-in-business are intertwined and because of this we can anticipate that networking will prove important for venture growth. At the very least, we can expect important and complex interactions. It might even be that networks provide external focal points to compare with the internalities of the family itself. What interests us is how do family firms who are engaged in the practices of entrepreneurship enhance, extend and evolve external network ties for venture growth?

Methodology

For the study, we selected three countries in which to carry out the fieldwork. These were Scotland, England and Greece. We also chose to look at family firms located in both rural and urban contexts from each country. Within these contexts, we also looked to choose family firms that we felt would be willing to share their experiences with members of the research team. Family firms are known for being secretive. So, to enhance the study and our exploration we purposefully sought to look at firms with whom some form of trust was already established as we felt this would lead to more depth in the detail of the data gathered. Sample firms tended to be known to the authors, their research assistants and/or university colleagues. Our selection criteria also involved only those firms who could demonstrate that they were entrepreneurial in their outlook, that growth had been achieved and where at least the second generation of family leader was actually running the venture. All firms also had to have more than one family member employed to work with the business and all had to be controlled by the owning families (Schulze & Gedajlovic, 2010, 197). Table 10.1 shows the features of the 12 firms which were used for this study. Our respondents of these firms were typically the current CEO, or led a strategic business unit of the family firm. In one case our respondent was the former CEO of the firm who then moved to the position of Chairman of the Board (President) of the group. Our sampling process was purposeful (Gartner & Birley, 2002; Pratt, 2009). Our sample was theoretical in having the characteristics that fitted our enquiry. Conceptually, our sample consisted of respondents who were all well placed to discuss entrepreneurial practice, growth strategies and how network ties were drawn on within the context of the family firm.

Semi-structured interviews with carried out with our 12 family firm entrepreneurs. Particular emphasis was placed on the themes and issues of interest for the study and which related to networking and growth. Interviews were then transcribed. For the Greek data interviews were also translated into English by the native-speaker interviewer. Following on from this, transcripts were read and reread, and notes on emergent themes were entered into research diaries (Easterby-Smith et al., 1991). We continued reviewing the material to clarify emergent themes, until few new insights occurred to us (Human & Provan, 1996). As the readings and reflections developed, categories and concepts emerged within our research notes. Incidents and experiences, observations and responses were continually compared with others within emerging categories. This constant comparative method (Glaser & Strauss, 1967; Alvesson & Sköldberg, 2000; Silverman, 2000) has become an accepted approach of dealing with entrepreneurial network analysis (Human & Provan, 1996; Hill et al., 1999; Jack, 2005). Throughout this process of theme emergence, in constant comparison to extant theory, we iteratively and simultaneously continued the development of our framework (Uzzi, 1997).

Table 10.1 Sample summary

Respondent	Age/sex	Generation	Role	Urban/rural	Country	Company alias	Sector/s	Number of employees (FTEs)
Andreas	53, male	5th of 5	President	Rural	Greece	HellasDrink	Manufacturing drinks	22
Babis	31, male	3rd of 3	CEO	Rural	Greece	HellasSupplies	Business supplies	2
Costas	32, male	3rd of 3	Function Head	Rural	Greece	HellasLogistics	FMCG shop supplies	40
Douglas	89, male	3rd of 4	President (was CEO)	Rural	Scotland	ScotFood	Food manufacturing	1,500
Elaine	60, female	3rd of 3	CEO (was SBU head)	Rural	England	EngStone	Diverse ventures around Stone: production and sales	10 (in spin off) 40 (in family group)
Freda	39, female	2nd of 3	SBU Head	Rural	England	EngFarm	Diverse ventures around Farm: production and sales	28
Giorgos	42, male	2nd of 3	SBU Head	Urban	Greece	HellasProduce	Diverse ventures around trading produce	17
Hari	44, male	2nd of 2	CEO	Urban	Greece	HellasInfo	Diverse ventures: information and media	300 (+)
Ioannis	55, male	2nd of 2	CEO	Urban	Greece	HellasDeli	Manufacturing branded gourmet product	110
Jock	35, male	2nd of 2	CEO	Urban	Scotland	ScotHome	Home improvements artisans	70
Keith	29, male	2nd of 2	Senior Manager	Urban	England	EngService	Complex industrial supplies and service	18
Larry	36, male	2nd of 2	Director	Urban	England	EngArtisan	Business service artisans	6 (+ contractors)

The research team presented and compared the three sets of initial coding, both with each other and with a working framework of expectations derived from the literature. As field data provided empirical evidence to compare with the framework, elements of it were "retained, revised, removed, or added" (Uzzi, 1997). Coding categories were agreed upon by the research team. We continued the development of our framework, in constant comparison to extant theory, returning to "fine tune" the categories and concepts in the light of this theoretical labor. We then jointly produce an illustrated summary of the major themes and the relationships between them. For the elements within the data which related to networking and venture growth, a simple explanatory framework emerged which encapsulated various aspects of two main themes. The first of these themes covers the origins of growth opportunities, whilst the second incorporates investigating and enacting growth paths. This framework is presented in the findings below, and provides the basis for our subsequent analysis and discussion.

Findings

Origins of growth opportunities

Growth strategies for many of the family firms studied tended to be driven by resources available within the family–firm nexus. We found a strong belief that ready to hand resources should be used as the fundamental basis for building growth opportunities. A variety of family assets was used in this fashion to spring board growth strategy. These included material resources, such as redundant buildings, or land. Also frequently viewed in this way were family human assets. The skills and knowledge of family members – especially younger ones – offered a resource base that could be leveraged to generate growth opportunities.

Interestingly, these growth opportunities often took the form of related diversification, so that a kind of hub and spoke pattern of strategic development emerged, with a range of new "ventures" being grown around the central conceptual and commercial core of the family firm. Several examples of such resource-driven growth paths are presented in Table 10.2. Instructive is Ioannis' comment that this type of development broadens the base of the firm, and reduces the risk exposure which overly specialized firms can experience. It may be that hub-and-spoke venture growth is especially suited to family firms, as they strive to combine a culture of entrepreneurship and innovation (expressed through the launch of new SBUs (strategic business units)), with protecting the family assets from certain external risks (through related diversification), whilst fully exploiting family firm skills, resources, "name" and knowledge (by spinning new SBUs out from the central core, or hub). Although not the main focus of this study, this is such an interesting finding in its own right that we intend to develop the insights further in future work.

Family human capital and growth opportunities

For many respondents, sources of growth opportunities included related diversification driven by the special skills, interests and passions of new generation leadership. It was interesting that examples of such growth were proffered during interview by new and old generations alike, and in a variety of commercial settings. As Table 10.3 shows, the types of family human capital described in this

Table 10.2 Origins of growth opportunities

Illustrative example	Respondent	Source of capital
"We realized that our location on this very busy main road was an opportunity for us and so my parents developed this idea of the farm shop, and having this building, a redundant barn, in which to develop the shop"	Freda EngFarm	Location and empty property drive new opportunity
"This building my Mother ran as a guest house for 10 years to make money for my Father to start his business ... this building became the offices for my Father's company which was growing. ... then ... the shop in 'CountryTown' which had been doing well for a few years, it came into the ground floor of this building"	Elaine EngStone	Multiple uses over time for a specific piece of family property; the largest capital asset in the family
Jock decided to cease one type of activity, upon which the original business had been founded, because it was an inefficient use of an expensive asset (space, capacity): "because *** was only a small part of the business as it is now the decision was basically made to utilize the space it was taking up"	Jock ScotHome	Under-utilized capacity and capital can also be re-configured to facilitate venture growth
"We decided to expand as we had the capacity"	Andreas HellasDrink	Excess capacity drives expansion motivation
"Everything was on ration ... at the end of the war ... we just had a small business, just doing some jam when we could get sugar and ... putting beetroot into vinegar when we could get jars"	Douglas ScotFood	Post-war growth totally driven by the production inputs made available during rationing; resource-driven
Q: Advantages of family firm? A: "Financially its capital is limited and small ... it cannot grow and it can raise limited debt"	Babis HellasSupplies	Lack of financial capital is a barrier to growth in family firms
Giorgos (and later his siblings) developed a diversified business around their produce trading, moving into B2B, distribution and gourmet importation as their skills, contacts and resources developed (e.g. from running their own produce distribution to managing B2B logistics for others)	Giorgos HellasProduce	Family firm skills, resources and contacts used as springboard for venture growth
"I inherited a good name. A brand name.... This helped me and I grew fast"	Babis HellasSupplies	Family "core" as foundation for growth
"Stone has always been part of what we do here. There is that thread of continuity and the people who have been coming here for 30 years remember it as such"	Elaine EngStone	Hub and spoke development of diversified ventures around "core" of stone
Hari's family firm has developed a range of diversified ventures around their core skills and brand in the information field, including conferences, print media, e-communication.	Hari HellasInfo	Hub and spoke development of diversified ventures around "core" of information
"The company has widened its product base, by including, apart from ***, products with ***. And we have also taken over distribution for some products. This has given the increase in turnover and has provided a broader base for endurance and growth"	Ioannis HellasDeli	Hub and spoke diversification explained as providing the protection of a broader base

Table 10.3 Family human capital and growth opportunities

Illustrative example	Respondent	Type of human capital
"My daughter ... runs the company, she was a management banker, so she is very good with money, that is why she does the takeover things"	Douglas ScotFood	Business experience outside the family firm fueling growth opportunities
Andreas, like his father, studied chemical engineering. He wanted to be a scientist, to stay in the University, but was tempted back to the family business because "I liked the scientific aspect, not the financial one". Andreas uses his scientific knowledge – and the large lab he built, to drive new product development	Andreas HellasDrink	Inclination and education fueling growth opportunities
"I came back into the business ... and my skills complemented theirs, that was to do with people and systems and strategizing ... I think my heart was here really, I had a strong connection with the place and was very passionate about what my parents had started here"	Freda EngFarm	Inclination, passion and education fueling growth opportunities
"Based on my own inclination to science, I managed to combine the experience that was scattered in the business with science. So, nowadays the company has fully covered the product in terms of organization, trading and scientific knowledge"	Ioannis HellasDeli	Inclination and education fueling growth opportunities
Babis' sole proprietorship is a sales and service representative for his former employer, but it is so closely linked to the family firm (which sells a different range of specialized supplies) that "we have the same customers, we share some suppliers; and the network"	Babis HellasSupplies	Adding new product range to existing firm, based on new generation prior employment

Quote	Name / Firm	Theme
"That experience of working outside of the business was vastly important to me … going out and measuring yourself against other people and creating your own identity and learning where your skills are…Then knowing what you really want to do, can you do that within your own business?"	Elaine EngFarm	Business experience outside the family firm fueling growth motivation
"My whole thing was doing things with my hands when I was young, it was making models … it is a very manual business … so when potential suppliers were coming in here with a new product and saying 'you should sell this', because of my technical background, you know, we could take it to bits, see if it was a good product"	Jock ScotHome	Screening new product opportunities using skills which have their roots in childhood passions
"I could have not studied correctly, could have flunked through school and then thought, it is alright, I can just go and work for my Dad … I went to University, I got a first, I got my Masters, went and worked for a big investment bank … so I always did everything to prove myself, so no one could say it is a silver spoon"	Keith EngService	New generation desire to prove itself generates the resources which fuel later growth
"I think if they went out and learnt something that they could bring to the business that would be better. If you are interested in … what we are doing, then go and find yourself a qualification first … something that you can bring to the business, so you are not tied to it"	Larry EngArtisan	Children, their education and the future of the family business (aged 5 and 8!)
"I used to have lego and make things and she would sit with her ponies and her dolls. Just not interested in this. It is not what drives her; she just likes babies so she is a midwife"	Keith EngService	Sibling chooses to *not* join family firm since interests and skills do not suit
"I have got the common sense, and he has got the intellect … he would be far too advanced for what this company needs … as a kid I was always the one mucking about helping my dad, and he was always the one reading a book or on the computer"	Jock ScotHome	Sibling chooses to *not* join family firm since interests and skills do not suit

way included business experience outside the family firm, formal education, and interests and passions. Interestingly, explanations for siblings choosing to *not* join the family firm were very often couched in terms of skills, passions and education not being complementary to the firm.

Also, when respondents were considering whether, and on what terms, youth and child family members might join the organization, this issue was again raised. In these contexts, many respondents explicitly stated that youth and child family members should *first* gather educational and experiential capital to bring into the business, as the basis for future growth, before formal employment within the business.

Some of the children discussed in such terms were not yet at school, whilst others were approaching the end of formal education. In some cases, the children themselves were depicted as expressing a desire to develop fully their own talents and potential so as to be able to offer something (other than just the family name) to the venture. Some younger respondents also emphasized how much they had wanted to bring something special to the venture, to be seen to have earned their position. The interest-specific training, experience and education of children was thus seen to offer multiple benefits to the firm: respect for the new entrants, as well as a foundation for future growth opportunities through the development of diverse human resources.

There was little constraint placed on what areas might be helpful for the firm; rather the focus was on the interests, passions and inherent strengths of these young people. However, the complete mismatch between some sibling interests and the family firm were cited as a rationale for them pursuing a career elsewhere, so the scope for the firm to make use of a range of diverse skills was not seen to be infinite, although wide indeed.

Commercial capital and growth opportunities

Another source of growth opportunities was the desire more fully to exploit under-utilized assets, such as property, or excess capacity. Again, these stimulated diversification growth strategies, dependent on the nature of the asset. An empty barn in a great location provided the basis for a shop and café; excess capacity in a manufacturing firm drove the development of a new more modern line of drinks; a large family home was turned into a guest house to generate funding for other family start-ups; the family brand name allowed a fast-start for a related business supplies venture. All the family firms which we encountered that utilized this approach were based in rural areas, in all three countries studied. It may be that the paucity of other resources available within the rural periphery is such as to enforce an enhanced thriftiness upon such family firms, so that maximizing the potential of all commercial capital is especially desirable.

It is instructive that where financial capital is mentioned, it is the *lack* of funds which is sometimes presented as a barrier to growth. The family firms in our study, as the research to date would predict, do not have substantial accumulations of financial assets to drive their growth paths forward. However, nor do they typically seek out substantial growth funds – either as debt or equity – from external stakeholders. There seems relatively little interest in financial capital as a growth tool, or in developing strong-tie relationships with angel investors, venture capitalists and so forth. One respondent only – Elaine – had borrowed substantially to upgrade her business: but even here her objective was clearly stated as being to make the venture esthetically perfect, rather than to pursue growth.

Investigating and enacting growth paths

Investigating growth possibilities, making strategic decisions and implementation of new strategies were largely enacted through ongoing, succinct conversations within the immediate group of family-firm employees. However, we also found quite frequent utilization of formal, rational, management techniques for researching, analyzing and planning growth paths. These two complementary processes contrast with those utilized by non-family entrepreneurs, who often articulate ideas in short intense periods of informal, detailed brainstorming within their firms, with large numbers of their (non-kin) staff. Idea validation and development for non-family entrepreneurs appears to typically occur through close innovative collaboration with external business friends, especially customers and suppliers.

Ongoing conversational process

An important element in investigating growth possibilities was also found to involve conversations within the firm. These were not lengthy, one-off brain storming conversations, but rather were typically a series of brief exchanges between family members going on over quite a substantial period of time. Many of these conversational snippets took place within the domestic environment, as well as in the workplace, for several of our respondents. Larry's long description of the process, shown below, is replicated in the processes described by many of our respondents (see Table 10.4).

> Informal, very informal. We just kind of meet up where we need to. We will just pitch some ideas and go away and think about it some more. Come back again, it is that kind of thing you know it grows in the mind, you touch base and it is this constant to-ing and fro-ing over the same thing. There is no formula, but this is an issue now we need some action. It is a just five or ten minutes, here or there, it is constant throughout the day. Nothing, just incidental, you know I am just going down … have you thought of this … yes, that is a good point, anyway I will speak to you later. It is that non-stop, the pair of us and he seems to come to me just as much now, it is very much a two way street, he is as dependent on me as I am on him now, that is the kind of relationship that we have got to.

Respondents told us that they used their family as sounding boards, to verify that their 80 percent certainty was valid, to present and approve suggestions. Occasionally, we found evidence that a single brief exchange might be enough to trigger agreement that a new opportunity should be tried out immediately. Empiricism seems highly valued, and family trust permits people to try ideas out in practice. This brevity in decision making appears to support perceptions of the family firm using centrality of control as a means to drive commercial flexibility and rapidity, as the scholarly literature has long suggested.

Table 10.4 Ongoing conversational process

Illustrative example	Respondent	Aspect of conversation
"We use each other as sounding boards, you know what are you thinking, what are your thoughts, give it a go"	Larry EngArtisan	Sounding boards
"One of us will come up with a suggestion and we go away and try it, so we do it between us"	Larry EngArtisan	Empiricism – trying ideas out
"We might say a word, 'we must do this thing. What is your opinion? Yes. Lets do it.' With very brief processes"	Giorgos HellasProduce	Brevity in decision making
"When I am 80% sure that I want to do something, I ask and then I might be certain that it is the right move"	Babis HellasSupplies	Confirmation, validation across the generations
"There are still always things that go on in your own head that still only involve discussion to get a conclusion in your own mind, by speaking to my father"	Jock ScotHome	Confirmation, validation across the generations
Q: *When were you actually introduced to the family business?* A: "A large part of what is talked about within the family … family meals and the like, so you just absorb a lot"	Elaine EngStone	Ubiquity of family firm conversations, in business and private life
"It is very informal … Christmas dinner, all the time, somebody will just spark something, a comment or discussion"	Freda EngFarm	Ubiquity of family firm conversations, in business and private life

Quote	Interviewee / Firm	Theme
Q: *How do discussions take place?* A: "Everywhere. We might meet by the stairs, in a meeting, at home over lunch"	Costas HellasLogistics	Ubiquity of family firm conversations, in business and private life
"When you are in an entrepreneurial family you will talk for a while about football, for a while about politics and then it is just your business you talk about"	Costas HellasLogistics	Very high quantity of business conversations within the family
Q: *Now your daughter runs the business do you communicate with each other? ... is it more formal or informal?* A: "Yes, every second or third day ... she will just say 'hello Dad' and we have a cup of coffee and we chat, the other thing is that we trust each other, you have got to have trust"	Douglas ScotFood	Continuous, detailed, informal conversations
"In a family business, the most significant issue is to make use of the experience, and ... in order to use it, you need a continuum. You cannot walk up to someone and say 'Father ... what would you do in this case?' They need continuous information and details. Otherwise they cannot offer you detached advice."	Hari HellasInfo	Continuous, detailed provision of information, to keep other family members informed enough to converse/contribute effectively
"With my sister and my aunt we discuss everything: thoughts, opinions, views"	Ioannis HellasDeli	Continuous, detailed conversations
"I would say do you not think that we ought to have meetings, and I can remember them both bursting out laughing and saying 'good God she wants meetings, what on earth do you want meetings for?'"	Elaine EngStone	Resistance to formalization of communication, conversational form of decision making

Formal evaluation process

Market and technology evaluations took place through quite formal, "professional" mechanisms in many cases (see Table 10.5). Douglas developed his internationalization strategy in the 1950s drawing closely upon "push–pull" conceptualizations to drive his market entry. This is a remarkably early adoption of a formal marketing tool, especially when we recall Douglas' peripheral geographic location in rural Scotland. Formal market research and feasibility studies were also mentioned by Freda and Elaine. Information search was not left to serendipity, but was highly focused and made use of professional publications, the internet and other media. We were surprised to find that all examples of such formal, rational evaluation were provided by respondents in rural environments (with the exception of Jock). Perhaps this can be explained by the difficulty in building informal growth networks from a peripheral setting necessitating a more structured approach.

Weak-tie utilization

External to the family, the usage of weak-ties, which has come to be seen of diminished importance for non-family entrepreneurs, appeared more significant for those family firms involved in entrepreneurship and growth. It is very important to note that even though these relationships were often of very long standing, they seldom developed a social aspect. New weak-ties were identified in a very calculating fashion on the basis of what the firm's needs were. Communication focused on specific business concerns.

Tie maintenance did not extend into socialization, but was built into the low-intensity routines of everyday life. It should be noted that, on a personal level,

Table 10.5 Formal evaluation process

Illustrative example	Respondent	Type of evaluation
"My brother did a feasibility study into pick your own strawberries"	Freda EngFarm	Formal feasibility study
"Harvard had come up with this idea of push–pull sell" (this refers to a market entry strategy in the 1950s)	Douglas ScotFood	Theoretical basis for market entry strategy
Q: *Sources of information and support?* A: "The Internet. The mass media"	Babis HellasSupplies	Rational, focused market information search
Jock literally takes potential new products to pieces to test them thoroughly, "to see if it was a good product, or whether it was going to fall to pieces when it was sold you know"	Jock ScotHome	Formal, physical new product testing
"You build up a database and I would do questionnaires and I would get them to fill them in and get some responses…"	Elaine EngStone	Formal market research
"I did a lot of work myself in finding out about customers and developing a brand to get people interested in coming here"	Freda EngFarm	Planned, managed, rational research and marketing activities driving growth

our respondents may indeed have close personal friends outside the venture – as Giorgos describes in Table 10.6 – but that the family firm does not seem to be on the list of topics routinely shared with such strong-ties.

The single exception to this practice that we encountered was Douglas, who showed many similar behaviors to non-family entrepreneurs in this area. Douglas, very early on in his long reign as CEO, recruited senior non-executive directors to his firm, and socialized these relationships extensively through the seductive and judicious use of salmon fishing and Scotch whisky. It is interesting that here we see Douglas' rurality turned into an asset to deepen his ties with key professional contacts.

Some evidence was also presented that long-term non-family employees had shouldered the responsibility for building and maintaining somewhat stronger network ties, especially within customer and supplier businesses. By spending perhaps an entire working career delivering to, selling to, collecting from and meeting with these partner ventures, trusted non-family employees developed relationships which provided an additional ongoing asset to the family firm. The Appendix figure summarizes our findings, showing the patterns of family firm networking-for-growth which we identified through this study, and which will be discussed further below.

Discussion

Family firms engaged in entrepreneurship in several instances appear closer to formal, rational models of interaction with the marketplace than non-family entrepreneurs (who typically develop well-embedded strong customer, supplier and other industry ties which act as the foundation for growth). Table 10.7 compares and contrasts the two modes of networking processes during venture growth, which highlight the importance of social capital in general, and strong ties in particular, for non-family entrepreneurs. Perhaps contrary to pervading stereotypes, it appears as though family firm growth patterns may be far more rational and "professional" than the socialized growth paths associated with non-family entrepreneurs.

As the fieldwork findings above have illustrated, it seems as though for family firms, commercial and family human capital are the starting point for venture growth paths, and not social capital. Idea articulation is carried out over a quite long period of time, via the vehicle of very brief interactions to frame specific elements in the opportunity conceptualization. The family becomes immersed in an ongoing conversation characterized by the exchange of a sentence or two several times a day, until clarity is reached. Much of the communication is tacit, perhaps since kin can "fill in the gaps" and more easily recognize what has been left unsaid.

It is especially noteworthy that family firms engaged in entrepreneurship use diverse existing resources as the dynamic to create growth opportunities, often around some core concept representing the firm's heart, such as "stone", "farm", "produce" or "information". We have suggested that such hub-and-spoke venture growth may offer family firms a way to combine elements of great importance to them. The core itself provides the stability, continuity and identity which demarcates the specific family firm over time. By diversifying around this core, using the broad interests and passions of family members, risks of over-specialization are mitigated, reducing risk. New generation members are enabled to build their own identities, and to earn individual respect, through their educational and professional labors. The pursuit of growth through creation of "spoke" SBUs

Table 10.6 Weak-tie utilization

Illustrative example	Respondent	Type of tie and utilization
"I might discuss business, with much less detail, with people I work with … mostly general discussion … 'how do you see the new tax measures?' … simple stuff"	Babis HellasSupplies	Simple ongoing scanning via weak-ties
Costas met key contacts – suppliers and customers – in a purely business setting "not at a café or a tavern … while working; delivering; receiving, etc.". He continues to rely on these business contacts: "daily contact with the customer in the market … tells me whether I need to change something"	Costas HellasLogistics	Even after many years, these key weak-ties have not become socialized, multiplex, friendship relationships
"Company issues … that is just kept in house and you sort things out … there are probably only two people that we get involved with outside of the company"	Jock ScotHome	Very limited external ties, ascribed to inherent secrecy
"We get on, we don't brag about what we do, we keep things in house … some customers know that 'Peter' [father] has retired, some probably aren't aware; you know we are quite a private company"	Keith EngService	Very limited external ties, ascribed to inherent secrecy
"The magazines would come and visit and try and get business from you, so I would make them sit there for 2 hours whilst I asked them everything about … who buys your magazine, why do they buy, adverts work"	Elaine EngStone	Calculative development of weak-tie to meet specific business need
"There were always people who helped us with their knowledge, for example … a professor at the University in GreekTown, a good contact, who helped us set up the quality control laboratory"	Ioannis HellasDeli	Calculative development of weak tie to meet specific business need
"I heard that Mr So-and-So is a specialist … and I invited him here. We had long discussions … I took the initiative"	Andreas HellasDrink	Calculative development of weak-tie to meet specific business need

Quote	Respondent	Interpretation
"I did an awful lot of searching out people to speak with while I was doing LEAD … it was laying the foundations for what I am doing now"	Freda EngFarm	Creating a purposive weak-tie network to support business growth
Hari talked with enthusiasm about an older long-standing "acquaintance of the company" from the industry who had been helpful because of "how free his mind is". But he then said that frequency of contact was "rare … formal … not once a month or every two months". When asked what the alter takes from the relationship he answered "they get satisfaction from the fact that the company has not discharged them"	Hari HellasInfo	Even the network relationships which are perceived as especially influential, are – given closeness of tie, formality and frequency of contact – weak-ties
"Our business can get very close to very large customers, and we have got a very low turnover of staff, very many people have been here for over ten plus years. So we have got good continuity, when customers ring up it always the same person that they are dealing with"	Keith EngService	Non-family employees maintain many customer and supplier ties
"Three very good friends that I love … special people, sometimes they know more than my brothers and sister. It has nothing to do with business. It can even take a year till I discuss something with them that has to do with the business"	Giorgos HellasProduce	Strong ties may be personally very important friendships, but interactions are not often related to the business
"When I went to America another discovery that I made was non-executive directors, to have important people, more significant people … these were men of great experience who were able to advise me … about 1964 I had my first non-executive director … they came fishing with me, they used to say we had our board meetings on the river bank, you had a glass of whisky in your hand over lunch"	Douglas ScotFood	Unlike the rest of our respondents, Douglas acts like high growth entrepreneurs, bringing in very senior non-execs and using socialization to develop rich, multiplex ties with them

Table 10.7 Networking processes during venture growth: family firms engaged in entrepreneurial practice

Identifying growth opportunities	Driven by under-utilized, or newly available, commercial and human capital held within the family firm
Articulating growth opportunities	Articulate ideas in longish periods of disrupted conversations: a few words here and there to move thinking onwards and clarify specific points
Investigating growth opportunities: formal techniques	Frequent utilization of formal, rational, management techniques for researching, analyzing and planning growth paths
Investigating growth opportunities: weak-tie development and maintenance	Family members take market readings as a routine part of their interactions with weak-tie contacts, who are kept at arms' length Seek out relevant specialists purposively, as new weak-ties

sustains the culture of entrepreneurship, change and excitement which is the lifeblood of the family firm.

It is also important to ask why family firms appear not to make extensive use of strong-ties. One possible answer is that some of the market-scanning and relationship management labor in family firms is, perhaps surprisingly, carried out by (non-family) employees. Because employees often spend very long periods of their working life – sometimes all of it – within a single family firm, they are well placed to develop substantive relationships with customers, suppliers and other market players. We found several instances where trusted, long-term employees were acting to manage such key relationships, rather than the family managers themselves. Could it be that family firms are delegating this most delicate task to their long-term staff? For non-family entrepreneurs we have found it is the everyday management of the firm which is delegated to trusted staff, freeing the entrepreneur to develop, maintain and exploit social capital in the external networked environment. Do family firm leaders prioritize internal managerial control so strongly that they retain responsibility for this, rather than managing social capital? Does the family firm tradition of control, and secrecy, deny them both the time and the inclination to embed fully in surrounding business networks? At the least, this intriguing juxtaposition demands further study.

A second possibility to explain the lack of networking for growth in family has to do with the liability of newness experienced by non-family entrepreneurs, especially solo founders, who experience a driving need to develop marketplace legitimacy. A strong family "brand" delivers a quality-guarantee within the business environment for new family firm ventures/growth paths, which legitimation an entrepreneur can only secure through enacting social capital.

A third explanation may have to do with the intensity of relationships within the family firm. Non-family entrepreneurs often experience professional loneliness and isolation, as they struggle to build their firms. The real warmth with which they discuss the strong-tie relationships in their embedded networks indicates the importance of their emotional aspects. Indeed, family metaphors are often encountered as entrepreneurs talk about strong-tie alters acting like their brother, grandfather, big sister and so on. Family firm leaders and members enjoy such close, deep and intense relationships within their own firms, where the strongest of all ties – those of kinship – bind the venture and family together.

It seems feasible that the very nature of these strong internal ties limits the possibilities of outside ties. Perhaps a helpful metaphor is to imagine some sort of family barrier which is very hard to permeate.

Conclusion

Our research question was how do family firms who are engaged in the practice of entrepreneurship enhance, extend and evolve external network ties for venture growth? In addressing this question, this study highlights the special nature of networking for growth which differentiates family from non-family firms. We find that the highly socialized nature of entrepreneurial growth does not appear to be practiced in family firms where exploiting internal resources, articulating ideas through special ongoing family discourse, applying formal rational evaluation tools and relying on weak-tie network contacts are found instead. Some initial explanations of this phenomenon are proposed, which include family firm leaders' preference for secrecy and control over embeddedness, the pre-legitimation which a family "brand" provides to new projects and the emotional intensity of bonds within the family firm. This is of significance for teachers, scholars, practitioners and policy makers alike. In particular, it raises the concern that the recent focus on life-cycle understanding of entrepreneurial networking configurations and processes may not adequately explain all forms of enterprise. Perhaps an extension of our theorization in this area is called for, exploring cases and contexts which are not amenable to stage model accounts.

Limitations inherent within the study include those traditionally associated with the small samples necessitated by qualitative work: especially generalizability and representativeness. Interview methods also have certain drawbacks, such as the potential for post-hoc rationalization of past actions, self-serving bias and so forth. We have attempted to tackle these limitations to some degree by crafting a sample which is diverse in terms of sector, location, size and generation. The strong consistency of our findings across this diverse sample adds to their confidence and robustness, as well as suggesting some degree of universalizability.

In terms of future research, we identify three main areas of potential interest. First, discourse within the family firm environment appears to play a special role as a mechanism for investigating and enacting growth. It seems likely that further research in this area would be beneficial, perhaps enriched by insights from other disciplines, most notably anthropology, into kin discourse. Second, the insight that the related diversification described by so many of our respondents seems to form some kind of hub-and-spoke pattern also offers substantial potential for deeper analysis. Whilst many new venture opportunities were pursued by the family firms we studied, they all seemed to center round some sustained, core vision of what the family firm is and does. Not only did this core form the foundation for venture creation but also the building blocks for growth.

Acknowledgments

Special thanks to research assistants, Alexis Komselis (of AHEAD, ALBA) and Artur Steiner (SRUC) for their support around some data collection activities. And, to the Institute for Entrepreneurship and Enterprise Development (IEED) and Lancaster University for its support for this project through Higher Education and Innovation Funding (HEIF).

Appendix

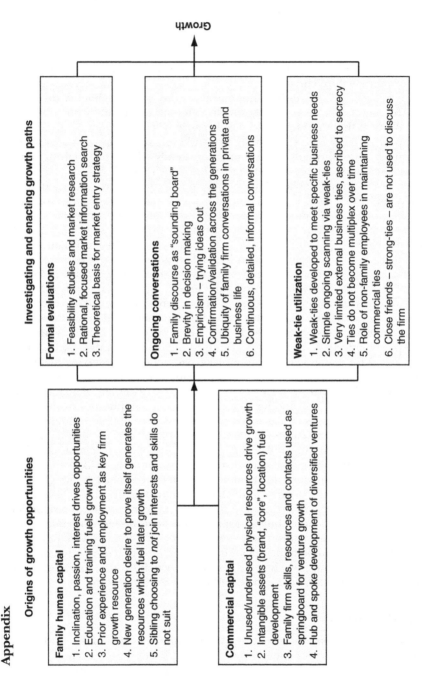

Origins of growth opportunities

Family human capital

1. Inclination, passion, interest drives opportunities
2. Education and training fuels growth
3. Prior experience and employment as key firm growth resource
4. New generation desire to prove itself generates the resources which fuel later growth
5. Sibling choosing to *not* join interests and skills do not suit

Commercial capital

1. Unused/underused physical resources drive growth
2. Intangible assets (brand, "core", location) fuel development
3. Family firm skills, resources and contacts used as springboard for venture growth
4. Hub and spoke development of diversified ventures

Investigating and enacting growth paths

Formal evaluations

1. Feasibility studies and market research
2. Rational, focused market information search
3. Theoretical basis for market entry strategy

Ongoing conversations

1. Family discourse as "sounding board"
2. Brevity in decision making
3. Empiricism – trying ideas out
4. Confirmation/validation across the generations
5. Ubiquity of family firm conversations in private and business life
6. Continuous, detailed, informal conversations

Weak-tie utilization

1. Weak-ties developed to meet specific business needs
2. Simple ongoing scanning via weak-ties
3. Very limited external business ties, ascribed to secrecy
4. Ties do not become multiplex over time
5. Role of non-family employees in maintaining commercial ties
6. Close friends – strong-ties – are not used to discuss the firm

Growth

Figure 10.A.1 Family firms: networking for growth.

References

段
Aldrich, H., & Sakano, T. (1995). "Is Japan different? The personal networks of Japanese business owners compared to those in four other industrialized nations". *KSU Economic and Business Review, 22*, 1–28.

Aldrich, H., Reese, P. R. & Dubini, P. (1989). "Women on the verge of a breakthrough: networking among entrepreneurs in the United States and Italy". *Entrepreneurship and Regional Development, 1*(4), 339–356.

Alvesson, M., & Skoldberg, K. (2000). *Reflexive Methodology*, London: Sage.

Anderson, A. R., & Lee, E. Y. C. (2008). "From tradition to modern: attitudes and applications of guanxi in Chinese entrepreneurship". *Journal of Small Business and Enterprise Development, 15*(4), 775–787.

Anderson, A. R., & Miller, C. J. (2003). " 'Class matters': human and social capital in the entrepreneurial process". *Journal of Socio-economics, 32*(1), 17–36.

Anderson, A. R., Dodd, S. D. & Jack, S. (2010). "Network practices and entrepreneurial growth". *Scandinavian Journal of Management, 26*(2), 121–133.

Anderson, A. R., Dodd, S. D. & Jack, S. L. (2012). "Entrepreneurship as connecting: some implications for theorising and practice". *Management Decision, 50*(5), 958–971.

Arregle, J. L., Hitt, M. A., Sirmon, D. G. & Very, P. (2007). "The development of organizational social capital: attributes of family firms". *Journal of Management Studies, 44*, 73–95.

Birley, S., Cromie, S. & Myers, A. (1991). "Entrepreneurial networks: their emergence in Ireland and overseas". *International Small Business Journal, 9*(4), 56–74.

Brüderl, J. and Preisendörfer, P. (1998). "Network support and the success of newly founded businesses". *Small Business Economics, 10*, 213–225.

Carney, M. (2005). "Corporate governance and competitive advantage in family-controlled firms". *Entrepreneurship: Theory and Practice, 29*, 249–265.

Chrisman, J. J., Chua, J. H. & Kellerman, F. (2009). "Priorities, resource stocks, and performance in family and nonfamily firms". *Entrepreneurship: Theory and Practice, 33*, 739–760.

Chrisman, J. J., Chua, J. H. & Steier, L. (2005). "Sources and consequences of distinctive familiness: an introduction". *Entrepreneurship: Theory and Practice, 29*, 237–247.

Chua, J. H., Chrisman, J. J. & Chang, E. P. C. (2004). "Are family firms born or made? An exploratory investigation". *Family Business Review, 17*(1), 37–54.

Clinton, E. A., Nason, R. S. & Zellweger, T. M. (2010). "The effect of reputation on entrepreneurial behavior in family firms: a resource perspective". Paper presented at the *Babson College Entrepreneurship Research Conference*, Lausanne, June.

Craig, J. B. L., & Moores, K. (2006). "A 10-year longitudinal investigation of strategy, systems, and environment on innovation in family firms". *Family Business Review, 19*(1), 1–10.

Curran, J., Jarvis, R., Blackburn, R. A. & Black, S. (1993). "Networks and small firms: constructs, methodological strategies and some findings". *International Small Business Journal, 11*(2), 13–25.

Davidsson, P., & Honig, B. (2003). "The role of social and human capital among nascent entrepreneurs". *Journal of Business Venturing, 18*, 301–331.

Dodd, S. D., & Patra, E. (2002). "National differences in entrepreneurial networking". *Entrepreneurship and Regional Development, 14*(2), 117–134.

Dodd, S. D., Jack, S. & Anderson, A. R. (2002). "Scottish entrepreneurial networks in the international context". *International Small Business Journal, 20*(2), 213–219.

Drakopoulou Dodd, S., & Theoharakis, V. (2010). "Which aspects of 'familiness' influence continuous strategic renewal in family firms?" Presented at the *Babson College Entrepreneurship Research Conference*, Lausanne, June.

Drakopoulou Dodd, S., Jack, S. L. & Anderson, A. R (2006). "The mechanisms and process of entrepreneurial networks: continuity and change". In Wiklund, J., Dimov, D., Katz, J. & Shepherd, D. (Eds), *Advances in Entrepreneurship, Firm Emergence and Growth* 9, Amsterdam: Elsevier.

Drakopoulou Dodd, S., Jack, S. L. & Anderson, A. R (2012). "Being in time and the family owned firm". *Scandinavian Journal of Management, 29*(1), 35–47.

Easterby-Smith, M., Thorpe, R. & Lowe, A. (1991). *Management Research: An Introduction*, London: Sage Publications.

Eddleston, K., Kellermanns, F. W. & Sarathy, R. (2008). "Resource configuration in family firms: linking resources, strategic planning and technological opportunities to performance". *Journal of Management Studies, 45*, 1 26–50.

Elfring, T., & Hulsink, W. (2007). "Networking by entrepreneurs: patterns of tie formation in emerging organizations". *Organization Studies, 28*(12), 1849–1872.

Foley, D. (2008). "Indigenous (Australian) entrepreneurship?" *International Journal of Business and Globalisation, 2*(4), 419–436.

Gartner, W. B., & Birley, S. (2002). "Introduction to the special issue on qualitative methods in entrepreneurship research". *Journal of Business Venturing, 17*, 387–395.

Glaser, B. G., & Strauss, A. L. (1971 [1967]). *The Discovery of Grounded Theory*, New York: Aldine.

Gómez-Meja, L. R., Makri, M. & Larraza Kintana, M. (2010) "Diversification decisions in family-controlled firms". *Journal of Management Studies, 47*(2), 223–254.

Gómez-Meja, L. R., Takács Haynes, K., Núñez-Nickel, M., Jacobsen, K. J. L. & Moyana-Fuentes, J. (2007) "Socioemotional wealth and business risks in family-controlled firms: evidence from Spanish olive oil mills". *Administrative Science Quarterly, 52*, 106–137.

Greve, A. (1995). "Networks and entrepreneurship: an analysis of social relations, occupational background, and use of contacts during the establishment process". *Scandinavian Journal of Management, 11*(1), 1–24.

Greve, A., & Salaff, J. (2003). "Social networks and entrepreneurship". *Entrepreneurship: Theory and Practice, 28*(1), 1–23.

Habbershon, T. G., & Williams, M. L. (1999). "A resource-based framework for assessing the strategic advantages of family firms". *Family Business Review, 12*, 1–25.

Habbershon, T. G., Williams, M. & MacMillan, I. C. (2003). "A unified systems perspective of family firm performance". *Journal of Business Venturing, 18*, 451–465.

Hill, J., McGowan, P. & Drummond, P. (1999). "The development and application of a qualitative approach to researching the marketing networks of small firm entrepreneurs". *Qualitative Market Research: An International Journal, 2*(2), 71–81.

Hite, J. (2005). "Evolutionary processes and paths of relationally embedded network ties in emerging entrepreneurial firms". *Entrepreneurship: Theory and Practice, 29*(1), 113–144.

Hite, J. M., & Hesterly, W. S. (2001). "Research notes and commentaries. The evolution of firm networks: from emergence to early growth of the firm". *Strategic Management Journal, 22*(3), 275–286.

Hoang, H., & Antoncic, B. (2003). "Network-based research in entrepreneurship: a critical review". *Journal of Business Venturing, 18*(2), 165–187.

Human, S., & Provan, K. (1996). "External resource exchange and perceptions of competitiveness within organizational networks: an organizational learning perspective". In Reynolds, P., Birley, S., Butler, J., Bygrave, W., Davidsson, P., Gartner, W. & McDougall, P. (Eds), *Frontiers of Entrepreneurship Research*, Wellesley, MA: Babson College.

Jack, S., Moult, S., Anderson, A. R. & Dodd, S. (forthcoming). "Using the constant comparative technique to consider network change and evolution". In Neergaard, H. & Leitch, C. (Eds), *Handbook of Qualitative Research Techniques and Analysis in Entrepreneurship*, Cheltenham: Edward Elgar.

Jack, S. L. (2005). "The role, use and activation of strong and weak network ties: a qualitative analysis". *Journal of Management Studies, 42*(6), 1233–1259.

Jack, S. L., Drakopoulou Dodd, S. & Anderson, A. R (2008). "Change and the development of entrepreneurial networks over time processual perspective". *Entrepreneurship and Regional Development, 20*(2), 125–159.

Johannisson, B. (1995). "Paradigms and entrepreneurial networks: some methodological challenges". *Entrepreneurship and Regional Development, 7*(3), 215–232.

Johannisson, B., & Mønsted, M. (1997). "Contextualizing entrepreneurial networking". *International Journal of Management and Organization, 27*(3), 109–137.

Johannisson, B., & Nilsson, A. (1989). "Community entrepreneurs: networking for local development". *Entrepreneurship and Regional Development*, *1*(1), 3–19.

Klyver, K., & Terjesen, S. (2007). "Entrepreneurial network composition: an analysis across venture development stage and gender". *Women in Management Review*, *22*(8), 682–688.

Klyver, K., Hindle, K. & Meyer, D. (2008). "Influence of social network structure on entrepreneurship participation: a study of 20 national cultures". *International Entrepreneurship and Management Journal*, *4*(3), 331–347.

Larson, A., & Starr, J. A. (1993). "A network model of organization formation". *Entrepreneurship: Theory and Practice*, *17*(2), 5–15.

Lechner, C., & Dowling, M. (2003). "Firm networks: external relationships as sources for the growth and competitiveness of entrepreneurial firms". *Entrepreneurship and Regional Development*, *15*(1), 1–26.

Lubatkin, M. H., Schulze, W. S., Ling, Y. & Dino, R. N. (2005). "The effects of parental altruism on the governance of family-managed firms". *Journal of Organizational Behaviour*, *26*, 313–330.

Miller, D., & Le Breton-Miller, I. (2006). "Family governance and firm performance: agency, stewardship, and capabilities". *Family Business Review*, *19*, 73–87.

Miller, D., Le Breton-Miller, I. & Echolike, B. (2008). "Stewardship vs. stagnation: an empirical comparison of small family and non-family businesses". *Journal of Management Studies*, *45*(1), 51–78.

Minchilli, A., Corbetta, G. & Macmillan, I. (2010). "Diversification decisions in family-controlled firms". *Journal of Management Studies*, *47*(2), 205–222.

Mitchell, B. C., & Co, M. J. (2004). "Entrepreneurial networks: findings from a South African study". *South African Journal of Economic and Management Sciences/Suid-Afrikaanse Tydskrif vir Ekonomiese en Bestuurswetenskappe*, *7*(4), 589.

Morck, R., & Yeung, B. (2003). "Agency problems in large family business groups". *Entrepreneurship Theory and Practice*, *27*, 367–382.

Morck, R., & Yeung, B. (2004). "Family control and the rent-seeking society". *Entrepreneurship: Theory and Practice*, *28*, 391–410.

Pages, E., & Garmise, S. (2003). "The power of entrepreneurial networking". *Economic Development Journal*, Summer, 20–30.

Pratt, M. (2009). From the editors: "For the lack of a boilerplate: tips on writing up (and reviewing) qualitative research". *Academy of Management Journal*, *52*(5), 856–862.

Ram, M. (1994). "Unravelling social networks in ethnic minority firms". *International Small Business Journal*, *12*(3), 42–53.

Ram, M. (2001). "Family dynamics in a small consultancy firm: a case study". *Human Relations*, *54*(4), 395–418.

Renzulli, L. A., & Aldrich, H. E. (2005). "Who can you turn to? Tie activation within core business discussion networks". *Social Forces*, *84*(1), 323–341.

Robson, P. J. A., Jack, S. L. & Freel, M. S. (2008). "Gender and the use of business advice: evidence from firms in the Scottish service sector". *Environment and Planning. C, Government and Policy*, *26*(2), 292.

Schulze, W. S., & Gedajlovic, E. R. (2010). "The family and enterprise: unpacking the connections – guest editors' introduction". *Journal of Management Studies*, *47*(2), 191–204.

Schulze, W. S., Lubatkin, M. H. & Dino, R. N. (2002). "Altruism, agency, and the competitiveness of family firms". *Managerial and Decision Economics*, *23*, 247–259.

Shane, S., & Venkataraman, S. (2000). "The promise of entrepreneurship as a field of research". *Academy of Management Review*, *25*(1), 217–226.

Shepherd, D., & Zahra, S. (2003). "From conservatism to entrepreneurialism: the case of Swedish family firms". Unpublished paper, University of Colorado, Boulder, CO.

Short, J. C., Payne, G. T., Brigham, K. H., Lumpkin, G. T. & Broberg, J. C. (2009). "Family firms and entrepreneurial orientation in publicly traded firms: a comparative analysis of the S&P 500". *Family Business Review*, *22*(1), 9–24.

Silverman, D. (2000). "Analyzing talk and text". In Denzin, N. K. & Lincoln, Y. S. (Eds), *Handbook of Qualitative Research* 2, Thousand Oaks, CA: Sage.

Sirmon, D., & Hitt, M. A. (2003). "Creating wealth in family business through managing resources". *Entrepreneurship: Theory and Practice, 27,* 339–358.

Slotte Kock, S., & Coviello, N. (2010). "Entrepreneurship research on network processes: a review and ways forward". *Entrepreneurship: Theory and Practice, 34*(1), 31–57.

Staber, U., & Aldrich, H. E. (1995). "Cross-national similarities in the personal networks of small business owners: a comparison of two regions in North America". *Canadian Journal of Sociology/Cahiers canadiens de sociologie,* 441–467.

Stevenson, H. H., & Jarillo, C. J. (1990). "A paradigm of entrepreneurship: entrepreneurial management". *Strategic Management Journal, 11*(5), 17–27.

Tagiuri, R., & Davis, J. (1996). "Bivalent attributes of the family firm". *Family Business Review, 9,* 199–208.

Uzzi, B. (1997). "Social structure and competition in interfirm networks: the paradox of embeddedness". *Administrative Science Quarterly, 42*(1), 35–67.

Witt, P., Schroeter, A. & Merz, C. (2008). "Entrepreneurial resource acquisition via personal networks: an empirical study of German start-ups". *Service Industries Journal, 28*(7), 953–971.

Zahra, S. A. (2005). "Entrepreneurial risk taking in family firms". *Family Business Review, 18,* 23–40.

Zahra, S. A. (2010). "Harvesting family firms' organizational social capital: a relational perspective". *Journal of Management Studies, 47*(2), 345–366.

Zahra, S. A., Hayton, J. C. & Salvato, C. (2004). "Entrepreneurship in family vs. non-family firms: a resource-based analysis of the effect of organizational culture". *Entrepreneurship: Theory and Practice, 28,* 363–381.

11 The impact of domestic drivers and barriers on the entrepreneurial start-up decision

Rob Lubberink, Vincent Blok, Johan A.C. van Ophem, and S.W.F. Onno Omta

Introduction

Many people would like to be an entrepreneur and enjoy the advantageous prospects of being their own boss and having greater job autonomy. However, only some of these people do become entrepreneurs whereas others do not. This may be due to different levels of access to resources (e.g. money, information, or advice) needed for firm founding (Kim, Aldrich, and Keister 2006). Social capital is a means to acquire and utilize these resources (Anderson and Jack 2002) during the firm founding process (Brüderl and Preisendörfer 1998; Stam 2010). Nahapiet and Ghoshal (1998, p. 243) describe it as 'the sum of the actual and potential resources embedded within, available through, and derived from the network of relationships possessed by an individual or social unit'.

Many scholars have studied the effect of strong ties with family and friends on entrepreneurship (e.g. Granovetter 1973; Jack 2005; Krackhardt 1992). Despite an increasing interest in the impact of the networks of relationships on the entrepreneurial process that can be found in the literature (Hoang and Antoncic 2003; Schutjens and Stam 2003; Greve and Salaff 2003; Drakopoulou-Dodd, Jack, and Anderson 2006), the household is a crucial but often overlooked part of this network. The impact of the family is often studied from the perspective of Family Entrepreneurship (Lumpkin, Brigham, and Moss 2010), where the family is seen as a bounded entity (Anderson, Jack, and Dodd 2005). However, the intersections between family, family company, and entrepreneurship are still under-examined (Hoy and Sharma 2010; Nordqvist and Melin 2010; Uhlaner *et al.* 2012). This is surprising, to say the least, as the family is a critical source of social capital (Bubolz 2001) and can be the breeding ground for the predisposition to entrepreneurship (Rogoff and Heck 2003). Rogoff and Heck (2003, p. 559) even call the family 'the oxygen that feeds the fire of entrepreneurship'. Besides, there is considerable evidence that family considerations are taken into account when making decisions in the work domain (Powell and Greenhaus 2012).

The work–family interface between the entrepreneur, household members, and the company is changing continuously. It is exactly this dynamic nature of environments and relationships that creates the need to examine the conditions under which social capital in the entrepreneur's network is in danger of being lost or becoming dissipated (Gedajlovic *et al.* 2013). Therefore, we look at social capital from the dimension of relational embeddedness (focus on the quality and type of relationships) instead of structural embeddedness (properties of the social system or network as a whole) while recognizing their interrelatedness

(Nahapiet and Ghoshal 1998). By integrating these arguments, this study aims to explore the impact of the household network on the entrepreneurial process by identifying domestic drivers of and barriers to the start-up decision. This will give the necessary insights into gaining and sustaining the social capital provided by the household members of entrepreneurs. This study also differs from typical Family Entrepreneurship studies because it is not confined to family enterprises, but instead includes all kinds of enterprises. Furthermore, we do not look at the whole family of the entrepreneur, instead our scope only includes members of the entrepreneur's household (i.e. the domestic network). In the end, this chapter will provide an answer to the following research question: What impact do the domestic drivers and barriers of entrepreneurs have on the entrepreneurial start-up decision?

In this research we have studied the impact of the household on the start-up decision from a work–family conflict perspective. Strong ties in social networks need to be developed and maintained (Adler and Kwon 2002) also in the household (Bubolz 2001). This needs investment of time and energy that cannot be invested then in the company. Entrepreneurs need to balance family and work domains to prevent conflicts and possible disintegration of the family or company. Therefore, in the theoretical framework, we first provide a brief overview of networks, how networks provide social capital, and what the connection is between social capital and entrepreneurship. Subsequently, we present the main theories in the field of work–family interface with a special focus on work–family conflict theory, since the conflict theory forms the basis of our framework.

Because of the objective of this study, and the limited sources available to us, we have carried out some essential exploratory research. In order to identify the drivers and barriers, 45 semi-structured interviews were conducted with entrepreneurs living in Oslo, Stockholm, Copenhagen, and Helsinki. These cities are located in countries where labour can be characterized by its high productivity and relatively low numbers of working hours. For that reason, western countries often use them as inspiration for improving conditions important to maintaining a good work–life balance (Khallash and Kruse 2012). The findings of this research can be used to help entrepreneurs, coaches who assist entrepreneurs, policy makers, and others involved in enhancing entrepreneurial careers.

Theoretical framework

Many different theories have been developed to understand the work and family interface (Michel *et al.* 2009). The dominant theories are included in the theoretical framework of this chapter. First, the concept of social capital and its importance for entrepreneurship is explained. Subsequently, there will be a literature review with the main theories regarding work–family interface. The review by Geurts and Demerouti (2003) provided a useful overview of different theories developed in this field over time. The literature review regarding work and family interface will be finished with work–family conflict theory as studied by Michel *et al.* (2011, 2009) and Amstad *et al.* (2011). This theory is based on role theory, which serves as a broad theoretical umbrella that includes many aspects of work–family conflict literature (Michel *et al.* 2009). The theoretical framework will be finished with the family life-cycle theory.

Social capital and entrepreneurial networks

An increasing number of studies show that next to the entrepreneur, his or her network is essential for his or her entrepreneurial adventure and ultimately company success as well (Aldrich and Zimmer 1986). Social capital theory is often used to understand the scope, nature, and quality of such entrepreneurial networks (Anderson and Jack 2002; Greve and Salaff 2003). Gaining and maintaining social capital is important for having access to resources that are necessary for starting and sustaining a company.

We distinguish between two specific assets of social capital; bonding social capital and bridging social capital. Bonding configurations of social capital are strong homogeneous ties between actors, often characterized by face-to-face interaction. Therefore, bonding configurations of social capital are often seen in networks consisting of family and friends. Bridging social capital is associated with the openness of networks. For example, openness to: clients, customers, friends-of-friends, etc. (Burt 1997). In line with the objective of this study, we focus on bonding social capital by the entrepreneur's household members.

Social capital consists of several dimensions (Nahapiet and Ghoshal 1998). The structural dimension involves: who you are connected with and how often you are in contact with them. The relational aspect involves the types of ties in terms of: trust, expectations, reciprocity, and obligations. The cognitive and normative dimensions focus more on micro processes that can help in gaining social capital, such as communication skills (Lans, Blok, and Gulikers 2014).

Family ties are often useful for financial resources, professional advice, and practical help throughout the entrepreneurial process but especially during the start-up phase (Werbel and Danes 2010). Where weaker ties might help recognize the opportunity, family ties can provide the resources to seize the identified opportunity and often influence the decision making process to become an entrepreneur in various ways. Self-employed parents influence attitudes, values, etc. of their children either when raising them (Aldrich, Renzulli, and Langton 1998), or through encouragement by family and friends who have entrepreneurial experience. However, the family can also be a fire blanket that extinguishes the fire when family and friends are unfamiliar with entrepreneurship.

On the basis of social capital theory, we expect that entrepreneurs need to develop and maintain the ties in their household network to get access to and keep the resources needed for their company. Therefore, it is important to understand the work–family interface of entrepreneurs. In the next sections, the main theories on work–family interface are presented.

First theories in work/non-work interface

The first theories embraced by scientists in the field of work–family interface were spill-over and compensation theories (Geurts and Demerouti 2003; Clark 2000). The first implies that (dis)satisfaction in one domain can affect the other domain, whereas the compensation theory assumes that one can compensate (dis)satisfaction in one domain by investing more in the other domain. Both spill-over and compensation may occur simultaneously. However, both theories are insufficient to understand the work–family interface (Clark 2000).

Later, work–family interface was often studied in terms of the role stress theory (Geurts and Demerouti 2003). In role theory one assumes that different roles are hard to manage at the same time. This can ultimately lead to time-, strain-, or behavioural-based work–family conflict. The first studies in role stress theory saw the work–family interface primarily from a conflict perspective. Current studies also look at possible role enhancement, where skills learned for one domain appear to be useful in the other domain as well. Having multiple roles is not necessarily a resource drain but can create energy as well in some circumstances. One of the more influential theories is the work–family border theory by Clark (2000).

Work–family border theory

The work–family border theory is used to study how individuals shape the work and family domain and the borders between them to achieve satisfaction and good functioning at home, with a minimum of role conflict.

According to the work–family border theory, the work and family domains consist of different rules, thought patterns, and behaviour. These different rules, behaviour, and thought patterns result in different cultures and different desired ends in both domains.

However, although the culture and desired ends are different between the domains, people manage (to some extent) to integrate them (Clark 2000). The level of integration of the two domains depends partly on the borders between the two. The physical borders involve the place or area where work or family life takes place, temporal borders when work or family life takes place, and psychological borders involve the rules regarding thinking, behaviour, and emotions in each domain (Clark 2000). The nearer the two domains are in space and time and the more permeable and flexible the border, the more integrated the domains will be. An example of integration between the two domains can be found in working at home for the company while at the same time taking care of your child.

People who influence the domains and borders are the so-called border crossers and border keepers. In the context of this chapter, the entrepreneur can be seen as the border crosser, because he or she moves between the domain of work (their firm) and the domain of the family. Because they are entrepreneurs, they are often more in control regarding the domains and the ability to cross borders compared with people who are employed; they are often dependent on the dominant culture and desired ends of the company. However, the border keepers (e.g. life partners in the family domain and the boss in the work domain) play an important role in managing the borders between the domains, and subsequently the opportunity to move across these borders as well. If a spouse for instance complains about the working hours of his wife, he keeps up the border and may prevent his wife crossing borders. Nevertheless, border keepers allow more flexible and permeable borders in case they are aware of the other domain and they are committed to the border crosser (e.g. the entrepreneur).

Sustainable family business theory

Sustainable family business theory (SFBT) (Danes *et al.* 2008) concentrates on family capital, which consists of human, social, and financial capital. This capital can be beneficial to the company directly (e.g. labour and money) or indirectly (e.g. positive relationships and patterns of activity) (Danes *et al.* 2009). The theory assumes that the sustainability of the family business depends not only on the firm's performance, but also on family functionality and the exchange of resources between these two domains.

Different studies regarding SFBT posit that resource processes and/or inter-personal processes in both domains can enhance or constrain the firm's sustainability (Danes *et al.* 2008). Resources may conflict in case there is a mismatch between supply and demands of resources in both domains. Such a situation may occur in case of a new start-up, because starting a new business is likely to require many resources (Werbel and Danes 2010). In order to manage sustainable growth of such a start-up, there should be continuous interaction between the family and the firm through exchange of resources. Ultimately, family members manage their firm and family jointly to improve the sustainability and family functionality.

Because work–family conflict is seen as a significant problem in firm foundation (Werbel and Danes 2010), we focus on the theory of work–family conflict theory in the next section.

Work–family conflict theory

Work–family conflict is explained from different theoretical perspectives, which are ranged under the 'umbrella concept' role theory (Michel *et al.* 2009). Family and work roles are the results of other people's expectations about how one should behave in both domains. Each of these domains entails multiple roles (e.g. as spouse, parent, boss, colleague, friend, or child) that place specific demands on the individual or, in our case, the entrepreneur.

According to meta-analyses by Michel *et al.* (2011, 2009) and Amstad *et al.* (2011) the theory of work–family conflict consists of three components: (1) antecedents in the work and family domain, such as: family–work time demands, involvement in each domain, social support from people in the domain, etc., (2) a combination of work, family, and general-life domain outcomes like: family-, work-, and general-life satisfaction, (3) a mediating work–family conflict and family–work conflict construct concerning: work interference with family and family interference with work.

According to Michel *et al.* (2011, 2009), there are five antecedents of work–family conflict. The first antecedent concerns the social support from people at work and home for the work role and family role. This entails instrumental aid, emotional concern for the other, informational- and appraisal functions of others in the work or family domain that benefit one's self-esteem. In this chapter, we conceptualize these four underlying dimensions of social support in terms of emotional and instrumental support. With regard to emotional support, one can think of providing advice and appraisal. Financial support and practical support (e.g. providing labour for the company) are considered as instrumental support. These types of support have positive effects on the personal competence of the entrepreneur, his or her personal control, and sense of stability (Langford *et al.* 1997).

The second antecedent of conflicts is role involvement, which concerns psychological and cognitive preoccupation and the immersion in one's work or family role. Yogev and Brett (1985) found that dual earners have similar involvement in work and family domains, opposed to single earner couples. Respondents indicating higher job involvement perform better (individually) at their job (Diefendorff *et al.* 2002). However, when respondents are too much involved, they often cannot disengage from work when being with their family (Carlson and Frone 2003). The same pattern applies when being too much involved in the family. However, there are mixed results found by different studies (Carlson and Frone 2003).

The third antecedents, internal work role conflict and internal family role conflict, are associated with experiences of incompatible role pressures within the work (e.g. incompatible requests by customers or colleagues) or family domain (e.g. having different goals from spouse).

The fourth antecedents of conflict concern work time demands and family time demands. It refers to the time devoted to work and family roles. In a meta-analysis by Van der Doef and Maes (1999) they showed that having control over the pace and method of working has a moderating effect on experienced work time demands (e.g. time pressure). However, in general the conclusion can be drawn that work time demands can be associated with an increase in work–family conflict (Voydanoff 2004).

The fifth antecedents of conflict concern work role ambiguity and family role ambiguity. It refers to the lack of information and/or clarity about one's duties, objectives, and responsibilities for the work or family role. In the meta-analyses by Tubre and Collins (2000) and Mesmer-Magnus and Viswesvaran (2005), the first found that role ambiguity is negatively related with job performance, where the latter found a positive effect of family role ambiguity on family interference with work.

The antecedents and the references used by Michel *et al.* (2011, 2009) are presented in Table 11.1.

These antecedents of conflict in the work or family domain affect the two mediating variables: work interference with family (WIF) and family interference with work (FIW). These interferences can be supportive or disruptive. Subsequently, the above-mentioned antecedents and the mediator variables WIF and FIW affect the three outcome variables: work satisfaction, family satisfaction (degree of satisfaction with work and family related aspects of their life), and general life satisfaction (degree of satisfaction with general quality of life).

Table 11.1 References of antecedents obtained from Michel *et al.* (2009, 2011)

Antecedents of work–family conflict	References
Work social support and family social support	Carlson and Perrewé 1999; House 1981; Matsui, Ohsawa, and Onglatco 1995
Work involvement and family involvement	Diefendorff *et al.* 2002; Frone 2003; Greenhaus and Parasuraman 1999; Kanungo 1982; Yogev and Brett 1985
Internal work role conflict and internal family role conflict	Bacharach, Bamberger, and Conley 1990; Beehr 1995; Kahn *et al.* 1964; Katz and Kahn 1978; Kopelman, Greenhaus, and Connolly 1983
Work time demands and family time demands	Carlson and Frone 2003; Judge, Boudreau, and Bretz 1994; Kirchmeyer 1992; Major, Klein, and Ehrhart 2002; Frone, Yardley, and Markel 1997
Work role ambiguity and family role ambiguity	Glazer and Beehr 2005; Cooper, Davies-Cooper, and Eaker 1988; Kahn *et al.* 1964; Peterson *et al.* 1995; Schuler 1980; Elloy and Smith 2003; Usita, Hall, and Davis 2004

We expect that imbalances in work–family interface will lead to work–family conflict. These conflicts will subsequently make it harder for the entrepreneur to be involved in both domains, and invest time, money, and energy in the firm. Ultimately, we expect that this will lead to less entrepreneurial behaviour. Therefore, it is expected that factors leading to increase of the conflict antecedents: high family involvement, time demands, internal conflict, ambiguity, and low social support are expected barriers to starting a company. Known reports of factors that can lead to conflicts are: dissimilar career orientations (Greenhaus and Beutell 1985), gender (i.e. women experience more conflicts (Byron 2005)), absence of social support (Byron 2005), and (more ambiguously) one's marital status (Byron 2005), and the number and ages of children (e.g. Greenhaus and Beutell 1985).

The theory of work–family conflict provides a model for analysing the dynamics between work and family, and is applied in our study to get an understanding about the impact of the family on the start-up decision. However, the values, social rules, individual and group objectives are different in the various family life-cycle stages. Therefore, the family life-cycle perspective is included for assessing the family impact on the start-up decision as well.

Family life-cycle theory

Theories involving the concept of family life cycles see family life as a sequence of states (e.g. engagement, marriage, birth of first and last child, and empty nest among others) (Elder 1977). Next to a sequence of stages, van Leeuwen (1976) identified aspects associated with different life cycles depending on connections between wealth, age, and the different life-cycle stages and demographic events in the different stages.

However, these descriptions do not leave room for deviation (Alwin 2012). Nowadays, family life-cycle theory should adopt a more flexible life course perspective, as marriage and parenting are not always in conjunction with each other, families are smaller and often non-traditional (De Hoog & van Ophem 2006), divorces occur more often, and children who once left the house return to their parents (Settersten 2003). Therefore, it is important to acknowledge the usefulness of the family life-cycle concept and take into account as well that current society harbours more variety of household settings.

Concepts like family life cycle (e.g. Glick 1977), life trajectory (e.g. Elder 1985), or life course (e.g. Clausen 1986) all have in common that the stages of an individual over his or her lifespan are marked by important events. One can think of leaving parental home, marrying, marriage dissolution, or labour force entry/exit (Willekens 1999). Families in different stages have dissimilar complexities of: tasks, allocation of power, number of interpersonal relationships, resources, networks, etc. (Mattessich and Hill 1987). The different stages in the lifespan of an individual can affect job preferences as one's priorities regarding work–life balance change with these stages (Martinengo, Jacob, and Hill 2010). Therefore, the family life-cycle stages might influence the presence or absence of drivers of and barriers to company formation as well.

Furthermore, there are gender differences regarding the development of work–family conflict over the family life cycle (Martinengo, Jacob, and Hill 2010). For example, when turning into parents, women become more family involved as opposed to men who tend to work more. Once the children are pre-school aged, women experience more family interference with work and vice versa due to caregiving and housework. Once the children are in adolescence, their presence works mainly relaxing and lowers work interference with family life (Martinengo, Jacob, and Hill 2010). However, parents engaged in flexible work (e.g. entrepreneurship) report lower levels of conflicts (Martinengo, Jacob, and Hill 2010).

By including the concept of the family life cycle in the work–family conflict model, we obtained a conceptual model based on work by Michel et al. (2009, 2011) (Figure 11.1) that can be used to analyse the dynamics in different household settings at the time of decision making. This model is mainly used to structure the interviews and interpretation of the results. The underlying assumption

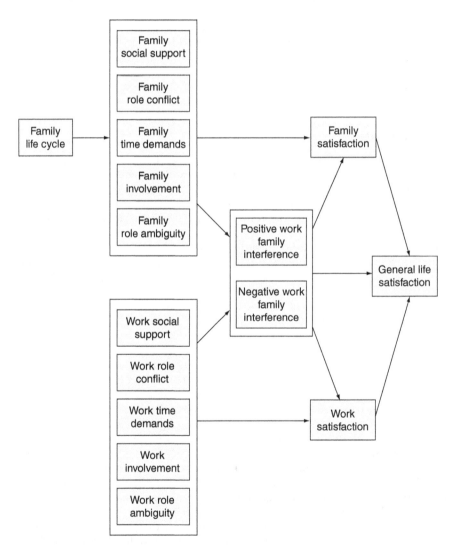

Figure 11.1 Conceptual model based on work–family conflict theory and family life-cycle theory, based on work by Michel et al. (2009, 2011).

is that less negative work–family interference and more positive work–family interference positively affect family satisfaction, work satisfaction, and, ultimately, general life satisfaction. We assume that people who expect to manage a family and a firm and to be satisfied in both domains are in favour of starting their firm.

Research methods

Research approach

Our qualitative exploratory study aims to identify drivers and barriers in start-up decisions experienced in the past, which makes this a retrospective research. We used in-depth semi-structured interviewing as a method of data collection, which is an approach to study the perceptions of participants and their experiences of an event in their own words (Taylor and Bogdan 1998), like the domestic drivers and barriers during the entrepreneurial process.

The interviews started with closed questions on: demographics, company information, and household characteristics. This was followed by open questions on: factors in the domestic environment experienced as stimuli and discouragements of entrepreneurship; factors in the work environment experienced as stimuli and discouragements of entrepreneurship; sources, types, and importance of social support. The interviews ended with questions about the entrepreneur's satisfaction with regard to family and household life, work life, general life, and health. Entrepreneurs were asked whether they experienced and/or could imagine different domestic drivers and barriers for the entrepreneurial start-up decision, when being in different household situations over time.

Data sample

In total 45 semi-structured interviews with a cross-section of entrepreneurs having various degrees of innovativeness were conducted in order to obtain first-person experiences. The sample includes entrepreneurs interviewed in Oslo ($n=11$), Stockholm ($n=12$), Copenhagen ($n=11$), and Helsinki ($n=11$). In 39 out of 45 cases, the interview took place at their work place. The sample includes entrepreneurs representing four small firms (10–50 employees), 27 micro firms (<10 employees), and 14 solo entrepreneurs. Nine entrepreneurs indicated being one-person households whereas 32 entrepreneurs indicated that they lived with their life partner. Sixteen of the entrepreneurs with a life partner also had one or more children. There were four entrepreneurs living with other family members or who were single parents. Since we want to look at the effect of the household network on the start-up decision, we also looked at one-person households as this enables comparison with other household types. This comparison is necessary for assessing the impact of other household members. The entrepreneurs in our sample were young and often at the beginning of their professional and family careers. In Table 11.2, the sample statistics are presented.

Data collection

The interviews were conducted successively in Oslo, Stockholm, Copenhagen, and Helsinki between August and November 2012. Next to the fact that the Nordic countries can be considered as best practices in balancing work and

Table 11.2 Sample statistics

Variable	Respondents	Male	Female	Household with child(ren)	Two-person household	One-person household
Male/female	29/16	n.a.	n.a.	10/5	10/4	9/4
Age resp.	34.8 (7.03)	32.6 (6.07)	38.9 (7.01)	38.4 (7.48)	31.86 (5.33)	32 (5.34)
Age life partner	35.44 (8.70)	32.1 (6.55)	42.8 (8.55)	37.87 (7.50)	34.54 (9.35)	n.a.
Company age	3.99 (3.76)	3.3 (3.28)	5.3 (4.33)	4.53 (3.96)	1.6 (0.96)	4.5 (3.5)
Age resp. when started the company	30.8 (6.05)	29.3 (4.99)	33.6 (6.93)	33.87 (6.90)	30.25 (5.41)	27.46 (4.59)
Working hours per week in the company	53.06 (19.37)	53 (22.28)	53.2 (12.62)	57.67 (17.02)	52.64 (22.55)	52.3 (16.85)
Number of employees, if any	4.1 (4.86)	5.2 (5.38)	1.4 (1.21)	4.75 (4.35)	3.05 (2.07)	6.1 (7.47)
Number of resp. with children	19 out of 46	11 out of 29	8 out of 16	15 out of 15	n.a.	n.a.
Number of children, if any	1.8 (1.23)	1.64 (0.81)	2 (1.69)	1.87 (1.36)	n.a.	n.a.
Working hours of life partner as employee	39.8 (8.11)	38.8 (8.36)	41.8 (7.64)	37.27 (10.17)	41.12 (4.67)	n.a.
Housework hours per week resp.	8.8 (8.57)	8.5 (10.24)	9.3 (4.96)	11.48 (8.5)	6.82 (2.63)	2.95 (1.63)
Housework hours per week life partner	11.4 (9.27)	12.9 (10.70)	9.2 (3.26)	13.58 (7.57)	7.07 (3.45)	n.a.

Notes
Standard deviation between brackets; resp. = respondent; n.a. = not applicable.

family combined with high productivity (Khallash and Kruse 2012), there were other reasons for data collection in these countries as well. These are homogeneous countries characterized by high social trust and high welfare. Due to their homogeneity, we do not expect to find differences attributable to institutional differences. Furthermore, a large share of the citizens in these countries are proficient in English which prevented a selection bias due to differences in language proficiency.

The 45 entrepreneurs were approached by applying convenience sampling and snowball sampling. Companies were entered, in neighbourhoods known for high start-up activity, if they appeared to be independent companies. Subsequently, the owner of the company was asked to participate in an interview. Social media was also used to approach entrepreneurs and convince them to participate in this study. Next to directly approaching the entrepreneurs, organizations that facilitate co-working spaces for entrepreneurs were contacted as well with the purpose of approaching their co-working space members. To a limited extent, snowball sampling was applied. Snowballing and convenience sampling are good methods to reach a desired sample. By approaching entrepreneurs in multiple areas of the city and by limiting the snowballing method as much as possible we attenuated a potential bias.

The interviews were conducted at places preferred by the interviewees. Each entrepreneur was interviewed for an average of 33 minutes. They were in-depth and face-to-face and entrepreneurs were given the opportunity to tell as much as they liked. The entrepreneurs talked from their own perspectives about their situation at the time of decision making, so it could be understood and expressed in their own words. Therefore, one has to take into account that perceptions of the entrepreneur's life partner, children, or other members, if any, are not included in our study. The interviews were in retrospective, but since most of the entrepreneurs started their company on average four years before the interview, they had little or no problems recalling the issues that played a role at the time of their decision making.

Data analysis

Transcripts were written verbatim from the recorded interviews. The transcripts retrieved from the interviews were reviewed and corrected before the content analysis. This content analysis was done using Atlas.ti as it facilitates management of coding and sorting of the data. Prior to the content analysis, a start list of codes was created based on the constructs (and survey questions that measure these constructs) obtained from articles underpinning the meta-analysis by Michel *et al.* (2011, 2009). To assign quotes to the right codes, the lists of survey questions measuring the constructs in work–family conflict theory are used to determine the boundaries for each concept (e.g. internal work role conflict by Rizzo, House, & Lirtzman (1970); work–family conflict by Kopelman, Greenhaus, and Connolly (1983), and Carlson, Kacmar, and Williams, (2000)). Subsequently, when quotes were within the determined boundaries they were labelled with that code. However, not all relevant quotes were within the scope of this deductive coding strategy. Therefore, open coding was used for the relevant text passages outside the scope of known concepts in work–family conflict theory. As the analysis went on, codes were revised and new codes were added when appropriate. Allowing for revision is a necessary step in the analysis process (Miles and Huberman

1994). After the coding was checked for appropriateness, reports were generated by Atlas.ti to identify all quotes assigned to each code and determine the fit of the quotation within the code. After this coding process, Atlas.ti provided information that helped to understand relationships and patterns of the household's impact on the entrepreneurial start-up decision. This way of systematic processing supports the validity.

In the results section, the drivers and barriers of one-person household stage, two-person household stage, and two-person household stage with children, are presented. The drivers and barriers mentioned in each of these family life-cycle stages are: experienced by the entrepreneurs in the household stage or expected to be present by entrepreneurs who are in different household stages from the ones they referred to. Also expected drivers and barriers are important since expectations can affect decisions whether to start a company in a specific household stage, or not. Therefore, in the results, reference is made to the total of 45 interviews.

Results

In the next sections the domestic drivers of and barriers to the entrepreneurial start-up decision are presented. First, we start with the one-person households. Subsequently, the influence of the life partner in the start-up decision is included. This is followed by the impact of children on the start-up decision.

One-person household stage

Data analysis revealed that one-person households share the characteristic that the level of intra-household social capital is relatively low, especially in terms of social support. Therefore, the resources are obtained from contacts outside the one-person household. Even though the level of intra-household social capital is low, findings in our study indicate that, overall, being in a one-person household is mainly supportive of the start-up decision, as ten entrepreneurs referred to this type of household situation as a positive influence, three entrepreneurs were neutral, and three entrepreneurs actually did see the one-person household as a constraint. The findings indicate that there are drivers present in a one-person household which outweigh the lack of intra-household social capital.

The drivers of being in a one-person household are mostly expressed in terms of money ($n=7$) and time ($n=8$). Looking at it from a financial point of view, many of the entrepreneurs were young and did not have high costs of living when they started their company. Furthermore, in one-person households, there were no responsibilities towards other household members, so decisions (e.g. to economize on expenses) solely affected the entrepreneurs themselves. The lower family responsibilities and the opportunity to make autonomous decisions are perceived as drivers for the start-up decision. The entrepreneurs in one-person households could take the financial risk, since negative financial outcomes solely affect them and no others. Examples of such advantages are expressed in the following quotes:

> R14: I am alone. I can live very, very tight if it is necessary, and so on. But that would not have been possible if you have a full family. [Then] you could not make the decision that there would be no holiday or no whatever. For me I could decide to do this.

R5: I don't have anyone at home waiting for me so I can make some extra hours.

What becomes clear from these quotes is that the entrepreneurs enjoy the fact that they do not have to invest much time and energy in bonding network ties compared to entrepreneurs who have multiple household members. Furthermore, they can make their decisions without running the risk of conflict resulting in weaker ties with household members and possible loss of social capital. Linking this to work–family border theory by Clark (2000), we see that respondents enjoy the absence of domain gatekeepers who influence the permeability of the borders between the family and work domain. Therefore, work-related decisions are free to affect the flexible family domain. Strong bonding ties are important for seizing the entrepreneurial opportunity (Werbel and Danes 2010). However, entrepreneurs in this study had already seized the opportunity. They found other ways to get access to resources necessary for taking the opportunity. Therefore, one-person households which still need access to the resources might be less positive about their household situation compared to entrepreneurs in this study.

The entrepreneurs also mentioned the advantage of their low costs of living in the early stages of the family life cycle. Nine entrepreneurs indicated that low, or flexible, costs of living was a driver for starting their company. The early stage of family life cycle is compatible with the company life cycle as the income in the first company year(s) is low but the fixed costs of living are low as well. Therefore, they do not experience the financial risk inherent in starting a company as a huge barrier. This becomes clear, for example, from the next quote:

R27: For me there wasn't any [financial constraint]. For me the only fixed costs that I have is my apartment. [...] I don't have a girlfriend that I need to take out to a fancy restaurant [once] in a while. I don't need to buy presents for anybody except my nearest family.

Next to financial advantages, entrepreneurs indicated the advantage of determining the number of working hours and level of involvement in their work role without neglecting family role responsibilities. Entrepreneurs talked the most about work involvement and the least about family involvement when describing the one-person household. Entrepreneurs face the risk of being immersed in their work role, making them cognitively preoccupied with the company. However, they did not indicate this as being problematic, probably because their immersion and preoccupation does not affect the rest of the household. The following quote is from an entrepreneur who thinks back to when he was single, and expresses the advantage in the following way:

R21: I met her very recently, it is mostly here in Stockholm that I am living with her. So before that I was living single in my house. I'm still in Tel Aviv single at my apartment so I am completely alone in this matter. That allows me, I guess, to be totally devoted to this thing [i.e. starting the company].

From the interviews it becomes clear that the low family time demands and low family involvement in one-person households allow entrepreneurs to devote many hours to and be highly involved in the start-up. One-person households experience low and flexible costs of living, which is compatible with the uncertain income associated with entrepreneurship. Therefore, having low and/or flexible costs of living is a driver for the start-up decision and is therefore to be added to the model of work–family conflict. It is also important to note that three entrepreneurs indicated that a one-person household would be a discouragement to start a company, as they do not receive emotional and economic support from other household members. Inherently, one-person households have one less source of income (instrumental support) than dual-earner households. Furthermore, they do not get emotional support from other household members when necessary. The absence of emotional and instrumental support for entrepreneurs in one-person households is therefore a barrier to the entrepreneurship. The social support must then come from sources outside the household like parents, siblings, or friends. Since these are one-person households, drivers or barriers related to family role ambiguity or internal family role conflict factors were little or not mentioned in the interviews.

Two-person household stage

The most important driver that results from the presence of a life partner is the family social support. The drivers with regard to family social support are divided into instrumental support (support by helping in the company, informational, or economic support) and emotional support (emotional concern and appraisal).

The life partners of entrepreneurs provide financial support ($n=7$), or would be willing to support financially if that is necessary. In two cases, entrepreneurs mentioned that their life partner invested money in their start-up. It was more common to use the income of the life partner to manage the household expenses ($n=5$). The reason why they prefer that income source to be spent on household costs may be to prevent the family from becoming involved in the company management. This is one of the reasons mentioned by Arregle *et al.* (2013). Using the life partner's income for the household expenses might be a coping strategy to manage the exchange of resources in both domains. The other ways of instrumental support mentioned by entrepreneurs, are life partners who help by: doing work tasks in the company ($n=10$) and/or doing the household tasks when work time demands prevent the entrepreneur from doing his or her share in the household ($n=7$) and by giving advice aiming to solve work-related problems ($n=4$). The latter is especially the case if the life partners are self-employed or work in a similar field and thus have the expertise to provide informational support. Here, the concept of other-domain awareness as part of the work–family border theory by Clark (2000) seems appropriate.

Emotional support is also an important domestic driver for the start-up decision. Looking at all 45 entrepreneurs, there were 41 who indicated that they received emotional support. In 28 cases, the entrepreneurs indicated that life partners are, or can be, considered as the main source of emotional support ($n=28$). This emotional support from life partners was expressed by showing empathy, concern, or affection, when the entrepreneur experienced work-related problems. The entrepreneurs who experienced time- or strain-based work–family conflict ($n=15$) state that the acceptance and understanding of their life partners is essential to combining work and household life. In the next quote it becomes clear that life partners who are entrepreneurial minded as well often show understanding about work–family role conflicts.

R25: She is also a bit entrepreneur, start-up, minded so she kind of understands what's going on.

These results are in line with many studies regarding work–family interface. However, the dynamics behind these types of support are also interesting. With regard to emotional support, the entrepreneurs seem to be in a struggle to find a good balance. On the one hand, emotional support from their life partner relieves and sometimes prevents stress. On the other hand, they want to separate work and household life and do not want to be preoccupied with work responsibilities at home. The life partners of entrepreneurs also struggle. They want to support the entrepreneurial activities of their life partner by showing understanding and accepting their lower family involvement, but at the same time they do complain about work time demands and high involvement in the company. This is expressed by one entrepreneur in the following way:

I: Does your girlfriend ... understand that [work priority]? Because she is self-employed as well?

R30: Yeah she does, but she is really tired of it obviously. ... I mean, I am so far away in my head, if you know what I mean. But, yeah she understands it. But she has hard times accepting it. If you know what I mean.

For entrepreneurs, to have a work–family balance where conflicts can occur, it is important to have a life partner who accepts, and empathizes with, their entrepreneurial career. It appears that communication and making decisions together positively affect the understanding and acceptance of the entrepreneurial endeavour. However, communication and coordination continues to be important, also after the decision is made. This confirms the importance of communication skills for gaining and maintaining social capital mentioned in the article by Lans, Blok, and Gulikers (2015).

I: How did she deal with the little time you had? Or how did you manage to combine the work with the studies and the family?

R9: With ... good communication. Good communication and understanding. She very much respects what I am doing here.

Next to the presence of drivers in two-person households, like emotional and instrumental support from the life partner, there are barriers as well. Namely, with more household members, the family involvement and family time demands increase as well. When the entrepreneurs are highly involved and devote many hours to the company, time- and strain-based conflicts can occur. It depends on the support and understanding of the life partner whether the entrepreneur experiences the increased family time demands and involvement as barriers to entrepreneurship. Life partners with dissimilar career and/or family orientations show lower support and understanding. However, this did not prevent the entrepreneurs in our sample from starting their company. Because the entrepreneurs did not mention an impact of family role ambiguity or internal family role, it cannot be determined to what extent these are drivers of or barriers to entrepreneurship.

Households with children stage

The impact of children on the start-up decision depends on the age of the children. Overall, after analysing 45 interviews, the conclusion can be drawn that many entrepreneurs see children as domestic barriers to self-employment ($n=20$). In most cases, the entrepreneur expressed that the presence of children caused conflict between work and household life. Only four entrepreneurs stated that children are supportive for their self-employment. Therefore, overall, children have a constraining impact on the start-up decision.

The birth of children is an important life event in family life-cycle theory that in our study appears to be linked with the start-up decision. This becomes clear from the interviews where maternity leave is repeatedly mentioned ($n=8$) as a point in time for a career change towards entrepreneurship. It is important to understand that most entrepreneurs already had entrepreneurial intentions and mentioned that they did not became entrepreneurs because of family reasons. However, it was one of the factors that determined the moment to start the company. Female nascent entrepreneurs use their paid leave to develop their initial idea into a full business plan. Subsequently, they will then start their company. Furthermore, if the company is started during maternity leave, the income that is obtained from maternity leave provides (to some extent) a secure income next to the uncertain income related to self-employment. When they have young children they try to work from home so they can take care of their children as well. The maternity leave is a positive external effect of children on the start-up decision.

Even though maternity leave is advantageous and enables recipients to determine their own working policies (e.g. working at home), the children (especially young children) are still perceived as constraints on entrepreneurship. This is mainly because they are a primary cause of time- and strain-based conflicts between the household and work. These conflicts between work and the household arise because the presence of children increases family time demands and family involvement, while simultaneously the company needs the same resources too. This is especially the case during the start-up phase, when the entrepreneur faces high work time demands and work involvement. Male entrepreneurs mentioned the presence of time-based conflict two times more often than female entrepreneurs. Next to time-based conflict, entrepreneurs also experience strain-based conflicts. Entrepreneurs are often exhausted in the start-up phase of the company, but the children still need involved parents. This puts pressure on the entrepreneur who still has his family role, which leads to strain-based work–family conflicts. The instrumental and emotional support from the life partner is essential for the entrepreneur in these households. When talking about the importance of social support, the entrepreneurs referred two times more often to households with children than in other situations. Furthermore, increasing fixed costs of living is conflicting with uncertain income from entrepreneurship, and is thus considered as a barrier. Especially when the company is in the start-up phase.

> R14: If I would have had children, I don't know if I would have started this company. Because I could not imagine working like this and keeping a family at the same time.... That would not be possible. So in that [respect] it is the lack of children [that] makes it possible to work like this.

However, few entrepreneurs mention that children do not solely create a negative relationship between self-employment and the household. Two examples of children as drivers of entrepreneurship are mentioned are:

> I: The fact that your girlfriend was pregnant and already had a child, what influence did [it] had on the company? And the decision to start your own company?

> R8: You know you always need money when you have children so the possibility to have your own shop was ... better than to sit five years in school and take an education to maybe get a job afterwards.

And

> R34: It was very hard for me to have an employment with two little children so that was a factor that was inspiring.

One of the major advantages which is frequently mentioned by the entrepreneurs, is the flexibility in time and work place as they are their own boss. This implies that the entrepreneurs can adjust their working times and place of work to their family needs. The most frequently mentioned example is that one of the parents takes the children to school and the other one picks them up. Even though it increases family interference with work when children are ill, the entrepreneur has the decisive power in the company to leave work in order to take care of their child.

Female entrepreneurs often manage their company in a way that is compatible with their family needs. If it is possible to work at home and beneficial to their household, then many (female) entrepreneurs would choose to work at home ($n=9$). This is especially the case in families with young children ($n=7$). They adjust the management of their company according to the family needs. One disadvantage of entrepreneurship is that female entrepreneurs will not get maternity leave when they want to have a child during their entrepreneurial career. Furthermore, when they are solo entrepreneurs they cannot stop working, as the company in that case will not be active either, and clients might switch to other companies. Then it can be the other way around in the sense that family planning is affected by the company.

Once the company and the children are older, there are fewer conflicts. The household and company can become more compatible to each other. First of all, the children can take care of themselves so family time demands decrease which leaves room for the entrepreneur's company. Second, children can provide instrumental support by doing more household tasks, which reduces family time demand for both the entrepreneur as well as their life partner. Third, in some cases the children assist in the company's work. Looking at this from the company perspective, the work time demands are expected to decrease after the start-up phase and the revenues will be less fluctuating. The strain due to time and finances seems to decline which is beneficial to both the household and the company.

Entrepreneurs experience important social support from their life partner, especially when being in households with children. When family time demands increase (e.g. due to the presence of young children) it is the life partner who often can prevent conflicts by increasing their share in the household. Emotional and instrumental support from the life partner is therefore a driver for the start-up decision. Increased family responsibilities in terms of family time demands and involvement are mainly barriers to entrepreneurship but decrease when children get older. The entrepreneurs did not mention the impact of family role ambiguity or internal family role conflict as barriers to the start-up decision.

When asked whether the presence of children in the household will affect the entrepreneurial start-up decision, many entrepreneurs respond that it would have made the choice harder but probably not different. An overview of the drivers for and barriers to the entrepreneurial start-up decision for the three different family life-cycle stages is presented in Table 11.3.

Conclusion and future research issues

The entrepreneurs in our study indicated that household reasons were not the key motivation to engage in entrepreneurship, which is in contrast with findings by McGowan *et al.* (2012) and Mattis (2004). The internal motivation to become an entrepreneur was already present or they could be considered as involuntary entrepreneurs (e.g. due to being unemployed and having low job prospects). Nevertheless, the family, and more precisely the household, has an impact on the entrepreneurial process. Entrepreneurs indicated that their household conditions were supportive and provided the opportunity to engage in their entrepreneurial endeavour. However, this does not mean that they started their firm motivated by a desire to balance family responsibilities. The conclusion can be drawn that the family and household situation does have an impact on the entrepreneurial process, as it is one of the elements determining entrepreneurial opportunities. Although in this study we did not take other influences into account than the household, we fully acknowledge the importance of factors such as internal motivation and involuntary or forced entrepreneurship (e.g. job loss or facing low job prospects). The same holds for the social capital outside the household, like the emotional and instrumental support by the parents, which appeared to be very important.

Furthermore, entrepreneurs appeared to manage their family planning and company planning in harmony with each other. Female entrepreneurs sometimes enjoy the benefits of maternity leave before starting their company. In other cases, their company had already passed the start-up phase before they started a family. In the case where women have young children, they try to manage their company in a way that enables them to take care of the children as well. The female entrepreneurs experience problems when they want to have a child after they have started a company because they cannot shut down the company.

What becomes clear from our study is that female entrepreneurs did not start their company because of family reasons but their household situation enabled them to start a company, which conflicts with findings by DeMartino and Barbato (2003). In the cases where the company had already started, they would like their company to be in a stable phase before expanding the family. Next to research that could shed light on drivers and barriers for female entrepreneurs in general, it could be interesting to study how perceptions of drivers and barriers develop when the relevant questions are asked before, at the moment of, and after the entrepreneurial start-up decision.

Table 11.3 Domestic drivers and barriers to the start-up decision in three family life-cycle stages

Drivers and barriers	One-person household	Two-person household	Family with children
Drivers	• Low family time demands	• Emotional support	• Instrumental and emotional support by the life partner
	• Low family involvement	• Instrumental support	• Instrumental support children when older
	• Flexible/low costs of living	• Shared living costs	• Emotional support children when older
			• High family time demands
			• High family involvement
			• High costs of living
Barriers	• Absence of intra-household instrumental support	When life partner has dissimilar career and family values:	
	• Absence of intra-household emotional support	• Higher family involvement	
	–	• Higher family time demands	

The life partner is essential for combining family responsibilities and work responsibilities, thereby preventing or mitigating work–family conflict. Couples with dissimilar career orientations can experience a lack of support by their life partner. The findings also indicate that there are important differences between the acceptance, understanding, and appreciation of the entrepreneurial career of their life partner. In this study, we did not examine in detail when these 'attitudes' change. We did find communication to be an important factor influencing the life partner's attitude. Also, other domain awareness (for instance in case the life partner has entrepreneurial experiences as well) seems an important factor.

The entrepreneurs in this study see children primarily as a constraint, as they increase family time demands, family involvement, and fixed costs of living. However, when children are older they have a relaxing effect and provide instrumental support by helping with the company or by doing household tasks. Since we did not focus on family businesses, we cannot study differences in the impact of children on work–family conflict between companies with and without succession. We think that there is still an area to be explored for future studies, to examine the influence of children on work–family conflict and the businesses of their entrepreneurial parents.

There are some limitations to this study. First of all, we did not interview the entrepreneur's partner. Therefore, we only have the perception of the entrepreneur. The entrepreneurs were not always sure whether the perceptions of their life partners were similar. Therefore, future research could study the perspectives of the entrepreneur's life partners and possible differences between them. The second limitation of this study is the fact that we interviewed people who had already made the decision to start a company. In future research it could be interesting to interview nascent entrepreneurs. This could give important insights, because they are at the point of decision making and therefore do not have to think in retrospect. The third limitation of this study is its limited generalizability. We only interviewed entrepreneurs in the dense urban areas of the capitals in the Nordic countries. Therefore, future research could shed new light on the work–family balance model by doing qualitative research in other settings and quantitative research with data from multiple countries. Our findings show that quantitative research regarding work–family conflict experienced by entrepreneurs should include the concept of low and flexible costs of living and family life-cycle stages. In this study, the concepts of internal family role conflict and family role ambiguity do not seem to be important factors affecting the start-up decision as entrepreneurs did not talk about them during the interviews.

Some practical implications follow from our research as well. Policy makers who want to stimulate entrepreneurship should take the family dimension into account when developing policies and policy makers responsible for paternal leave policies should take entrepreneurship into account. Especially, for female entrepreneurs this means that they should do some proactive thinking regarding family and company planning. Entrepreneurs should communicate about their difficulties in maintaining a work–family balance and make their life partners aware of their work domain so they understand why work–family balance is often hard to manage. This can prevent or mitigate conflicts in the household and loss of social capital.

References

Adler, Paul S., and Seok-Woo Kwon. 2002. 'Social Capital: Prospects for a New Concept'. *Academy of Management Review* 27 (1): 17–40.

Aldrich, H., and C. Zimmer. 1986. 'Entrepreneurship through Social Networks'. In *The Art and Science of Entrepreneurship*, edited by D. Sexton and R. Smilor, 2–32. New York: Ballinger Publishing Company.

Aldrich, Howard, Linda A. Renzulli, and Nancy Langton. 1998. 'Passing on Privilege: Resources provided by Self-Employed Parents to their Self-Employed Children'. *Research in Social Stratification and Mobility* 16: 291–318.

Alwin, Duane F. 2012. 'Integrating Varieties of Life Course Concepts'. *Journal of Gerontology Series B: Psychological Sciences and Social Sciences* 67 (2): 206–220.

Amstad, Fabienne T., Laurenz L. Meier, Ursula Fasel, Achim Elfering, and Norbert K. Semmer. 2011. 'A Meta-Analysis of Work-Family Conflict and Various Outcomes with a Special Emphasis on Cross-Domain versus Matching-Domain Relations'. *Journal of Occupational Health Psychology* 16 (2): 151.

Anderson, Alistair R., and Sarah L. Jack. 2002. 'The Articulation of Social Capital in Entrepreneurial Networks: A Glue or a Lubricant?' *Entrepreneurship and Regional Development* 14 (3): 193–210.

Anderson, Alistair R., Sarah L. Jack, and Sarah Drakopoulou Dodd. 2005. 'The Role of Family Members in Entrepreneurial Networks: Beyond the Boundaries of the Family Firm'. *Family Business Review* 18 (2): 135–154.

Arregle, Jean-Luc, Bat Batjargal, Michael A. Hitt, Justin W. Webb, and Anne S. Tsui. 2013. 'Family Ties in Entrepreneurs' Social Networks and New Venture Growth'. *Entrepreneurship: Theory and Practice* 39 (2): 1–32.

Bacharach, Samuel B., Peter Bamberger, and Sharon C. Conley. 1990. 'Work Processes, Role Conflict, and Role Overload: The Case of Nurses and Engineers in the Public Sector'. *Work and Occupations* 17 (2): 199–228.

Beehr, Terry A. 1995. *Psychological Stress in the Workplace*. London and New York: Routledge.

Brüderl, Josef, and Peter Preisendörfer. 1998. 'Network Support and the Success of Newly Founded Business'. *Small Business Economics* 10 (3): 213–225.

Bubolz, Margaret M. 2001. 'Family as Source, User, and Builder of Social Capital'. *Journal of Socio-Economics* 30 (2): 129–131.

Burt, Ronald S. 1997. 'The Contingent Value of Social Capital'. *Administrative Science Quarterly* 42 (2): 339–365.

Byron, Kristin. 2005. 'A Meta-Analytic Review of Work–Family Conflict and its Antecedents'. *Journal of Vocational Behavior* 67 (2): 169–198.

Carlson, Dawn S., and Michael R. Frone. 2003. 'Relation of Behavioral and Psychological Involvement to a New Four-Factor Conceptualization of Work-Family Interference'. *Journal of Business and Psychology* 17 (4): 515–535.

Carlson, Dawn S., and Pamela L. Perrewé. 1999. 'The Role of Social Support in the Stressor–Strain Relationship: An Examination of Work–Family Conflict'. *Journal of Management* 25 (4): 513–540.

Carlson, Dawn S., K. Michele Kacmar, and Larry J. Williams. 2000. 'Construction and Initial Validation of a Multidimensional Measure of Work–Family Conflict'. *Journal of Vocational Behavior* 56 (2): 249–276.

Clark, S. C. 2000. 'Work/Family Border Theory: A New Theory of Work/Family Balance'. *Human Relations* 53 (6): 747–770.

Clausen, John A. 1986. *The Life Course: A Sociological Perspective*. Englewood Cliffs, NJ: Prentice-Hall.

Cooper, Cary L., Rachel Davies-Cooper, and Lynn H. Eaker. 1988. *Living with Stress*. London and New York: Penguin Books.

Danes, S. M., K. Stafford, G. Haynes, and S. S. Amarapurkar. 2009. 'Family Capital of Family Firms: Bridging Human, Social, and Financial Capital'. *Family Business Review* 22 (3): 199–215.

Danes, Sharon M., Jinhee Lee, Kathryn Stafford, and Ramona Kay Zachary Heck. 2008. 'The Effects of Ethnicity, Families and Culture on Entrepreneurial Experience: An Extension of Sustainable Family Business Theory'. *Journal of Developmental Entrepreneurship* 13 (3): 229–268.

De Hoog, Kees, and Johan van Ophem. 2006. 'Families and Changing Life Cycles'. In *Heterodox Views on Economics and the Economy of the Global Society*, edited by G. Meijer, W. J. M. Heijman, J. A. C. van Ophem, and B. H. J. Verstegen, 143–154. Wageningen, Wageningen Academic Publishers.

DeMartino, Richard, and Robert Barbato. 2003. 'Differences between Women and Men MBA Entrepreneurs: Exploring Family Flexibility and Wealth Creation as Career Motivators'. *Journal of Business Venturing* 18 (6): 815–832.

Diefendorff, James M., Douglas J. Brown, Allen M. Kamin, and Robert G. Lord. 2002. 'Examining the Roles of Job Involvement and Work Centrality in Predicting Organizational Citizenship Behaviors and Job Performance'. *Journal of Organizational Behavior* 23 (1): 93–108.

Drakopoulou-Dodd, Sarah, Sarah L. Jack, and Alistair R. Anderson. 2006. 'The Mechanisms and Processes of Entrepreneurial Networks: Continuity and Change'. In *Advances in Entrepreneurship, Firm Emergence and Growth, Volume 9: Entrepreneurship: Frameworks and Empirical Investigations from Forthcoming Leaders of European Research*, edited by J. Wiklund, D. Dimov, J. A. Katz, and D. A. Shepherd, 107–145. Bingley, UK: Emerald.

Elder, Glen H. 1985. *Life Course Dynamics: Trajectories and Transitions, 1968–1980*. Ithaca, NY: Cornell University Press.

Elder Jr, Glen H. 1977. 'Family History and the Life Course'. *Journal of Family History* 2 (4): 279–304.

Elloy, David F., and Catherine R. Smith. 2003. 'Patterns of Stress, Work–Family Conflict, Role Conflict, Role Ambiguity and Overload among Dual-Career and Single-Career Couples: An Australian Study'. *Cross Cultural Management: An International Journal* 10 (1): 55–66.

Frone, Michael R. 2003. 'Work–Family Balance'. In *Handbook of Occupational Health Psychology*, edited by James Campbell Quick and Lois E. Tetrick, 17th edn, 143–162. Washington, DC: American Psychological Association.

Frone, M. R., J. K. Yardley, and K. S. Markel. 1997. 'Developing and Testing an Integrative Model of the Work–Family Interface'. *Journal of Vocational Behavior* 50 (2): 145–167.

Gedajlovic, Eric, Benson Honig, Curt B. Moore, G. Tyge Payne, and Mike Wright. 2013. 'Social Capital and Entrepreneurship: A Schema and Research Agenda'. *Entrepreneurship: Theory and Practice* 37 (3): 455–478.

Geurts, Sabine A. E., and Evangelia Demerouti. 2003. 'Work/Non-Work Interface: A Review of Theories and Findings'. In *The Handbook of Work and Health Psychology*, edited by Marc J. Schabracq, Jacques A. M. Winnubst, and Cary L. Cooper, 279–312. Chichester: John Wiley & Sons.

Glazer, Sharon, and Terry A. Beehr. 2005. 'Consistency of Implications of Three Role Stressors across Four Countries'. *Journal of Organizational Behavior* 26 (5): 467–487.

Glick, Paul C. 1977. 'Updating the Life Cycle of the Family'. *Journal of Marriage and the Family* 39: 5–13.

Granovetter, Mark S. 1973. 'The Strength of Weak Ties'. *American Journal of Sociology* 78 (6): 1360–1380.

Greenhaus, Jeffrey H., and Nicholas J. Beutell. 1985. 'Sources of Conflict between Work and Family Roles'. *Academy of Management Review* 10 (1): 76–88.

Greenhaus, Jeffrey H., and Saroj Parasuraman. 1999. 'Research on Work, Family, and Gender: Current Status and Future Directions'. In *Handbook of Gender and Work*, edited by Gary N. Powell, 391–412. Thousand Oaks, CA: Sage Publications Limited.

Greve, Arent, and Janet W. Salaff. 2003. 'Social Networks and Entrepreneurship'. *Entrepreneurship: Theory and Practice* 28 (1): 1–22.

Hoang, Ha, and Bostjan Antoncic. 2003. 'Network-Based Research in Entrepreneurship: A Critical Review'. *Journal of Business Venturing* 18 (2): 165–187.

House, James S. 1981. *Work Stress and Social Support*. Reading, MA: Addison-Wesley Publishing Company.

Hoy, Frank, and Pramodita Sharma. 2010. *Entrepreneurial Family Firms*. Englewood Cliffs, NJ: Prentice Hall.

Jack, Sarah L. 2005. 'The Role, Use and Activation of Strong and Weak Network Ties: A Qualitative Analysis'. *Journal of Management Studies* 42 (6): 1233–1259.

Judge, Timothy A., John W. Boudreau, and Robert D. Bretz. 1994. 'Job and Life Attitudes of Male Executives'. *Journal of Applied Psychology* 79 (5): 767–782.

Kahn, Robert L., Donald M. Wolfe, Robert P. Quinn, J. Diedrick Snoek, and Robert A. Rosenthal. 1964. *Organizational Stress: Studies in Role Conflict and Ambiguity*. Oxford: John Wiley & Sons.

Kanungo, Rabindra N. 1982. 'Measurement of Job and Work Involvement'. *Journal of Applied Psychology* 67 (3): 341–349.

Katz, Daniel, and Robert Louis Kahn. 1978. *The Social Psychology of Organizations*, 2nd edn. New York: John Wiley & Sons, Inc.

Khallash, Sally, and Martin Kruse. 2012. 'The Future of Work and Work–Life Balance 2025'. *Futures* 44 (7): 678–686.

Kim, Phillip H., Howard E. Aldrich, and Lisa A. Keister. 2006. 'Access (not) Denied: The Impact of Financial, Human, and Cultural Capital on Entrepreneurial Entry in the United States'. *Small Business Economics* 27 (1): 5–22.

Kirchmeyer, Catherine. 1992. 'Perceptions of Nonwork-to-Work Spillover: Challenging the Common View of Conflict-Ridden Domain Relationships'. *Basic and Applied Social Psychology* 13 (2): 231–249.

Kopelman, Richard E., Jeffrey H. Greenhaus, and Thomas F. Connolly. 1983. 'A Model of Work, Family, and Interrole Conflict: A Construct Validation Study'. *Organizational Behavior and Human Performance* 32 (2): 198–215.

Krackhardt, David. 1992. 'The Strength of Strong Ties: The Importance of Philos in Organizations'. *Networks and Organizations: Structure, Form, and Action* 216: 239.

Langford, Catherine Penny Hinson, Juanita Bowsher, Joseph P. Maloney, and Patricia P. Lillis. 1997. 'Social Support: A Conceptual Analysis'. *Journal of Advanced Nursing* 25 (1): 95–100.

Lans, Thomas, Vincent Blok, and Judith Gulikers. 2015 (forthcoming). 'Show Me Your Network and I'll Tell You Who You Are: Social Competence and Social Capital of Early-Stage Entrepreneurs'. *Entrepreneurship and Regional Development*. DOI: 10.1080/08985626.2015.1070537.

Lumpkin, G. T., Keith H. Brigham, and Todd W. Moss. 2010. 'Long-Term Orientation: Implications for the Entrepreneurial Orientation and Performance of Family Businesses'. *Entrepreneurship and Regional Development* 22 (3–4): 241–264.

McGowan, Pauric, Caroline Lewis Redeker, Sarah Y. Cooper, and Kate Greenan. 2012. 'Female Entrepreneurship and the Management of Business and Domestic Roles: Motivations, Expectations and Realities'. *Entrepreneurship and Regional Development* 24 (1–2): 53–72.

Major, Virginia Smith, Katherine J. Klein, and Mark G. Ehrhart. 2002. 'Work Time, Work Interference with Family, and Psychological Distress'. *Journal of Applied Psychology* 87 (3): 427–435.

Martinengo, Giuseppe, Jenet I. Jacob, and E. Jeffrey Hill. 2010. 'Gender and the Work–Family Interface: Exploring Differences across the Family Life Course'. *Journal of Family Issues* 31 (10): 1363–1390.

Matsui, Tamao, Takeshi Ohsawa, and Mary-Lou Onglatco. 1995. 'Work–Family Conflict and the Stress-Buffering Effects of Husband Support and Coping Behavior among Japanese Married Working Women'. *Journal of Vocational Behavior* 47 (2): 178–192.

Mattessich, Paul, and Reuben Hill. 1987. 'Life Cycle and Family Development'. In *Handbook of Marriage and the Family*, edited by Marvin B, Sussman and Suzanne K, Steinmetz, 437–469. New York: Springer.

Mattis, Mary C. 2004. 'Women Entrepreneurs: Out from under the Glass Ceiling'. *Women in Management Review* 19 (3): 154–163.

Mesmer-Magnus, Jessica R., and Chockalingam Viswesvaran. 2005. 'Convergence between Measures of Work-to-Family and Family-to-Work Conflict: A Meta-Analytic Examination'. *Journal of Vocational Behavior* 67 (2): 215–232.

Michel, Jesse S., Lindsey M. Kotrba, Jacqueline K. Mitchelson, Malissa A. Clark, and Boris B. Baltes. 2011. 'Antecedents of Work–Family Conflict: A Meta-analytic Review'. *Journal of Organizational Behavior* 32 (5): 689–725.

Michel, Jesse S., Jacqueline K. Mitchelson, Lindsey M. Kotrba, James M. LeBreton, and Boris B. Baltes. 2009. 'A Comparative Test of Work–Family Conflict Models and Critical Examination of Work–Family Linkages'. *Journal of Vocational Behavior* 74 (2): 199–218.

Miles, Matthew B., and A. Michael Huberman. 1994. *Qualitative Data Analysis: An Expanded Sourcebook*. Thousand Oaks, CA: Sage Publications.

Nahapiet, Janine, and Sumantra Ghoshal. 1998. 'Social Capital, Intellectual Capital, and the Organizational Advantage'. *Academy of Management Review* 23 (2): 242–266.

Nordqvist, Mattias, and Leif Melin. 2010. 'Entrepreneurial Families and Family Firms'. *Entrepreneurship and Regional Development* 22 (3–4): 211–239.

Peterson, Mark F., Peter B. Smith, Adebowale Akande, Sabino Ayestaran, Stephen Bochner, Victor Callan, Nam Guk Cho, Jorge Correia Jesuino, Maria D'Amorim, and Pierre-Henri Francois. 1995. 'Role Conflict, Ambiguity, and Overload: A 21-Nation Study'. *Academy of Management Journal* 38 (2): 429–452.

Powell, Gary N., and Jeffrey H. Greenhaus. 2012. 'When Family Considerations Influence Work Decisions: Decision-Making Processes'. *Journal of Vocational Behavior* 81 (3): 322–329.

Rizzo, John R., Robert J. House, and Sidney I. Lirtzman. 1970. 'Role Conflict and Ambiguity in Complex Organizations'. *Administrative Science Quarterly* 15 (2): 150–163.

Rogoff, Edward G., and Ramona Heck. 2003. 'The Evolving Family/Entrepreneurship Business Relationship (Special Issue)'. *Journal of Business Venturing* 18 (5): 559–687.

Schuler, Randall S. 1980. 'Definition and Conceptualization of Stress in Organizations'. *Organizational Behavior and Human Performance* 25 (2): 184–215.

Schutjens, Veronique, and Erik Stam. 2003. 'The Evolution and Nature of Young Firm Networks: A Longitudinal Perspective'. *Small Business Economics* 21 (2): 115–134.

Settersten, Richard A. 2003. 'Age Structuring and the Rhythm of the Life Course'. In *Handbook of the Life Course*, edited by Jeylan T. Mortimer and Michael J. Shanahan, 81–98. New York: Springer.

Stam, Wouter. 2010. 'Industry Event Participation and Network Brokerage among Entrepreneurial Ventures'. *Journal of Management Studies* 47 (4): 625–653.

Taylor, Steven J., and Robert Bogdan. 1998. *Introduction to Qualitative Research Methods: A Guidebook and Resource*, 3rd edn. New York: John Wiley & Sons.

Tubre, T. C., and J. M. Collins. 2000. 'Jackson and Schuler (1985) Revisited: A Meta-Analysis of the Relationships Between Role Ambiguity, Role Conflict, and Job Performance'. *Journal of Management* 26 (1): 155–169.

Uhlaner, Lorraine M., Franz W. Kellermanns, Kimberly A. Eddleston, and Frank Hoy. 2012. 'Erratum to: The Entrepreneuring Family: A New Paradigm for Family Business Research'. *Small Business Economics* 38 (1): 13.

Usita, Paula M., Scott S. Hall, and Jonathan C. Davis. 2004. 'Role Ambiguity in Family Caregiving'. *Journal of Applied Gerontology* 23 (1): 20–39.

Van der Doef, Margot, and Stan Maes. 1999. 'The Job Demand-Control (-Support) Model and Psychological Well-Being: A Review of 20 Years of Empirical Research'. *Work and Stress: An International Journal of Work, Health and Organisations* 13 (2): 87–114.

Van Leeuwen, L. T. 1976. 'Het Gezin Als Sociologisch Studie-Object: Een Historisch Overzicht van de Ontwikkeling van Een Sub-Discipline, Speciaal Met Het Oog Op de Situatie in Nederland'. Wageningen:[sn].

Voydanoff, Patricia. 2004. 'The Effects of Work Demands and Resources on Work-to-Family Conflict and Facilitation'. *Journal of Marriage and Family* 66 (2): 398–412.

Werbel, James D., and Sharon M. Danes. 2010. 'Work Family Conflict in New Business Commitment to the New Business Venture'. *Journal of Small Business Management* 48 (3): 421–440.

Willekens, Frans J. 1999. 'The Life Course: Models and Analysis'. In *Population Issues*, edited by Leo J.G. van Wissen and Pearl A. Dykstra, 23–51. Dordrecht, Netherlands: Springer.

Yogev, Sara, and Jeanne Brett. 1985. 'Patterns of Work and Family Involvement among Single- and Dual-Earner Couples'. *Journal of Applied Psychology* 70 (4): 754–768.

12 Habitual entrepreneurship and the socioemotional wealth of dynastic family enterprise

A synthesis of arguments and directions for future research

Robert V.D.G. Randolph, James Vardaman, and Hanqinq "Chevy" Fang

Introduction

Habitual entrepreneurship – the practice of establishing and simultaneously governing multiple new ventures – is a unique phenomenon that has the potential to significantly develop our fundamental understanding of entrepreneurship (MacMillan, 1986; Wright, Westhead, & Sohl, 1998). Extant research has found that habitual entrepreneurs differ from novice entrepreneurs in terms of motivation and growth intentions, which in turn influence the organizing mode of their founded firms and their subsequent entrepreneurial strategies (Westhead & Wright, 1998; Wiklund & Shepherd, 2008). While commonly studied at the individual level, habitual entrepreneurship can also emerge in collective contexts, such as within corporations or non-commercial social groupings such as families (Rosa, 1998). In this regard, business families can promote the entrepreneurial activities of family members by providing human, knowledge, or financial capital (Birley & Westhead, 1993; Sieger, Zellweger, Nason, & Clinton, 2011). Nevertheless, while scholars largely acknowledge the presence of business families in cases of habitual entrepreneurship (Plate, Schiede, & Schlippe, 2010), their impact on the entrepreneurial process of family members is widely unknown.

The study of the influence of family characteristics on entrepreneurial and organizational behavior has significantly developed over the last decade (De Massis, Sharma, Chua, & Chrisman, 2012; Gedajlovic, Carney, Chrisman, & Kellermanns, 2012). The salience of socioemotional wealth (SEW) – the multidimensional affective endowment of family owners that motivates their pursuit of non-economic goals (Berrone, Cruz, & Gomez-Mejia, 2012) – in particular serves as an idiosyncratic characteristic of family firms that fundamentally differentiates them from non-family firms, and provides a mechanism to distinguish family firms with differing levels of family-centered goals and motivations (Gómez-Mejía, Haynes, Núñez-Nickel, Jacobson, & Moyano-Fuentes, 2007). Broadly, the importance of SEW in family firms drives them toward an increased consideration of the preservation of family ideals, even when doing so may weaken the firm's financial performance or competitiveness (Berrone et al., 2012; Chrisman, Chua, Pearson, & Barnett, 2012). The rapid expanse of research regarding the organizational implications of this desire to preserve a family's SEW has allowed scholars to better understand family firms, and particularly the multigenerational motivations characteristic of family business.

A dominant characteristic of family firms, owed to their goals of preserving SEW, is the desire to maintain family control of the firm through multiple generations. Over time these transgenerational desires may lead to multiple family members owning and operating shared or disparate operations integrated into an overarching familial schema known as a family dynasty (Chua, Chrisman, & Sharma, 1999; Jaffe & Lane, 2004). The process and goals of venture creation in family dynasties is distinct from those in traditional habitual entrepreneurship as such ventures primarily serve as a mechanism to create or preserve the collective SEW of the family, not merely the individual goals of its founders or as profit-seeking opportunities (Casillas, Moreno, & Barbero, 2011; Sieger et al., 2011). These characteristics suggest a variety of implications regarding the mechanisms through which SEW influences the process of habitual family entrepreneurs, yet remains widely unstudied in family business research.

We explore the above arguments as the general thesis of this chapter. In so doing, we synthesize complementary arguments from habitual entrepreneurship, dynastic family business, and the SEW literature to study the entrepreneurial process of habitual family entrepreneurs. The following research questions guide this exploration.

Research Question 1: How does being associated with a dynastic family influence and/or motivate family entrepreneurs in such a way that differentiates them from firms founded by entrepreneurs not affiliated with a dynastic family?

Research Question 2: How does the association with a dynastic business family impact the entrepreneurial process of habitual family entrepreneurs, specifically with regard to opportunity recognition and exploitation?

Utilizing these questions as the framework of this chapter, we contribute to the current understanding of habitual Family Entrepreneurship by detailing how SEW goals in dynastic families potentially catalyze habitual Family Entrepreneurship. We posit that SEW influences fundamentally alter the process of Family Entrepreneurship – specifically entrepreneurial opportunity recognition and exploitation – distinguishing such ventures from those that have been traditionally explored in the study of habitual entrepreneurship. As a result, we introduce the perspective of SEW into the domain of habitual entrepreneurship, which may guide future research in this area.

Socioemotional wealth in dynastic business families

Over time as business families grow they often dynastically expand and diversify their business portfolios in such a way that results in multiple firms being owned by various members of a centralized family (Jaffe & Lane, 2004). We suggest a key motive to this phenomenon is the family members' shared desire to create or preserve the family's SEW (Gómez-Mejía et al., 2007). SEW is a multi-dimensional construct that captures the affective endowment of members of the owning family, including family control and influence, shared identification among family members within the firm, social ties with stakeholders, emotional attachments of family members to the firm, and family bonds renewed through dynastic succession (FIBER; Berrone et al., 2012). The notion of SEW is extremely relevant to the study of family dynasties, given the family's intention to maintain control over their firms, to strengthen familial ties among clustered firms, and to succeed ownership of family firms into later generations (Jaffe & Lane, 2004; Kellermanns, Eddleston, Barnett, & Pearson, 2008; Lambrecht, 2005).

Studies have suggested that owners of family firms tend to place higher priority on preserving SEW than on maximizing economic performance due to the fact that the former is directly related to family intimacy, status, reputation, and ability to provide resources to family members (Gómez-Mejía et al., 2007). The family business literature suggests a desire to preserve SEW can lead to strategic decisions inconsistent with economic rationale such as a tendency to avoid R&D investment (Block, 2012; Chrisman & Patel, 2012), international diversification (Gómez-Mejía, Makri, & Kintana, 2010), and unstandardized human resource practices (Schulze, Lubatkin, Dino, & Buchholtz, 2001). Overall, SEW has become a widely recognized paradigm in family business research that speaks to the fundamental factors that define family firms and differentiate them from non-family firms (Berrone et al., 2012).

Despite its relevance, the application of the SEW perspective in Family Entrepreneurship is limited. Extant literature primarily highlights that idiosyncrasies of family entrepreneurs, such as their entrepreneurial orientations (Nordqvist & Melin, 2010), access to resource endowments provided by families (Sieger et al., 2011), or the dynamics of entrepreneurial teams made up of family members (Schjoedt, Monsen, Pearson, Barnett, & Chrisman, 2013). While insightful, these findings are reported from the perspective of individually founded ventures and thus tend to overlook the role of their SEW, which is tied to their family. This is not an issue when studying novice entrepreneurs whose ventures are a commercial mechanism for pursuing the singular goals of its founder. However, SEW's influence in the process of habitual Family Entrepreneurship is much more complex and requires analysis beyond the singular study of individual family entrepreneurs or the firms they found. We posit that this atomistic focus on singular outcomes erroneously leads to assumptions that habitual entrepreneurship is equally driven by economic goals in both family and non-family settings. As a result of this restricted focus there is a concomitant lack of research exploring the SEW of entrepreneurs belonging to dynastic business families. To fill this gap, we present an outline of study that suggests that SEW preservation significantly impacts the motivations, cognitions, and capabilities of habitual family entrepreneurs.

Habitual entrepreneurship in dynastic families

The proposition driving our arguments thus far is that membership in a dynastic family could materially alter the process of Family Entrepreneurship. Extant research suggests family firms are driven by a desire to preserve SEW not merely the desire to maximize profit (e.g., Gómez-Mejía, Cruz, Berrone, & De Castro, 2011; Gómez-Mejía et al., 2007). As a result, the motivations and outcomes of habitual entrepreneurship might differ significantly among family and non-family firms. We expand the use of SEW to explore its role in differentiating habitual entrepreneurship in family and non-family settings. We posit this exploration as vital to the continued study of habitual Family Entrepreneurship because the interweaving of family and business values may impact the opportunity recognition and exploitation of family entrepreneurs.

The broader literature on habitual entrepreneurship highlights the importance of opportunity recognition and the pursuit of those opportunities as a key to new venture creation (Bhave, 1994). Research suggests habitual entrepreneurs engage in new venture creation when they recognize profitable opportunities (Venkataraman, 1997). Where family entrepreneurs differ in this regard is that the values and interests of the family play a role in their evaluation and plan on pursuing entrepreneurial opportunities. Family businesses are infused with values and interests that are unique to organizations formed by individuals with family ties (Chrisman, Chua, & Sharma, 2005; Corbetta & Salvato, 2004), and these values drive the SEW considerations for such firms (Schulze et al., 2001). As such, the values of the dynastic family may influence entrepreneurial activities by creating a standard of behavior and decision-making infused with family values. While entrepreneurially minded individuals might pursue a new venture upon recognizing a profitable opportunity, those belonging to business families might be more likely to have additional screening criteria based upon the inherently greater emphasis of SEW in family firms (Chrisman et al., 2005).

The goals of family firms are considerably expanded beyond simple profit-seeking and efficiency (Habbershon, Williams, & MacMillan, 2003), and the manifestation of SEW may be more salient in the pursuit of opportunities by family entrepreneurs. When incumbent business families explore entrepreneurial opportunities, a cognitive process of screening is triggered. For non-family entrepreneurs, the screening criteria is predominantly the profit potential of the new venture (Rosa, 1998; Shane, 2003). However, because of the high degree of salience that SEW has in business families, if the opportunity does not align with the SEW of the family, the opportunity will not be pursued even if it is potentially profitable. For example, if a business family derives SEW by being socially responsible and environmentally conscious in its local community, a profitable but environmentally suspect opportunity would be viewed as undesirable and thus would likely be passed by (Berrone, Cruz, Gomez-Mejia, & Larraza-Kintana, 2010; Zellweger, Nason, Nordqvist, & Brush, 2013). While non-family habitual entrepreneurs might seize such an opportunity to create a portfolio of profitable businesses, family entrepreneurs would perceive it as ineligible, opting instead only to engage in entrepreneurial activities when they are aligned with the SEW of their family.

Business families may differ in other aspects of habitual entrepreneurship as well. Due to the desire to preserve SEW, business families have goals beyond financial performance, such as maintaining family control or insuring leadership succession by a family member (Chua et al., 1999). Business families sometimes seek to create new ventures in order to provide an avenue for younger family members to lead an organization (Au, Chiang, Birch, & Ding, 2013; Gomez-Mejia et al., 2011). For instance, a father who owns a successful auto body company might start a new venture in an associated field, such as auto engine repair, for his son or daughter to manage despite that venture having only moderate profit potential. What is unique to business families is that the recognition of the opportunity has less to do with its potential for profit than its potential to reinforce and preserve the SEW of the family dynasty. While non-family habitual entrepreneurs would not be pressured to pursue such an opportunity, dynastic business families are more likely to do so if it creates or preserves SEW.

Our above arguments are logical extensions of the SEW perspective to the study of habitual entrepreneurship. The broad implication of which is that the wholly financially driven arguments of habitual entrepreneurship research may not be adequate for study of Family Entrepreneurship. However, we extend these arguments to suggest that SEW of family entrepreneurs not only alter their entrepreneurial goals, but may also fundamentally alter the very process through which they recognize, value, and pursue entrepreneurial opportunities. In essence, to wholly explore the implications of SEW in habitual Family Entrepreneurship we must study their influence on the process of Family Entrepreneurship. While we maintain a SEW perspective, we follow the works of Alvarez and Busenitz (2001) and utilize elements of the resource-based view (RBV) to suggest that the familial association of habitual family entrepreneurs fundamentally alter the methods through which they conduct business.

Opportunity recognition

In entrepreneurship research, opportunity recognition is a fundamental precursor to new venture creation. Entrepreneurs perceive the alignment of the creation of a new venture with the achievement of their goals, and the opportunity's potential for profitability and success (Shane & Venkataraman, 2000). Opportunity recognition is necessary for the founding of a new venture and is equally present in both novice and habitual entrepreneurship (Ucbasaran, Westhead, Wright, & Binks, 2003). While the RBV broadly suggests that the consequences of entrepreneurial activities are aligned with entrepreneur's individual capabilities, the initial awareness and the evaluation of an opportunity are dominantly diffused through their professional and social network associations (Singh, 2000). This suggests an entrepreneur's recognition of an opportunity is a function of both objective requirements and subjective expectations regarding the detail of the opportunity itself. This has a variety of implications for the arguments of this chapter, with the most pressing being that the recognition and valuation of opportunities by habitual family entrepreneurs will be diffused through their family network and thus their feasibility recognized as a function of their distinct familial resources.

Family business research has long recognized the implications of the convergence of family and business networks (Habbershon et al., 2003). So much so that recent family business research posits that viewing the family network as external to the firm may be erroneous, suggesting instead a set of binding social ties and integration of the two networks (Cruz, Justo, & De Castro, 2012). Hitherto, family business research regarding the implications of this integration primarily has focused on the role of non-economic family goals on the behaviors and performance of family firms. We extend this perspective to suggest additional implications for the opportunity recognition of family entrepreneurs. Specifically, we suggest that the opportunity recognition of family entrepreneurs, particularly habitual entrepreneurs affiliated with a dynastic business family, will be molded in such a way that emphasizes opportunities that both preserve and reinforce the SEW of their family. We develop our arguments toward this end to suggest that the opportunity recognition of family entrepreneurs is unique in that it conforms to the multiple dimensions of SEW in family firms; family control, identity, binding social ties, emotional attachment, and renewal of family bonds (Berrone et al., 2012).

The expansion and preservation of a family dynasty requires at least some form of continued entrepreneurship. However, as opposed to traditional conceptualization of opportunity recognition which emphasizes the conformity toward the entrepreneur's skillset as well as mobility of resources from previously founded firms (Ucbasaran et al., 2003), we suggest that habitual Family Entrepreneurship is further constrained by the SEW of the family. Particularly, we suggest that through adherence to the FIBER dimensions of SEW, the opportunity recognition of habitual family entrepreneurs will be constrained toward those that may be feasibly incorporated into the long-term strategy of the family dynasty (Jaffe & Lane, 2004). While we argue that the overarching SEW goals of the family dynasty impact the opportunity recognition, it should be noted that the individual dimensions themselves may have distinct implications.

The importance of sustained *family control* suggests that, while habitual entrepreneurs commonly pursue opportunities with high growth potential and short-term gains (Rosa, 1998; Shane, 2003), family entrepreneurs would be constrained to opportunities with long-term applicability that can be used to ensure maintained and complete family control. The family entrepreneur's *identification* with the family dynasty may place priority on opportunities that reinforce the traditions of the owning family. Hence, unlike in traditional conceptualizations of habitual entrepreneurship, opportunities that are consistent with the core focus of the business family may be pursued even when they might not be considered feasible in other contexts. Similarly the *bonding social ties* that may be forged through the founding of a new venture that reinforce or forge ties with important community or societal stakeholders even with reduced, or non-existent, economic profitability. The *emotional attachment* of family members may have a variety of influences on the opportunity recognition of family entrepreneurs. Primarily, the founding of a new venture may be a strategic tactic of entrepreneurs to pursue family, and not necessarily commercial goals, such as expanding the family dynasty to create governance roles for multiple successors to mitigate relational conflict. Finally, *renewal through succession* is a paramount aspect of the entire argument of this chapter. The concept of a family dynasty requires that family firms not only continue to exist, but expand. With this in mind, family entrepreneurs are constrained to only those opportunities that they believe will be incorporated into the long-term multi-generational strategy of the family dynasty, thus restricting opportunities from the high-risk, short-term, high-reward opportunities commonly pursued by habitual entrepreneurs.

Together these arguments suggest that membership in a dynastic family will influence the opportunity recognition of habitual entrepreneurs in such a way that fundamentally differentiates them from traditional conceptualizations of habitual entrepreneurship due to the desire to create or preserve the SEW of the family and expand their family dynasty. We expect this to result in an alignment between habitual family entrepreneurs and opportunities that reinforce and preserve family control, family identity, binding social ties, family members' emotional attachment, and the renewal of family bonds within the overarching family dynasty. While together these arguments suggest that a family's SEW alters the opportunity recognition of habitual family entrepreneurs, we extend these arguments to suggest that these elements will also have a residual impact on the tactics through which entrepreneurs pursue and exploit those opportunities.

Opportunity exploitation

Opportunity exploitation refers to the venture creation stage of entrepreneurship wherein entrepreneurs act upon previously identified opportunities (Shane & Venkataraman, 2000). Although considerable scholarly attention has been given to the entrepreneurial process, the majority of this research is focused on the recognition of opportunities with opportunity exploitation being a logical outcome of recognizing said opportunity, thus having somewhat of a "black box" quality (Busenitz & Barney, 1997). Alvarez and Busenitz (2001) propose that the RBV offers considerable potential to assist scholars in addressing opportunity exploitation, as entrepreneurial resources define the boundary conditions of exploitative strategies and new venture performance (Chrisman, Bauerschmidt, & Hofer, 1998; Eckhardt & Shane, 2003).

While SEW is predominantly discussed as a constraint for family entrepreneurs, it also suggests a unique bundle of resources available to the family entrepreneur as a result of their familial associations (Chrisman, Steier, & Chua, 2008; Abdellatif, Amann, & Jaussaud, 2010). Family entrepreneurs, particularly members of dynastic business families, may utilize these potentially significant resources when pursuing entrepreneurial opportunities. This may impact the new venture's strategic resources, such as startup or knowledge capital, as well as social resources, such as by providing a salient organizational identity which is commonly under-developed and malleable in new ventures (Sirmon & Hitt, 2003; Sundaramurthy & Kreiner, 2008). We argue that these resources not only facilitate the exploitation of opportunities by habitual family entrepreneurs but that they do so in a way that is aligned with the SEW of their family. In this regard, the resources of habitual family entrepreneurs are conceptualized as being dynamically managed by family entrepreneurs but potentially coordinated through their dynastic family and its members. Hence, the practice of habitual Family Entrepreneurship is wholly tied with the development and preservation of SEW with the attempts of structuring, bundling, and leveraging resources across multiple businesses. Maintaining a SEW perspective, we believe that opportunity exploitation of habitual family entrepreneurs differs from both novice Family Entrepreneurship and non-family habitual entrepreneurship in four primary aspects of opportunity exploitation: *resource creation, resource accumulation, resource leveraging,* and *resource retention.*

At its most basic level, opportunity exploitation largely depends on the ability of entrepreneurs to *create the critical resources* necessary for success, such as human, knowledge, and social capital, which are necessary to effectively exploit an opportunity in an innovative way that results in the creation of a competitive firm (Shane, 2003; Sieger et al., 2011). We expect SEW concerns of dynastic families will assist habitual family entrepreneurs in the creation of human and social capital in three distinct ways. First, an entrepreneur's identification with the dynastic family and experience in long-term collaborations create genetic human capital (Gedajlovic & Carney, 2010). This genetic human capital is directly tied to the familial association of the entrepreneur and can be applied in variant industrial and business settings, across multiple businesses in the family dynasty. Examples of genetic human capital are skills in interfacing with customers, facilitating collaboration and agreement in groups, as well as transmitting tacit information without formal explanation and written codification. Second, family bonding ties with external stakeholders may provide habitual family entrepreneurs access to unique resources and capital, thus aligning their resource creation toward those that exploit previously established social ties. Finally, the two resources mentioned above are not contingent upon industrial or temporal relevance. Meaning that the human and social capital provided to family entrepreneurs can be broadly applied across industrial settings, which can facilitate the ambidextrous utilization of the resources they create and thus may in turn further promote and reinforce the inherently habitual nature of entrepreneurship in dynastic business families.

Resources are not all naturally endowed and entrepreneurs are required to engage in *resource accumulation* in order to successfully exploit opportunities (Sirmon & Hitt, 2003). We expect resource accumulation in habitual Family Entrepreneurship to significantly differ from non-family and novice entrepreneurship. For instance, it has been argued that resource accumulation tactics of entrepreneurs are wholly driven by economic concerns, with perceptions of value or strengthened market position motivating the accumulation of particular resources (Schmidt & Keil, 2013). This may not be true for habitual family entrepreneurs. In their case, resources accumulation may primarily be driven by the noneconomic concerns of family owners and particularly the SEW of dynastic families.

In order to maintain family members' emotional attachment and their identification with the family, dynastic families may intentionally acquire resources that satisfy the entrepreneurial goals of specific family members or work to develop their managerial skill, even when the opportunity pursued is not perceived as economically promising (Schulze et al., 2001; Au et al., 2013). Pressures from the dynastic family may fundamentally alter the methods of exploitation, and as a result the opportunity's profitability toward those that reinforce the bonding social ties between stakeholder and family reputation, such as when a dynastic family chooses to exploit opportunities in socially conscious but profit restrictive ways (Berrone et al., 2010). Additionally, due to the long-term orientation and SEW motivations of dynastic families, the resource accumulation tactics of habitual family entrepreneurs are not under immediate or urgent economic pressure. This means that dynastic families can intentionally accumulate resources that are supportive of multiple and possibly future businesses instead of individual and immediate opportunities that would not be expected to be salient in non-family settings.

Under the context of opportunity exploitation in habitual entrepreneurship, *resource leveraging* refers to resources that can be mobilized and/or integrated for the purpose of venture creation (Brush, Greene, & Hart, 2001). Nevertheless, resources are not perfectly mobile, either because managers in multiple businesses are not willing to risk the resources they rely on for sustained performance, or because these resources are not applicable in different contexts. Again, the SEW motivations of dynastic families may impact resource leveraging in the opportunity exploitation of family entrepreneurs. Specifically, we posit that the emotional ties among family members may reduce the reluctance of other family managers in mobilizing and coordinating resources for new venture creation. Even when doing so conflicts with their business strategy, due to the recognized necessity of habitual Family Entrepreneurship in fulfilling the overarching goals of the family dynasty. This dynamic for collaborative resource leveraging among members of a family dynasty may also impact the *resource retention* tactics of habitual family entrepreneurs. Specifically, family entrepreneurs may be motivated to retain entrepreneurial resources after they have outlived their direct utility in order to make them available for future endeavors either by themselves or other family members. This may be due to the long-term orientation of dynastic family business as well as the family dynasties' promotion of habitual entrepreneurship (Miller & Le Breton-Miller, 2005; Nordqvist & Melin, 2010), or because business families are more inclined to keep these resources in the company in order to avoid feelings of nostalgia and incur emotional costs (Sharma and Manikutty, 2005). Hence, the association with a dynastic family may reduce barriers to resource mobility and cost of resource retention thus facilitating the preservation of entrepreneurial resources to be leveraged by members of the dynastic family in pursuit of future opportunities.

Overall, we posit that the SEW of dynastic families fundamentally alters the opportunity exploitation tactics of habitual family entrepreneurs in terms of resource creation, resource accumulation, resource leveraging, and resource retention. Considering the potentially significant role SEW can play in entrepreneurial opportunity recognition, as discussed in the previous section, we suggest that the SEW of a dynastic family serves as a primary differentiating aspect of habitual Family Entrepreneurship. With residual implications in all stages of the entrepreneurial process. In doing so we reinforce our overarching arguments that the underlying goals of Family Entrepreneurship includes the dynastic expansion of the family itself. This suggests that, at least to some degree, Family Entrepreneurship is inherently habitual when the entrepreneur's goals include the creation of a transgenerational family dynasty, which in turn fundamentally alters the methods through which family entrepreneurs exploit opportunities. While we believe that these arguments are justified as an extension of the SEW paradigm of family business research, we believe that these arguments will have a variety of implications for future research in Family Entrepreneurship.

Discussion and directions for future research

The arguments of this chapter defend our general position that the SEW of dynastic families fundamentally alters the process of habitual Family Entrepreneurship. We conceptually develop these arguments by suggesting that many of the traditionally accepted concepts of habitual entrepreneurship, such as the accumulation of resources for future opportunities, short-term strategic orientation, and economic opportunity recognition (Wright, Hmieleski, Siegel, & Ensley, 2007), are neither invariably nor perfectly applicable in the context of habitual Family Entrepreneurship. Instead, we posit that habitual family entrepreneurs not only leverage family resources in their entrepreneurial pursuits but may bilaterally establish and govern firms in such a way that reinforces the socioemotional goals of the overarching family. While the significance of familial associations has been recognized in the study of habitual Family Entrepreneurship (Plate et al., 2010; Sieger et al., 2011), we further develop these notions by implementing an SEW perspective to holistically study the motivational and procedural distinction of family entrepreneurs.

By considering the role of SEW in the process of Family Entrepreneurship we explore the residual impact on the goals and strategies of the firms they establish. In so doing, we contribute to current understandings of habitual Family Entrepreneurship in two primary ways. First, we provide an initial conceptualization of the SEW perspective in the study of habitual Family Entrepreneurship which we posit as an underexplored area of study. Second, while the presence of family dynasties is well-established in seminal conceptualizations of family firms, their role in Family Entrepreneurship has not yet been explored in family business research. Additionally, we present conceptual evidence that traditional non-family conceptualizations of habitual entrepreneurship are inappropriate in the context of family firms. To ameliorate this, we propose the use of the SEW perspective that binds the strategy of habitual family entrepreneurs to the motivations and resources of their overarching family. We suggest this perspective as a counter to the traditional perspective in entrepreneurial research that focuses on the individual motivations of the entrepreneurs themselves.

The arguments of this chapter highlight turbulent topics in the study of habitual Family Entrepreneurship and synthesize its study with that of SEW in dynastic family enterprise. Taken together, the ideas put forth here suggest that the entrepreneurial process of family entrepreneurs is diffused by the motivations of their family, resulting in the establishment of firms with fundamentally altered goals and strategies that are aligned with the overarching family dynasty. Our aim is for this chapter to help guide future research on habitual Family Entrepreneurship in a variety of ways that will continue to develop our understanding of the phenomenon.

Directions for future research

Multi-business family dynasties are common throughout the world and are considered a natural long-term progression when family businesses achieve success and growth (Almeida, Park, Subrahmanyam, & Wolfenzon, 2011; Jaffe & Lane, 2004). However, to date, extant research has primarily been concerned with the development and preservation of SEW within the family dynasty from the perspective of the centralized family or dominant firm. As a result, the inherent entrepreneurial concerns involved in the development of family dynasties have only recently become a topic of interest in Family Entrepreneurship research. To assist in guiding research in this line of inquiry we suggest in this chapter a synthesis of arguments in the study of habitual Family Entrepreneurship.

Our arguments revolve around our position that the SEW of the overarching family fundamentally alters the entrepreneurial process of family entrepreneurs in such a way that aligns their opportunity recognition and exploitation with the SEW of the family dynasty. While these arguments are heavily grounded in extant family business research and are a logical extension of the SEW perspective that drives much of the broader research on family businesses, they have a variety of implications for future research in the area of habitual Family Entrepreneurship. By increasing our understanding of the vital function(s) of habitual entrepreneurship in the creation and preservation of SEW in family dynasties we can better understand the bilateral nature of Family Entrepreneurship. A number of recent studies and case analyses provide an adequate foundation for research in this area. We hope that by incorporating this holistic approach, this chapter may inspire a thematic shift in the study of habitual Family Entrepreneurship. Specifically, we intend to support future research paying a greater consideration for the specific pressures and motivations of the family, as opposed to merely their outcomes on the founded firms, which is in our opinion constrictive to the holistic understanding of the phenomena of interest in Family Entrepreneurship research.

Recent findings support our notion that the function of Family Entrepreneurship differs when entrepreneurs belong to a dynastic family. Specifically, for novice entrepreneurs the decision to found a family vs. non-family firm may have little influence on the actual entrepreneurial process and instead manifest more in the strategy, goals, and long-term orientation of the firm post-founding (Heck, Hoy, Poutziouris, & Steier, 2008). However, this is not the case when family entrepreneurs belong to a dynastic family and as a result the very essence of the entrepreneurial process may be fundamentally altered in various ways. For example, a recent case study by Au and colleagues (2013) found that dynastic families motivated family members to found new ventures, not as part of a broader corporate strategy, but to assist in the grooming process of younger family members prior to them taking executive roles in the central family firm. While arguably circumstantial, this case provides an ideal example of dynastic families motivating family entrepreneurs toward incorporating strategies that differ from the growth and profit oriented strategies commonly associated with habitual entrepreneurs.

Future research can hopefully expand on this trend by discovering and validating explicit characteristics of habitual Family Entrepreneurship. While this chapter presents the case that the SEW of the dynastic family will fundamentally alter the entrepreneurial process of family members, the impact of this alignment on the actionable strategies of entrepreneurs still requires substantial research. Example topics of study are the pursuit of horizontally or vertically integrative strategies of dynastic Family Entrepreneurship. In such cases, we expect the motivations of family members are expectedly less focused on the potential for profit or growth of their new business venture and instead revolve around their venture being integrated into the overarching strategy of a dynastic family. Additionally, we present the salience of SEW as a characteristic of family dynasties and firms when in fact it is a multi-dimensional construct that can emerge with varying degrees of significance (Berrone et al., 2012). Meaning that by implementing the SEW approach into the study of habitual Family Entrepreneurship may not only provide insight into the distinction between family and non-family strategies, but may also provide insight into the heterogeneous strategies among family entrepreneurs based on the significance and salience of their family's SEW. Future research might consider the heterogeneity of business families by emphasizing that they can use each of the SEW dimensions as a reference point in decision-making (Cennamo, Berrone, Cruz, & Gomez-Mejia, 2012), which is likely to alter habitual Family Entrepreneurship behavior.

Finally, the idea of SEW as a reference point brings contingency factors to the fore. Future research might consider conditions that make financial considerations more important for habitual entrepreneurship. Christman and Patel (2012) found that when family firms fall below aspiration level, the reference point for decision-making shifts from SEW to financial concerns. In the context of habitual entrepreneurship, future research should consider the conditions under which financial concerns take precedence in driving this behavior.

More broadly we hope this chapter provides at least a rudimentary foundation for the study of habitual Family Entrepreneurship from the perspective of the family as opposed to the individual entrepreneur. While initially this recommendation may seem contradictory to the general study of entrepreneurship, of which the primary unit of analysis in most cases is either the entrepreneur or newly founded ventures, we submit that the idiosyncratic nature of Family Entrepreneurship must directly account for familial influence in order to distinguish it as a unique field of inquiry. Future research in this area should account for pre-existing family businesses or the presence of a family dynasty in order to truly explore the process, strategy, and motivations of family entrepreneurs. If this is the case, then adjusting the lens of study from a purely entrepreneurial focus to a habitual one may be appropriate for future Family Entrepreneurship research. In other words, the idiosyncratic strategies and goals of family entrepreneurs may seem irrational from a purely entrepreneurial perspective. However, when taking into account the presence of familial motivations to preserve and expand the family dynasty and its SEW, the strategy of family entrepreneurs may be more easily reconciled into traditional entrepreneurship and strategy research. Future research in this area would benefit from developing an explicit understanding of these idiosyncrasies, such as the role of image congruence, network governance, or access to shared resources in multi-business family dynasties.

Conclusions

In this chapter we synthesize research on habitual Family Entrepreneurship and dynastic family enterprise to provide foundational arguments regarding the impact of SEW on the process of habitual family entrepreneurs. The arguments of this chapter provide general insights into the impact that the SEW of family dynasties have on the process of habitual family entrepreneurs. We hope that the arguments of this chapter can be used by future research in these burgeoning areas of inquiry to take greater consideration of these idiosyncratic characteristics in order to more effectively study habitual Family Entrepreneurship, dynastic business families, and indeed Family Entrepreneurship as a whole.

References

Abdellatif, Mahamat, Amann, Bruno, & Jaussaud, Jacques. (2010). Family versus nonfamily business: A comparison of international strategies. *Journal of Family Business Strategy, 1*(2), 108–116.

Almeida, H., Park, S. Y., Subrahmanyam, M. G., & Wolfenzon, D. (2011). The structure and formation of business groups: Evidence from Korean chaebols. *Journal of Financial Economics, 99*(2), 447–475.

Alvarez, S. A., & Busenitz, L. W. (2001). The entrepreneurship of resource-based theory. *Journal of Management, 27*(6), 755–775.

Au, K., Chiang, F. F., Birtch, T. A., & Ding, Z. (2013). Incubating the next generation to venture: The case of a family business in Hong Kong. *Asia Pacific Journal of Management, 30*(3), 749–767.

Berrone, P., Cruz, C., & Gomez-Mejia, L. R. (2012). Socioemotional wealth in family firms theoretical dimensions, assessment approaches, and agenda for future research. *Family Business Review, 25*(3), 258–279.

Berrone, P., Cruz, C., Gomez-Mejia, L. R., & Larraza-Kintana, M. (2010). Socioemotional wealth and corporate responses to institutional pressures: Do family-controlled firms pollute less? *Administrative Science Quarterly, 55*(1), 82–113.

Bhave, M. P. (1994). A process model of entrepreneurial venture creation. *Journal of Business Venturing, 9*(3), 223–242.

Birley, S., & Westhead, P. (1993). A comparison of new businesses established by "novice" and "habitual" founders in Great Britain. *International Small Business Journal, 12*(1), 38–60.

Block, J. H. (2012). R&D investments in family and founder firms: An agency perspective. *Journal of Business Venturing, 27*(2), 248–265.

Brush, C. G., Greene, P. G., & Hart, M. M. (2001). From initial idea to unique advantage: The entrepreneurial challenge of constructing a resource base. *Academy of Management Perspectives, 15*(1), 64–78.

Busenitz, L. W., & Barney, J. B. (1997). Differences between entrepreneurs and managers in large organizations: Biases and heuristics in strategic decision-making. *Journal of Business Venturing, 12*(1), 9–30.

Casillas, J. C., Moreno, A. M., & Barbero, J. L. (2011). Entrepreneurial orientation of family firms: Family and environmental dimensions. *Journal of Family Business Strategy, 2*(2), 90–100.

Cennamo, C., Berrone, P., Cruz, C., & Gomez-Mejia, L. R. (2012). Socioemotional wealth and proactive stakeholder engagement: Why family-controlled firms care more about their stakeholders. *Entrepreneurship: Theory and Practice, 36*(6), 1153–1173.

Chrisman, J. J., & Patel, P. C. (2012). Variations in R&D investments of family and nonfamily firms: Behavioral agency and myopic loss aversion perspectives. *Academy of Management Journal, 55*(4), 976–997.

Chrisman, J. J., Bauerschmidt, A., & Hofer, C. W. (1998). The determinants of new venture performance: An extended model. *Entrepreneurship: Theory and Practice, 23*, 5–30.

Chrisman, J. J., Chua, J. H., Pearson, A. W., & Barnett, T. (2012). Family involvement, family influence, and family-centered non-economic goals in small firms. *Entrepreneurship: Theory and Practice, 36*(2), 267–293.

Chrisman, J. J., Chua, J. H., & Sharma, P. (2005). Trends and directions in the development of a strategic management theory of the family firm. *Entrepreneurship: Theory and Practice, 29*, 555–575.

Chrisman, James J., Steier, Lloyd P., & Chua, Jess H. (2008). Toward a theoretical basis for understanding the dynamics of strategic performance in family firms. *Entrepreneurship: Theory and Practice, 32*(6), 935–947.

Chua, J. H., Chrisman, J. J., & Sharma, P. (1999). Defining the family business by behavior. *Entrepreneurship: Theory and Practice, 23*(4), 19–40.

Corbetta, G., & Salvato, C. (2004). Self-serving or self-actualizing? Models of man and agency costs in different types of family firms: A commentary on "comparing the agency costs of family and non-family firms: Conceptual issues and exploratory evidence." *Entrepreneurship: Theory and Practice, 28*(4), 355–362.

Cruz, C., Justo, R., & De Castro, J. O. (2012). Does family employment enhance MSEs performance? Integrating socioemotional wealth and family embeddedness perspectives. *Journal of Business Venturing, 27*(1), 62–76.

De Massis, A., Sharma, P., Chua, J. H., & Chrisman, J. J. (2012). *Family Business Studies: An Annotated Bibliography*. Cheltenham: Edward Elgar.

Eckhardt, J. T., & Shane, S. A. (2003). Opportunities and entrepreneurship. *Journal of Management, 29*(3), 333–349.

Gedajlovic, E., & Carney, M. (2010). Markets, hierarchies, and families: Toward a transaction cost theory of the family firm. *Entrepreneurship: Theory and Practice, 34*(6), 1145–1172.

Gedajlovic, E., Carney, M., Chrisman, J. J., & Kellermanns, F. W. (2012). The adolescence of family firm research: Taking stock and planning for the future. *Journal of Management, 38*(4), 1010–1037.

Gómez-Mejía, L. R., Cruz, C., Berrone, P., & De Castro, J. (2011). The bind that ties: Socioemotional wealth preservation in family firms. *Academy of Management Annals, 5*(1), 653–707.

Gómez-Mejía, L. R., Haynes, K. T., Núñez-Nickel, M., Jacobson, K. J., & Moyano-Fuentes, J. (2007). Socioemotional wealth and business risks in family-controlled firms: Evidence from Spanish olive oil mills. *Administrative Science Quarterly, 52*(1), 106–137.

Gómez-Mejía, L. R., Makri, M., & Kintana, M. L. (2010). Diversification decisions in family-controlled firms. *Journal of Management Studies, 47*(2), 223–252.

Habbershon, T. G., Williams, M., & MacMillan, I. C. (2003). A unified systems perspective of family firm performance. *Journal of Business Venturing, 18*, 451–465.

Heck, R. K., Hoy, F., Poutziouris, P. Z., & Steier, L. P. (2008). Emerging paths of family entrepreneurship research. *Journal of Small Business Management, 46*(3), 317–330.

Jaffe, D. T., & Lane, S. H. (2004). Sustaining a family dynasty: Key issues facing complex multigenerational business and investment owning families. *Family Business Review, 17*(1), 81–98.

Kellermanns, F. W., Eddleston, K. A., Barnett, T., & Pearson, A. (2008). An exploratory study of family member characteristics and involvement: Effects on entrepreneurial behavior in the family firm. *Family Business Review, 21*(1), 1–14.

Lambrecht, J. (2005). Multigenerational transition in family businesses: A new explanatory model. *Family Business Review, 18*(4), 267–282.

MacMillan, I. (1986). To really learn about entrepreneurship, let's study habitual entrepreneurs. *Journal of Business Venturing, 1*(3), 241–243.

Miller, D., & Le Breton-Miller, I. (2005). Management insights from great and struggling family businesses. *Long Range Planning, 38*(6), 517–530.

Nordqvist, M., & Melin, L. (2010). Entrepreneurial families and family firms. *Entrepreneurship and Regional Development, 22*(3–4), 211–239.

Plate, M., Schiede, C., & Schlippe, A. V. (2010). Portfolio entrepreneurship in the context of family owned businesses. In M. Nordqvist & T. M. Zellweger (Eds.), *Transgenerational Entrepreneurship: Exploring Growth and Performance in Family Firms Across Generations.* Northampton, MA: Edward Elgar Publishing.

Rosa, P. (1998). Entrepreneurial processes of business cluster formation and growth by "habitual" entrepreneurs. *Entrepreneurship: Theory and Practice, 22*(4), 43–61.

Schjoedt, L., Monsen, E., Pearson, A., Barnett, T., & Chrisman, J. J. (2013). New venture and family business teams: understanding team formation, composition, behaviors, and performance. *Entrepreneurship: Theory and Practice, 37*(1), 1–15.

Schmidt, J., & Keil, T. (2013). What makes a resource valuable? Identifying the drivers of firm-idiosyncratic resource value. *Academy of Management Review, 38*(2), 206–228.

Schulze, W. S., Lubatkin, M. H., Dino, R. N., & Buchholtz, A. K. (2001). Agency relationships in family firms: Theory and evidence. *Organization Science, 12*(2), 99–116.

Shane, S., & Venkataraman, S. (2000). The promise of entrepreneurship as a field of research. *Academy of Management Review, 25*(1), 217–226.

Shane, S. A. (2003). *A General Theory of Entrepreneurship: The Individual–Opportunity Nexus.* Cheltenham, UK: Edward Elgar Publishing.

Sharma, P. and Manikutty, S. (2005), Strategic divestments in family firms: Role of family structure and community culture. *Entrepreneurship: Theory and Practice, 29*, 293–311.

Sieger, P., Zellweger, T., Nason, R. S., & Clinton, E. (2011). Portfolio entrepreneurship in family firms: A resource-based perspective. *Strategic Entrepreneurship Journal, 5*(4), 327–351.

Singh, R. P. (2000). *Entrepreneurial Opportunity Recognition through Social Networks.* New York: Garland.

Sirmon, D. G., & Hitt, M. A. (2003). Managing resources: Linking unique resources, management, and wealth creation in family firms. *Entrepreneurship: Theory and Practice, 27*(4), 339–358.

Sundaramurthy, C., & Kreiner, G. E. (2008). Governing by managing identity boundaries: The case of family businesses. *Entrepreneurship: Theory and Practice, 32*(3), 415–436.

Ucbasaran, D., Westhead, P., Wright, M., & Binks, M. (2003). Does entrepreneurial experience influence opportunity identification? *Journal of Private Equity, 7*(1), 7–14.

Venkataraman, S. (1997). The distinctive domain of entrepreneurship research: An editor's perspective. In J. A. Katz & R. H. Brockhaus (Eds.), *Advances in Entrepreneurship, Firm Emergence and Growth* (Vol. 3). Greenwich, CT: Jai Press.

Westhead, P., & Wright, M. (1998). Novice, portfolio, and serial founders: Are they different? *Journal of Business Venturing, 13*(3), 173–204.

Wiklund, J., & Shepherd, D. A. (2008). Portfolio entrepreneurship: Habitual and novice founders, new entry, and mode of organizing. *Entrepreneurship: Theory and Practice, 32*(4), 701–725.

Wright, M., Hmieleski, K. M., Siegel, D. S., & Ensley, M. D. (2007). The role of human capital in technological entrepreneurship. *Entrepreneurship: Theory and Practice, 31*(6), 791–806.

Wright, M., Westhead, P., & Sohl, J. (1998). Habitual entrepreneurs and angel investors. *Entrepreneurship: Theory and Practice, 22*(4), 5–22.

Zellweger, T. M., Nason, R., Nordqvist, M., & Brush, C. (2013). Why do family firms strive for nonfinancial performance? *Entrepreneurship: Theory and Practice, 37*(2), 229–248.

13 Typology of interactions and data content in qualitative family case study research

Céline Barrédy

Family business research has grown a lot over the last decade but is still an emerging field (Chrisman et al., 2008). Since the seminal papers of Handler (1989) and Daily and Dollinger (1993), few studies, except recently (De Massis & Kotlar, 2014; Melin et al., 2013; De Massis et al., 2012, Dawson & Hjorth, 2012, Litz et al., 2012), have focused on issues related to research methods that may provide greater understanding of the family business field. Even if they don't represent the majority of the research process in the field of family business, qualitative methods could be the best approach to analyze many issues in family business (Reay & Zhang, 2014). Using our experience on qualitative case study research in family business,[1] this chapter makes a step forward by the objective of identifying the type of interactions entering in family business research and their influence on the data collected in qualitative case study research approach.

The development of the field of family business and Family Entrepreneurship is based on the assertion that "family businesses are different from non-family business in some important ways" (Chrisman et al., 2005). Family entrepreneurship is quite new and defines the role of families in entrepreneurial activities (Heck et al., 2008). As explained by Zachary et al. (2013), the family is very important because it is from the family context that entrepreneurial behavior is created. Family entrepreneurship relies on a family business following an entrepreneurial dynamic. However, there is still no consensus on the exact definition of family business although there is great effort to find an acceptable definition (Miller & Le-Breton-Miller, 2007). Even today the question "What is family business?" asked by Lansberg et al. (1988) in the first paper of *Family Business Review*, remains valid and proves the high complexity of family business (Peredo, 2003). The reason why the field has grown a lot lies in the fact that *researchers believe that the family components shape the business in a way that the family members of the executive in non-family firms do not and cannot* (Chua et al., 1999; Lansberg 1983). The systemic approach defines the family business as composed of subsystems driven by different rationalities (Donnelley, 1964; Whiteside & Brown, 1991; Beckhard & Dyer, 1983; Davis, 1983). Considering Family Entrepreneurship, the subsystems identified are individual, entrepreneurs, the family, and the business. All these systems interfere together and enter into interactions to create the whole organization. Because of the place of family, informal relations inside the business, relationship, attitudes, behaviors, values, both individual and familial, play an essential role. Interactions inside the business led by a family appear to be very specific and an interesting way to explore the uniqueness of family firms.

The question of methodology has a high relevance for research into family business and Family Entrepreneurship. Between 1961 and 2008, 22 percent of the articles on family business examine small samples. Concerning empirical studies, 10.1 percent are based on the case study method (Benavides-Velasco et al., 2013). Qualitative research methods, which include descriptive articles (Handler, 1989) dominated the early work in the field (Sharma et al., 2012). But they were very descriptive and the field needed a more rigorous approach. Nowadays, most of the research in family business follows quantitative methods (Sharma et al., 2012; Dyer & Sanchez, 1998; Sharma, 2004). Vought et al. (2008) show many differences between practical and theoretical aspects of family business research. Many authors criticize the lack of primary data (Ibrahim et al., 2008) and highlight the interest that could represent qualitative methods coming from the field (Glaser & Strauss, 1967; Strauss & Corbin, 1990) to evaluate specific aspects of family business, like values (Klein et al., 2005). Quantitative methods show limits "to understand the forces that drive the empirical observations" (Zahra & Sharma, 2004). "There is a need for qualitative and interpretive research in the field of family business" (Nordqvist et al., 2009). Nowadays, the field is enriching of different kinds of qualitative approaches (Sharma et al., 2012). Qualitative methods are "an umbrella term covering a range of interpretive techniques which seek to describe, decode, translate and otherwise come to terms with the meaning, not frequency, of certain more or less naturally occurring phenomena in the social world" (Van Maanen 1979). They cover a plurality settled by three major methodological milestones (Easterby-Smith et al., 2008): Glaser and Strauss (1967) *Discovery of Grounded Theory*, Van Maanen (1979) "reclaiming qualitative methods for organizational research," and Denzin and Lincoln (1994) *Handbook of Qualitative Research*. "Qualitative methods are especially well suited because they allow to understand the most complex elements (relationship, power, intangible knowledge transfer)" (De Massis et al., 2012). Among the large number of qualitative methods, the case study method caught our attention because it fits well with the particularity and complexity of the family business field including the context (Stake, 1995). Case studies represent one of the most used qualitative methods in organizational studies (Eisenhardt, 1989; De Massis & Kotlar, 2014). As explained by De Massis and Kotlar (2014), case studies are a powerful methodology that can be used in a rigorous, creative, and wide-ranging variety of ways to advance family business research. Moreover, "case studies could be particularly relevant to family business research because family firms exist at the intersection of two systems – the family and the business (Tagiuri & Davis, 1992) – that interact in producing idiosyncratic organisational outcomes" (De Massis & Kotlar, 2014). This method allows the researcher to pay attention to the role played by individuals in the process observed and the interactions between them. Yin (1994) was one of the first to define the case study, stating that it is an empirical study that examines a contemporary phenomenon in its real context when the boundaries with the context are not clearly defined and for which several data sources are used. "In qualitative case study, we seek greater understanding of the case. We want to appreciate the uniqueness and complexity, its embeddedness and interaction with its context" (Stake, 1995). Case studies can be conducted following different orientations (De Massis & Kotlar, 2014) from positivism (Yin, 2009), which is dominant in family business research (De Massis & Kotlar, 2014; Kontinen et al., 2013), to inductive approach (Glaser & Strauss, 1967) based on grounded theory. The qualitative research in family business and Family Entrepreneurship based on interactions focus mainly on interpretivism approach (Stake, 2005; Miles & Huberman, 1994). It is an abductive approach of the research that considers data and existing theory in tandem (Alvesson & Karreman, 2007). According to this approach, the knowledge is created in the mind of the researcher (Stake, 1995, 2005).

> This means that knowledge is constructed rather than revealed, and the researcher works towards reconstructing events and believes that humans are active in the construction of knowledge rather than being passive recipients of knowledge. Thus, knowledge is constructed through the creation of concepts, models, and schemes to make sense of human experience and are continually interpreted and modified by the researcher.
>
> (De Massis & Kotlar, 2014)

The aim of those studies is to "understand the human experience" (Stake, 1995). It is based on interactions between players and between players and researcher, which fits perfectly with the purpose of advancing family business research as explained by Nordqvist et al. (2009) or De Massis and Kotlar (2014). This chapter focuses on the interpetativist approach of qualitative research and case study research. Researchers do not intend any action, or try to influence the actors, but interact with them, themselves also being interacting together. It is one of the most interesting aspects of this method of research. The researcher engages in a process of interactions with players in order to catch interactions as they develop inside the whole system. The knowledge created from those interactions is new, it depends on the nature of those interactions (Kahn, 1989).

There are many references in the literature relating to the access of data (interviews, observation etc.), recommendations on the data collection process, the question of subjectivity, and the risk in interpretation. If qualitative research is rich, it is also very often critiqued for lacking in rigor (Gioia et al., 2013). As explained by De Massis and Kotlar (2014), this lack of understanding as to what makes "quality" research (Easterby-Smith et al., 2008; Gioia et al., 2013; Graebner et al., 2012) is unfortunate because papers that build theory from case studies are frequently considered the "most interesting" (Bartunek et al., 2006; Eisenhardt & Graebner, 2007) and are also among the most impactful papers in the academic community (Eisenhardt, 1989). One of the main points concerns biases in data collection, particularly when data are collected by interviews. Interview is the main method to collect data in case studies (Reay & Zhang, 2014), even if it is not the unique one (De Massis & Kotlar, 2014). In this chapter, we mainly focus our analysis on interviews because they lead to data produced by interactions. Interviews are often presented to have weaknesses and bias. As explained by De Massis and Kotlar (2014), hindsight bias, attributional bias, subconscious attempts to maintain self-esteem, or impression management can then occur (Huber & Power, 1985; Salancik & Meindl, 1984). In the different recommendations about the way data must be collected, very little is said about the role played by interactions in the data content (Eisenhardt & Graebner, 2007) which explains that this chapter contributes significantly to the literature about family business and methodological aspects.

It leads to four main contributions in the field of family business and in the field of qualitative case study research in entrepreneurship. The first contribution is the analysis of what makes qualitative research in organizations where there is a family influence or commitment, totally different. It is not simply applying a research method to a field, it is also taking into account the specificity of the family business. The second contribution is the identification of typologies of interactions coming from inside the company and the family and coming from the entering of the researcher into the business. The third contribution considers the influence made by the different type of interactions on the data collected. It links the player interviewed to the other components of the system he belongs to. Then, the data delivered by the player contains several levels coming from his interactions with other players and the researcher. Those levels must be identified in order to understand properly the different dimension of the player's speech and the place each component of the system has in his representations. The fourth contribution is the attention of the data content on a methodological point of view. The speech of players is produced by the embeddingness of data expressing different levels of interactions coming from subsystems of the whole system.

The chapter is organized as follows. It first explores the place of interactions in family business specificity. Then we show why the qualitative case study method is relevant to capture specific family business interactions. A typology linking interactions, actor's intentions, and data content in family business research can be developed and explained. We finish by propositions of recommendations for qualitative data collection in family business research.

Interactions: the art of family business specificity

Interaction is an interplay expressed by a verbal expression, an attitude, or an action. The concept of interaction comes from psycho-sociology. According to Goffman (1983) interactions arise from social situations when two or more individuals are physically in one another's response presence. It occurs as a response to an impulse and causes another response from the person whom receives it. It creates a dynamic coming from the interplay of a system component. They can be verbal or non-verbal, take the form of gestures and actions. According to Vion (1996), interactions are part of joint conflict or cooperative actions. They are grounded in the *verstehen* approach according to which, human beings are active in the creation and re-creation of their social reality (Berger & Luckmann, 1967). Therefore, human actors interpret the meaning of their own and others' actions (Schwandt, 1994).

The approach by interactions gives an interesting grid to analyze family business. The specificity of research in family business comes from the commitment of the family in the business (Chrisman et al., 2012). Decisions come from people who are, at the same time, member of the business and member of the family. Throughout time, the family goals are intertwined with those of the business (Ward, 1987). The two sub-systems, the company and the family have different values and interact with each other (Whiteside & Brown, 1991). So, the first level of interactions entering in the specificity of family business is between the two subsystems; family and business. According to Durkheim (1888), a company exists because its members share common values and common rules and transmit them. This set of values and norms generates specific habits to the family. To maintain his place in the family, each member must respect the customs and transmit them, it "does not simply represent what is most often, but what must be done. It is a rule that everyone is obliged to obey and which is under the authority of any sanction" (Durkheim, 1888). Failure to comply would be perceived as a treatise by the other family members. This is also why these habits go through generations. This knowledge, communicated to all family members, would represent social values and standards of conduct. Within the company, a behavior consistent with these values and standards is consecutively developing. Implicit rules are created by the family socialization. A collective consciousness is built, regulating individual behavior for the benefit of the family community. So, to move outside the family expectations would be treason. The peculiarities of individual family members can express themselves but they are integrated into the overall regulatory mechanism. The community of interest in the family therefore outweighs the individual interest, including that of the head of the family.

The family looks like a clan and is an effective system of control that works from the strong socialization of its members to eliminate the differences in individual goal (Ouchi, 1979). He speaks of shared social understanding, establishing "good behavior" and strongly urging its members to adopt appropriate behaviors. They are "shared expectations of the group ... that provide a set of principles and procedures judge for good behavior and resolve conflicts." The family can bring up standards of behavior that tell the individual how he should act. The actions of one family member affect and reflect the well-being of others (Becker, 1974, 1993; Kepner, 1983; Bergstrom, 1995).

In a family, the individual level is also very interesting because relations between actors are very different compared to those developed in a non-family business (Harvey & Evans, 1994), they are more complex because of the multiple role of each member in the family business context (Nordqvist et al., 2009). The entrepreneurship dynamic is contextualized by the family but frequently becomes individual. Shane (2003) talks about the nexus of individual and opportunity. The individual level is an important part of the entrepreneurial orientation of the family business. Moreover, a family is made of people with very close relations and are particularly well known to each other (Sjöstrand, 1997).[2] The key difference is made by "blood ties" that create a "glue" and "determines the structure and organizational behavior" of the family business (Hirigoyen, 2002). Each member is very sensitive to his role inside the family and the other family members' opinion about him. This makes a great influence on the nature of interaction individuals have together. Links with family members are primarily emotional (Ben-Porath, 1980). They are also financial (Pollak, 1985) since each family member is associated with the volume and structure of capital owned by others, and informational (Lundberg, 1994) since the family members communicate as parents and as colleagues and this may cause a burden to both emotion and rationality. The information is contained in rituals, history, ceremonies which include values and beliefs. It is not formalized but transmitted between generations and within generations. The desire to enroll in the family group can sometimes be dominant and influence the speech given by actors. All these relations create values, history, tradition, links that create a small world of very specific interactions that are part of the specific constitution of family business. "This shapes the identity of individuals" (Nordqvist et al., 2009). To understand the real influence of the family on the business, it is necessary to capture "family members individuals, relations, emotions, values, power, roles ... needs and motives" (Nordqvist et al. 2009). The social identify theory (Ashforth & Mael, 1989) allows the development of a link between the individual level and the family social group level. Social identification is a perception of oneness with a group of persons. It stems from the categorization of individuals, the distinctiveness and prestige of the group, the salience of outgroups, and the factors that traditionally are associated with group formation. The social identification leads to activities that are congruent with the identity, support for institutions that embody the identity, stereotypical perceptions of self and others, and outcomes that traditionally are associated with group formation, and it reinforces the antecedents of identification. Therefore, it is not only the individual level that is interesting when interviewing a player but it is also taking into account what part of the speech concerns the individual preference and what part concerns the influence of the social group on the individual speech. It means understanding the tacit, the less unconscious aspects that do not appear and are not traceable but underlying, give sense to interactions between family members and between them and all other members of the organization (Nordqvist et al., 2009). Then, one challenge coming from the family business research is to understand and to analyze those interactions (Habbershon et al., 2003).

Therefore, a set of interactions can be highlighted coming from the family relationships and involvement in the firm. An actor can give a story consistent with his own representations. In that case, he will express his proper stake. There is an interaction between each actor in the global system of family business on an individual level. His representations are different from other actors' ones. The specificity of family business is the underlying family links that appears between family members' individual interactions. At the same time, the actor is part of his family taken globally. So there is an interaction between him and the family he belongs to. It is the family institutional level. The actor is also part of the business, so he can express data referring to his interactions with the business: the professional level interactions. Then, he can include interactions between him and the family business global system.

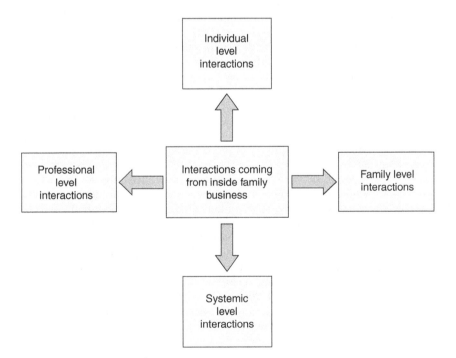

Figure 13.1 Set of interactions inside a family business.

The professional level takes into account all the interactions linked with running the business in a rational way. This level concerns the organizational structure and all the professional relationships inside the firm. They are influenced by the individual level, particularly the entrepreneurial orientation and, at the same time, they are influenced by the family social identity which creates routines, know-how, specific skills inside the family business. This has a consequence on the specific advantage of the firm and the governance of the firm, through the *familiness* (Habbershon et al., 1999), for example. This level includes relations with players who don't belong to the family. They could be external practitioners like outside directors, consultants, experts etc. They bring a different view of the business and they are considered as professional. Then the systemic level concerns the functioning of the whole, which includes the image and the reputation of the whole family business. The relationship with the researcher for example enters this level.

Qualitative case study: a relevant method to capture specific family business interactions

"Currently, family business research is dominated by traditional research methods" (Nordqvist et al., 2009) and "determining 'how' and 'why' family firms differ from nonfamily firms has been problematic for researchers who are trying to build theory and contribute to practice" (Vought et al., 2008). There is a need for deeper insights.

The case study method is suitable for understanding complex phenomena related to the management and dynamics in family business settings. "Qualitative case studies are apt to capture the specific characteristics of family business, to reach an in-depth understanding of the complex and tacit phenomena and processes related to ownership, management and the development that are typical for family business" (Nordvist et al., 2009). The interpretative approach through the case study method is particularly adapted to catch all those complex, tacit unconscious dimensions of the relationships in family business (Nordqvist et al., 2009). The very interest of family business research is to analyze how the family business specificity influences the content of data collected because of interactions. According to Eisenhardt (1989) and Stake (1995), the case study method allows studying actors, processes, and events, taking into account the context and longitudinal dimension which lacks in family business research (Benavides-Velasco et al., 2013). The researcher enters the actor's world in order to "see the situation as it is seen by the actor, observing what the actor takes into account, observing how he interprets what is taken into account" (Blumer, 1969). The case study methods present the advantages of

> grounding observations and concepts about social actions and structures by studying actors' day-to-day activities at close hand in their natural settings; providing information from a number of sources and over an extended period of time, allow the study of complex social processes and meanings; highlighting the dimension of time and history and it facilitates theoretical and conceptual development.
>
> (Orum et al., 1991)

Case study method is based on interactions and is made to capture and understand them in order to create a new knowledge which does not derive from one or the other but is the product of both (Kahn, 1989). The main question raised by the method is about the correct interpretation of data given by the actor: interpretation given by himself and interpretation coming from the researcher (Silverman, 1993). The idea is to create interpretive constructs to better understand what people do or say.

The researcher faces many challenges in the way to interpret data because the content of the data collected is not only revealing the individual level coming from the interviewed player but the player expresses also data influenced by the other levels with which he interacts. Those levels don't necessarily fit together. An important part of the sensemaking comes from the ability of the researcher to identify which data belong to what level even if the data come from the same medium, for example a player. This could explain why it is necessary to change the units of analysis when exploring family business (De Massis & Kotlar, 2014).

The typical access to data in case studies comes from interviews, observations, and documents. In this chapter we particularly focus on data content produced by interviews because it is a very interesting way to capture data coming directly from actors. It gives access to the way they live and interpret their life and their interactions with other people (Stake, 2000). Therefore, interview is particularly relevant for creating and capturing interactions and it is the only way to capture tacit and informal data. Then, interaction can occur in a context where the real recipient of the speech content is not necessarily the one who interacts (Maingueneau, 2007). He is taken in a kind of interactivity with other virtual or real actors entering the construction of the speech. The family member interviewed by the researcher will introduce in his speech tacit interactions he entertained with family members and business members, even if they don't attend the interview. The accuracy of this question is particularly high in family business research because, as we explained previously, the researcher interacts with individuals and the family community.

Then, each family member is stuck in a system of interactions. The content of the speech can come from his proper representation or the interaction with the other subsystems because each individual takes part in least at one subsystem; family or business or both. So, the content of the speech can refer to different parts of that system according to the group the individual refers to. But this question is very important in the data analysis. It is not possible to interpret equally a content that refers to the individual representations or the family representation through the individual speech for example.

This raises questions of the quality of interpretation that can be made on the data content collected. How close is the interpreted meaning to the original meaning expressed by the actor? The process of interpretation is a clarification of the meaning and understanding (Denzin, 2001). It is the "double hermeneutics" (Giddens, 1979). The researcher and the actor join an ongoing dialogue (Denzin, 2001) to co-create a new knowledge. The researcher ceases to be an objective finder of the truth but turns into a subject: a socially and culturally situated co-producer of the social reality (Nordqvist et al., 2009). Therefore, it means defining intentions of actors and consequences (Denzin, 2001) to the content of data delivered. "Every understanding is a product of negotiated meanings, and, as such, it is open to reconstruction" (Nordvist et al., 2009). According to Golden-Biddle & Locke (1993), "the data-generating strategies indicate the investment in attempting to be faithful to the complexity and variability in the dimension of organizational life into which our research inquiries."[3] The quality of the research in that context is internalized with the underlying research philosophy (Amis & Silk, 2008). Moreover, as the position of the researcher is well known in an interpretive qualitative research, it is less studied to analyze the position of the interviewed. Hlady-Rispal (2002) states that "the principle of interaction also acknowledges the influence of the researcher on how the actors will reflect on the phenomenon studied and (re) act against it."

However, the interviewed actor will also react in terms of the different subsystems of family business he belongs to and in terms of the interaction created by the researcher. The professional actor, however, sought to fill this data, adopts attitudes and different strategies that the researcher must understand in order to interpret correctly the data content.

A typology linking interactions, intentions, and data content in family business research

As Nordqvist et al. (2009), we use our research experience in grounded analysis and qualitative longitudinal case studies in the field of family business governance. The aim of those research projects was to conceptualize the complexity of the family business governance[4] by in-depth analysis of family business actors' practice. The cases were chosen following Glaser and Strauss (1967), because they had a strong family specificity according to the ownership and the family commitment into the business. Cases were run during a minimum of three years through secondary data collection (annual reports, dissertations made by managers, notes etc.) and essentially through primary data collection interviewing several times separated along time,[5] board members, and family members not involved in the business.[6] We use all through the chapter, examples and *verbatims* coming from those cases studies to illustrate the analysis we want to highlight.

Two sets of interactions

The system of interactions that the interviewed actor enters, creates an intention which determines the content of data (see Figure 13.2).

The analysis must focus first on the type of interactions. Two sets of interactions can be revealed. They are casually linked together. A first set of interactions is caused by the researcher entering into contact with an actor in order to collect primary data. This first interaction will produce the second set of interactions coming from the actor belonging to a family involved in the business (see Figure 13.3).

The case study is particularly interesting in family business research because the interaction caused by the researcher highlights family members' interactions between them and with business members.

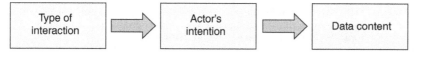

Figure 13.2 Influence of interactions on data content through an actor's intentions.

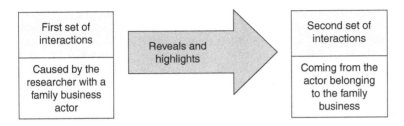

Figure 13.3 Relations between the two sets of interactions.

Interaction caused by the researcher implementing his research design

In case study methods, the researcher does not aim to change any actor's behavior. He aims to collect and understand the practice by collecting primary data and interpreting them. Interviews create an interaction between an actor and the researcher. As an individual, being interviewed by a researcher will produce different intentions influencing the data content of his story.

Two noticeable intentions are coming from two different kinds of interaction.

The first one is affective. It is created by the will to be well considered by the researcher. For the sake of his image and sometimes a lack of self-confidence, the actor tries to understand the research design, he listens carefully to the researcher, asks many questions showing his interest. He attempts to identify what "to think or respond." It creates an intention to satisfy the researcher by giving him a story relevant to the actor's interpretation of the researcher's objectives. Therefore, the data express a "seductress" content (Barrédy, 2009).

The second is a cognitive interaction. It is created by the actor's will to prove his ability, skills, and knowledge concerning the research topic. In this case, the actor wants to prove he knows how to respond "correctly." Therefore, the data express a "leader" content.

These types of interactions create a major challenge to the researcher because data content is not reliable. The researcher faces a lack of relevance.

Table 13.1 Details of the set of interactions between the researcher and an actor

Set of interactions	Nature of the interaction	Actor's intention	Data content
Between the researcher and an actor	Affective	Satisfy the researcher	"Seductress"
	"I do not really know if I can tell you what you expect." "I do not know if I give you the answers you expect."[*]		
	Cognitive	Prove his ability, skills, and knowledge concerning the research topic	"Leader"
	"I like to think about the concept of corporate governance, you know I spend a lot of time studying reviews and journals that talk about that topic. So I think I am up to date on that topic."[*]		

Note
* In Barrédy (2005).

Table 13.2 Details of the set of interactions between the researcher and an actor

Set of interactions	Nature of the interaction	Actor's intention	Data content
Between members of the family business system	Individual	To know the opinion of family member on his behavior and decisions	Instrumentalized
	Illustration: "I don't know if my father talked to you about that…" "My brother certainly explained that to you before." "My brother explained to you that we both think…"		
	Family	To detect the representations of other family members involved in the research design to insert himself in the main stream.	Socialized
	Illustration: "In remember, during the first six months of 1990 when we decided on a major reorganization of the company and then we felt the need, my brother, may have talked about this time with you, to bring in a banker, a CEO of Southwest, an entrepreneur. We made a committee that was not a strategic committee but that helped us making decisions…. First we have two people at a high level, my brother had to tell you, who are not directors."**		
	Professional	To prove competencies and professional skills	Business
	Illustration: "I want the board of directors to be very active because I need them to take part of the decisions in a stakeholder's vision."***		
	Systemic	To give a good image of the family business and to respect the community strategy of communication as a spokesman of the family business.	Community
	Illustration: The family firm is owned and run by three brothers.* The aim was to meet each of them and the two external directors separately, at least twice. Between two meetings, we noted a change in answers and a homogenization of their story: • After a first meeting with one of the brothers, each other brother met afterwards told us they knew the purpose of the research. • The topics that the first actors met didn't want to develop, remained unavailable with the others. • They all refused to allow us to enter in contact with outside directors, there was no way of negotiation.		

Notes

* In Barrédy and Batac (2009).

** Barrédy (2005).

Interaction coming from inside the family business between actors

The first set of interactions between the researcher and a family business actor gives way to the researcher to access to those interactions. The researcher interacts with the different components of the family business system, by the means of his interaction with each actor.

This set of interactions comes from the different circles of the family firm to which the actor belongs. Therefore, the actor can answer a same question taking different "hats" which has an influence on the content of his answer. Each level gives way to different intentions in the story given by the actor. If we integrate specific levels of interaction in family business described in Figure 13.1, a typology can be detailed including the type of interactions, actor's intention, and the data content.

The challenge is crucial for the researcher at two levels. First, when the actor expresses an intention, the data content gives clues to the nature and the quality of interactions family members have. Therefore, it gives access to interactions and the interpretation the actor has on them. Second, the researcher must catch those intentions linked with the underlined interaction because the actor's story is oriented in order to satisfy the intention and not necessarily to cooperate in the data process. The researcher must be very careful not to send signals that could be interpreted by the actor and modify the data content he gives to the researcher. At the same time, to pay attention to those intentions can help the researcher to understand why the data content from one actor can change between two interviews. The sense of community in family business creates interactions between family business members between two interviews and they can adapt their story fits with the community strategy of communication, decided together. So they will work together not only in substance but also on the form of the speech. This strategy also extends to the choices they make about the family members allowed to meet the researcher which is meaningful for the researcher. Therefore, the risk to be outside the main stream or excluded from the family community can lead a family member to decide to stop any relationship with the researcher.

Illustration[7]

The research began with meetings with the CEO and the relationship with the researcher was very good. After the first two interviews, inconsistencies such as a very strong attachment to performance, excluding the family interests on the one hand and a desire to satisfy the majority family shareholder of the other hand remained. The CEO proposed a meeting with his father and promised to organize that meeting but after that last meeting he totally broke contact with the researcher. His behavior was, for the researcher, proof the case was worth it. A contact with a non-family manager was tried successfully. He helped to understand the reason why the CEO stopped any contact and they were linked to his interactions with his father. Their relationship was very high conflict and he expected his father to tell evils about him. At the same time, he did not want the researcher to catch that information.

The typology raises the question of how a qualitative researcher can be aware of that during data collection.

Recommendations for qualitative data collection in family business research

The typology highlighted prove the data content collected during interviews in case studies refers to different levels of the family business and it raises the importance to take that information into account in order to make a relevant analysis. So the question of detecting the different levels used by the actor during interviews is relevant. Some recommendations can be presented. It is a topic that requires further analysis and developments.

Suggestion of tools to be used during case study data collection

The technique of data collection has a strong influence on the data content.

- *Make interview accompanied*

The accompanying researcher is more an observer. He is able to quickly step back. The interaction between the two researchers during the interview adds complexity to the actor's perception of the research's design. It is therefore more difficult for him to build an accurate representation of what he "should" answer. Indeed, the accompanying researcher can play the role of "trouble-maker" to break a pattern too clearly identifiable by the actor.

Illustration

Case study about the role of outside directors in family firm[8]

The beginning of the research was conducted alone. Then a second researcher was involved in the work. The change produced several contributions. First, the research was depersonalized. The subject was no longer attached to a person but a team. Second, it was much more difficult to anticipate the research strategy led by the duo. The intentions in the content changed to focus more on professional and family aspects.

- *The question of recording interviews*

Because of the question of quality of qualitative research methods, recording interviews is often recommended. It contributes to all the actor's words and expressions. This produces advantages for processing and analyzing data, but at the same time, it causes problems during data collection. The recording of the actor's voice promotes his willingness to expose arguments that he considers to be consistent with the family business communication. He rarely expresses at his individual level but more at the family level with the intention to stay in the main stream. There is, from his point of view, always the risk the recording could be listened to by another family member.

> **Illustration**[9]
>
> When I met the professional manager after all contact stopped with the family CEO, at the beginning of the interview, he told me:
>
> > Ok, you want to record this interview. No problem, I just inform you that my speech will be commercial, conventional. I can't allow myself according to the circumstances to preserve any traces, nor openly criticize the management of the company I've just left. You decide. In any case I ask you to sign a letter that engages you to confidential data.

Note-taking presents advantages. It enables the actor to slow down and to take time. Interviews last longer. Note-taking indeed leaves time to the researcher to respond to the comments and to enter into a true reflection. He is no more giving a show that is recorded but this technique helps to refocus him on the concepts of the study. He quits his search for answers consistent with what the other actor would have said.

- *The choice of the period of time when interviews are made*

The period of time data are collected makes a strong influence. It became extremely detrimental to collect data at the same time as the event studied is occurring. If actors are in a situation of high uncertainty and risk, they will rely more on the institutional communication and less on the real topic. They naturally will have intent to justify and rationalize decisions. They could even try to use the researcher as an expert who could help them.

> **Illustration**
>
> The case Delta[10] started from the introduction of outside directors in the board. The case Office Furniture BtoB[11] started much later after the introduction of outside directors in the board. In the Delta case, actors followed the conventional discourse on the image and the reason to request outside directors. Data collected in Office Furniture BtoB were deeper and multi-level. They focused on professionalization, family relationships, and competencies transfers. In the Delta case, they stayed on the professional conventional level. We had to wait three years after to collect data under family and individual level.
>
> It was the same for the Oak case study about the choice of the two tier system. Research started at the same time as they were changing the leadership structure to adopt a two tiers system. None of the actors could express himself about the new leadership structure, it was too new.

Tricks to use during interviews

- *Randomly raise topics during interviews*

Before entering the field, when the research is not totally inductive, as suggested by Huberman and Miles (2002), the researcher designs a protocol with the principal axes to explore. Usually, at the beginning of the interview, the researcher explains the purpose of the research, the design, and sometimes the way of analysis. The researcher's intention is most of the time to create a relationship of trust with actors. To facilitate the data analysis process, researchers mostly follow the interview guide. Some disadvantages can appear. It creates for the actor the ability to rebuild the researcher's intention and expectations. It is more useful to raise research topics randomly during the interview according to the story content given by the actor. It is much better to let the actor speak and reduce the researcher talking time to a minimum.

- *Not just one meeting, and the use of tables, figures*

Transcripts, field notes, and interpretations can be periodically returned to actors met to allow participants to check facts and logic and to see if the account "rings true" (Hanson & Newburg, 1992; Lincoln & Guba, 1985). The use of diagrams summarizing the topics discussed during previous meetings helps the actor to explore different levels. It helps him to disinhibit and allows him to express data coming from his interactions with the family in a more personal way. It requires meeting each actor many times. This approach also helps to develop trust, and leads to identification of the different levels on which the actor expresses. Returning to the topics discussed during previous meetings, the actor can then unwittingly provide information valuable to the researcher on the interactions between themes.

Illustrations

The research was about the choice of a two tier system in family listed firms.[12] During the second interview, as we were presenting to the chairman a table summarizing the key topics of the previous meeting and how they are related together, he told us showing the relationship between two topics: "You do not understand this, yet it seemed that it was what you were expected!" Back on this part of his speech, under cover of a misunderstanding, we could access to two different explanations, within two different kinds of interactions, of the same topic.

Add other ways to collect data

It is important in the family business research to use a variety of

> different data, including the combination of subjective or interpretative and more objective factual information, can add much to our understanding of organizational processes and outcomes. The use of multiple data sources enhances data credibility (Patton, 1990.) Each data source is one piece of the "puzzle", with each piece contributing to the researcher's understanding of the whole phenomenon.
>
> (De Massis & Kotlar, 2014)

It introduces a triangulation of data which strengthen the accuracy of the case study analysis (Tracy, 2010) because it gives different ways to analyze a same phenomenon (Denzin & Lincoln, 1994; Jick, 1979; Pettigrew, 1990; Stake, 2013; Yin, 1984). It is particularly accurate according to the interaction influence that we exposed previously. This is reinforced by Wright and Kellermanns (2011) who insist on the need for multi-level research with data collected from multiple respondents at different levels of the organization to reduce biases.

Adding direct observations to interviews also helps to reducing biases (De Massis & Kotlar, 2014; Barrédy, 2009). Observation is another way to collect data and to capture what level of interaction it refers to in family business. This method is a process that includes voluntary attention and intelligence, guided by a target device or organizer and directed on to an object to gather information (De Ketele & Roegiers, 1996). The observation helps to become familiar with situations, to perceive the context in which the actor evolves, their relations with other actors. It is very complementary to interviews because data collected by observation can be crossed with those collected during the interview. These may reveal the nature of interactions.

Illustration

In the Sparkling Wine case,[13] several contexts of observation allowed revelation of some new explanations of what was studied. On several occasions, particularly in three cases where the third or fourth generation was in power, observation of sites in which the interviews took place was very meaningful. In both cases, sites showed a dual front. The first case was a wine castle in the champagne region. When I arrived for the first interview, the chairman of the supervisory board came to pick me up at the railway station. I realized that his approach was not only courteous. He wanted to show me the most symbolic places of his family history. So, before we went to the castle, we traveled the city to show me the church where his family celebrates weddings, baptisms, and funerals for three generations. He also wished to introduce me to the castle; his wife is an heiress. Finally when we arrived, two nested elements were striking. At first glance, the castle was a beautiful property. Once back in his office, the surprise was to find alongside the stylish furniture basins for collecting water from gutters flooded the room through the ceiling. The contrast between the external appearance and internal condition, so hidden, was meaningful. This observation has been made in other cases.

During an interview the chairman of the supervisory board was very clear his will to let his children run the business freely. One of his daughters, aged 50, came into the office asking her father for the key to the winery. This harmless object for a wine chateau required permission from the father. Indeed, he kept it jealously with him all the time. The observed relationship did not match with what he was expressing with words. It was the behavior of a father to his "little girl." It showed a strong relationship of power.

It can be very interesting to use observation when the interviews are conducted by several researchers. One of them may take the time to observe. However Silverman (1993) warns the researcher on the encoding methods for observation data. The observation is up to the eye of the researcher and what he retains or not. Then, it is subject to cognitive filters. Holding a real diary with questions and reflections is then essential. His confrontation with other researchers and experts in the field and the methods employed foster future analysis.

- *Peer debriefing with a qualified person who can play the "devil's advocate"* (*Lincoln & Guba, 1985*)

"Exposing oneself to a disinterested peer in a manner paralleling an analytical session and for the purpose of exploring aspects of inquiry that might otherwise remain only implicit within the inquirer's mind" (Lincoln & Guba, 1985: 308). It is important, as the opposite of a partnership in the research process, that the colleague is not involved in the research project. It helps to clarify interpretations. According to Lincoln and Guba (1985), the researcher has to establish the trustworthiness of the research by demonstrating the credibility of his or her work through prolonged engagement with actors, member checking, and triangulation. Other kind of tools like a mechanical approach that directs and draws on the creative and conceptual ability of the analyst can be used to determine the meaning, salience, and connecting logic of emerging themes (Ritchie et al., 1994).

Conclusion

The aim of the chapter was to start from the specificity of family business to identify a typology of interactions and to analyze the influence they have on the data collected by the researcher during interviews in a qualitative case study. The results prove the existence of multi-level interactions in family business coming from individuals, the family social group, the professional community, which can be composed of non-family members and the whole systemic family business. Those interactions are present in the speech delivered by interviewees and in order to understand properly the phenomenon observed by the researcher, it is necessary to identify which interactions the data are linked to. Therefore, interaction influences the data collected by researchers. The chapter leads to four main contributions in the field of family business and in the field of qualitative case study research in entrepreneurship. The first contribution is the analysis of what makes qualitative research in organizations where there is a family influence or commitment, totally different. It is not simply applying a research method to a field, it is also taking into account the specificity of the family business. The second contribution is the identification of typologies of interactions coming from inside the company and the family and coming from the entering of the researcher into the business. The third contribution considers, the influence made by the different type of interactions on the data collected. It links the player interviewed to the other components of the system he belongs to. Then, the data delivered by the player contents several levels coming from his interactions with other players and the researcher. Those levels must be identified in order to understand properly the different dimension of the player's speech and the place each component of the system has in his representations. The fourth contribution is the attention about the data content on a methodological point of view. The speech of players is produced by the embeddingness of data expressing different levels of interactions coming from subsystems of the whole system.

Appendix

Table 13.A.1 Case descriptions*

	Electronic Components	Distribution	Office Furniture BtoB	Sparkling Wine	The Maull	Conglomerate	Raw Materials	Delta	Gambling	Oak
Date of creation	1952	1913	1966	1849	1893	1855	1941	1946	1973	1900
Generation in power	Second	Third	Second	Sixth	Fourth	Fifth	Second	Second	Second	Third
Capital owned by the family	>50%	<33%	>50%	>50%	>50%	<50%	>50%	>50%	>50%	>50%
Management	Two generations of family members	Two generations of family members	Two generations of family members	One family member and an external member	Two generations of family members	One family member and an external member	One family member and an external member	Two generations of family members	Two generations of family members	Two generations of family members
Research question	Organization and board structure change Mechanism of entrenchment	Organization and board structure change Mechanism of entrenchment	Organization and board structure change Mechanism of entrenchment	Organization and board structure change Mechanism of entrenchment	Organization and board structure change Mechanism of entrenchment	Organization and board structure change Mechanism of entrenchment	Organization and board structure change Mechanism of entrenchment	Social capital and learning External directors and board process	Organization and board structure change Mechanism of entrenchment	Organization and board structure change Mechanism of entrenchment

Note
* Because of the high confidentiality of the data given during interview, it is not possible to give the real names of the cases.

Notes

1 We approach the family business governance through qualitative research methods by case studies.
2 In Nordqvist et al. (2009).
3 In Easterby-Smith et al. (2008).
4 The case study method was chosen to explore the determinants of the leadership structure, the entrenchment, and the role of external directors on the board process.
5 Four times each on average.
6 A detailed description of the cases is available in the chapter Appendix.
7 Case: Office Furniture BtoB (Barrédy, 2005).
8 Case: Delta (Barrédy & Batac, 2010, 2013).
9 Case: Office Furniture BtoB (Barrédy, 2005).
10 Barrédy and Batac (2010, 2013).
11 Barrédy (2005).
12 Barrédy (2005).
13 Barrédy (2005).

References

Alvesson, M., & Karreman, D. (2007). Constructing mystery: Empirical matters in theory development. *Academy of Management Review*, 32(4), 1265–1281.
Amis, J.M., & Silk, M.L. (2008). The philosophy and politics of quality in qualitative organizational research. *Organizational Research Methods*, 11(3), 456–480.
Ashforth, B.E., & Mael, F. (1989). Social identity theory and the organization. *Academy of Management Review*, 14(1), 20–39.
Barrédy, C. (2005). *Le choix de la structure en directoire et conseil de surveillance dans la société familiale cotée comme mode de gouvernance*. Thèse de Doctorat en Sciences de Gestion, Bordeaux, Université Brdeaux IV, 447p.
Barrédy, C. (2009). Quelles stratégies "qualité" d'accès aux données pour le chercheur qualitatif? Le cas particulier des entreprises familiales. *Revue Internationale de Psychologie*, XV(35), 73–94.
Barrédy, C., & Batac, J. (2010). Un nouveau regard sur le rôle des administrateurs extérieurs dans l'entreprise familiale: Pompiers ou partenaires? *Revue Française de Gouvernance d'Entreprise*, 6, 35–57.
Barrédy, C., & Batac J., (2013). Faire de la stratégie en famille 60 ans d'histoire dans une entreprise familiale. *Gérer et Comprendre*, premier trimestre.
Bartunek, J.M., Rynes, S.L., & Ireland, R.D. (2006). What makes management research interesting, and why does it matter? *Academy of Management Journal*, 49(1), 9–15.
Becker, G. (1974). On the relevance of the new economics of the family. *American Economic Review*, 64(2), 317–319.
Becker, G. (1993). *Treatise on the Family*, Cambridge, MA, Harvard University Press.
Beckhard, R., & Dyer Jr., G. (1983). Managing continuity in the family-owned business. *Organizational Dynamics*, 12(1), 5–12.
Ben-Porath, Y. (1980). The F-connection: Families, friends and firms and the organization of exchange. *Population and Development Review*, 6(1), 1–30.
Benavides-Velasco, C., Quitana-Garcia, C., & Guzman-Parra, V. (2013). Trends in family business research. *Small Business Economics*, 40, 41–57.
Berger, P., & Luckmann, T. (1967). *The Social Construction of Reality: A Treatrise in the Sociology of Knowledge*, London, Penguin Books.
Bergstrom, T.C. (1995). On the evolution of altruistic ethical rules for siblings. *American Economic Review*, 85(1), 58–82.
Blumer, H. (1969). *Symbolic Interactionism: Perspective and Method*, Berkeley, CA, University of California Press.

Chrisman, J., Chua, J., Pearson, A., & Barnett, T. (2012). Family involvement, family influence, and family-centered non-economic goals in small firms. *Entrepreneurship: Theory and Practice*, 36(2), 267–293.

Chrisman, J., Chua, J., Kellermans, F., & Matherne, C. (2008). Management journals as venues for publication of family business research. *Entrepreneurship: Theory and Practice*, 32(5), 927–934.

Chrisman, J., Chua, J., & Sharma, P. (2005). Trends and directions in the development of a strategic management theory of the family firm. *Entrepreneurship: Theory and Practice*, 29(5), 555–575.

Chua, J., Chrisman, J., & Sharma, P. (1999). Defining the family business by behaviour. *Entrepreneurship: Theory and Practice*, 23(4), 19–39.

Daily, C., & Dollinger, M. (1993). Alternative methodologies for identifying family- versus nonfamily-managed businesses. *Journal of Small Business Management*, 31(2), 79–90.

Davis, P. (1983). Realizing the potential of the family business. *Organizational Dynamics*, 12(1), 47–56.

Dawson, A., & Hjorth, D. (2012). Advancing family business research through narrative analysis. *Family Business Review*, 25(3), 339–355.

De Ketele, J.-M., & Roegiers, X. (1996). *Méthodologie de Recueil d'Informations*, Bruxelles, DeBoeck Université.

De Massis, A., & Kotlar, J. (2014). Case study method in family business research: Guidelines for qualitative scholarship. *Journal of Family Business Strategy*, 5(1), 15–29.

De Massis, A., Sharma, P., Chua, J.H., & Chrisman, J.J. (2012). *Family Business Studies: An Annotated Bibliography*, Northampton, MA, Edward Elgar Publishing.

Denzin, N. (2001). *Interpretive Interactionism*, Thousands Oaks, CA, Sage.

Denzin, N., & Lincoln, Y. (1994). *Handbook of Qualitative Research*, London, Sage.

Donnelley, R.G. (1964). The family business. *Harvard Business Review*, 42(4), 93–105.

Durkheim, É. (1888). Introduction à la sociologie de la famille. *Extrait des Annales de la Faculté des lettres de Bordeaux*, 10, 257–281.

Dyer, W., & Sanchez, M. (1998). Current state of family business theory and practice as reflected in family business review 1988–1997. *Family Business Review*, 11(4), 287–295.

Easterby-Smith, M., Golden-Biddle, K., & Locke, K. (2008). Working with pluralism: Determining quality in qualitative research. *Organizational Research Methods*, 11, 419–430.

Eisenhardt, K. (1989). Building theories from case study research. *Academy of Management Review*, 15(4), 532–550.

Eisenhardt, K.M., & Graebner, M.E. (2007). Theory building from cases: Opportunities and challenges. *Academy of Management Journal*, 50(1), 25–32.

Giddens, A. (1979). *Central Problems in Social Theory: Action, Structure and Contradiction in Social Theory*, London, Macmillan Press.

Gioia, D.A., Corley, K.G., & Hamilton, A.L. (2013). Seeking qualitative rigor in inductive research notes on the Gioia methodology. *Organizational Research Methods*, 16(1), 15–31.

Glaser, B., & Strauss, A. (1967). *The Discovery of Grounded Theory: Strategies for Qualitative Research*, New York, Aldine.

Goffman, E. (1983). The interaction order. *American Sociological Review*, 48(1), 1–17.

Golden-Biddle, K., & Locke, K. (1993). Appealing work: A study of how ethnographic text convince. *Organization Science*, 4(4), 1–22.

Graebner, M.E., Martin, J.A., & Roundy, P.T. (2012). Qualitative data: Cooking without a recipe. *Strategic Organization*, 10(3), 276–284.

Habbershon, T., Williams, M., & MacMillan, I. (2003). A unified systems perspective of family firm performance. *Journal of Business Venturing*, 18(4), 451–465.

Habbershon, T.G., & Williams, M.L. (1999). A resource-based framework for assessing the strategic advantages of family firms. *Family Business Review*, 12(1), 1–25.

Handler, W. (1989). Methodological issues and considerations in studying family businesses. *Family Business Review*, 2(3), 257–276.

Hanson, T., & Newburg, D. (1992). Naturalistic inquiry as a paradigm for doing applied performance enhancement research. *Contemporary Thought on Performance Enhancement*, 1, 71–105.

Harvey, M., & Evans, R.E. (1994). Family business and multiple levels of conflict. *Family Business Review*, 7(4), 331–348.

Heck, R.K., Hoy, F., Poutziouris, P.Z., & Steier, L.P. (2008). Emerging paths of family entrepreneurship research. *Journal of Small Business Management*, 46(3), 317–330.

Hirigoyen, G. (2002). Le gouvernement des entreprises familiales. In Caby, J. & Hirigoyen, G. (Eds.), *La Gestion des Entreprises Familiales*, Paris, Economica.

Hlady-Rispal, M. (2002). *Méthode des Cas, Application à la Recherche en Gestion*, Bruxelles, DeBoeck Université.

Huber, G.P., & Power, D.J. (1985). Retrospective reports of strategic-level managers: Guidelines for increasing their accuracy. *Strategic Management Journal*, 6(2), 171–180.

Huberman, M., & Miles, M.B. (2002). *The Qualitative Researcher's Companion*, Thousand Oaks, CA, Sage.

Ibrahim, N.A., Angelidis, J.P., & Parsa, F. (2008). Strategic management of family businesses: Current findings and directions for future research. *International Journal of Management*, 25(1), 95–110.

Jick, T.D. (1979). Mixing qualitative and quantitative methods: Triangulation in action. *Administrative Science Quarterly*, 602–611.

Kahn, J. (1989). Culture: Demise or resurection? *Critique of Anthropology*, 2(9), 15–25.

Kepner, E. (1983). The family and the firm: A coevolutionary perspective. *Organizational Dynamics*, 12(1), 57–70.

Klein, S.B., Astrachan, J.H., & Smyrnios, K.X. (2005). The F-PEC scale of family influence: Construction, validation, and further implications for theory. *Entrepreneurship: Theory and Practice*, 29, 321–339.

Kontinen, T., Plakoyiannaki, E., & Ojala, A. (2013). The case study in family business: A review of research practice. *Academy of Management Proceedings*, 2013(1), 15871.

Lansberg, I. (1983). Managing human resources in family firms: The problem of institutional overlap. *Organizational Dynamics*, 21(1), 39–46.

Lansberg, I.S., Perrow, E.L., & Rogolsky, S. (1988). Family business as an emerging field. *Family Business Review*, 1(1), 1–8.

Lincoln, Y., & Guba, E. (1985). *Naturalistic Inquiry*, Beverly Hills, CA, Sage.

Litz, R.A., Pearson, A.W., & Litchfield, S. (2012). Charting the future of family business research perspectives from the field. *Family Business Review*, 25(1), 16–32.

Lundberg, S. (1994). Unravelling communication among family members. *Family Business Review*, 7(1), 29–37.

Maingueneau, D. (2007). *Analyser les Textes de Communication*, Paris, Armand Colin.

Melin, L., Nordqvist, M., & Sharma, P. (Eds.). (2013). *The SAGE Handbook of Family Business*, London, Sage.

Miles, M.B., & Huberman, A.M. (1994). *Qualitative Data Analysis: An Expanded Sourcebook*, Thousand Oaks, CA, Sage.

Miller, D., & Le Breton-Miller, I. (2007). Kicking the habit: Broadening our horizon for studying family businesses. *Journal of Management Inquiry*, 16(1), 27–30.

Nordqvist, M., Hall, A., & Melin, L. (2009). Qualitative research on family businesses: The relevance and usefulness of the interpretive approach. *Journal of Management and Organization*, 15(3), 294–308.

Orum, A., Feagin, J., & Sjoberg, G. (1991). Introduction: The nature of the case study, Orum, A., Feagin, J., & Silverman, D. (Eds.), *Interpreting Qualitative Data: Methods for Analyzing Talk, Text and Interaction*, London, Sage.

Ouchi, W.G. (1979). A conceptual framework for the design of organizational control mechanisms. *Management Science*, 25, 833–848.

Patton, M.Q. (1990). *Qualitative Evaluation and Research Methods*, Thousand Oaks, CA, Sage.

Peredo, A.M. (2003). Nothing thicker than blood? Commentary on "Help one another, use one another: toward an anthropology of family business." *Entrepreneurship: Theory and Practice*, summer, 397–400.

Pettigrew, A.M. (1990). Longitudinal field research on change: Theory and practice. *Organization Science*, 1(3), 267–292.

Pettigrew, A.M. (1997). What is a processual analysis? *Scandinavian Journal of Management*, 13(4), 337–348.

Pollak, R.A. (1985). A transaction cost approach to families and households. *Journal of Economic Literature*, XXIII, 581–609.

Reay, T., & Zhang, Z. (2014). Qualitative methods in family business research. In Melin, L., Nordqvist, M., & Sharma, P. (Eds.), *The SAGE Handbook of Family Business*, London: Sage.

Ritchie, J., Spencer, L., Bryman, A., & Burgess, R.G. (1994). *Analysing Qualitative Data*. London: Routledge.

Salancik, G.R., & Meindl, J.R. (1984). Corporate attributions as strategic illusions of management control. *Administrative Science Quarterly*, 29(2), 238–254.

Schwandt, T. (1994). Constructivist, interpretivist approach to human inquiry. In Denzin, N.K., & Lincoln, Y.S. (Eds.), *Handbook of Qualitative Research*, Thousands Oaks, CA, Sage.

Shane, S.A. (2003). *A General Theory of Entrepreneurship: The Individual–Opportunity Nexus*, Cheltenham, UK, Edward Elgar Publishing.

Sharma, P. (2004). An overview of the field of family business studies: Current status and directions for the future. *Family Business Review*, 17(1), 1–36.

Sharma, P., Chrisman, J.J., & Gersick, K.E. (2012). 25 years of family business review: Reflections on the past and perspectives for the future. *Family Business Review*, 25(1), 5.

Shotter, J. (1993). *Conversational Realities: Contructing Life through Language*, London, Sage.

Silverman, D. (1993). *Interpreting Qualitative Data: Methods for Analyzing Talk, Text and Interaction*, London, Sage.

Sjöstrand, S.E. (1997). *The Two Faces of Management: The Janus Factor*, Cengage Learning Business Press.

Spencer, L., Ritchie, J., & O'Connor, W. (2003). Analysis: Practices, Principles and Processes. In Ritchie, J., & Lewis, J. (Eds.), *Qualitative Research Practice: A Guide for Social Science Students and Researchers*, London, Sage.

Stake, R. (1995). *The Art of Case Study Research*, Sage, London.

Stake, R. (2000). Case studies. In Denzin, N., & Lincoln, Y. (Eds.), *Handbook of Qualitative Research*, Thousands Oaks, CA, Sage.

Stake, R.E. (2005). Qualitative case studies. In Denzin, N., & Lincoln, Y. (Eds.), *Handbook of Qualitative Research*, Thousand Oaks, CA, Sage.

Stake, R. E. (2013). *Multiple Case Study Analysis*, New York: Guilford Press.

Strauss, A., & Corbin, J. (1990). *Basics of Qualitative Research: Grounded Theory Procedures and Techniques*, Newbury Park, CA, Sage.

Tagiuri, R., & Davis, J.A. (1992). On the goals of successful family companies. *Family Business Review*, 5(1), 43–62.

Tracy, S.J. (2010). Qualitative quality: Eight "big-tent" criteria for excellent qualitative research. *Qualitative Inquiry*, 16(10), 837–851.

Van Maanen, J. (1979). Reclaiming qualitative methods for organizational research: A preface. *Administrative Science Quarterly*, 24(4), 520–526.

Vion, R. (1996). L'analyse des interactions verbales. *Publication du Centre de Recherches sur la Didacticité des Discours Ordinaires*, 4, 19–32.

Vought, K., Baker, L., & Smith, G. (2008). Practitioner commentary: Moving from theory to practice in family business research. *Entrepreneurship: Theory and Practice*, 32(6), 1111–1121.

Ward, J.L. (1987). *Keeping the Family Business Healthy*, San Francisco, CA, Jossey Bass.

Whiteside, M.F., & Brown, H. (1991). Drawbacks of dual systems approach to family firms: Can we expand our thinking? *Family Business Review*, 4(4), 383–395.

Wright, M., & Kellermanns, F.W. (2011). Family firms: A research agenda and publication guide. *Journal of Family Business Strategy*, 2(4), 187–198.

Yin, R. (1984) *Case Study Research*, Beverly Hills, CA, Sage.

Yin R. (1994). *Case Study Research: Design and Methods*, Beverly Hills, CA, Sage.

Yin, R.K. (2009). *Case Study Research: Design and Methods* (Vol. 5), Beverly Hills, CA, Sage.

Zachary, R.K., Rogoff, R.G., & Phinisee, I. (2013). Defining and identifying family entrepreneurship: A new view of entrepreneurs. In Minniti, M. (Ed.), *The Dynamics of Entrepreneurship: Evidence from Global Entrepreneurship Monitor Data*, Oxford: Oxford University Press.

Zahra, S.A., & Sharma, P. (2004). Family business research: A strategic reflection. *Family Business Review*, 17(4), 331–346.

Conclusion to Part III

Giovanna Dossena

The chapters of this third part each explore specific questions and contribute to building knowledge at the junction of the fields of family and entrepreneurship. As the literature review in the Introduction to this book shows, much of the extant literature focuses on how the family influences the family business; much less is known about how the family influences entrepreneurship at other times (e.g., pre-start up, the dynastic family), other levels of analysis (e.g., the family business group), to the firm in its context (e.g., its network). These questions raise other important research issues, in particular related to appropriate research methods to capture and understand these phenomena.

The collective contributions of the chapters in Part III address each of these lacunae. The framework offered to understand the influence of the couple's relationship on launch decision and firm survival can inspire further research in that, being grounded in the Sustainable Family Business Theory, admits that families and businesses are not all identical and they can evolve differently in times of stability and change. Using Network theory to understand the family business in its context can be developed beyond the contribution in this volume by, for example, integrating social and cultural specificities of the conceptualization of family, by developing a Network theory view to entrepreneurship as effectuation, and by focusing more specifically on structural gaps. Dynastic families are at the origin of family business groups: this raises interesting questions such as how individual family members' entrepreneurial identity influences their choice of opportunity to pursue and the mode of exploitation.

In addition to the specific suggestions for further research detailed in each chapter, here we note the main common points which deserve more attention:

- the family business group can be explored as an additional level of analysis for entrepreneurial behaviors (in addition to the individual, the family and the family business);
- the Network theory can be used to better understand the composition and configuration of family evolution;
- effectuation can support research on decision-making of families in the pre-start up phase.

Entrepreneurial activities stem more and more from families endowed with human resources: wives and husbands of entrepreneurs represent potential boosters for development as well as influencers of behaviors such as risk taking and initiating (serially) new ventures. Different generations may hold different values or demonstrate different entrepreneurial identities; this is related to socio-emotional characteristics of course, but also to the relative strength of the individual, family, and business identity. This "observation" is at the heart of this new field of research: in order to fully grasp it, research needs to delve into the intersection of family business, entrepreneurship, and family. The dynamics between individual family members, the family business (and family business group), and the family influence each other, and many of these relationships are dramatically unexplored.

Final conclusion

What we need to know about Family Entrepreneurship

Alain Fayolle

In the Introduction to this work we showed how Family Entrepreneurship can be an integrating framework to bring together family, family business, and entrepreneurship research. This framework is the fruit of our understanding of Family Entrepreneurship and we share it in the hopes of encouraging dialogue and debate. It can first be used to build a more robust and holistic body of knowledge because it integrates extant research previously disconnected and second it can be used to provide an overarching framework to support future research. The scope of this framework induces bolder, rather than incremental, research questions.

Recently, the question of whether Family Entrepreneurship could be considered as a field of research was asked (Bettinelli, Fayolle, & Randerson, 2014; Randerson, Fayolle, & Dossena, forthcoming). The preliminary answer was that

> being or becoming a field of research depends strongly on the level of academic legitimacy. Legitimacy is a process of building, influenced by key drivers like salience of the issues studied, the production of strong results and the maintenance of disciplinary plasticity (Lyytinen & King, 2004).
>
> (Bettinelli et al., 2014: 53–54)

If Family Entrepreneurship can be qualified as a developing field (Bettinelli et al., 2014), this field can grow and gain in legitimacy in several manners. Family Entrepreneurship can indeed reunite scholars around a common understanding, integrate extant knowledge (in entrepreneurship, family business, and family) into an overarching framework, and encourage new research. The contributions in this volume represent a first attempt in this direction. The issues studied here include various aspects of Family Entrepreneurship and all seem equally relevant for the advancement of our knowledge, both from a theoretical point of view and from a practical one. The disciplinary elasticity that the authors of the contributions in this book have implemented – for example by integrating theoretical perspectives that belong to different fields – and the soundness of the first empirical findings are both indicators that we are moving toward a greater legitimacy of Family Entrepreneurship as a field of research.

As shown in this volume, there is a greenfield for future research at the intersection of the fields of family business and entrepreneurship. Entrepreneurship is a "coat of many colors" (Zahra & Dess, 2001) and many aspects of entrepreneurship have not yet been explored in the family business context. For example, the chapter by Sarasvathy and colleagues is the first to research effectuation in the family business context: this effort deserves to be pursued and expanded.

Another important aspect which is currently understudied is the commonalities in the entrepreneurial processes of family businesses and non-family businesses. Indeed, much of family business research concentrates on understanding the differences between family firms and non-family firms or the heterogeneity of family firms. Here we suggest that research focusing on understanding what is common in these processes can provide important building-blocks to further knowledge.

With reference of research themes at the intersection of Family Business and Family, the main focus of previous research was "how does the family affect the family business?" There are important blind spots in our understanding of how the family business affects the family. In addition, not enough is known about how the dynamics evolve over time, for example according to the life cycles of family members, family, and family business, or how changes in family composition (divorce, re-partnership) interact with changes in the family business (sales, spin off, internationalization, for example). It is now paramount to create knowledge which integrates the heterogeneousness of families. There are different conceptualizations of family according to cultures, religions, and systems of law. The vast majority of extant research is based in the US, which precludes understanding or offering pertinent knowledge to cultures which adopt the stem rather than the nuclear family as norm. For example, the nuclear family is based on a monogamous partnership whereas some religions support polygamous partnerships. Similarly, different legal systems can play a significant role in the definition of family boundaries. Finally the *common law* system (US, UK, Australia, New Zealand) is embedded in an individualistic political philosophy which grants autonomy to the individual to decide which moral rights and duties family members have toward each other, whereas the *civil law* system, collectivistic, establishes rules which aim at establishing legally, formally, rights and responsibilities. These examples are to stress the importance of the context in which Family Entrepreneurship is studied. In the case of Family Entrepreneurship indeed, taking into proper account the heterogeneousness of families and the context where they exist, is even more salient as families are clearly the locus for human development and behaviors from various points of view (Bronfenbrenner, 1986).

Another intriguing stream of research was identified at the intersection of Entrepreneurship and Family. In this case, there is much more knowledge on how the family influences entrepreneurial behaviors than how entrepreneurial behaviors influence the family. It could also be interesting to research effectuation as a logic in the family context. In other terms, is effectual logic proper to entrepreneurship (expert entrepreneurs) or can effectual and causal logics support other types of decision-making in the family or domestic realm?

Does familiness "spill over" to non-family businesses? And also, does socioemotional wealth develop and in what form when members of a family work in the same organization (a non-family business)?

Beyond these specific suggestions, it is also important to support this new knowledge creation with appropriate research design. Extant literature reviews in family business have shown how important it is to pay attention to the theoretical lenses that are used when one interprets empirical findings (Gedajlovic, Carney, Chrisman, & Kellermanns, 2012). What has emerged from the contributions offered in this book is that, while some theories seem to be more appropriate than others to explore and explain Family Entrepreneurship, there is a need to adopt a complementary theoretical framework. In order to be sound, this framework has to integrate theories from family business, from entrepreneurship, and from family science (Randerson, Bettinelli, Fayolle, & Anderson, 2015). Indeed, Family Entrepreneurship involves issues and phenomena that are ontologically diverse; this is why it is only with the adoption of a multi-theoretic framework that we could be able to offer a coherent view of the phenomena that occur in Family Entrepreneurship. Additionally, since Family Entrepreneurship aims at understanding causal and circular effects between and among the family, the individual, and the family business' features and entrepreneurial behaviors, the application of empirical studies that adopt a longitudinal perspective seems particularly suitable. Not only does this allow better observation of causal effects, it also offers a more complete view of behaviors that can only be observed over time. Additionally, a suggestion for future research is also to take into account that the field involves different levels of analysis. For the moment we focus on two elements at a time, but research can also be undertaken at the intersection of the three fields.

We would like to close this book with saying that we are really grateful to the authors who a couple of years ago accepted to take part into this audacious project and contributed with such a challenging research output. Their enthusiasm and sharpness in the development of this common project have illuminated our pattern toward a better understanding of Family Entrepreneurship. However, we are well aware that this volume and the considerations that we include here represent only the tip of an iceberg that we are eager to explore in the future.

References

Bettinelli, C., Fayolle, A., & Randerson, K. 2014. Family Entrepreneurship: A Developing Field. *Foundations and Trends® in Entrepreneurship*, 10(3): 161–236.
Bronfenbrenner, U. 1986. Ecology of the Family as a Context for Human Development: Research Perspectives. *Developmental Psychology*, 22(6): 723–742.
Gedajlovic, E., Carney, M., Chrisman, J. J., & Kellermanns, F. W. 2012. The Adolescence of Family Firm Research: Taking Stock and Planning for the Future. *Journal of Management*, 38(4): 1010–1037.
Lyytinen, K. & King, J. L. 2004. Nothing at the Center? Academic Legitimacy in the Information Systems Field. *Journal of the Association for Information Systems*, 5(6): 8.
Randerson, K., Bettinelli, C., Fayolle, A., & Anderson, A. forthcoming. Family Entrepreneurship as a field of research: Exploring its Contours and Contents. *Journal of Family Business Strategy*, 6(3): 143–154, ISSN 1877-8585, http://dx.doi.org/10.1016/j.jfbs.2015.08.002.
Randerson, K., Fayolle, A., & Dossena, G. forthcoming. The Future of Family Entrepreneurship. *Futures*.
Zahra, S. & Dess, G. G. 2001. Entrepreneurship as a Field of Research: Encouraging Dialogue and Debate. *Academy of Management Review*, 26(1): 8–10.

Index

Page numbers in *italics* denote tables, those in **bold** denote figures.

dynastic business families 265, 302;
expansion and preservation of 269;
habitual entrepreneurship in 266–8;
socioemotional wealth in 265–6, 272;
transgenerational 272

effectual SEW (ESEW) 39–40; as modified
subset of SEW **39**
effectuation, principles of: affordable loss
principle 17; bird-in-hand principle
16–17; crazy quilt principle 17; lemonade
principle 17–18; mapping *20–9*; pilot-in-
the-plane principle 18
emotions, within business families:
attributes of 159; emotional attachment
160; emotional intelligence 160; forms
and effects of 160; relevance of 159; role
of 158–60; trustworthiness 159
enterprising families, definition of 1
entrepreneurial family: business 1–2;
concept of 1–2
entrepreneurial family firms: auto-
referential tendency of 175; behavior of
94–5, 172–4; capacity to work in a team
175–6; competitive growth of 176–8;
decision-making in 176; economic and
social sustainability 176; "ephemeral"
activities 174; factors influencing 174–6;
idea-invention 178; initial development
stage 177; innovation, process of 175;
innovative-financial phase of 178; long-
term vision and value orientation 174;
personalisation of 176–7; product-
market-technology mix 176; risk taking,
conditions for 174–5; stakeholder theory
174; start-up phase 177; technical–design
phase of 178; "virtuous" evolution of 174
entrepreneurial networking and growth
213–18; commercial capital and growth
opportunities 224–5; co-opetition
networks 214; development of new
network contacts 214; elements of 215;
investigating and enacting growth paths
225–9; pre-start phase 214; social capital
and 241; start-up networking patterns
215; story of growth in family firms
216–17; technological partnering 214;
venture establishment phase 214
entrepreneurial start-up decision: data
analysis 249–50; data collection 247–9;
data sample 247; domestic drivers and
barriers to *257*; family life cycles 245–7;
family responsibilities in terms of 256;
households with children stage 254–6;
networks of relationships, impact of 239;
one-person household stage 250–2;
research methods for analysis of 247–50;
social capital and entrepreneurial

networks 241; sustainable family business
theory (SFBT) 242–3; theoretical
framework of 240–7; time- and strain-
based conflicts 253; two-person
household stage 252–3; work–family
border theory 242; work–family conflict
theory 243–5, 249, 252, 258; work–family
interface and 239–40, 242
entrepreneurs: behaviors 3; characteristics
of 171; expert 305; spouses of 189;
virtuous 175

F-PEC scale 34, 77, 79
family bonds, through dynastic succession
149
family business: behavioral assumptions at
18–19; capital structure of 31–2;
classification of 121; competitive success
of 137; dualist representation of **113**;
effectuation, mapping of *20–9*;
effectuation, principles of 16–18;
effectuation research 15–16; elements of
the effectual process of 16; empirically
derived propositions 35–7;
entrepreneurial development of 2, 5–6;
family and 6–8; global system of 284;
growth-strategies adopted by 173;
identity construction in *see* identity
construction, in family business; meta-
identity structure 120; *versus* non-family
businesses 113; nonfamily stakeholders
and familiness 32–4; product portfolios
156; revenue-generating capacity 7;
review of extant empirical work in 19–35;
scope of 14; self-identification in 83; set
of interactions inside **284**; small- and
medium-sized 5; social elements,
influence of 33; stakeholder self-selection
process **17**; strategic flexibility 34–5;
succession in 31, 171
family capital 187, 190; classification of 189;
human capital and growth opportunities
220–4; spousal capital 189
family dynamics, influence on family firm
behaviour 139
family dynasty *see* dynastic business families
family entrepreneurial orientation 51
family entrepreneurship: conceptualization
of **3,** 185–7; definition of 1; discursive
psychology and 119–24; fields involved in
4; importance of 3; risk-taking behaviors
94; unified systems view of identity in **114**
family firms: agency theory of 172; capital
structure of 31–2; concept of 170;
corporate venturing in 49; debt-capital
ratios 32; decentralized control on
entrepreneurial activity 33; decision
making 32; economic goals *versus*